Between Stress and Hope

BETWEEN STRESS AND HOPE

*From a Disease-Centered to a
Health-Centered Perspective*

Edited by Rebecca Jacoby and Giora Keinan

Praeger Series in Health Psychology
Barbara J. Tinsley, Series Editor

Westport, Connecticut
London

Library of Congress Cataloging-in-Publication Data

Between stress and hope : from a disease-centered to a health-centered perspective / edited by Rebecca Jacoby and Giora Keinan.

     p. cm.—(Praeger series in health psychology, ISSN 1543–2211)

Includes bibliographical references and index.

ISBN 0–275–97640–8 (alk. paper)

1. Clinical health psychology. 2. Stress (Psychology)—Health aspects. 3. Hope—Health aspects. 4. Medicine and psychology. I. Jacoby, Rebecca. II. Keinan, Giora. III. Series.

R726.7.B48 2003

155.9'042—dc21   2003042014

British Library Cataloging in Publication Data is available.

Library of Congress Catalog Card Number: 2003042014

ISBN: 0–275–97640–8

ISSN: 1543–2211

First published in 2003

Praeger Publishers, 88 Post Road West, Westport, CT 06881

An imprint of Greenwood Publishing Group, Inc.

www.praeger.com

Printed in the United States of America

The paper used in this book complies with the Permanent Paper Standard issued by the National Information Standards Organization (Z39.48–1984).

10 9 8 7 6 5 4 3 2 1

Copyright Acknowledgments

The authors and publisher gratefully acknowledge permission to use the following material:

From *The Neverending Story* by Michael Ende, translated by Ralph Manheim, copyright © 1979 by K. Thienemanns Verlag, Stuttgart. Translation copyright © 1983 by Double-day & Co. Inc., 1983. First published in Germany under the title *Die Unendliche Geschichte*. Used by permission of Dutton Children's Books, an imprint of Penguin Putnam Books Inc. All rights reserved. Reproduced by permission of Penguin Books Ltd.

To my mentor and dear friend, Shlomo Breznitz,
who illuminated the pathway between stress and hope.

Rebecca

To my granddaughter Alma, a ray of hope in this stressful period.

Giora

CONTENTS

ILLUSTRATIONS

FIGURES

TABLES

SERIES PREFACE

The field of health psychology has experienced tremendous growth during the past 20 years. This growth reflects an increasing recognition of the many social and psychological factors affecting health and illness, and the realization that physical health can no longer be addressed solely from a biomedical perspective.

The books in this series focus primarily on how social, psychological, and behavioral factors influence physical health. These volumes will serve as important resources for lay readers, as well as students and scholars in psychology, medicine, sociology, nursing, public health, social work, and related areas.

PREFACE

The 1999 annual meeting of the European Health Psychology Society (E.H.P.S.) was held in Florence, Italy, on the topic of "Psychology and the Renaissance of Health." In this meeting, the first editor of this book (R.J.) presented a poster titled "Between stress and Hope" (see Figure P.1). The idea of editing this book was born and developed in conversations that took place after the meeting with the second editor (G.K.).

The book's title, *Between Stress and Hope*, embraces two meanings. One relates to the transition psychology underwent during the twentieth century from an almost exclusive focus on anxiety and stress to an occupation with optimism and hope. This transition reflects a more general process of transition from the pathogenic model that focuses on illness and vulnerability to a saluthogenic model that focuses on health and resilience. The second relates to the transitions between stress and hope often experienced by individuals or groups exposed to stressful circumstances.

While in the past stress and hope were treated separately, today it is clear that these concepts are mutually interrelated; stress, particularly when it is perceived as uncontrollable, promotes hopelessness, whereas positive resources such as optimism and hope aid in coping with stressful situations, either serving as coping mechanisms or as moderators between stress, coping, and quality of life.

The book contains three parts. The first part discusses the theoretical aspects of stress and hope as well as the nature of their interrelationships. The chapters included in this part represent the most updated thinking on the concepts of hope and optimism. However, conceptual differences can easily be discerned in the writings of our contributors derive from different theoretical approaches (e.g., see the approach of Snyder versus that of Carver & Scheier or that of Hobfoll). These differences attest to the state of the field, which is one of continuous development. Further empirical studies are necessary to support or refute hypotheses derived from the different models.

The second part deals with coping processes of individuals or groups that have been exposed to various situations of stress, and it illuminates the role of hope in these processes. The situations include a variety of psychological, physical, and social stressors, such as racial prejudice, illness, and imprisonment. This part of the book reveals the power of unique coping strategies adopted by individuals in the most extreme situations.

The third part of the book presents two therapeutic approaches demonstrating the application of the knowledge and understanding of the "work of hope" in psychotherapy, either by means of working through the body, or by using literature.

We hope that in these times, when the world is exposed to extreme threats, the materials presented in this volume will aid clinicians and researchers to unravel the inner workings and the complexity of human beings facing these threats and stimulate new directions for research.

Rebecca Jacoby and Giora Keinan

Presented at the 13th Conference of the European Health Psychology Society (E.H.P.S.): Psychology and the Renaissance of Health. Florence, Italy, 1999.

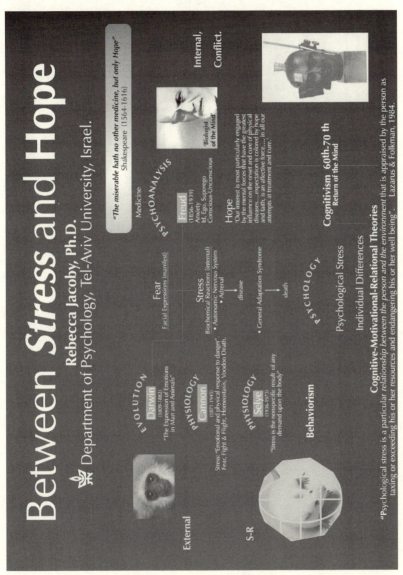

Figure P.1 (continued)

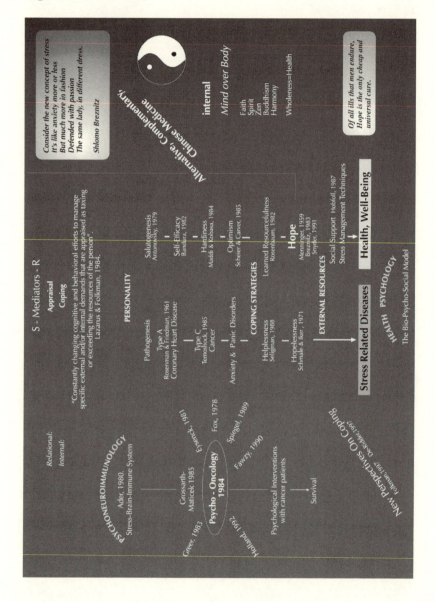

ACKNOWLEDGMENTS

We are grateful to all the individuals who helped us with this book. First and foremost, to each of our distinguished contributors for sharing their expertise and knowledge with us; to Yael Meilijson-Nachumi for her editorial work and for her excellent input; and last but not least, to Debby Carvalko, our acquisitions editor from the Greenwood Publishing Group for her encouragement, empathy, and patience.

Part I

THEORETICAL UNDERPINNING OF STRESS AND HOPE

Chapter 1

BETWEEN STRESS AND HOPE: A HISTORICAL PERSPECTIVE

Rebecca Jacoby

Forces that threaten to negate life
must be challenged by courage,
which is the power of life to affirm itself
in spite of life's ambiguities.
This requires the exercise
of a creative will
that enables us
to hew out a stone of hope
from a mountain of despair.

Martin Luther King Jr.

INTRODUCTION

The concept of stress has come to occupy an increasingly central place in psychology during the twentieth century, as the modern human has been continuously bombarded with new and rapidly changing demands. While at the cognitive level, the human being has adjusted to the technological and scientific innovations, physiological systems and to a large extent emotional capacity had not undergone an adaptation process. The price of this discrepancy has been paid in an increased rate of stress-related diseases (see Sapolsky, 1994), anxiety, and depression (Kessler, 1997; Buss, 2000). Consequently, individuals were searching for instant remedies, leading to other problems such as substance abuse and violence.

Psychology addressed these developments with new theories in which the focus shifted from the person to his or her interaction with the outside world (Lazarus & Folkman, 1984). Research on stress flourished. In parallel, new treatment approaches were developed, centered on psycho-physiological and cognitive-behavioral techniques (see Cotton, 1990; Lehrer and Woolfolk, 1993), with the underlying premise that these interventions (usually short term and focused) can improve the individual's functioning with regard to the psychological and physiological parameters related to stress. But, while focusing on cognition and techniques, the human spirit had been largely ignored.

Social movements have responded with an appeal to a return to nature, using slogans such as "make love not war," "don't worry be happy," and so on. The scientific and technological developments "shortened distances" and enabled people to travel the world. The Far East with its different pace of living has become increasingly attractive. In many fields such as medicine, nutrition, and music, the borders between East and West have dissolved, transforming the world into a "global village."

Psychology too underwent some major transitions. During the last two decades, there has been an increasingly growing movement towards approaches emphasizing the role of the human spirit in coping with life's adversities (e.g., preventing and fighting diseases). Concepts used solely by poets and clergy previously entered the world of psychology. Hope, faith, and spirituality were no longer considered a foreign culture.

Although research in this area is only at its initial stages, it is already impossible to ignore the developments indicating that positive psychological variables can influence physiological systems either by reducing stress or by affecting chemical substances that have not been fully identified, and thus enhance health (Scheier & Carver 1987, 1992; Scheier et al. 1989; Carver et al. 1993; Segerstrom et al., 1998; Taylor et al., 2000; Salovey et al., 2000; Udelman, 1986; Udelman & Udelman, 1991; Valdimarsdottir & Bovbjerg, 1997). It appears that at the beginning of the new millennium psychology is returning to search for the individual's internal resources and shifting its focus from stress to hope.

In this chapter I will briefly discuss some of these transitions from a historical perspective. My analysis is largely speculative and relies on research and theories published in relation to these concepts, while focusing on a number of milestones and central figures who have contributed to the field. The process of selecting the materials was complex, mainly because the field of psychology abounds with diverse theoretical and methodological approaches and there is "no standard method or technique (that) integrates the field" (Miller, cited in Schultz & Schultz, 2000, p. 20). At the same time, the lack of a unified method allows for the examination of the issues at hand from several perspectives and for a more stimulating discussion.

HISTORICAL DEVELOPMENTS

The concepts of stress and hope in various versions (such as anxiety and fear vs. optimism and happiness) have been known for many years. While in the past, stress was studied mainly by physiologists (Darwin, Cannon, Selye), and hope belonged in the realm of philosophy and poetry, from the middle of the twentieth century the concepts of stress and hope have come to occupy a central position in modern psychology in general and in health psychology in particular.

In their book *The History of Modern Psychology,* Schultz and Schultz (2000) note that the various approaches in psychology evolved from protest movements against existing approaches, and that this process resulted many times in fluctuations between extremes. According to these writers, two main factors have contributed to the development of new schools of thought in psychology; environmental events such as innovations, revolutions, or war, which fostered the development of new ideas, and the individuals who brought these ideas forward when the time was ripe:

> A science such as psychology does not develop in a vacuum, subject only to internal influences. Because it is part of the larger culture, it is also affected by external forces that shape its nature and direction. An understanding of psychology's history must consider the context in which the discipline evolved, the prevailing ideas in the science and culture of the day—the Zeitgeist or intellectual climate of the times—as well as the existing social, economic and political forces. (p. 10)

Viewing the development of the concepts of stress and hope from such a perspective, it is clear that their antecedents were known long before the development of modern science, but they had been mainly related to the attempts to understand the relationship between mind and body.

> The body grows without—
> The more convenient way—
> That if the Spirit—like to hide

Its Temple stands always,
Ajar—secure—inviting—
It never did betray
The soul that asked its shelter
In solemn honesty.

                                                    Emily Dickinson

MIND AND BODY

The relationship between mind, soul, and body has puzzled humankind throughout its history. Ancient cultures tended to attribute both physical and emotional illnesses to supernatural causes such as demons, spirits, and witches. The widespread belief was that destiny is determined by a superior power stronger than humanity. The healing ceremonies were conducted by the shaman using symbols, objects, and suggestions presumably containing hypnotic elements.

You will recover
You will walk again
My power is great
Through our white shell
I will enable you to walk again.
                        Healing Songs of the American Indians (1965)

Claude Levi-Strauss (1963) claimed that shamanistic healing methods can be positioned somewhere between modern medicine and psychotherapy, and that their uniqueness lies in the application of psychotherapeutic methods for healing an organic condition.

Remnants of this ancient belief can be found today among people who believe that they were cursed or given the evil eye and search for a cure not in modern medicine but in magical healing methods, or in someone who promises to free them of the curse or chase out the demon who lurks in their body (Bilu, 1993; Somer, 1993, 1997).

Graeco-Roman medicine was radically somatic and opposed to all previous super naturalistic beliefs. However, Greek philosophers had contributed to the psychosomatic orientation in medicine. For example, the Hippocratic writings contain some causal remarks on soul and disease such as "anger contracts the heart and good feelings dilate it"; or "if the soul is simultaneously set on fire, it consumes the body" (Hippocrates, cited in Ackerknecht, 1982, p. 17). Hippocrates classified humans into four types according to their temperament (sanguine, phlegmatic, melancholic, choleric), based on four bodily humors. The ancient Greeks believed that health was related to the equilibrium between these four humors. Plato wrote that the principal mistake physicians make in the healing of the human body is in dissociating between the body and the mind. Galen referred to the relationship between mind and body by stressing the role of passions in pathogenesis, and he adhered to the hygienic approach according to which a person must be freed from his or her passions in order to be cured. Susan Sontag (1977), in her book *Illness as Metaphor*, quotes W. H. Auden's (1937) poem, "Miss Gee," which illustrates a similar approach. People who have no outlet for their drives ("creative fire") such as "childless women" and "men when they retire," are mostly vulnerable to get cancer.

The belief that emotions influence the body was applied to practice by Maimonides, the Jewish physician, who treated asthma by stimulating psychic energies through perfume, music, and enjoyable stories. This belief has lasted for a number of generations and has found a widespread expression in folklore, literature, poetry, and play.

The Renaissance witnessed a reawakening of ancient medical knowledge and an effort to free the medical science from religion and sever the body from the soul. The belief that the mind can influence the body was considered unscientific and frivolous. The understanding of the mind came to be regarded as the province of religion and philosophy, while the treatment of the body became a separate domain. In the literature and poetry of that time we find descriptions implying that the soul is divine and eternal while the body is material and temporary. The Arab poet Abu-Al-Taib remarkably describes this in his words: "... and in the body lies a soul which will not gray with age."

The discovery of the nineteenth century that diseases are caused by microorganisms sharpened this approach further and culminated in the establishment of separate hospitals for physical and mental illnesses. It was only during the twentieth century, when the bio-medical model was replaced by the bio-psycho-social model, that the mind-body interaction has returned to occupy a respectful niche in medical and psychological discourse.

In light of the above it can be claimed that the dualistic approach that endorsed the belief that body and soul are separate entities set the foundations for the split between stress and hope, with stress belonging to the realm of physiological/physical processes, and hope delegated to the poets and prophets dealing with the mysteries of the soul.

THE DEVELOPMENT OF SCIENCE AND TECHNOLOGY

The widespread belief of the seventeenth century was that all natural processes are mechanically determined and can be explained by the laws of physics and chemistry. Consequently, it was believed that once scientists unraveled the laws by which the universe functioned, they could predict how it would run in the future. The image of the universe was of a great machine, and the clock and automaton have come to serve as models of the human mind and body. This lay the foundation for the idea that mechanical laws govern human functioning and behavior, and that the experimental and quantitative methods used for uncovering the laws of the physical universe can be used to elucidate the secrets of human nature (Murray, 1983; Stanger, 1988; Leahey, 1994; Schultz & Schultz, 2000). The application of the clockwork mechanism to the human body had been the center stage of the monumental work of the French philosopher René Descartes, who also forwarded the revolutionary idea that mind and body, although distinct, interact and influence each other.

Descartes represents the optimistic approach in philosophy, because he believed that science will succeed in providing solutions to the human plight and free the world from fear and disease. The belief that humans can make their world a better place and that science will enable people to be masters of the world and control natural phenomena, which opposes the deterministic world view, was provocative, innovative, and optimistic, as well as presumptuous and immodest. The consequences of this viewpoint in the Western culture of the twentieth century are manifested in the belief that humans can overcome the laws of nature, ignore their limits, and seek eternal youth and immortality.

It should be noted that this so-called optimistic approach could be a source of difficulty, because it contains omnipotent elements that are often unrealistic and may prevent a person from being aware of his or her limits and accepting them. The fall, which comes after the frustration, is harmful and painful (such as in the case of the high-tech crisis) and may result in severe disturbances. This is the model of the narcissistic personality disorder in which the individual finds it difficult to maintain a balance and therefore experiences repetitive fluctuations between omnipotence and impotence (Kohut, 1971).

THE DEVELOPMENT OF MODERN PSYCHOLOGY

Modern psychology was founded formally in Germany in the nineteenth century by Wilhelm Wundt (1832–1920) and has been influenced by the intellectual spirit of the time. Wundt was an empiricist who focused his work on consciousness and introspection. He initiated the development of a science of psychology independent of philosophy.

In the United States it was William James (1842–1910) who laid the foundations of the science of psychology. James argued against the mechanistic approach, termed by him "psychology without a soul" (James, 1890/1983) and stated that humanity must be understood as a complete entity. He also opposed Wundt's atomistic approach, which reduced all conscious experience to sensations and feelings. James insisted on a holistic approach, while using the metaphor of a stream to describe how consciousness functions. James's biography is a model of coping, as he himself had overcome depression. He declared that consciousness commands the body and granted human will a central place in his philosophy.

An important contribution to shaping the questions of modern psychology was made by Friedrich Nietzsche (1844–1900), who wrote about pain, coping, and the "work of hope" (see Jacoby, 1993):

> You must be ready to burn yourself in your own flame:
> How could you become new, if you had not first become ashes?
>
> From: *Thus Spoke Zarathustra*

These words of Nietzsche resemble closely the metaphor of the Phoenix as a coping model.[1] Like James, Nietzsche symbolized coping with his life. Thus, Morgan (1975) wrote about him: "He has the courage to experience the myriad anxieties that fester the modern soul, and a will to overcome them with new vision" (p. vii).[2]

During the same period Sigmund Freud (1856–1939) developed his theory on the unconscious and inner psychological constructs, emphasizing that anxiety is the outcome of inner conflicts between the id and the superego. In this way, he viewed anxiety as resulting from needs that are higher than survival needs as described by Charles Darwin.

For many years the main streams that dominated psychology were behaviorism and psychoanalysis. In the early 1960s the zeitgeist invited a change and two new movements have been established in American psychology, humanistic psychology and cognitive psychology.

Humanistic psychology opposed the mechanistic aspects of behaviorism as well as psychoanalytic approaches emphasizing unconscious and mental dysfunction. Humanistic psychologists, led by Carl Rogers (1902–1987) and Abraham Maslow (1908–1970), argued that humans are complex and cannot be objectified and quantified and emphasized the role of consciousness and emotional health. The basic themes of humanistic psychology included a belief in the wholeness of human nature, and a focus on free will, spontaneity, and the individual's creative power. Humanistic psychology had set the cornerstones for positive psychology, which became prevalent towards the end of the twentieth century (See Seligman & Csikszentmihalyi, 2000; Snyder, 2000; Snyder & Lopez, 2002).

The recognition that the stimulus-response model of behaviorism is not sufficient to deal with the complexity of human behavior has led to the development of the cognitive movement, which had been largely influenced by the innovation of the computer. The cognitive movement has had an immense and widespread impact on the field of psychology, while exploring the mind and its diverse functions such as appraisal, information processing, and decision making. The cognitive revolution has contributed immensely also to the theory and research on stress (see below). Although the cognitive revolution received a great boost by the end of the twentieth century, it was also criticized for overemphasizing cognition while neglecting other important variables such as motivation and emotion.

A question arises as to why, in spite of the scientific and technological advances during the twentieth century, people have not become healthier or happier (see Myers, 2000). Buss (2000) attributes this in part to the "discrepancies between modern and ancestral environments which interfere with the quest of a high quality of life" (p. 17). Stress is one of the prices humanity pays for these discrepancies.

STRESS

The concept of stress has occupied a central place in the psychological literature and research from the second half of the twentieth century, as one of the characteristics of modern society and the price paid by its members for competitiveness, desire for achievement, unfulfilled goals, and the need for immediate gratification. However, the concept of stress dates back to the eighteenth century. The first to have dealt with it was Darwin (1809–1882), who studied responses of animals and humans to emotional situations and published his findings in his book *The Expression of Emotions in Man and Animals* (1872/1965). Darwin was mainly interested in the observable responses and not in the biochemical changes that occur in response to stress. He claimed that fear, as long as it is at an optimal level, has an adaptive function of warning about danger. As such, fear response is essential for the survival of the organism and plays a central role in the successful adaptation to the environmental circumstances to which they are exposed. Since species that cannot adapt do not survive, and only survivors can pass on their adaptive qualities to future generations, it follows that fear is an adaptive response.

An immense stride towards the understanding of stress responses and their physiological basis had been made in the work of two physiologists, Walter Cannon (1871–1945) and Hans Selye (1907–1982). Cannon (1929) studied the homeostatic mechanisms underlying the "fight or flight" response in stressful situations. He argued that when homeostasis is disturbed, the organism enters a state of stress. Later, Selye developed the theory of the General Adaptation Syndrome, which describes the process of adaptation to chronic stress. Although Selye and others after him tried to expand the concept of stress to include a psychological dimension, this was mainly cast in terms of stimulus-response relationships, consistent with the dominant physiological and behavioral approaches of the period.

The "cognitive revolution" enabled an understanding of the concept of stress not only at the physiological but also at the psychological level. A seminal contribution to the conceptualization of stress was made by Lazarus and Folkman (1984), who emphasized the importance of appraisal as a mediator in the process of coping with stress. Since the 1980s, research on stress has flourished, rising to the major challenge of revealing the psychological and physiological variables underlying the link between stress and disease. While at the psychological level research has focused on personality (Friedman & Booth-Kewley, 1987; Friedman & Rosenman, 1959; Friedman et al., 1968; Temoshok, 1987; Grossarth-Maticek et al., 1985; Eysenck, 1993, 1994; Sanderman & Ranchor, 1997), the development of psychoneuroimmunology (Ader, 1980) has fostered the discovery of complex relationships between mind, brain, the immune system and disease (see: Weisse, 1992; Maier et al., 1994; Cohen & Herbert, 1996; Kiecolt-Glaser et al., 2002). This is one of the most promising fields that will enable us to gain insights into the mind-body enigma.

The broadening of the concept of stress has fostered the understanding of human behavior but complicated the research in the field because of the difficulty in reaching unified definitions and measures of psychological variables related to stress. For example, despite the widespread agreement between researchers concerning the concept of stress, there is still a lack of consensus on the basic properties of related concepts such as coping. Thus, in a recent article on coping assessment, De-Ridder (1997) pointed out that there are over 30 definitions of coping, and that this is paralleled by a large number of questionnaires used to assess coping. She also pointed out that many instruments are not grounded in theory. In addition, most instruments are based on self-report and do not consider important external resources such as social support (see also Miceli & Castelfranchi, 2001).

During the mid-twentieth century, a considerable body of reports has accumulated on individuals who succeeded in coping with severe stresses such as handicaps, incapacitating illness (Cousins, 1979; Sacks, 1986), the terror of the holocaust (Frankl, 1963; Pisar, 1981; Breznitz, 1992) and so on. Although this literature cannot be considered as empirical evidence, it does provide an indication that positive psychological variables may exert a remarkable influence on individuals' coping with stress, at times enabling them to overcome and gain mastery of the threatening situation, both at the psychological and the physiological level.

These reports have drawn the attention of investigators concerned with the effects of stress, leading to a growing shift of interest from the traumatic influences of stressful situations to the influence of positive factors on functioning and dealing with stress. This line of research seeks to identify variables that aid in effective coping, faster recovery, and fewer long-term residues of trauma.

HOPE AND POSITIVE PSYCHOLOGY

> The miserable hath no other medicine but only hope.
>
> Shakespeare

In the past, the subject of hope was the exclusive province of writers, poets, and prophets, and was not subject to psychological inquiry. Early psychological theory and research into human behavior did not treat hope as a variable of importance or a unique quality. Until the 1960s, both psychological and physiological theories focused on the explanation of animal and human behavior as directed towards drive reduction and satisfaction of basic needs, serving the pleasure principle (Freud, 1955) or maintenance of homeostasis (Cannon, 1932). These approaches did not distinguish between desire and hope. Likewise, for researchers in the area of learning, hope was merely a motivating factor underlying an organism's propensity to learn new responses in order to obtain reward, whose strength varied as a function of the past experiences of the organism. Thus, Mowrer (1960) described the "emotion of hope" as follows:

> Hope is something which motivated organisms like to have (since it implies imminent drive reduction), just as fear is something they do not like to have (since it implies a threat of drive increase), so that we may legitimately infer

that a motivated organism will show a strong tendency to make those responses which have, as one may say, a hopeful feedback. The tendency to seek response-correlated stimulation which arouses hope is biologically useful in that it disposes a motivated organism to make responses which in the past led to (or produced) satisfaction. (p. 10)

In the 1950s, Olds and Milner (1954, 1958) accidentally discovered that electrical stimulation to certain parts of the rat's brain produced a rewarding effect, which was not associated with the reduction of a primary drive state. These authors assumed that they had located a system within the brain whose peculiar function is to produce a rewarding effect on behavior. Additional studies found that in many cases the drive for brain stimulation was more powerful than hunger. Therefore it seems that there is a hopeful expectation that exists beyond the primary drives.

The understanding of the positive influences of hope were closely tied to the negative influence of hopelessness and helplessness. Richter (1957) demonstrated sudden death of wild rats by drowning in response to conditions of hopelessness such as restraint and confinement, in contrast to an active and aggressive struggle of the control group, lasting for up to 60 hours of swimming. Richter claims that during the experimental situation in which the rats found themselves unable to apply the "fight or flight" response to stress, they simply gave up and died. According to Richter, the rats' death resulted from an overstimulation of the parasympathetic system, which slows down heart and breathing rate and lowers blood pressure and muscle tone. On the basis of these results, Richter suggested that sudden death in other animals and in humans may also result from a state of hopelessness. When all the roads to escape or survival are blocked, there is resignation, culminating in death. Additional manifestations of this phenomenon are found in folklore. Cannon (1957) described primitive tribes in South America, Africa, Australia, and New Zealand in which persons who were condemned and sentenced by a so-called medicine man and therefore expelled from the community died shortly after the event. This phenomenon, known as "voodoo death," was explained by this writer as "due to shocking emotional stress in response to obvious or repressed terror" (p. 189). Richter sees in this another manifestation of a reaction to hopelessness. The classical work of Seligman (1975) on learned helplessness in animals and humans has provided an additional demonstration that exposure to an uncontrollable threat leads to resignation, helplessness, and depression. In his remarkable book on the power of human hope, Frankl (1963) described a higher incidence of death in concentration camp prisoners during the week between December 25, 1944 and January 1, 1945, because of their unfulfilled expectations of being liberated on New Year's Eve.

On the other hand, medical practitioners always have some exceptional stories about terminal patients who survive against all odds when expecting an extremely important family event such as a wedding or holidays. After the awaited event they die. It is probably not surprising that the first to touch upon the subject of hope were the nurses who have described their clinical experience, especially with cancer patients. Research has become a natural sequel (Dufault & Martocchio, 1985; Nowotny, 1991).

During the 1980s researchers began to develop theories and concepts that focused on the person's sources of strength. A review of their writings reveals a long list of variables and concepts such as hope (Breznitz, 1982; Snyder, 1991), dispositional optimism (Scheier & Carver, 1985), learned resourcefulness (Rosenbaum, 1982), self-efficacy (Bandura, 1982), hardiness (Kobasa, 1982), sense of coherence (Antonovsky, 1979), happiness (Argyle et al., 1989), social support (Donald & Ware, 1982), conservation of resources (Hobfoll, 1989), and resilience (Ryff & Singer, 1996) as well as outcomes such as subjective well being (Diener, 1984) and quality of life (Patrick & Erickson, 1993).

Toward the end of the twentieth century we have witnessed an encompassing shift in psychology whereby the field that for years has been primarily concerned with stress, disease, and pathology, has turned to dealing with health, optimism, and hope. This might be the beginning of a positive revolution in psychology. Interestingly, while revolutions are usually said to occur when theoreticians and researchers oppose existing schools of thought, the transition to positive psychology appears to be more of an internal reaction of the field whereby the same writers who had focused on the effects of stress on functioning and illness began to examine the effects of positive variables on coping with stress and health.

How did this transition come about? It is too early to answer this question, but we can assume that the spirit of the time, which stresses health over illness, resilience over vulnerability and hope over stress, was influenced by reports of people who survived extreme situations such as the Holocaust. Another possibility is that individuals tired of chasing after material wealth and began searching for spiritual experiences. Finally, it is possible that just as psychology severed its ties with philosophy at the beginning of the twentieth century, at the end of the century it freed itself from dependence on the medical model. Consequently, it could lean on its own models and research methods while maintaining a relationship with the medical professions as well as with philosophy, in which all the sides benefit from the other's knowledge. One of the great challenges facing health psychology today is to reveal how positive variables like hope influence parameters of health and aid in coping with illness.

HEALTH PSYCHOLOGY

> ...I will do all that science, so far as it may filter through my efforts, can accomplish. But whenever my patient begins to count the carriages in her funeral procession I subtract 50 per cent from the curative power of medicines. If you will get her to ask one question about the new winter styles in cloak sleeves I will promise you a one-in-five chance for her, instead of one in ten.
>
> From: *The Last Leaf* (O. Henry, 1995, p. 179)

Health psychology is a rapidly growing field that aims to cope with a core philosophical question of mind-body relationship, at the theoretical, clinical, and empirical levels. This exciting field holds the potential of fostering the understanding of complex psychophysiological processes and attracts professionals from diverse disciplines.

Albeit the field is relatively new, in a short period it has succeeded in gaining a reputation as an interdisciplinary field. A review of the titles of journals, books, and articles published in the field of health psychology shows that this field, more than any other in psychology, incorporates the concepts of stress and hope. Of particular interest are the reciprocal relations between stress and hope and their health-related outcomes (see Culver et al., chapter 2 this volume).

The advances in medicine and technology during the twentieth century opened new possibilities for interventions that can create and prolong life, using innovative techniques such as in-vitro fertilization and organ transplants. These advances decreased the mortality rate from acute diseases while in parallel increasing the prevalence of chronic diseases, and the latter trend was compounded by the twentieth-century lifestyle. These changes required a reassessment of the factors contributing to illness and health, and the development and application of appropriate treatment techniques. During the past 30 years there has been an increasing awareness of the importance of understanding the relationship between physiological and psychosocial factors that can affect the outburst of diseases and ways of coping with them and preventing them. As a result of these developments, new channels of communication have been created among the various disciplines concerned with health and illness, and interdisciplinary fields of research such as psycho-oncology and psychoneuroimmunology have been developed.

The advancement in medical treatment and the subsequent increase in chronic illnesses, especially heart disease, cancer, diabetes, and AIDS, have fostered research in health psychology, applying cognitive models that have focused on appraisal processes (Folkman et al., 1995, 1997) illness representations (Leventhal et al., 1980, 1984), positive illusions (Taylor, 1983; Taylor et al., 1984, 1996), optimism (Scheier & Carver, 1985; Scheier et al., 1989; Carver et al. 1993) and hope (Snyder et al., 1991; Irving et al., 1998), and the interaction between these variables and coping with illness. Another direction has focused on the efficacy of psychosocial interventions with regard to coping, quality of life, and its health/illness outcomes (Spiegel et al., 1983, 1989; Kiecolt-Glaser & Glaser, 1988, 1992; Fawzy et al., 1990a, 1990b, 1995; Andersen, 1992; Walker et al., 1999; Cunningham et al., 2000; Schneiderman et al., 2001; De-Ridder & Schreurs, 2001).

Health psychology is a meeting ground between psychology and medicine. The development of the discipline has incorporated a shift from the traditional medical model to the biopsychosocial model, which considers the psychological and social factors involved in illness and in health (see Baum & Poslusny 1999). In parallel, clinical psychologists who for many years emphasized only the spoken word began to take into account physiological processes and developments in brain research, so that the body, which has been ignored for so many years, has regained centrality. Thus, at the onset of the twenty-first century we witness a process in which psychology again seeks to cope with the body-mind relationship, from the theoretical, empirical, and clinical perspectives.

DISCUSSION

> In America...I have seen the freest and best educated of men in the circumstances the happiest to be found in the world; yet it seemed to me that a cloud habitually hung on their brow, and they seemed serious and almost sad in their pleasure...because they never stop thinking of the good things they have not got.
>
> Alex de Tocqueville

While technological and scientific developments have improved human life economically and medically by increasing wealth and health, these developments as well as environmental changes (urbanization, media) and lifestyle (nutrition) have produced new ills and suffering. The transition to the big cities has fostered the breakdown of the family as a supportive net. People became more competitive, centralistic, and alienated. Aggressive and destructive forces have reached unprecedented proportions (World Wars, Holocaust) as if humans were losing inhibitory mechanisms that lower species possess (see Lorenz, 1967). Life has become increasingly stressful and people have become increasingly unhappy.

Since World War II, psychology has offered, side by side with the medical professions, to repair damage and to heal. Although the new treatment modalities (psychological and pharmacological) have helped people to control better their stress and depression, the almost exclusive attention to pathology has been at the expense of neglecting meaning, fulfillment, and spirituality.

Like in the fairy tale about the unhappy king who was looking for the shirt of a happy man and discovered that the only happy man in his land had no shirt, people have come to realize that hope and happiness belong to the human spirit and cannot be purchased. At the end of the twentieth century humanity returns to search for our internal resources, and psychology addresses this change by shifting its focus from stress to hope.

In parallel, Eastern treatment methods began influencing the disciplines of medicine and psychology. The medical establishment, which for years refused to include alternative medicine (given this name not by accident), has begun to acknowledge its advantages. In the field of psychotherapy, new techniques were introduced as an addition to the "talk cure." In recent years there has been an increasing trend for people coping with life-threatening illnesses to resort to coping by means of art, spirituality, or religion. Indeed, in 1999 *Psycho-Oncology* dedicated a special issue to the role of religion and spirituality in cancer patients' coping with the illness, and urged that such coping strategies be taken into account both in research on coping and in interventions with cancer patients. It appears that the spirit, which has been neglected for so many years is regaining its place. Is it one of the outcomes that feminism has brought?

At the turn of the twenty-first century, the human is no longer seen as a sophisticated machine, a computer, or a box of drives, but as a creature that combines within itself both yin and yang, body and mind, stress and hope.

However, as we enter the new millennium, levels of stress and helplessness in our lives have not decreased, but on the contrary have increased and in fact have reached enormous dimensions due to the outbreak of hitherto unfamiliar powers such as international terrorism. It is especially at times like these that there is a necessity to provide the younger generation with tools that will enable them to use hope in order to cope with the stressors of life and as buffers against mental and physical illness (see Roberts et al., 2002; Seligman & Csikszentmihalyi, 2000).

Are we at the beginning of a new revolution in psychology? Seligman & Csikszentmihalyi (2000) believe that we are: "Much of the task of prevention in this new century will be to create a science of human strength whose mission will be to understand and learn how to foster these virtues (courage, future mindedness, optimism, interpersonal skill, faith, work ethic, hope, honesty, perseverance and the capacity for flow and insight) in young people" (p. 7).

As I was about to finish writing this chapter and was collecting the books and articles that were scattered on my table, I came across an illuminating article by Schneider (1998) in which he calls for the return of Romanticism, or "the science of the heart," into the field of psychology. "Science of the heart," explains Schneider, characterizes an ancient Israelite conception of wisdom, or *hochma,* which "combines intelligence, feeling and perception" (p. 277).

This comment arouses in me two thoughts: one, many empirical findings in the area of psychology were long known to philosophers, writers, and poets, but only empirical support lent this knowledge validity in the eyes of the scientific community. Second, intuition and emotion (*hochma*) never disappeared from the stage of psychology; they have always served clinical psychologists, but the split that transpired between the scientists and the practitioners turned the world of psychologists into a more limited and constrained one. Today, we face the need to bridge the gap and to develop open channels of communication (Beutler et al., 1995; Stricker & Trierweiler, 1995).

I will conclude with Kanwall's (1997) citation on the Pandora box myth as a metaphor for the analytic process, which can be used as a metaphor for processes of development and scientific thinking in general, and those about stress and hope in particular:

> If the opening of Pandora's forbidden box (or jar) is taken as a metaphor for the analytic process, what is described in myth can be equated with what has happened in our field. We have let out the many vices of human nature and have examined them to no end. Some of us feel that psychoanalysis tends to overly pathologize living experiences, while hope still remains in the box. Before we ever get to discover hope, we replace the lid. Is it that we

dread the analysis of hope, lest our own exploration take away the power of this magical experience from us? (p. 136)

I would like to add that it is not by accident that hope was among the inhabitants of the box: hope is essential where there is suffering.

> When I hoped, I recollect
> Just the place I stood –
> At a Window facing West –
> Roughest Air – was good –
> Not a Sleet could bite me –
> Not a frost could cool –
> Hope it was that kept me warm-
> Not Merino shawl-
> When I feared – I recollect
> Just the day it was –
> Worlds were lying out to sun –
> Yet how Nature froze –
> Icicles upon my soul
> Prickled Blue and Cool –
> Bird went praising everywhere –
> Only Me – was still –
> And the Day that I despaired –
> This – if I forgot
> Nature will – that it be Night
> After Sun has set –
> Darkness intersect her face –
> And put out her face –
> And put out her eye –
> Nature hesitate – before
> Memory and I –

Emily Dickinson

NOTES

The author wishes to thank Arie Nadler for sharing his ideas, Ina Weiner for her helpful comments, encouragement, and support in writing this chapter, and Andres Konichezky, my assistant, who has become a colleague.

1. The Phoenix is a sacred bird in Egyptian religion. According to the legend, only one such bird is alive on earth at any given time. It has a beak with holes in it like that of a flute to play sweet songs at dawn. It resembles an eagle and has

flaming red and gold feathers. The phoenix lives 500 years and builds a nest of herbs at the end of its time. There it fans its wings until it catches fire, thereby burning itself to death. Then, out of the ashes, arises a new Phoenix to continue the musical tradition of its heritage.

2. I would like to refer the reader to the fictional book *When Nietzsche Wept* (Yalom, 1992), in which Breuer discusses with Nietzsche his hypothesis on stress as being the cause of his migraine attacks (pp. 94–95).

REFERENCES

Ackerknecht, E. H. (1982). The history of psychosomatic medicine. *Psychological Medicine, 12,* 17–24.

Ader, R. (1980). Psychosomatics and psycho immunologic research. *Psychosomatic Medicine*, 42(3), 307–321.

Andersen, B. L. (1992). Psychological interventions for cancer patients to enhance the quality of life. *Journal of Consulting and Clinical Psychology,* 60, 552–568.

Antonovsky, A. (1979). *Health, stress, and coping.* San Francisco: Jossey-Bass.

Argyle, M., Martin, M., & Crossland, J. (1989). Happiness as a function of personality and social encounters. In J.P. Forgas and J.M. Innes (Eds.), *Recent advances in social psychology: an international perspective.* North Holland: Elsevier Science.

Auden, W. H. (1937/1991). Miss Gee. In E. Mendelson (Ed.), *Collected poems* (pp. 158–161). London: Faber & Faber.

Bandura, A. (1982). Self-efficacy mechanism in human agency. *American Psychologist, 37,* 122–147.

Baum, A., & Posluszny, D. M. (1999). Health psychology: mapping biobehavioral contributions to health and illness. *Annual Review of Psychology,* 50, 137–163.

Beutler, L. E., Williams, R. E., Wakefield, P. J., & Entwistle, S. R. (1995). Bridging scientist and practitioner perspectives in clinical psychology. *American Psychologist, 50* (12), 984–994.

Bilu, Y. (1993). *Without bounds: The life and death of Rabbi Yaacov Wazana.* Jerusalem: The Magnes Press, The Hebrew University. (Hebrew).

Breznitz, S. (1982). The psychology of hope. Paper presented at the annual conference of the Israeli Psychological Association. Haifa University, Israel.

Breznitz, S. (1992). *Memory fields.* New York: Alfred A. Knopf.

Buss, D. M. (2000). The evolution of happiness. *American Psychologist, 55,* 15–23.

Cannon W. B. (1929). *Bodily changes in pain, hunger, fear & rage.* New York: Appleton-Century-Crofts.

Cannon W. B. (1932). *The wisdom of the body.* New York: W.W. Norton.

Cannon W. B. (1957). "Voodoo" death. *Psychosomatic Medicine, 19,* 182–190.

Carver, C. S., Pozo, C., Harris, S., Noriega, V., Scheier, M., Robinson, D., Ketchman, A., Moffat, F., & Clark, D. (1993). How coping mediates the effect of optimism on distress: A study of women with early stage breast cancer. *Journal of Personality and Social Psychology,* 65, 375–390.

Cohen, S., & Herbert, T. B. (1996). Health psychology: Psychological factors and physical disease from the perspective of human psychoneuroimmunology. *Annual Review in Psychology,* 47, 113–142.

Cotton, D.H.G. (1990). *Stress management: An integrated approach to therapy.* New York: Brunner & Mazel.

Cousins, N. (1979). *Anatomy of an illness as perceived by the patient.* New York: W.W. Norton.

Cunningham, A. J., Edmonds, C.V.I., Phillips, C., Soots, K. I., Hedley, D., & Lockwood, G. A. (2000). A prospective longitudinal study of the relationship of psychological work to duration of survival in patients with metastatic cancer. *Psycho-Oncology,* 9, 323–339.

Darwin (1965). *The Expression of emotions in man and animals.* Chicago: University of Chicago Press.

Dickinson, E. (1960). In T.H. Johnson (Ed.), *The complete poems of Emily Dickinson.* Boston: Little, Brown.

Diener, E. (1984). Subjective well-being. *Psychological Bulletin,* 95, 542–575.

De-Ridder, D. (1997). What is wrong with coping assessment? A review of conceptual and methodological issues. *Psychology and Health,* 12, 417–431.

De-Ridder, D., & Schreurs, K. (2001). Developing interventions for chronically ill patients: Is coping a helpful concept? *Clinical Psychology Review,* 21(2), 205–240.

Donald, C. A., & Ware, J. E. (1982). *The quantification of social contacts and resources.* Santa Monica, CA: Rand Corporation: R-2937-HHS.

Dufault, K., & Martocchio, B. C. (1985). Hope: its spheres and dimensions. *Nursing Clinics of North America,* 20(2), 379–391.

Eysenck, H. J. (1993). Prediction of cancer and coronary heart disease mortality by means of a personality inventory: Results of a 15-year follow up study. *Psychological Reports,* 72(2), 499–516.

Eysenck, H. J. (1994). Cancer, personality and stress: prediction and prevention. *Advances in Behavior Research and Therapy,* 16(3), 167–215.

Fawzy, I. F., Cousins, N., Fawzy, N.W., Kemeny, M. E., Elashoff, R., & Morton, D. (1990a). A structured psychiatric intervention for cancer patients. 1. Changes over time in methods of coping and affective disturbance. *Archives of General Psychiatry,* 47, 720–725.

Fawzy, I. F., Kemeny, M. E., Fawzy, N. W., Elashoff, R., Morton, D., & Cousins, N. (1990b). A structured psychiatric intervention for cancer patients. 2. Changes over time in immunological measures. *Archives of General Psychiatry,* 47, 729–735.

Fawzy, I. F., Fawzy, N. W., Arndt, L. A., & Pasnau, R. O. (1995). Critical review of psychosocial interventions in cancer care. *Archives of General Psychiatry, 52,* 100–113.

Folkman, S., & Chesney, M. (1995). Coping with HIV infection. In M. Stein & A. Baum (Eds.), *Chronic Diseases: Perspectives in Behavioral Medicine* (p. 115–133). New Jersey: Lawrence Erlbaum Associates.

Folkman, S., Moskowitz, J. T., Ozer, E. M., & Park, C. L. (1997). Positive meaningful events and coping in the context of HIV/AIDS. In B.H. Gottlieb (Ed.), *Coping with chronic stress: The Plenum series on stress and coping.* (p. 293–314). New York: Plenum Press.

Frankl, V. E. (1963). *Man's search for meaning.* New York: Washington Square Press.

Freud, S. (1955). *Beyond the pleasure principle.* Standard Edition. London: Hogarth Press.

Friedman, H. S., & Booth-Kewley, S. (1987). The "disease prone personality." *American Psychologist, 42*(6), 539–555.

Friedman, M., & Rosenman, R.H. (1959). Association of specific overt behavior pattern with blood and cardiovascular findings. *Journal of the American Medical Association,* 169, 1286–1296.

Friedman, M., Rosenman, R.H., Straus, K., Wurn, M., & Kositchek, R. (1968). The relationship of behavior pattern A to the state of coronary vasculature. *American Journal of Medicine,* 44, 525–537.

Grossarth-Maticek, R., Bastiaans, J., & Kanazir, D. T. (1985). Psychosocial factors as strong predictors of mortality from cancer, ischemic heart disease and stroke: The Yugoslav prospective study. *Journal of Psychosomatic Research,* 29, 167–176.

Healing Songs of the American Indians (1965). New York: Ethnic Folkway Library Album. No. FE 4251.

Henry, O. (1995). *100 selected stories.* Great Britain: Wordsworth Classics.

Hobfoll, S. E. (1989). Conservation of resources: A new attempt at conceptualizing stress. *American Psychologist, 44*(3), 513–524.

Irving, L. M., Snyder, C. R., & Crowson, J. J. Jr. (1998). Hope and coping with cancer by college women. *Journal of Personality,* 66 (2), 195–214.

Jacoby, R. (1993). "The miserable hath no other medicine but only hope": some conceptual considerations on hope and stress. *Stress Medicine,* 9, 61–69.

James, W. (1890/1983). *The principles of psychology.* Cambridge: Harvard University Press.

Kanwall, G. S. (1997). Hope, respect, and flexibility in the psychotherapy of schizophrenia. *Contemporary Psychoanalysis, 33*(1), 133–150.

Kessler, R. C. (1997). The effects of stressful life events on depression. *Annual Review of Psychology,* 48, 191–214.

Kiecolt-Glaser, J. K., & Glaser, R. (1988). Psychological influences on immunity: Implications for AIDS. *American Psychologist,* 43, 892–898.

Kiecolt-Glaser, J. K., & Glaser, R. (1992). Psychoneuroimmunology: Can psychological interventions modulate immunity? *Journal of Consulting and Clinical Psychology,* 60, 569–575.

Kiecolt-Glaser, J. K., McGuire, L., Robles, T. F., & Glaser, R. (2002). Emotions, morbidity, and mortality: New perspectives from psychoneuroimmunology. *Annual Review in Psychology,* 53(1), 83–107.

Kobasa, S. C. (1982). The hardy personality: Toward a social psychology of stress and health. In J. Suls & G. Sanders (Eds.), *Social Psychology of Health and Illness* (pp. 3–33). Hillsdale, NJ: Erlbaum.

Kohut, H. (1971). *The analysis of the self: A systematic approach to the psychoanalytic treatment of narcissistic personality disorder.* New York: International Universities Press, Inc.

Lazarus, R. S., & Folkman, S. (1984). *Stress, appraisal and coping.* New York: Springer.

Leahey, T. H. (1994). *A history of modern psychology.* New Jersey: Prentice-Hall.

Lehrer P. M., & Woolfolk, R. L. (1993). *Principles and practice of stress management.* New York: Guilford.

Leventhal, H., Meyer, D., & Nerez, D. (1980). The common sense representation of illness danger. In S. Rachman (Ed.), *Medical Psychology.* Vol. 2 (pp. 7–30). New York: Pergamon Press.

Leventhal, H., Nerez, D., & Steele, D. (1984). Illness representations and coping with health threats. In A. Baum & J. Singer (Eds.), *A handbook of psychology and health,* Vol. 4 (pp. 219–252). New Jersey: Lawrence Erlbaum Associates.

Levi-Strauss, C. (1963). *Structural anthropology.* Middlesex: Penguin Books.

Lorenz, K. (1967). *On aggression.* Great Britain: University Paperback Edition.

Maier, S. F., Watkins, L. R. & Fleshner, M. (1994). Psychoneuroimmunology: The interface between behavior, brain and immunity. *American Psychologist,* 49(12), 1004–1017.

Miceli, M., & Castelfranchi, C. (2001). Further distinctions between coping and defense mechanisms? *Journal of Personality,* 69(2), 287–296.

Morgan, G.A. (1975). *What Nietzsche means.* Westport, Connecticut: Greenwood Press.

Mowrer, O. H. (1960). *Learning theory and the symbolic processes.* New York: Wiley.

Murray, D. J. (1983). *A history of western psychology.* New Jersey: Prentice-Hall.

Myers, D. G. (2000). The funds, friends, and faith of happy people. *American Psychologist,* 55(1), 56–67.

Nowotny, M. L. (1991). Every tomorrow, a vision of hope. *Journal of Psychosocial Oncology,* 9(3), 117–126.

Olds, J. (1958). Satiation effects in self-stimulation of the brain. *Journal of Comparative and Physiological Psychology,* 51, 675–678.

Olds, J., & Milner, P. (1954). Positive reinforcement produced by electrical stimulation of sepal area and other regions of rat brain. *Journal of Comparative and Physiological Psychology,* 47, 419–427.

Patrick, D. L., & Erickson, P. (1993). *Health status and health policy: Quality of life in health care evaluation and resource allocation.* New York: Oxford University Press.

Pisar, S. (1981). *Of blood and hope.* Tel-Aviv: Schocken.

Richter, C. P. (1957). On the phenomemenon of sudden death in animals and man. *Psychosomatic Medicine,* 19, 191–198.

Roberts, M. C., Brown, K. J., Johnson, R. J., & Reinke, J. (2002). Positive psychology for children. In C. R. Snyder & S. J. Lopez (Eds.), *Handbook of positive psychology* (pp. 663–675). New York: Oxford University Press.

Rosenbaum, M. (1982). *Learned resourcefulness.* New York: Springer.

Ryff, C. D., & Singer, B. (1996). Psychological well-being: Meaning, measurement, and implications for psychotherapy research. *Psychotherapy and Psychosomatics,* 65(1), 14–23.

Sacks, O. (1986). *A leg to stand on.* London: Picador.

Salovey, P., Rothman, A. J., Detweiler, J. B., & Steward, W. T. (2000). Emotional states and physical health. *American Psychologist,* 55, 110–121.

Sanderman, R., & Ranchor, A. V. (1997). The predictor status of personality variables: Etiological significance and their role in the course of disease. *European Journal of Personality,* 11, 359–382.

Sapolsky, R. M. (1994). *Why Zebras don't get ulcers.* New York: Freeman.

Scheier, M. F., & Carver, C. S. (1985). Optimism, coping and health: Assessment and implications of generalized outcome expectancies. *Health Psychology,* 4, 219–247.

Scheier, M. F., & Carver, C. S. (1987). Dispositional optimism and physical well-being: The influence of generalized outcome expectations on health. *Journal of Personality,* 55(2), 169–210.

Scheier, M. F., & Carver, C. S. (1992). Effects of optimism on psychological and physical well-being: Theoretical overview and empirical update. *Cognitive Therapy and Research,* 16, 201–228.

Scheier, M. F., Matthews, K. A., Owens, J. F., Magovern, G. J., Sr., Lefebvre, R. C., Abbott, R. A., & Carver, C. S. (1989). Dispositional optimism and recovery from coronary artery bypass surgery: The beneficial effects on physical and psychological well being. *Journal of Personality and Social Psychology,* 57, 1024–1040.

Schneider, K. J. (1998). Toward a science of the heart. Romanticism and the revival of psychology. *American Psychologist,* 53(3), 277–289.

Schneiderman, N., Antoni, M. H., Saab, P. G., & Ironson, G. (2001). Health psychology: Psychosocial and biobehavioral aspects of chronic disease management. *Annual Review in Psychology,* 52, 555–580.

Schultz, D. P., & Schultz, S. E. (2000). *A history of modern psychology* (7th ed.). Fort Worth: Harcourt Brace.

Segerstrom, S. C., Taylor, S. E., Kemeny, M. E., & Fahey, J. L. (1998). Optimism is associated with mood, coping and immune change in response to stress. *Journal of Personality and Social Psychology,* 74(6), 1646–1655.

Seligman, M. E.P. (1975). *Helplessness.* San Francisco: Freeman.

Seligman, M. E.P., & Csikszentmihalyi, M. (2000). Positive psychology: an introduction. *American Psychologist, 55,* 5–14.

Shakespeare, W. (1980). *Measure for Measure.* In *The Complete Works of William Shakespeare.* London: Atlantis. Act III.

Snyder, C. R. (2000). *Handbook of hope: Theory, measures and applications.* San Diego: Academic Press.

Snyder, C. R., Irving, L., & Anderson, J. R. (1991). Hope and health: Measuring the will and the ways. In C .R. Snyder & D. R. Forsyth (Eds.), *Handbook of social and clinical psychology: The health perspective* (pp. 285–305). Elmsford, NY: Pergamon.

Snyder, C. R., & Lopez, S. J. (2002). *Handbook of positive psychology.* New York: Oxford University Press.

Somer, E. (1993). Possession syndrome in a histrionic personality: Exorcism and psychotherapy. *Dialogue: Israel Journal of Psychotherapy, 3* (1), 40–48. (Hebrew).

Somer, E. (1997). Paranormal and dissociative experiences in Middle Eastern Jews in Israel: Diagnostic and treatment dilemmas. *Dissociation, 10* (3), 174–181.

Sontag, S. (1977). *Illness as metaphor.* N.Y.: Vintage Books.

Spiegel, D., & Bloom, J. R. (1983). Group therapy and hypnosis reduce metastatic breast carcinoma pain. *Psychosomatic Medicine, 45,* 333–339.

Spiegel, D., Bloom, J. R., Kraemer, H. C., & Gottheil, E. (1989). Effect of psychosocial treatment on survival of patients with metastatic breast cancer. *Lancet, 2,* 888–891.

Stanger, R. (1988). *A history of psychological theories.* New York: Macmillan.

Stricker, G., & Trierweiler, S. J. (1995). The local clinical scientist: A bridge between science and practice. *American Psychologist, 50*(12): 995–1002.

Taylor, S. E. (1983). Adjustment to threatening events: A theory of cognitive adaptation. *American Psychologist, 38,* 1161–1173.

Taylor, S. E., Lichtman, R. R., & Wood, J. V. (1984). Attributions, beliefs about control and adjustment to breast cancer. *Journal of Personality and Social Psychology, 46,* 489–502.

Taylor, S. E., & Armor, D. A. (1996). Positive illusions and coping with adversity. *Journal of Personality (special issue), 64* (4), 873–898.

Taylor, S. E., Kemeny, M. E., Reed, G. M., Bower, J. E., & Gruenwald, T. L. (2000). Psychological resources, positive illusions, and health. *American Psychologist, 55,* 99–109.

Temoshok, L. (1987). Personality, coping style, emotion and cancer: Towards an integrative model. *Cancer Survival, 6,* 545–567.

Udelman, D. L. (1986). Hope and the immune system. *Stress Medicine, 2,* 7–12.

Udelman, D. L., & Udelman, H. D. (1991). Affects, neurotransmitters, and immunocompetence. *Stress Medicine, 7,* 159–162.

Valdimarsdottir, H. B., & Bovbjerg, D. H. (1997). Positive and negative mood: association with natural killer cell activity. *Psychology and Health,* 12, 319–327.

Walker, L. G., Heys, S. D., & Eremin, O. (1999). Surviving cancer: Do psychosocial factors count? (Editorial). *Journal of Psychosomatic Research,* 47 (6), 497–503.

Weisse, C. S. (1992). Depression and immunocompetence: A review of the literature. *Psychological Bulletin,* 111(3), 475–489.

Yalom, I. D. (1992). *When Nietzsche wept.* New York: Harper Perennial.

Chapter 2

DISPOSITIONAL OPTIMISM AS A MODERATOR OF THE IMPACT OF HEALTH THREATS ON COPING AND WELL-BEING

*Jenifer L. Culver, Charles S. Carver,
and Michael F. Scheier*

Health threats represent an important source of stress in people's lives. Many variables, including differences in personality, influence how people respond to health threats. One variable with an important role in this context is optimism versus pessimism. People's levels of optimism influence how much distress they experience when facing a health threat. Optimism also influences the ways people cope with the health threat.

This chapter examines evidence on both of these assertions. We begin by placing optimism within the broad framework of expectancy-value models of motivation, to show the dynamics that we believe underlie the influence of optimism and pessimism on coping and well-being.

OPTIMISM AND EXPECTANCY-VALUE MODELS OF MOTIVATION

Optimism is the expectation of good outcomes; pessimism is the expectation of bad outcomes. Folk wisdom has long held that this difference has implications for many aspects of living, and contemporary research supports this position. Optimists and pessimists differ in ways that have major impacts on their lives. They differ in how they approach problems, and they differ in the manner—and the success—with which they cope with adversity.[1]

The fact that the optimism construct is grounded in expectancies links it to a long tradition of expectancy-value models of motivation. These theories assume that behavior is organized around goals. Goals are states or actions that people view as either desirable or undesirable. People try to fit their behaviors—indeed fit their very selves—to what they see as desirable, and they try to avoid what they see as undesirable (what Carver & Scheier, 1998, called "anti-goals").

In this view, two factors underlie motivation. The first is the *value*, or importance, of the goal. If the goal is not important, there is no reason to act. The second is *expectancy*—the sense of confidence about the attainability of the goal. The person who believes a goal is unattainable will not strive for it. Doubt can impair effort before or during action. Only with enough confidence will people move into action and only if they retain confidence will they continue their efforts. When people are confident about an outcome, effort will continue even in the face of great adversity.

Goals Vary in Breadth and Abstractness

Goals vary in specificity. Some are very general, some pertain to a particular domain of life, some are very concrete and specific. This suggests that expectancies may have a comparable range of variation (Armor & Taylor, 1998; Carver & Scheier, 1998). That is, you can be confident or doubtful about (for example) having a satisfying career, making good impressions in social situations, winning a particular golf game, preparing an enjoyable dinner, or peeling a potato.

Which level of expectancies matter? Perhaps all. Expectancy-based theories often suggest that behavior is predicted best when the level of the expectancy fits the level of the behavior being predicted. Sometimes it is argued that prediction is best when you take into account several levels of specificity at once. People often face novel situations, however, and situations that evolve over time. It has been suggested that in such cases, generalized expectations may be particularly useful in predicting people's behavior (Scheier & Carver, 1985).

The same principles that apply to focused confidence also apply to the generalized confidence that defines optimism. When we talk about optimism, the sense of confidence is just broader in scope. Thus, when confronting a challenge (and it shouldn't matter greatly what the challenge is), optimists should tend to assume a posture of confidence and persistence (even if progress is difficult or slow), whereas pessimists should be more doubtful and hesitant. This divergence may even be amplified under conditions of serious adversity. Optimists are likely to assume the adversity can be handled successfully, pessimists are likely to anticipate disaster. These differences in how people approach adversity have important implications for how they cope with stress (Scheier & Carver, 1992).

Conceiving and Assessing Optimism

Expectancies are pivotal in contemporary theories of optimism, but there are at least two ways to assess expectancies. One way is to measure them directly, asking people to rate the extent to which they believe that their outcomes will be good or bad. This approach underlies the Life Orientation Test (LOT, Scheier & Carver, 1985) and its revision (LOT-R, Scheier, Carver, & Bridges, 1994).

Another approach to assessing optimism is less direct, assessing expectancies by examining attribution style (Peterson & Seligman, 1984; Seligman, 1991). Explaining bad outcomes in terms of causes that are stable (will persist into the future) and global (influence many events) indicates a pessimistic outlook. That is, such interpretations imply the expectation that bad outcomes will occur again in the future and in many aspects of life. Explaining bad outcomes by causes that are unstable and specific suggests the bad outcomes are less likely to recur and thus reflect greater optimism.

These approaches to conceptualizing and measuring optimism have led to their own research literatures. In this chapter, we focus on optimism as operationalized directly—that is, as self-reported generalized expectancies for the future.

Optimism and pessimism are qualities of personality that influence how people orient to many kinds of events. They influence people's subjective experiences when confronting problems, and they influence the actions people take to deal with the problems. When we ask the question "Do optimists and pessimists differ in how they react to health threats?" the answer has at least two parts. The first is whether they differ in distress. The second is whether they differ in how they act to deal with the adversity. These two themes are explored in the next two sections.

OPTIMISM AND PSYCHOLOGICAL WELL-BEING

When people confront adversity, a variety of emotions emerge, ranging from excitement and eagerness to anger, anxiety, and depression. The balance among these feelings appears to relate to optimism versus pessimism. Optimists expect to have good outcomes, even when things are hard. This should yield a mix of feelings that is relatively positive. Pessimists expect bad outcomes. This should yield a greater tendency toward negative feelings—anxiety, guilt, sadness, or despair (Carver & Scheier, 1998; Scheier & Carver, 1992; see also Snyder et al., 1996).

Relationships between optimism and distress have been examined in many groups of people facing adversity. Studies have examined students entering college (Aspinwall & Taylor, 1992; Brissette, Scheier, & Carver, 2002); employees of businesses (Long, 1993); survivors of missile attacks (Zeidner & Hammer, 1992); and people caring for cancer patients (Given et al., 1993) and Alzheimer's patients (Hooker, Monahan, Shifren, & Hutchinson, 1992; Shifren & Hooker, 1995). Research has examined people dealing with childbirth (Carver & Gaines, 1987), abortion (Cozzarelli, 1993), coronary artery bypass surgery (Fitzgerald, Tennen, Affleck, & Pransky, 1993; Scheier et al., 1989), attempts at in vitro fertilization (Litt, Tennen, Affleck, & Klock, 1992), bone marrow transplantation (Curbow, Somerfield, Baker, Wingard, & Legro, 1993), cancer (Carver, Pozo, Harris et al., 1993; Friedman et al., 1992), and the progression of AIDS (Taylor, Kemeny, Aspinwall et al., 1992). As indicated by the latter examples, many of these studies focus on people undergoing truly serious crises, rather than ordinary problems of daily life.

These studies vary in complexity, and thus in what they tell us. In many cases researchers examined responses to a difficult event, but at only one time point. These studies show more distress among pessimists than optimists. What they can *not* show is whether pessimists also had more distress beforehand. It is better to examine people repeatedly, to see how distress shifts over circumstances. Even if people cannot be assessed before the key event, more can be learned about the process of adapting if distress is assessed at several points afterward. We focus here on studies in which people were assessed at multiple time points.

Coronary Disease

One early project examined the relationship between optimism and the reactions of men undergoing coronary artery bypass surgery (Scheier, Matthews, Owens et al., 1989). Patients completed a set of psychosocial measures the day before surgery, a week after surgery, and six months post-surgery. Prior to surgery optimists reported less hostility and depression than pessimists. A week after surgery, optimists reported more relief and happiness, more satisfaction with medical care, and more satisfaction with emotional support from friends. Six months after surgery, optimists reported higher quality of life than pessimists. In a follow-up five years later (described in Scheier & Carver, 1992), optimists had greater subjective well-being and general quality of life than pessimists. Optimists reported greater work satisfaction, greater satisfaction with relationships, and less sleep disturbance (even when medical factors were statistically controlled).

Another study on optimism and quality of life after coronary artery bypass (Fitzgerald et al., 1993) assessed participants one month before surgery and eight months afterward. Optimism related to less presurgical distress. Further, controlling for presurgical life satisfaction, optimism related to post-surgical life satisfaction. Further analyses revealed that the general sense of optimism operated on feelings of life satisfaction through a more focused confidence about the surgery. That is, the general sense of optimism about life was channeled into a specific optimism about the surgery, and from there to satisfaction with life.

Similar beneficial effects of optimism have been observed in women undergoing coronary artery bypass surgery (King, Rowe, Kimble, & Zerwic, 1998). In this study, optimism was assessed one week after surgery. Additional measures were obtained at the same time point and again 1, 6, and 12 months post surgery. Optimism predicted more positive mood, less negative mood, and more satisfaction with life at all points. Optimism even predicted more positive and less negative mood at one month when controlling for initial mood.

An additional research project (Leedham, Meyerowitz, Muirhead, & Frist, 1995) explored the effects of positive expectations on experiences surrounding heart transplant surgery (this study did not examine optimism per se, but variables conceptually tied to optimism). Patients (and nurses) completed measures before surgery, at discharge, and three and six months post-surgery. Initial items assessed confidence about the efficacy of treatment, confidence about future health and survival, and broader confidence for the future. Positive expectations related to higher quality of life in the future, even among patients who had health setbacks.

Finally, in a more recent study, cardiac patients hospitalized with ischemic heart disease were assessed one month after discharge and a year later (Shnek, Irvine, Stewart, & Abbey, 2001). Optimism related inversely to depressive symptoms at the initial assessment and at the one year follow-up. Indeed, optimism related to follow-up depression even when controlling for initial depression.

Reproductive Medical Issues

Other research has examined optimism and emotional well-being in the context of reproductive medical issues. In an early study Carver and Gaines (1987) examined the development of depressed affect following childbirth. Women reported optimism and depression in the last trimester of their pregnancy, and reported depression again three weeks after the baby was born. Optimism related to less depression at the initial assessment. More important, optimism predicted less depression postpartum, even when controlling for initial levels.

Similar results were found by more recent studies. Fontaine and Jones (1997) also assessed optimism and depression before and after childbirth. Optimism was again associated with fewer depressive symptoms, both during pregnancy and at two weeks postpartum. Park, Moore, Turner, and Adler (1997) assessed women's optimism during their first prenatal clinic visit. During the last trimester of the pregnancy, they assessed the women's anxiety and the extent to which they were maintaining positive states of mind. Optimism related negatively to anxiety and positively to positive states of mind.

Optimism and psychological well-being have also been studied in women dealing with issues of infertility. In vitro fertilization sometimes overcomes fertility problems, but not always. Litt, Tennen, Affleck, and Klock (1992) examined reactions among people whose attempts at in vitro fertilization were unsuccessful. Approximately eight weeks before the attempt, they assessed optimism, expectancies for fertilization success, coping strategies, distress levels, and the impact of the infertility on participants' lives. Two weeks after notification of a negative pregnancy test, distress was assessed again. Neither demographics, obstetric history, marital adjustment, nor the rated effect of infertility on subjects' lives predicted distress following the negative pregnancy test, but pessimism did, even controlling for previous levels of distress.

Additional studies have examined the influence of optimism on adjustment to abortion. In one study (Cozzarelli, 1993), women completed measures of optimism, self-esteem, self-mastery, self-efficacy, and depression one hour prior to the abortion. Depression and psychological adjustment were assessed 30 minutes after the abortion and again three weeks later. Optimists had less pre-abortion depression, better post-abortion adjustment, and better three-week adjustment than pessimists. A second similar study was conducted by Major et al. (1998), who were interested in personal resources that might protect women from distress. Optimism proved to be a key component in a style of personal resilience that facilitated post-abortion adjustment.

Cancer

Optimism has also been studied in the context of adjusting to diagnosis and treatment for cancer. One study examined effects of optimism on adaptation to treatment for early-stage breast cancer (Carver et al., 1993). Diagnosis and treatment for breast cancer is traumatic, because the disease is life threatening. But because the prognosis for early-stage cancer is relatively good, there is enough ambiguity about the future to permit individual differences to be readily expressed. Patients were interviewed six times over the course of a year: at the time of diagnosis, the day before surgery, 7 to 10 days after surgery, and 3, 6, and 12 months later. Optimism predicted less distress over time, even when controlling for the effects of medical variables and the prior level of distress. Thus, optimism predicted not just lower initial distress, but also resilience to distress during the next year.

Johnson (1996) demonstrated the beneficial effects of optimism among a group of men receiving radiation therapy for prostate cancer. Optimism was assessed before the first radiation treatment. Mood was assessed through the treatment period and at two weeks, one month, and three months after the end of treatment. Optimism predicted emotional responses both during and after treatment, with less optimistic patients being particularly vulnerable to negative moods.

Finally, Christman (1990) examined adjustment among a group of patients receiving radiation for diverse cancers. Patients entered the project at one of three times: on the first day of treatment, the 15th day of treatment, or the last day of treatment. Multiple assessments were made on patients who were enrolled before the conclusion of their treatment. Optimism related to less adjustment problem at all assessment points, as well as to illness uncertainty at the first and second assessment points.

Other Health Contexts

The majority of the research that relates optimism to psychological well-being in health settings focused on heart disease, reproductive issues, and cancer. Research from other domains makes similar points, however. For example, Taylor et al. (1992) examined psychological well-being in a cohort of gay and bisexual men at risk of developing Acquired Immunodeficiency Syndrome (AIDS). Among both HIV+ and HIV− men, greater optimism was associated with lower levels of subsequent distress.

Chamberlain et al. (1992) demonstrated the beneficial effects of optimism in joint replacement patients. Data were collected before surgery, the third day following surgery, and approximately six weeks following surgery. Presurgical optimism related positively to follow-up life satisfaction and well-being, and negatively to distress and pain.

In addition to having positive effects on well-being among people dealing with medical conditions, optimism also influences the well-being of people who act as caregivers to medical patients. For example, Given et al.

(1993) studied a group of cancer patients and their caregivers, and found that caregivers' optimism related to a number of caregiver well-being variables—lower depression, less impact of caregiving on physical health, and less impact on caregivers' daily schedules. Similar effects have been found among caregivers of Alzheimer's patients (Hooker et al., 1992; Shifren & Hooker, 1995) and caregivers of patients suffering from stroke (Tompkins, Schulz, & Rau, 1988). In each case, optimism predicted lower levels of depression and higher levels of psychological well-being.

Adjustment in Nonhealth-Related Contexts

Although much of the evidence that optimism relates to psychological well-being comes from samples such as people facing health threats and people caring for seriously ill relatives, others have studied samples undergoing events that are difficult but far less extreme. For example, the start of a person's college years is a difficult and stressful time. Two groups of researchers have examined students adjusting to the first semester of college (Aspinwall & Taylor, 1992; Brissette et al., 2002). In this research, optimism was assessed when the students first arrived, and measures of psychological and physical well-being were obtained at the end of the semester.

In the study by Aspinwall and Taylor (1992), higher levels of optimism upon entering college predicted less distress at the end of the semester. This relationship was independent of effects due to self-esteem, locus of control, desire for control, and baseline mood. Brissette et al. (2002) added the demonstration that these effects on emotional well-being were independent of initial well-being. They also added the discovery that the better adjustment of optimistic students was mediated in part by developing better social support during that period.

In a similar vein, Stewart et al. (1997) examined adjustment among a group of first-year medical students. Students were surveyed prior to the beginning of their medical training. Two months later, students who initially had high levels of anxiety and low levels of optimism were more likely to develop symptoms of depression and anxiety. Another study, involving first-year law students (Segerstrom, Taylor, Kemeny, & Fahey, 1998) assessed optimism and mood disturbance at the beginning of classes. The same measures were readministered at midsemester, eight weeks later. Baseline optimism predicted fewer mood disturbances at follow-up, even after controlling for initial level of mood disturbance.

In a community population of middle-aged adults, Räikkönen et al. (1999) assessed ambulatory blood pressure for three days and asked participants to keep a diary of daily moods and daily stressful events. In examining the average rating of mood across the three assessment days, they found that optimism (assessed before monitoring began) predicted lower negative mood and higher positive mood. They also found that optimists rated the day's most negative event as less stressful than did pessimists.

Another study involving a middle-aged sample (Bromberger & Matthews, 1996) focused on women approaching menopause. Optimism, depressive symptoms, and life stress were assessed at baseline and again three years later. Women who were more pessimistic at baseline were at higher risk for depression at follow-up. This effect was particularly pronounced among women who reported an ongoing stressor at the time during which pessimism was assessed. All these effects remained significant after baseline depression was controlled.

OPTIMISM, PESSIMISM, AND COPING

One conclusion is clear from the findings just described. When experiencing a health threat, optimists experience less distress than pessimists. Is this just because optimists are more cheerful than pessimists? Apparently not, because the differences often remain even when controls are included for *previous* distress. There must be other explanations. Do optimists do anything to cope that helps them adapt better than pessimists? Many researchers have investigated this possibility.

In this section we consider the strategies that optimists and pessimists use to cope with health threats, and we link those coping differences to differences in distress. As discussed earlier, people who are confident continue to exert effort, even when dealing with adversity. People who are doubtful withdraw effort. They are more likely to try escaping from the adversity by wishful thinking. They are more likely to do things that provide temporary distractions but don't help solve the problem. Sometimes they even give up completely. Both the effort of optimists and the reduced effort of pessimists can be expressed in a variety of ways, and those expressions—people's coping reactions and coping strategies—are the focus of this section.

Differences in Coping

Differences in coping methods used by optimists and pessimists have been found in many studies. One early project (Scheier, Weintraub, & Carver, 1986) asked undergraduates to recall their most stressful event of the previous month and report their coping responses to that event. Optimism related to problem-focused coping, especially when the situation was perceived to be controllable. Optimism also related to use of positive reframing and (when the situation was uncontrollable) with the tendency to accept the reality of the situation. In contrast, optimism related negatively to use of denial and attempts to distance oneself from the problem.

These findings provided the first indication that optimists are not just problem-focused copers, which might have been many people's first assumption. Optimists also use emotion-focused coping techniques, including accepting the reality of difficult situations and putting the situations in the best possible light. Because emotion-focused coping is so often tied to situations that cannot be changed, these findings hint that optimists may enjoy a coping advantage even in this sort of situation.

Other research has studied differences in dispositional coping styles among optimists and pessimists (Billingsley, Waehler, & Hardin, 1993; Carver, Scheier, & Weintraub, 1989; Fontaine, Manstead, & Wagner, 1993). As with situational coping, optimists report a general tendency to use problem-focused coping, and they report being more planful. Pessimism relates to a tendency to disengage from goals with which the stressor is interfering. While optimists report a tendency to accept the reality of stressful events, they also report trying to see the best in bad situations and to learn something from them. Pessimists report tendencies toward overt denial and substance abuse—strategies that temporarily lessen their awareness of the problem. Thus, in general terms, optimists appear to be active copers and pessimists appear to be avoidant copers.

Other projects studied relationships between optimism and coping in specific contexts. Strutton and Lumpkin (1992) studied coping in the work environment. They found optimists using problem-focused coping (e.g., directed problem solving) more than pessimists. Pessimism related to avoidant coping (self-indulgent escapism including sleeping, eating, and drinking). Another study in the workplace, focusing on executive women (Fry, 1995), found that optimists react to daily hassles differently than pessimists. Optimistic women expected gain or growth from stressful events and reported coping indicating acceptance, expressiveness, and tension reduction. They also reported using their social support, rather than withdrawing, distancing, or engaging in self-blame.

A study of AIDS patients described earlier (Taylor et al., 1992) also provides information about coping. In general, optimism related in this study to active coping. Optimism related to positive attitudes and tendencies to plan for recovery, seek information, and reframe bad situations so as to see their most positive aspects. Optimists made less use of fatalism, self-blame, and escapism, and they neither focused on the negative aspects of the situation nor tried to suppress thoughts about their symptoms. Optimists also appeared to accept situations that they could not change, rather than trying to escape those situations.

It is important to realize that the associations between optimism and coping do not simply reflect a difference in the manner in which optimists and pessimists appraise events. Chang (1998) found that optimists and pessimists did not differ in their primary appraisal of an upcoming exam (i.e., how threatening it was). They differed, though, in their secondary appraisals. Optimists perceived the exam to be more controllable and their efforts to cope with it more effective than pessimists. Significant differences still emerged between optimism and several varieties of coping, even after the effect of secondary appraisals was statistically controlled.

Promoting Well-Being When Faced with Health Threats

In describing how optimists and pessimists cope with adversity, several other studies are worth noting. These studies do not deal with coping per se, but they make points closely related to those we've made regarding coping. Many of these studies involve responses to particular health threats or illness episodes. As a group, they show that optimists are more likely than pessimists to face health threats head-on, and do whatever they can to improve the situation they are confronting. In this respect, the behavior reflects problem-focused coping, an attempt to engage in proactive processes that promote good health and well-being (Aspinwall, 1997; Aspinwall & Taylor, 1997).

One study bearing on this theme looked at health promotion among heart patients participating in a cardiac rehabilitation program (Shepperd, Maroto, & Pbert, 1996). Optimism related to greater success in lowering levels of saturated fat, body fat, and global coronary risk. Optimism also related to increased exercise across the rehabilitation period. Another study (Scheier & Carver, 1992) investigated lifestyles of coronary artery bypass patients five years after their surgery. This study found that optimists were more likely than pessimists to be taking vitamins, eating low-fat foods, and to be enrolled in a cardiac rehabilitation program.

An obvious health risk related to behavior is HIV infection. By avoiding certain sexual practices, people reduce their risk of infection. One study of HIV-negative gay men revealed that optimists reported fewer anonymous sexual partners than pessimists (Taylor et al., 1992). Another study examined the intentions of sexually active inner-city minority adolescents (Carvajal, Garner, & Evans, 1998). Optimists reported stronger intentions of avoiding unsafe sex. Taken together, the findings suggest that optimists were making efforts or intending to make efforts to reduce their risk, thereby safeguarding their health.

One more study relevant here (Friedman, Weinberg, Webb, et al., 1995) examined health behavior and intentions among a group of hospital employees at risk for skin cancer. Optimists were significantly more likely than pessimists to report intentions to engage in skin cancer-relevant health prevention behaviors (e.g., regular sunscreen use). In addition, among those identified at screening as having suspicious lesions, optimists were more likely to comply with recommended follow-up care.

Although they are perhaps less impressive than studies of health patients, other studies have examined health-related habits of people with no salient health concerns. At least two such projects have found optimists report more health-promoting behaviors, in general, than pessimists (Robbins, Spence, & Clark, 1991; Steptoe, Wardle, Vinck et al., 1994). These studies also suggest that optimism relates to behaviors aimed at promoting health and reducing health risk.

Consistent with this pattern is research showing conclusively that optimists aren't simply people who stick their heads in the sand and ignore threats to their well-being. Rather, they display a pattern of attending selectively to risks—risks that both are applicable to them and also are related to serious health problems (Aspinwall & Brunhart, 1996). If the potential health problem is minor, or if it is unlikely to affect them personally, optimists don't show this elevated vigilance. Only when the threat matters does it emerge. This fits the idea that optimists scan their surroundings for threats to their well-being but save their active coping efforts for threats that are truly meaningful.

Linking Coping to Emotional Distress

The studies just described help establish that optimists cope differently than pessimists, but none of what we have said thus far indicates that these differences in coping produce differences in psychological well-being. As it happens, however, a number of the studies reviewed in the context of optimism and distress contained measures of coping along with measures of well-being. This allowed the researchers to examine whether differences in well-being were mediated by differences in coping.

One of the studies reviewed earlier (Scheier et al., 1989) assessed the use of attention-cognitive strategies as ways of dealing with the experience of coronary artery bypass. Before surgery, optimists were more likely than pessimists to report they were making plans for their future and setting goals for recovery. Optimists also tended to report being less focused on negative aspects of their experience—distress emotions and physical symptoms. After the surgery, optimists were more likely than pessimists to report seeking out and requesting information about what physicians would be requiring of them in the months ahead. Optimists reported less effort to suppress thoughts about their physical symptoms. Path analyses suggested that the positive impact of optimism on quality of life six months post-surgery occurred through the effect of differences in coping.

Similarly, King et al. (1998) assessed coping in their study of women undergoing coronary bypass. Although their results were not entirely consistent across all the assessment points in their study, optimists displayed more positive thinking during the week following surgery, engaged in more attempts at finding meaning at 1 month, and used less escapism at 12 months. Mediation analyses showed that finding meaning and using less escapism were partly responsible for the relation between optimism and negative mood.

The study of adaptation to failed in vitro fertilization that was described earlier (Litt et al., 1992) also examined coping. Although the researchers did not find a relationship in this study between optimism and instrumental coping, they found that pessimism related to escape as a coping strategy. Escape, in turn, related to greater distress after the fertilization failure. In addition, optimists were more likely than pessimists to report feeling that they benefited somehow from the failed fertilization experience (e.g., by becoming closer to their spouse).

Several studies have examined relationships between optimism, coping, and distress among cancer patients. One study followed women undergoing breast biopsy (Stanton & Snider, 1993). Optimism, coping, and mood were assessed the day before. Women receiving a cancer diagnosis were reassessed 24 hours before surgery and 3 weeks after surgery. Women with a benign diagnosis completed a second assessment that corresponded to either the second or the third assessment of the cancer group. Pessimists used more cognitive avoidance in coping with the upcoming diagnostic procedure than optimists. This contributed to elevated distress prior to biopsy, and also predicted post-biopsy distress among women with positive diagnoses.

Another study of cancer patients, mentioned earlier in the chapter, examined the ways women cope with treatment for early stage breast can-

cer during the first full year after treatment (Carver et al., 1993). Optimism, coping (with the diagnosis of cancer), and mood were assessed the
day before surgery. Coping and mood were also assessed 10 days post surgery, and at 3 follow-up points during the next year. Both before and after
surgery, optimism was tied to a pattern of coping tactics that revolved
around accepting the reality of the situation, placing as positive a light on
the situation as possible, trying to relieve the situation with humor, and (at
presurgery only) taking active steps to do whatever there was to be done.
Pessimism was linked to denial and behavioral disengagement (giving up)
at each measurement point.

The coping tactics that related to optimism and pessimism also related
to distress. Positive reframing, acceptance, and use of humor all related
inversely to self-reports of distress, both before surgery and after. Denial
and behavioral disengagement related to greater distress at all measurement points. At six months a new association emerged, with distress positively related to another kind of avoidance coping: self-distraction. Further
analyses revealed that the effect of optimism on distress was largely indirect through coping, particularly at post surgery.

A more recent study by Epping-Jordan et al. (1999) assessed breast cancer patients at diagnosis and at three and six month follow-ups. They found
that initial pessimism related to higher symptoms of anxiety and depression
at all time points. They also found this was partially mediated by pessimists'
use of disengagement coping strategies at two of the three time points.

Other studies have also looked for a mediational role of coping in the
relationship between optimism and psychological well-being. In one college adaptation study described earlier (Aspinwall & Taylor, 1992), optimistic students were more likely than pessimistic students to engage in
active coping and less likely to engage in avoidance coping. Avoidance
coping related to poorer adjustment, and active coping was (separately)
associated with better adjustment. The paths from optimism to well-being
through coping were significant. In the other college adaptation study
described earlier (Brissette et al., 2002), optimists made more use of positive reframing, which related to better adjustment. Further, the path from
optimism through coping to adjustment was significant. Thus, as in the
health studies, the beneficial effects of optimism in adapting to college
seem to operate partly through differences in coping.

Similar effects have emerged in other contexts. In the study described earlier on adjustment to pregnancy (Park et al., 1997), optimistic women were
more likely than pessimistic women to engage in constructive thinking
(thinking about and solving daily problems in effective ways). Constructive
thinking also correlated negatively with later anxiety and positively with

positive states of mind. The association between optimism and each of these markers of psychological adjustment was mediated through the tendency of optimists to engage in constructive thinking.

Finally, recall the study by Segerstrom et al. (1998) of law students. Additional data from that study showed that optimists used less avoidant coping than pessimists. Mediational analyses showed that the differences between optimists and pessimists in mood disturbance was at least partially due to the differences in their use of avoidant coping strategies.

In sum, these studies indicate that optimists differ from pessimists both in stable coping tendencies and in the coping responses they spontaneously generate when confronting stressful situations. Optimists also differ from pessimists in how they cope with serious disease. In general, findings suggest that optimists tend to use more problem-focused coping than pessimists. When problem-focused coping is not a possibility, optimists turn to adaptive emotion-focused coping strategies such as acceptance, use of humor, and positive reframing. Pessimists tend to cope through overt denial and by mentally and behaviorally disengaging from the goals with which the stressor is interfering.

Acceptance, Overcoming Adversity, and Continued Goal Engagement

It is perhaps particularly noteworthy that optimists turn toward acceptance in uncontrollable situations, whereas pessimists turn more toward overt denial. Although both seem to reflect emotion-focused coping, there are important differences between them. Overt denial (a refusal to accept the reality of the situation) means trying to adhere to a world view that is no longer valid. Acceptance implies a restructuring of one's experience so as to come to grips with the reality of the situation that one confronts. Acceptance thus may involve a deeper set of processes, in which the person actively works through the experience, attempting to integrate it into an evolving world view.

The active attempt to come to terms with the existence of problems may confer special benefits on acceptance as a coping response. We should be very clear here, however, about the "acceptance" we are discussing. The acceptance we have in mind is a willingness to admit that a problem exists or that an event has happened—even an event that may irrevocably alter the fabric of the person's life. We are *not* talking about a stoic resignation, or a fatalistic acceptance of negative consequences to which the problem or event might lead, no matter how likely those consequences might be. This kind of acceptance does not confer a benefit at all.

Consider, for example, the situation faced by someone diagnosed with an illness such as terminal cancer. The ultimate outcome will be death. Yet, the person can accept the fact that he or she is terminally ill without simultaneously succumbing to the feeling that he or she is "as good as dead." The latter sort of resignation may well promote a kind of functional death, in which the person prematurely disengages from the opportunities of life. Consistent with this idea, there are findings suggesting that people who react to illness diagnoses with stoic resignation, or passive acceptance of their own impending death, actually die sooner than those who do not (Greer, Morris, & Pettingale, 1979; Greer, Morris, Pettingale, & Haybittle, 1990; Pettingale, Morris, & Greer, 1985; Reed, Kemeny, & Taylor, 1994; for further discussion, see Scheier & Carver, 2001).

In contrast to resignation to the ultimate consequence, an acceptance of the diagnosis per se may have very different consequences. It may cause people to reprioritize their lives, to realistically revise and cut back on long-term goals, and to use what time they have left in optimal ways. By accepting the fact that life may be compromised (but not ended), people in this situation may be impelled to develop a more adaptive set of guidelines within which to live the life they have left (Moskowitz, Folkman, Collette, & Vittinghoff, 1996).

Why is a revised outlook on life potentially so important, and why should it lead to enhanced well-being? To answer these questions fully, we must revisit some ideas we introduced earlier, regarding theoretical underpinnings of optimism (see also Carver & Scheier, 1998). In particular, recall the central role played by goals. In the view described earlier, people live life by identifying goals and working and behaving in ways to attain these goals (Figure 2.1, Loop 1). Obviously, the goals themselves can take a variety of forms, both social and nonsocial, both personal and communal (Carver & Scheier, 1998). Regardless of their nature, however, goals provide the structure that defines people's lives and imbues life with meaning.

As we indicated earlier, keeping people goal engaged requires two things. One is the ability to identify goals that are valued. People don't take up goals that don't matter to them. Valued goals are purposes for living. The second factor is the perceived attainability of the goal. If a goal seems unattainable at the outset, effortful behavior never even begins. If people continually fail to make progress toward goals they are committed to, they will begin to withdraw effort and start to perceive the goals as out of reach. In contrast, hope enables people to hold onto valued goals, stay engaged in the process of striving, and stay committed to the attempt to move forward (Figure 2.1, Loop 2).

Figure 2.1
Successful Self-Regulation

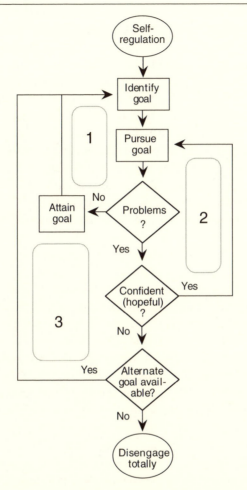

Successful self-regulation is a continuing process of identifying goals, pursuing them, attaining them, and identifying further ones (Loop 1). Given adversity, a step of evaluating chances of success may be added (Loop 2), but sufficient confidence places the person back into the first loop. If confidence is low enough, the person may seek an alternative goal (Loop 3); if available, it returns the person to goal pursuit and attainment. If, however, the original goal is seen as unattainable and no alternative is available, the person may disengage completely. (From C. S. Carver and M. F. Scheier, *On the self-regulation of behavior*, 1998, Cambridge University Press; reproduced with permission of the publisher and authors.)

One final part of the overall picture is that the loss of engagement in a goal does not necessarily lead to a vacuum of goallessness. The ebb and flow of engagement and disengagement can be seen in terms of competition among goals (Carver & Scheier, 1998). Disengagement from one goal may reflect a weakening of commitment to it, but because people usually have many goals at once, this weakening of commitment permits another goal to become focal and thus permits behavior to shift toward *its* pursuit. Thus, the loss of one goal is often followed directly by pursuit of another one.

Sometimes this means scaling back to a less ambitious goal in the same domain as the abandoned goal. By taking up an attainable alternative, the person remains engaged in goal pursuit and forward movement (Figure 1, Loop 3). This is particularly important when the blocked path concerns a value that is central to the self. People need multiple paths to these core values (cf. Linville, 1985, 1987; Showers & Ryff, 1996; Wicklund & Goll-witzer, 1982). If one path is barricaded, people need to be able to jump to another one.

It seems apparent that the ability to shift to a new goal, or a new path to a continuing goal, is a very important part of remaining goal-engaged. What happens if there is no alternative to take up? In such a case disengagement from an unattainable goal is not accompanied by a shift, because there is nothing to shift to. This is the worst situation, where there is noth-ing to pursue, nothing to take the place of what is seen as unattainable (cf. Moskowitz et al., 1996; Scheier & Carver, 2001). If commitment to the unattainable goal remains, the result is great distress. If the commitment wanes, the result is emptiness. There is reason to suspect that such a state might also be implicated in premature death (Carver & Scheier, 1998).

Pessimism and Health-Defeating Behaviors

We have characterized optimists as persistent in trying to reach desired goals. This includes efforts to deal with adversity and efforts to promote well-being apart from adversity. Theory holds that pessimists are less likely to struggle to ensure their well-being. There is, in fact, evidence that pessimists engage in behaviors that reflect a tendency to give up. Some of these behaviors have adverse consequences for well-being. Some even have deadly consequences.

Various forms of substance abuse can be seen as reflecting a giving-up tendency. Substance abuse in general, and excessive alcohol consumption in particular, is often seen as an escape from problems. If so, it follows that pessimists should be more vulnerable than optimists to this pattern of maladaptive behavior. At least three studies have produced findings that fit this picture.

One was a study of women with a family history of alcoholism. Pessimists in this group were more likely than optimists to report drinking problems (Ohannessian, Hesselbrock, Tennen, & Affleck, 1993). In another study of people who had been treated for alcohol abuse and were now entering an aftercare program, pessimists were more likely to drop out and return to drinking than optimists (Strack, Carver, & Blaney, 1987). Finally, optimistic women have been found less likely to engage in substance abuse during the course of their pregnancies than pessimists (Park et al., 1997).

Giving up can be manifested in many ways. Alcohol consumption dulls awareness of failures and problems. People can disregard their problems by distracting themselves. Even sleeping can help us escape from situations we don't want to face. Sometimes, though, giving up is more complete. Sometimes people give up not on specific goals, but on all the goals that form their lives. Such extreme cases can prompt suicide (though Snyder, 1994, points out that successful suicide also requires effortful pursuit of one last goal). Some people are more vulnerable to suicide than others. It is commonly assumed that depression is the best indicator of suicide risk. But pessimism (as measured by the Hopelessness scale) is actually a stronger predictor of this act, the ultimate disengagement from life (Beck, Steer, Kovacs, & Garrison, 1985).

In sum, a sizeable body of evidence indicates that pessimism can lead people into self-defeating patterns. The result can be less persistence, more avoidance coping, health-damaging behavior, and potentially even an impulse to escape from life altogether. With no confidence about the future, there may be nothing left to sustain life (Carver & Scheier, 1998).

IS OPTIMISM ALWAYS BETTER THAN PESSIMISM?

The picture painted throughout this chapter is one in which optimists are virtually always better off than pessimists. The evidence indicates they are less distressed when times are tough, they cope in ways that foster better outcomes, and they are more proactive in their responses to adversity. Although there are certainly times and situations in which optimists are only a *little* better off than pessimists, and probably cases where they have no advantage at all, there is remarkably little evidence that optimists are ever *worse* off than pessimists.

Several people have suggested the possibility that such situations may exist, that optimism may be potentially damaging (Schwarzer, 1994; Tennen & Affleck, 1987). Indeed, there is logic behind this hypothesis. For example, too much optimism might lead people to ignore a threat until it's too late, or might lead people to overestimate their ability to deal with an adverse situation, resulting in poorer outcomes.

Most of the data reviewed in the preceding sections indicate, however, that this is generally not the case. On the other hand, there are a couple of studies that suggest the possibility that optimists may not always take action to enhance future well-being. Goodman, Chesney, and Tipton (1995) studied whether adolescent girls at risk for HIV infection sought out information about HIV testing and agreed to have a test performed. Those higher in optimism were less likely to expose themselves to the information, and were less likely to follow through with an actual test (see also Perkins, Lesserman, & Murphy, 1993).

These findings contradict the bulk of evidence reviewed earlier. Why the findings diverge in this way is not clear. Goodman et al. noted that the average level of optimism among the adolescent girls they studied was substantially lower than the levels typically seen. This may have played a role in the results. Alternatively, perhaps the results do not really contradict previous findings at all. For example, no information was gathered about the girls' knowledge concerning the serostatus of their sexual partners. Perhaps optimists had gone to greater lengths than pessimists to verify that their partners were HIV-negative. If so, they would have less need for HIV-relevant information or testing. Perhaps they took greater steps to avoid engaging in unsafe sex, and for this reason had less need to pursue information about their HIV-status. Consistent with this latter possibility are findings reported by Carvajal et al. (1998), in which optimistic adolescent girls expressed stronger intentions to avoid unsafe sex than did their more pessimistic counterparts. Obviously, however, more work is needed for these questions to be resolved.

The idea that optimists may fail to take steps to protect themselves is one potential way in which optimism might work against a person. Another possibility worth considering is that the world view of an optimist might be especially vulnerable to the shattering impact of a traumatic event, an event more consistent with the pessimist's world view. Given the diagnosis of metastatic cancer, the experience of a violent rape, or having one's home destroyed by fire or flood, will the optimist react worse than the pessimist? Will optimists be less able to rebuild their shattered lives? All these possibilities are legitimate to raise. Any of them might occur. However, we are aware of no evidence that any of them sys-tematically *does* occur.

Perhaps the lack of evidence that optimists respond worse to a shatter-ing event reflects a more general lack of information about how personal-ity predicts responses to trauma or to experiences more extreme than those reviewed here—such as terminal illness. There is not much information on these questions. However, we do not expect optimists to be harmed by these experiences more than pessimists. Rather, we expect them to re-set their sights on their changed realities, and to continue to make the best of what they are facing. Pessimists may find that their world views are con-firmed by trauma or disaster, but we doubt that they will take much satis-faction in this confirmation. Rather, their experience will revolve around anticipation of continued adversity, along with the feelings of distress to which such expectancies lead.

CAN PESSIMISTS BECOME OPTIMISTS?

Given the many ways in which the life of the optimist is better than that of the pessimist, there is good reason to want to be in the former category instead of the latter. There is at least a small problem, though, for those who are not already optimistic: Twin research suggests that optimism is genetically influenced (Plomin et al., 1992). There remains a question about whether optimism is heritable, or whether it displays heritability because of its relation to other aspects of temperament. That is, optimism relates both to neuroticism and to extraversion, and both are genetically influenced. Although optimism is distinguishable from these tempera-ments (Scheier et al., 1994), the observed heritability of optimism may depend on these associations.

Another influence on people's outlook on life is early childhood experi-ence. In discussing personality development, Erikson (1968) held that infants who experience the social world as predictable develop a sense of "basic trust," whereas those who experience it as unpredictable develop a sense of "basic mistrust." These qualities are not so different from opti-mism and pessimism. Similarly, attachment theorists hold that some infants are securely attached in their relationships, but others are not (Ainsworth, Blehar, Waters, & Wall, 1978; Bowlby, 1988). This has also been extended to discussions of adult attachments (Hazan & Shaver, 1994). As it happens, insecurity of adult attachment is related to pes-simism. Perhaps optimism derives partly from the early childhood experi-ence of secure attachment (see also Snyder, 1994). This is only one example, of course, of many possible ways in which the environment might influence the development of optimism.

Whether one views the origins of optimism and pessimism in inheritance or in early childhood experience, these pathways suggest that optimism and pessimism are relatively stable. Genetically determined qualities are by definition part of your fundamental make-up, exerting a virtually unending influence on your behavior. Similarly, aspects of your world-view that are acquired early in life are the foundation from which you experience the *rest* of the events in your life. The more firmly shaped that foundation, the more enduring is its influence.

If pessimism is that deeply embedded in a person's life, can it be changed? The cautious answer seems to be yes. However, there remain questions about how large a change can be expected and how permanent the change will be. There also remain questions about whether an induced optimism will act in the same way—have the same beneficial effects—as a naturally occurring optimism.

Of the many ways to try to turn a pessimist into an optimist, the most straightforward may be the techniques known collectively as cognitive-behavioral therapies. Indeed, trying to turn pessimists (focused or generalized) into optimists seems an apt characterization of the thrust of these therapies. Their earliest applications were to problems such as depression and anxiety (Beck, 1967). The logic was that people with these problems make a variety of unduly negative distortions in their minds (e.g., "I can't do anything right"). The negative thoughts cause negative affect (dysphoria, anxiety) and set people up to stop trying to reach their goals. These distortions closely resemble what we would imagine to be the interior monologue of the pessimist.

If unduly negative cognitions and self-statements define the problem, the goal of the cognitive therapies is to change the cognitions, make them more positive, and thereby reduce distress and foster renewed effort. Many techniques exist for producing such changes. In general, this approach to therapy begins by having people pay close attention to their experience, to identify points where distress arises and the thoughts associated with (or immediately preceding) these points. The idea is to make the person more aware of what are now automatic thoughts. In many cases, the thoughts turn out to be pessimistic beliefs. Once the beliefs are isolated, they can be challenged and changed. (This attempt to deal with pessimistic beliefs by shifting them has an interesting resemblance to positive reframing, described earlier as a useful coping strategy.)

At least one study has found that cognitive-behavioral therapy can increase optimism (Antoni et al., 2001). It compared breast cancer patients who underwent a ten-week cognitive-behavioral stress management intervention with those who underwent a one-day stress-management seminar. Women completed questionnaires post-surgery, and three, six, and twelve months later. The intervention proved to increase women's optimism, an effect that was maintained at assessments three months and nine months after the intervention.

Another method for change is personal efficacy training. The focus of such procedures is on increasing specific kinds of competence (e.g., by assertiveness or social skill training). However, the techniques often address thoughts and behaviors that relate to a more general sense of pessimism. Training in problem-solving, selecting and defining obtainable sub-goals, and decision making all improve the ways in which a person handles a wide range of everyday situations.

Although development of positive expectations is an important goal, it should also be recognized that it can be counterproductive to substitute an unquestioning optimism for an existing doubt. Sometimes people are pessimistic because they have unrealistically high aspirations. They demand perfection, hardly ever see it, and develop resulting doubts about their adequacy. This must be countered by establishing realistic goals and identifying which situations must be accepted rather than changed. People must learn to relinquish unattainable goals and set alternative goals to replace those that cannot be attained (Carver & Scheier, 1998, in press; Wrosch, Scheier, Carver, & Schulz, in press).

CONCLUDING COMMENT

The research reviewed here makes clear that an optimistic orientation to life is beneficial in many circumstances, including the facing of an illness or health threat. Put simply, optimists are less distressed than pessimists in such circumstances. In part, this "optimistic advantage" stems from differences in the manner in which optimists and pessimists cope with difficulties. Optimists remain engaged with their goals and their lives, facing problems head-on and taking active and constructive steps to solve them. They use their support resources effectively, giving them an extra measure of resilience. Pessimists, in contrast, tend to avoid facing their problems and are more likely to abandon their efforts to reach their goals. These differences in coping are potent moderators of the impact of stress on emotional well-being.

NOTES

Correspondence: Charles S. Carver, Department of Psychology, University of Miami, Coral Gables, FL 33124–2070, Phone: (305) 284–2817, FAX: (305) 284–3402, E-mail: ccarver@miami.edu.

Preparation of this chapter was facilitated by support from the National Cancer Institute (grants CA64710, CA64711, CA78995, and CA84944) and the National Heart, Lung, and Blood Institute (grants HL65111 and HL 65112).

1. We note that although we often refer to optimists and pessimists as though they were distinct groups, this is a matter of verbal convenience. This dimension is distributed relatively normally: People range from the very optimistic to the very pessimistic, with most falling somewhere in the middle.

REFERENCES

Ainsworth, M. D. S., Blehar, M. C., Waters, E., & Wall, T. (1978). *Patterns of attachment.* Hillsdale, NJ: Erlbaum.

Antoni, M. H., Lehman, J. M., Kilbourn, K. M., Boyers, A. E., Culver, J. L., Alferi, S. M., Yount, S. E., McGregor, B. A., Arena, P. L., Harris, S. D., Price, A. A., & Carver, C. S. (2001). Cognitive-behavioral stress management intervention decreases the prevalence of depression and enhances benefit finding among women under treatment for early-stage breast cancer. *Health Psychology, 20,* 20–32.

Armor, D. A., & Taylor, S. E. (1998). Situated optimism: Specific outcome expectancies and self-regulation. In M. Zanna (Ed.), *Advances in experimental social psychology* (Vol. 30, 309–379). San Diego: Academic Press.

Aspinwall, L. G. (1997). Where planning meets coping: Proactive coping and the detection and management of potential stressors. In S. L. Friedman & E. K. Scholnick (Eds.), *The developmental psychology of planning: Why, how, and when do we plan?* (pp. 285–320). Mahwah, NJ: Erlbaum.

Aspinwall, L. G., & Brunhart, S. M. (1996). Distinguishing optimism from denial: Optimistic beliefs predict attention to health threats. *Personality and Social Psychology Bulletin, 22,* 993–1003.

Aspinwall, L. G., & Taylor, S. E. (1992). Modeling cognitive adaptation: A longitudinal investigation of the impact of individual differences and coping on college adjustment and performance. *Journal of Personality and Social Psychology, 63,* 989–1003.

Aspinwall, L. G. & Taylor, S. E. (1997). A stitch in time: Self-regulation and proactive coping. *Psychological Bulletin, 121,* 417–436.

Beck, A. T. (1967). Depression: Clinical, experimental, and theoretical aspects. New York: Harper & Row.

Beck, A. T., Steer, R. A., Kovacs, M., & Garrison, B. (1985). Hopelessness and eventual suicide: A 10-year prospective study of patients hospitalized with suicidal ideation. *American Journal of Psychiatry, 142,* 559–563.

Billingsley, K. D., Waehler, C. A., & Hardin, S. I. (1993). Stability of optimism and choice of coping strategy. *Perceptual and Motor Skills,* 76, 91–97.

Bowlby, J. (1988). *A secure base: Parent–child attachment and healthy human development.* New York: Basic Books.

Brissette, I., Scheier, M. F., & Carver, C. S. (2002). The role of optimism in social network development, coping, and psychological adjustment during a life transition. *Journal of Personality and Social Psychology,* 82, 102–111.

Bromberger, J. T., & Matthews, K. A. (1996). A longitudinal study of the effects of pessimism, trait anxiety, and life stress on depressive symptoms in middle-aged women. *Psychology and Aging,* 11, 207–213.

Carvajal, S. C., Garner, R. L., & Evans, R. I. (1998). Dispositional optimism as a protective factor in resisting HIV exposure in sexually active inner-city minority adolescents. *Journal of Applied Social Psychology,* 28, 2196–2211.

Carver, C. S., & Gaines, J. G. (1987). Optimism, pessimism, and postpartum depression. *Cognitive Therapy and Research,* 11, 449–462.

Carver, C. S., Pozo, C., Harris, S. D., Noriega, V., Scheier, M. F., Robinson, D. S., Ketcham, A. S., Moffat, F. L., & Clark, K. C. (1993). How coping mediates the effect of optimism on distress: A study of women with early stage breast cancer. *Journal of Personality and Social Psychology,* 65, 375–390.

Carver, C. S., & Scheier, M. F. (1998). *On the self-regulation of behavior.* New York: Cambridge University Press.

Carver, C. S., & Scheier, M. F. (2003). Three human strengths. In L. G. Aspinwall & U. M. Staudinger (Eds.), *A psychology of human strengths: Perspectives on an emerging field.* Washington, DC: American Psychological Association.

Carver, C. S., Scheier, M. F., & Weintraub, J. K. (1989). Assessing coping strategies: A theoretically based approach. *Journal of Personality and Social Psychology,* 56, 267–283.

Chamberlain, K., Petrie, K., & Azaria, R. (1992). The role of optimism and sense of coherence in predicting recovery following surgery. *Psychology and Health,* 7, 301–310.

Chang, E. C. (1998). Dispositional optimism and primary and secondary appraisal of a stressor: Controlling for confounding influences and relations to coping and psychological and physical adjustment. *Journal of Personality and Social Psychology,* 74, 1109–1120.

Christman, N. J. (1990). Uncertainty and adjustment during radiotherapy. *Nursing Research,* 39, 17–20, continued on 47.

Cozzarelli, C. (1993). Personality and self-efficacy as predictors of coping with abortion. *Journal of Personality and Social Psychology,* 65, 1224–1236.

Curbow, B., Somerfield, M. R., Baker, F., Wingard, J. R., & Legro, M. W. (1993). Personal changes, dispositional optimism, and psychological adjustment to bone marrow transplantation. *Journal of Behavioral Medicine,* 16, 423–443.

Epping-Jordan, J. E., Compas, B. E., Osowiecki, D. M., Oppedisano, G., Gerhardt, C., Primo, K., & Krag, D. N. (1999). Psychological adjustment in breast cancer: Processes of emotional distress. *Health Psychology,* 18, 315–326.

Erikson, E. H. (1968). *Identity: Youth and crisis.* New York: Norton.

Fitzgerald, T. E., Tennen, H., Affleck, G., & Pransky, G. S. (1993). The relative importance of dispositional optimism and control appraisals in quality of life after coronary artery bypass surgery. *Journal of Behavioral Medicine,* 16, 25–43.

Fontaine, K. R., & Jones, L. C. (1997). Self-esteem, optimism, and postpartum depression. *Journal of Clinical Psychology,* 53, 59–63.

Fontaine, K. R., Manstead, A. S. R., & Wagner, H. (1993). Optimism, perceived control over stress, and coping. *European Journal of Personality,* 7, 267–281.

Friedman, L. C., Nelson, D. V., Baer, P. E., Lane, M., Smith, F. E., & Dworkin, R. J. (1992). The relationship of dispositional optimism, daily life stress, and domestic environment to coping methods used by cancer patients. *Journal of Behavioral Medicine,* 15, 127–141.

Friedman, L. C., Weinberg, A. D., Webb, J. A., Cooper, H. P., & Bruce, S. (1995). Skin cancer prevention and early detection intentions and behavior. *American Journal of Preventive Medicine,* 11, 59–65.

Fry, P. S. (1995). Perfectionism, humor, and optimism as moderators of health outcomes and determinants of coping styles of women executives. *Genetics, Social, and General Psychology Monographs,* 121, 211–245.

Given, C. W., Stommel, M., Given, B., Osuch, J., Kurtz, M. E., & Kurtz, J. C. (1993). The influence of cancer patients' symptoms and functional states on patients' depression and family caregivers' reaction and depression. *Health Psychology,* 12, 277–285.

Goodman, E., Chesney, M. A., & Tipton, A. C. (1995). Relationship of optimism, knowledge, attitudes, and beliefs to use of HIV antibody test by at-risk female adolescents. *Psychosomatic Medicine,* 57, 541–546.

Greer, S., Morris, T., & Pettingale, K. W. (1979). Psychological response to breast cancer: Effect on outcome. *Lancet,* ii, 785–787.

Greer, S., Morris, T., Pettingale, K. W., & Haybittle, J. L. (1990). Psychological response to breast cancer and 15-year outcome. *Lancet,* i, 49–50.

Hazan, C., & Shaver, P. R. (1994). Attachment as an organizational framework for research on close relationships. *Psychological Inquiry,* 5, 1–22.

Hooker, K., Monahan, D., Shifren, K., & Hutchinson, C. (1992). Mental and physical health of spouse caregivers: The role of personality. *Psychology and Aging,* 7, 367–375.

Johnson, J. E. (1996). Coping with radiation therapy: Optimism and the effect of preparatory interventions. *Research in Nursing and Health,* 19, 3–12.

King, K. B., Rowe, M. A., Kimble, L. P., & Zerwic, J. J. (1998). Optimism, coping, and long-term recovery from coronary artery bypass in women. *Research in Nursing & Health,* 21, 15–26.

Leedham, B., Meyerowitz, B. E., Muirhead, J., & Frist, W. H. (1995). Positive expectations predict health after heart transplantation. *Health Psychology,* 14, 74–79.

Linville, P. (1985). Self-complexity and affective extremity: Don't put all of your eggs in one cognitive basket. *Social Cognition,* 3, 94–120.

Linville, P. (1987). Self-complexity as a cognitive buffer against stress-related illness and depression. *Journal of Personality and Social Psychology,* 52, 663–676.

Litt, M. D., Tennen, H., Affleck, G., & Klock, S. (1992). Coping and cognitive factors in adaptation to in vitro fertilization failure. *Journal of Behavioral Medicine,* 15, 171–187.

Long, B. C. (1993). Coping strategies of male managers: A prospective analysis of predictors of psychosomatic symptoms and job satisfaction. *Journal of Vocational Behavior,* 42, 184–199.

Major, B., Richards, C., Cooper, M.L., Cozzarelli, C., & Zubek, J. (1998). Personal resilience, cognitive appraisals, and coping: An integrative model of adjustment to abortion. *Journal of Personality and Social Psychology,* 74, 735–752.

Moskowitz, J. T., Folkman, S., Collette, L., & Vittinghoff, E. (1996). Coping and mood during AIDS-related care giving and bereavement. *Annals of Behavioral Medicine,* 18, 49–57.

Ohannessian, C. M., Hesselbrock, V. M., Tennen, H., & Affleck, G. (1993). Hassles and uplifts and generalized outcome expectancies as moderators on the relation between a family history of alcoholism and drinking behaviors. *Journal of Studies on Alcohol,* 55, 754–763.

Park, C. L., Moore, P. J., Turner, R. A., & Adler, N. E. (1997). The roles of constructive thinking and optimism in psychological and behavioral adjustment during pregnancy. *Journal of Personality and Social Psychology,* 73, 584–592.

Perkins, D. O., Leserman, J., Murphy, C., & Evans, D.L. (1993). Psychosocial predictors of high-risk sexual behavior among HIV-negative homosexual men. *AIDS Education and Prevention,* 5, 141–152.

Peterson, C., & Seligman, M. E.P. (1984). Causal explanations as a risk factor for depression: Theory and evidence. *Psychological Review,* 91, 347–374.

Pettingale, K. W., Morris, T., & Greer, S. (1985). Mental attitudes to cancer: An additional prognostic factor. *Lancet,* i, 750.

Plomin, R., Scheier, M. F., Bergeman, C. S., Pedersen, N. L., Nesselroade, J.R., & McClearn, G. E. (1992). Optimism, pessimism, and mental health: A twin/adoption analysis. *Personality and Individual Differences,* 13, 921–930.

Räikkönen, K., Matthews, K. A., Flory, J. S., Owens, J. F., & Gump, B. B. (1999). Effects of optimism, pessimism, and trait anxiety on ambulatory blood pressure and mood during everyday life. *Journal of Personality and Social Psychology,* 76, 104–113.

Reed, G. M., Kemeny, M. E., Taylor, S. E., Wang, H-Y.J., & Visscher, B. R. (1994). Realistic acceptance as a predictor of decreased survival time in gay men with AIDS. *Health Psychology,* 13, 299–307.

Robbins, A. S., Spence, J. T., & Clark, H. (1991). Psychological determinants of health and performance: The tangled web of desirable and undesirable characteristics. *Journal of Personality and Social Psychology,* 61, 755–765.

Scheier, M. F., & Carver, C. S. (1985). Optimism, coping and health: Assessment and implications of generalized outcome expectancies. *Health Psychology,* 4, 219–247.

Scheier, M. F., & Carver, C. S. (1992). Effects of optimism on psychological and physical well-being: Theoretical overview and empirical update. *Cognitive Therapy and Research,* 16, 201–228.

Scheier, M. F., & Carver, C. S. (2001). Adapting to cancer: The importance of hope and purpose. In A. Baum & B. L. Andersen (Eds.), *Psychosocial interventions for cancer* (pp. 15–36). Washington, DC: American Psychological Association.

Scheier, M. F., Carver, C. S., & Bridges, M. W. (1994). Distinguishing optimism from neuroticism (and trait anxiety, self-mastery, and self-esteem): A reevaluation of the Life Orientation Test. *Journal of Personality and Social Psychology,* 67, 1063–1078.

Scheier, M. F., Matthews, K. A., Owens, J. F., Magovern, G. J., Lefebvre, R. C., Abbott, R. A., & Carver, C. S. (1989). Dispositional optimism and recovery from coronary artery bypass surgery: The beneficial effects on physical and psychological well-being. *Journal of Personality and Social Psychology,* 57, 1024–1040.

Scheier, M. F., Weintraub, J. K., & Carver, C. S. (1986). Coping with stress: Divergent strategies of optimists and pessimists. *Journal of Personality and Social Psychology,* 51, 1257–1264.

Schwarzer, R. (1994). Optimism, vulnerability, and self-beliefs as health-related cognitions: A systematic overview. *Psychology and Health,* 9, 161–180.

Segerstrom, S. C., Taylor, S. E., Kemeny, M. E., & Fahey, J. L. (1998). Optimism is associated with mood, coping, and immune change in response to stress. *Journal of Personality and Social Psychology,* 74, 1646–1655.

Seligman, M. E. P. (1991). *Learned optimism.* Knopf: New York.

Shepperd, J. A., Maroto, J. J., & Pbert, L. A. (1996). Dispositional optimism as a predictor of health changes among cardiac patients. *Journal of Research in Personality,* 30, 517–534.

Shifren, K., & Hooker, K. (1995). Stability and change in optimism: A study among spouse caregivers. *Experimental Aging Research,* 21, 59–76.

Shnek, Z. M., Irvine, J., Stewart, D., & Abbey, S. (2001). Psychological factors and depressive symptoms in ischemic heart disease. *Health Psychology,* 20, 141–145.

Showers, C. J., & Ryff, C. D. (1996). Self-differentiation and well being in a life transition. *Personality and Social Psychology Bulletin,* 22, 448–460.

Snyder, C. R. (1994). *The psychology of hope: You can get there from here.* New York: Free Press.

Snyder, C.R., Sympson, S.C., Ybasco, F.C., Borders, T.F., Babyak, M.A., & Higgins, R.L. (1996). Development and validation of the state hope scale. *Journal of Personality and Social Psychology, 70,* 321–335.

Stanton, A.L., & Snider, P.R. (1993). Coping with breast cancer diagnosis: A prospective study. *Health Psychology, 12,* 16–23.

Steptoe, A., Wardle, J., Vinck, J., Tuomisto, M., Holte, A., & Wichstrøm, L. (1994). Personality and attitudinal correlates of healthy lifestyles in young adults. *Psychology and Health, 9,* 331–343.

Stewart, S. M., Betson, C., Lam, T. H., Marshall, I. B., Lee, P. W., & Wong, C. M. (1997). Predicting stress in first year medical students: A longitudinal study. *Medical Education, 3,* 163–168.

Strack, S., Carver, C. S., & Blaney, P. H. (1987). Predicting successful completion of an aftercare program following treatment for alcoholism: The role of dispositional optimism. *Journal of Personality and Social Psychology, 53,* 579–584.

Strutton, D., & Lumpkin, J. (1992). Relationship between optimism and coping strategies in the work environment. *Psychology Reports, 71,* 1179–1186.

Taylor, S.E., Kemeny, M.E., Aspinwall, L.G., Schneider, S.G., Rodriguez, R., & Herbert, M. (1992). Optimism, coping, psychological distress, and high-risk sexual behavior among men at risk for Acquired Immunodeficiency Syndrome (AIDS). *Journal of Personality and Social Psychology, 63,* 460–473.

Tennen, H., & Affleck, G. (1987). The costs and benefits of optimistic explanations and dispositional optimism. *Journal of Personality, 55,* 377–393.

Tompkins, C.A., Schulz, R., & Rau, M.T. (1988). Post-stroke depression in primary support persons: predicting those at risk. *Journal of Consulting and Clinical Psychology, 56,* 502–508.

Wicklund, R.A., & Gollwitzer, P.M. (1982). *Symbolic self-completion.* Hillsdale, NJ: Erlbaum.

Wrosch, C., Scheier, M.F., Carver, C.S., & Schulz, R. (2003). The importance of goal disengagement in adaptive self-regulation: When giving up is beneficial. *Self and Identity, 2,* 1–20.

Zeidner, M., & Hammer, A.L. (1992). Coping with missile attack: Resources, strategies, and outcomes. *Journal of Personality, 60,* 709–746.

Chapter 3

THE HOPEFUL ONES: A PSYCHOLOGICAL INQUIRY INTO THE POSITIVE MIND AND HEART

C. R. Snyder, Laura Yamhure Thompson, Hal S. Shorey, and Laura Heinze

"THE HOPEFUL ONES" AND WHY WE NEED THEM

I (CRS) used to dread that point on airline flights when a fellow passenger asked, "What do you do for a living?" My "I'm a clinical psychologist" answer was a conversation stopper. Things have improved in the last three years, however. To this question, I now answer, "I am a positive psychologist." It is as if I have won a popularity contest. My fellow travelers are fascinated with positive psychology, and we may chat about it until the plane lands. Recently I was sitting next to two men in their 50s when one popped the WDYDFAL question. I talked about my little corner of positive psychology, which is hope. In turn, information poured out of these two guys, including the fact that they were fraternal twins. One brother pointed toward his brother and, in a tone of admiration said, "He is the hopeful one." Based on the rest of our conversation, this observation seemed quite accurate.

This story relates to this chapter because there is much to learn from such high-hope people. In the subsequent pages, my colleagues and I will share what we have uncovered about these "hopeful ones," and what they can teach us about coping. Perhaps most importantly, these lessons on living hopefully can be applied to help the generational waves of hopeless people. On this latter point, consider that an estimated 500,000 American adolescents attempt suicide every year (Popenhagen & Qualley, 1998). Moreover, fully half of all teenagers have had thoughts of killing themselves (Dickstra, 1995; Jacobs, 1999). Unfortunately, hopelessness abounds in those very young people who soon will be the stewards of our society.

THREE QUESTIONS IN SEARCH OF HOPE

In the 1960s motivational literature, scholars described hope as a desire to seek goals (e.g., Stotland, 1969). Indeed, this goal-directed thought consistently emerged in my (CRS) interviewing of people about their daily thoughts. Additionally, two other components appeared in these conversations. First, people talked about finding routes to their goals. Second, they described their motivations to use those routes. Beyond their thoughts about a specific goal, however, people also had views about their capabilities in goal pursuits more generally. As such, these routing and motivating thoughts manifested themselves at a state, situation level, as well as at a cross-situational, trait-like one. People have recounted these routing and motivational thought processes to our research team members in countless subsequent conversations over the years. What do you want (goals)? How are you going to get there (pathways)? How are you going to get motivated (agency)? By answering this trilogy of questions, we can gain insights about hope.

Goals: What We Want

Goals represent the cognitive targets for hope (Snyder, 1994). They vary temporally from short- to long-term (e.g., "I want to get this sentence written" versus "I want to build a house on my farm"). Goals also vary in specificity, with more clearly defined goals typifying high-hope thinking. Moreover, goals must be of sufficient value for people to pursue them. Furthermore, goals may reflect something positive that we want to happen (approach goals), or something negative that we want to prohibit from happening (prevention goals; Snyder, Feldman, Taylor, Schroeder, & Adams, 2000).

Averill, Catlin, and Chon (1990) have suggested that hope is aimed at goals with intermediate probabilities of attainment. We agree, but would add that goals with seemingly very high or low probabilities of attainment actually may fall into this intermediate range. Our reasoning is that people sometimes rework easy goals so as to inject some uncertainty. They do this by setting stringent personal standards that render the outcomes less certain (e.g., setting shorter time limits). Moving to the other end of the goal difficulty continuum, people sometimes achieve "impossible" goals through supreme planning and efforts. On this point, many physicians can recount examples of patients who have been cured from the "incurable." Because "impossible" goals sometimes are reached, we would suggest extreme care in criticizing people for their "false hopes" (see Snyder, Rand, King, Feldman, & Taylor, in press).

Pathways: How We Are Going to Get There

A goal is but a tantalizing possibility, however, without a route to attain it. On this point, the pioneering cognitive psychologist Craig has suggested in *The Nature of Explanation* (1943) that the purpose of the human brain is to envision chains linking where we are now to where we want to go (i.e., "A to B" sequences). (Pinker [1997] has made a similar point in his more recent *How the Mind Works* volume.)

Using a variety of methodologies, we (Snyder, LaPointe, Crowson Jr., & Early, 1998) have found that high-hope persons report positive and affirming self-talk about being able to find pathways to their goals (e.g., "I'll find a way to solve this"). High-hope persons also should be certain about the pathways for their goals, whereas their low-hope counterparts should be uncertain and have difficulty in articulating their routes (see Woodbury, 1999).

In addition to advantages in goal pursuits under normal circumstances, higher hope should become especially beneficial during those instances in which the preferred routes are blocked. For example, higher hope has related to more flexibility and the actual production of alternate routes during impeded circumstances (Irving, Snyder, & Crowson Jr., 1998; Tierney, 1995).

Agency: How We Are Going to Get Motivated

Agency thinking involves the perceived motivation to begin and continue using a pathway in one's goal pursuits. As experimental support for this definition, we have found that high- as compared to low-hope research participants advocate agentic self-talk (e.g., phrases such as "I can do it," "I can," and "I won't give up"; Snyder, LaPointe et al., 1998).

Agency thinking provides the requisite motivation for our daily goal-directed activities. What happens, however, when we encounter blockages? We have theorized that during such impeding circumstances, agency thought becomes especially important in terms of applying the motivation to the appropriate alternate pathway (for support, see Snyder, Harris et al., 1991; Snyder, Shorey et al., in press).

BARRIERS, STRESSORS, AND EMOTIONS

Life has a way of placing barriers in our paths. If we perceive that a barrier may thwart our goal pursuit, we may appraise that impeding circumstance as stressful. As Lazarus, Deese, and Osler (1952) put it, "stress occurs when a particular situation threatens the attainment of some goal" (p. 295). Thus, negative and positive emotions should result from the perception of unsuccessful or successful goal pursuits, respectively (see Brunstein, 1993). Positive emotions may occur in the context of successful goal pursuit under unimpeded circumstances, and even more enhanced positive emotions should result after overcoming blockages. Although the stress and negative emotions can result from lack of success under unimpeded circumstances, typically there is a thwarting circumstance that has stymied the person (Ruehlman & Wolchik, 1988). In hope theory, therefore, it should be emphasized that the perceptions of the success of goal pursuits are posited to causally drive subsequent overall positive and negative emotions (see Snyder, Sympson et al., 1996 for empirical support). Although a person may further refine the general positive ("yahoo") or negative emotions ("yuck") into seemingly more specific emotions depending on the nature of the particular goal attainment or nonattainment, we hold that the key to important reinforcing (positive or negative) feedback properties derives from the overall general positive or negative emotional experience.

Thus, the perception of probable success or failure in a given goal pursuit, which is moderated by emotional feedback in a particular situation, comprises the person's immediate experience, or "state," of hope. Such state of hope is subject to upward or downward temporal fluctuations as the individual either experiences adverse emotions and attempts to change course, or experiences positive emotions that reinforce the choice of pathways and strengthen the cognitive momentum, or agency, to pursue those pathways. In this way, a spiral is created in which higher or lower levels of state of hope continually are reinforced by the positive or negative emotional experiences that then feed back to further impact the individual's current state of hope.

Over time, the person will come to develop a cognitive set, or character logical outlook on his or her goal pursuits. As such, the overall sense that a person has of being capable of achieving goals in general will become a relatively stable disposition or "trait."

Generally, persons who are high as compared to low in trait hope should be less likely to construe impediments as stressful; moreover, the high-hoper's thoughts and actions often should make the impediment less stressful over time. Because of a history of successfully dealing with stres-sors and positive outcomes in their various goal pursuits, high-hopers should experience overall positive emotions, a sense of zest, happiness, and confidence (Snyder, Sympson, Michael, & Cheavens, 2000). Low-hopers, however, having histories of unsuccessfully dealing with stressors along with negative outcomes in their various situational goal pursuits, should exhibit overall negative emotions, affective flatness, and passive feelings. These positive and negative moods or emotional sets represent the residue from myriad previous goal pursuits. Associated with trait hope levels, these emotional sets should be brought to bear on any goal-related activities.

We also believe that memories are catalogued by emotions, along with the contents of the particular events. One applied implication here is that these stored emotions can serve as clues for helping clients to locate the underlying sources of their problems. Although the pathology model would suggest that our efforts should focus on the circumstances under-girding the experience of negative emotions, a positive psychology approach would advise that there are benefits in tracing the roots of one's positive emotions.

PUTTING HOPE TOGETHER

The various components in hope theory are shown in Figure 3.1. Con-sider this figure as a heuristic for understanding how, in moving from left to right, goal-directed thoughts and emotions lead to (in each new goal-pursuit) actual behaviors to reach desired goals. This figure includes both the learning history of goal-directed thought, as well as the instantiation of any given goal-directed activity (the pre-event and event sequence). In the far right of the figure, the person either has succeeded or not in his or her particular goal pursuit actions.

At the far left, the etiologies of the pathways and agency thoughts are shown as the pathways and agency components iterate. Pathways and agency thinking are a normal part of the developmental learning sequence, and these two components are fairly well established by age three. (For in-depth descriptions of the developmental antecedents of the hope process, see: McDermott and Snyder, 2000, pp. 5–18; Snyder, 1994, pp. 75–114; and Snyder, McDermott, Cook, and Rapoff, 2002, pp. 1–32.) Just to the right of agency-pathways thoughts, we see the trait-like moods (i.e., emo-

Figure 3.1
Hope Theory Schematic of Feed-forward and Feed-back Functions Involving Agency and Pathway Goal-Directed Thoughts as an Individual Begins and Completes Behaviors Aimed at a Given Goal.

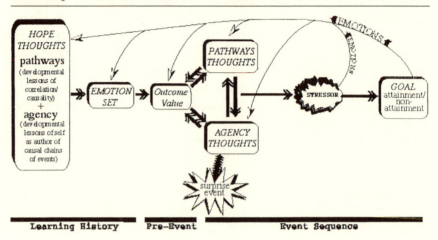

tional sets) that the person brings to the goal-pursuit process. Thus, people's learning histories are comprised of trait hope levels and the associated emotion sets. This learning history and mood predisposition provides the starting context for specific goal pursuits.

Having more goals facilitates a person's ability to consider a new goal if an original one is unobtainable. Therefore, higher hope should be related to the propensity to consider more goals. In support of this postulate, high-hope adults (ages 20 through 60) have reported having significantly more goals in their lives than their low-hope counterparts (Langelle, 1989). Thus, the "hopeful one" appears to have an investment portfolio replete with life goals.

Next in the progression (as shown in the pre-event analysis phase of Figure 1), we see that the protagonist considers the values associated with the particular goal pursuit that is being considered. The high-hopers appear to place more value on goals that reflect their own standards rather than goals reflecting other people's standards (Snyder, 1994). Whenever possible, the "hopeful one" also is likely to select and value "stretch goals" (i.e., goals that build upon previous personal outcomes in the same or similar arena; Harris, 1988). Assuming that the goal is a valued one, the person then decides that the given goal pursuit should be undertaken, and he or she then moves into the event sequence analysis phase. Here, there is an ongoing iteration of the pathways and agency thinking for the particular goal. Note also that there is an outcome value check-back process once the agency-pathways process has begun (arrows going both ways); this enables the person to make certain that the goal still is valued. It should be emphasized that at this point in time, the person actually has launched behaviors aimed at achieving the desired goal. In other words, more than sheer thinking is involved as the person now has moved into goal-directed action.

If matters appear to be going well in this "getting started" phase, then the feedback loop allows positive emotions to cycle back so as to reinforce the process. At this stage, the "hopeful one" should be very focused on the relevant cues, and should have an internal challenge-like dialogue (e.g., "I am ready for this!"). This focused/challenged set should produce positive emotions that are very functional in sustaining attention and motivation. At this same initial goal pursuit stage, less hopeful people are apprehensive and filled with thoughts such as "I'm not doing very well." Already having a general level of negative emotions, they experience a rush of strong negative emotions, self-critical ruminations, and an inability to attend to the task at hand. Research findings support the differential thoughts and feelings for high- and low-hope persons as hypothesized here (Snyder, in press; Snyder, Cheavens, & Michael, 1999).

Before moving farther, we would like to clarify the important roles played by emotions. We have suggested that the goal-directed cognitions are responsible causally for the enduring emotional set and the state of ongoing emotions in a specific goal-pursuit sequence. We would emphasize, however, that those raw emotions shape and inform a person's thoughts and actions. We are using emotions in a functional manner (Clore, 1994). Levenson (1994) succinctly captured this functionalist perspective when he wrote, "Emotions serve to establish our position vis-à-vis our environment, *pulling us toward certain people, objects, actions, and ideas, and pushing us away from others* (p. 123, emphasis added). As we have noted previously, in hope theory, emotions are causally derived from the perceived success, or lack thereof, in a given goal pursuit. Moreover, general positive emotion (what we previously have called "yahoo") should reinforce the continuation of ongoing goal pursuit thoughts and activities, whereas general negative emotions (what we previously have called "yuck") should lessen such affirmative thoughts and goal pursuit activities.

Let's return to the goal pursuit sequence, and focus upon the point where a stressor is encountered (see Figure 3.1). (This stressor may occur, however, at an earlier or later point in the sequence.) The stressor in this context represents a barrier to the progression of the actual goal pursuit. High-hopers see the barrier as a challenge and should be open to alternate pathways and the rechanneling of their agency to the new pathways (Snyder, 1994). They often are successful in working around the stressor, and this success cycles back via approach emotions to reinforce dispositional and situational hopeful thinking. Low-hopers, however, are likely to become sidetracked by, or stuck in, disruptive, self-critical thoughts and accompanying negative emotions. In following people through the various stages of goal pursuits, support has emerged for these hypothesized responses of high- and low-hope people to stressors (Anderson, 1988).

If the person has made it past the stressor, or there is no stressor, then the pathways and agency thoughts should iterate (note bidirectional arrows) along the course of the event sequence. The success (or lack thereof) perceptions and the associated approach emotions can cycle back to inform the subsequent progress toward the goal. (In Figure 3.1, it can be noted that there is an emotional feedback arrow stationed toward the end of the sequence of encountering a stressor, but in fact such feedback occurs throughout the event sequence.)

Before finishing this section, we need to discuss surprise events (see Figure 3.1, lower center). These surprises may be positive (e.g., watching your child walk for the first time) or negative (e.g., watching your five-year-old fall from a tree branch). Such surprise events happen outside of the normal goal-pursuit thought process, but they quickly produce emotions because of the contrast (positive or negative) that they offer in relation to that which is expected for the ongoing events. These surprise-based emotions cause arousal that, in turn, is transformed quickly into ongoing agency thinking. Thereafter, this agency motivation is "attached" to a goal and pathways that are appropriate to the situation (e.g., helping the child who has fallen from the tree). Although these surprise-based emotions start outside the goal-pursuit corridor, they quickly are incorporated into the goal-pursuit process.

In Figure 3.1, it can be seen that the pathways and agency thinking has both feed-forward and feedback emotion-laden mechanisms that modulate the person's success in attaining a given goal. Accordingly, hope theory is an interrelated system of goal-directed thinking that is responsive to feedback at various points in the temporal sequence of actual behavior aimed at reaching a goal.

MEASURING HOPE

Using this hope model, we have developed and validated several individual-differences measures of hope. We briefly summarize three major scales in this section.

Trait Hope Scale

The adult Trait Hope Scale (Snyder, Harris et al., 1991) has four agency, four pathways, and four distracter items. Respondents are asked to imagine themselves across time and situational contexts, and to respond on an eight-point Likert scale as to the applicability of each item (1 = Definitely False, to 8 = Definitely True). The scale is internally reliable (alphas of .74 to .88) and temporally stable (test-retests of .85 for three weeks to .82 for ten weeks). There are two separate yet related agency and pathways factors (they typically correlate .50), as well as an overarching hope factor (using traditional and confirmatory procedures; Babyak, Snyder, & Yoshinobu, 1993). Moreover, the scale has received considerable concurrent and discriminant validational support (Snyder, Harris et al., 1991). No differences in the scores of males and females have been reported.

State Hope Scale

The State Hope Scale (Snyder, Sympson et al., 1996) has three agency and three pathways items on which respondents describe the applicability of each item using an eight-point Likert continuum (1 = Definitely False, to 8 = Definitely True). Respondents are asked to complete the items according to how they are "right now." Studies support the scale's internal reliability (alphas of .90 to .95), factor structure, and concurrent and discriminant validities (Snyder, Sympson et al., 1996). The State Hope Scale has correlated .48 over a 30-day interval and .93 over a two-day interval, thereby manifesting the expected greater malleability over longer time periods.

Children's Hope Scale

The Children's Hope Scale (ages 8 to 16; Snyder, Hoza et al., 1997) is made up of three agency and three pathways items. Children are asked to think about themselves across various situations, and then to place a check mark in one of six boxes (reflecting a Likert continuum of "none of the time" to "all of time"). Studies support its internal reliability (alphas of .72 to .86, with a median of .77), temporal stability (test-retest correlations of .71 to .73 over one month), two-factor structure, and convergent and discriminant validities (Snyder, Hoza et al., 1997). No differences in the scores of boys and girls have been reported.

HOPE THEORY COMPARED WITH OTHER THEORIES

There are three other recent theories that bear similarities to hope theory. In this section, we review hope in relation to the self-efficacy theory of Bandura, the optimism theory of Scheier and Carver, and the optimism theory of Seligman. In Table 3.1, the shared and not-shared components and the relative emphases of all four theories are depicted. Although we will emphasize the differences in these theoretical approaches, they all are variants of expectancy-based motives.

Table 3.1 Implicit and Explicit Components and Their Respective Emphases in Hope Theory as Compared to Selected Positive Psychology Theories

Theory Component	Hope– Snyder	Self Efficacy - Bandura	Optimism– Scheier-Carver	Optimism- Seligman
Attributions	.	.	.	ΔΔΔ
Outcome Value	ΔΔ	ΔΔ	ΔΔ	Δ
Goal-Related Thinking	ΔΔΔ	ΔΔΔ	ΔΔ	Δ
Perceived Capacities For Agency-Thinking	ΔΔΔ	ΔΔΔ	ΔΔΔ	.
Perceived Capacities for Pathways Thinking	ΔΔΔ	ΔΔ	Δ	.

Notes: Δ —component is implicit in model.
        ΔΔ—component is explicit in model.
        ΔΔΔ —component is explicit and emphasized in model.
(More triangles represent greater emphasis on a specific component).

Self-Efficacy—Bandura

Similar to hope theory, Bandura (1997) suggests that an important goal-related outcome is necessary in self-efficacy theory. Bandura has held that self-efficacy thinking must be based on situation-specific goals. Goals are emphasized in hope theory, but they may be either at the enduring, cross-situational, or situational levels. Somewhat similar to pathways thinking, in self-efficacy theory people are hypothesized to analyze the contingencies of a specified goal-attainment situation (called outcome expectancies). In hope theory, however, the focus of pathways thought is on the self-analysis of one's overall capabilities at finding initial routes to goals and thereafter producing alternate routes if blockages occur.

Of primary importance in Bandura's theory is the efficacy expectancy, which bears some similarity to agency thinking. Self-efficacy reflects the evaluation of the degree to which a person *can* carry out the actions inherent in the outcome expectancies, and these situation-based self-efficacy thoughts are the most important and last step prior to beginning the particular goal-directed action. In hope theory, however, both the pathways and agency thinking are emphasized prior to and during the goal-pursuit sequence. In a comparison of these two theories, Magaletta and Oliver (1999) have reported differing factor structures, along with the fact that hope produced unique variance beyond self-efficacy in predicting well-being.

Optimism—Scheier and Carver

The Scheier and Carver (1985) theory of optimism, similar to hope theory, assumes that optimism is a goal-based cognitive process that operates with outcomes of substantial value. These generalized outcome expectancies of optimism tap into people's perceptions of being able to move toward desired goals (or, away from undesirable goals; Carver & Scheier, 2000). Although agency- and pathways-like thinking are implicit in this optimism model, the outcome expectancies (similar to agency) appear to be the prime elicitors of goal-directed behaviors (Scheier & Carver, 1987). Related to this issue, Magaletta and Oliver (1999) report that the pathways component is orthogonal to the items on the Scheier and Carver optimism measure in a factor analysis (the optimism measures are the Life Orientation Test [Scheier & Carver, 1985] and the Life Orientation Test-Revised [Scheier, Carver, & Bridges, 1994]). Differing from the emphasis on agency-like thought, in hope theory the pathways and agency thinking are posited to have equal (and constantly iterative) emphases (see Table 3.1).

Both of these two theories are cognitive and focus on behaviors across situations; also, the Hope Scale and LOT correlate around .50 (Snyder, Harris et al., 1991). Relative to scores on the LOT, scores on the Hope Scale have reliably augmented the variance in predicting several variables (Magaletta & Oliver, 1999).

Optimism—Seligman and Colleagues

Building on the reformulated helplessness model (Abramson, Seligman, & Teasdale, 1978), Seligman (1991) postulated that an optimistic explanatory style reflects the pattern of making external, variable, and specific attributions for negative outcomes. As such, this theory of optimism focuses implicitly upon goal-directed cognitions that distance the person from negative outcomes. In contrast, hope focuses on the moving toward desired goals, with explicit emphases placed on pathways and agency goal-directed cognitions. In both theories, the outcome must be of high importance, but this is emphasized more in hope theory.

EXAMINING THE RESUMES OF "THE HOPEFUL ONES"

In this section, we will examine the outcomes of high- as compared to low-hope people in the areas of academics, athletics, physical health, psychological adjustment, and psychotherapy. Although we expected to find that high-hopers *usually* fare better than their low-hoper counterparts, we instead have found that the high-hopers are advantaged *in every instance*.

Outcomes in Academics

In samples of grade school (Snyder, Hoza et al., 1997), high school (Snyder, Harris et al., 1991), and college students (Chang, 1998), higher hope has correlated significantly with better grades. In a longitudinal study tracing college students over six years, their Hope Scale scores taken at the beginning of college significantly predicted higher overall grade point, higher rate of graduation, and lower rate of dropout (Snyder, Shorey et al., in press). These findings regarding the predictive power of hope remained significant when controlling for intelligence (grade school), self-esteem and previous grades (college/cross-sectional), and entrance exam scores (college/longitudinal).

High-hopers should do well in academics because they can stay focused on the appropriate ("on-task") cues in both the learning and testing environments, whereas low-hopers are prone to anxious, self-critical ruminations (see Michael, 2000). Support for this reasoning has been found with student samples (see Snyder, Shorey et al., in press).

Outcomes in Athletics

Curry, Snyder, Cook, Ruby, and Rehm (1997) gave the Hope Scale to male athletes (from seven universities) at the beginning of their track seasons; additionally, coaches rated their athletes' natural physical abilities. Even when the natural athletic ability variance was removed statistically, the high-hope athletes' performances were significantly better than those of their low-hope counterparts. In a modified replication, the trait Hope Scale scores of female track athletes taken at the beginning of the season significantly predicted the actual track performances; moreover, the State Hope Scale scores taken prior to each track meet also significantly predicted performances. Furthermore, trait and state hope together accounted for 56 percent of the variance related to the track performances.

In a study of girls at a summer sport camp, the high-hopers set more sport-specific goals than the low-hopers (Brown, Curry, Hagstrom, & Sandstedt, 1999). The high-hope girls also were less likely to think about quitting their sports (mirroring the academic dropout findings).

Curry, Maniar, Sondag, and Sandstedt (1999) started a college class aimed at imparting hopeful thinking to athletes. Comparing those who have to those who have not taken the course, there were reliable improvements in their athletic performance confidence (maintained at a one-year follow-up). Although sport confidence is considered the "gold standard" for predicting performance, hope scores have significantly augmented its predictive capabilities.

Outcomes in Physical Health

Primary prevention involves activities to eliminate or reduce physical health problems *before* they occur. In this regard, Snyder, Feldman et al. (2000) proposed that higher-hope people use information about physical illness as a pathway for prevention efforts. Related to this proposition, high- as compared to low-hope women have performed significantly better on a cancer knowledge test, and they reported having stronger intentions to undertake cancer-prevention activities (Irving, Snyder, &

Crowson Jr., 1998). In another study of health prevention behaviors by Harney (1990), high-hope people reported engaging in more physical exercise than their low-hope counterparts. Finally, Floyd and McDermott (1998) reported that gay men with high relative to low hope are more likely to practice safe sex.

Secondary prevention taps activities aimed at eliminating or reducing problems *after* they have appeared. In this regard, higher hope has correlated with better coping with major burn injuries (Barnum et al., 1998), spinal cord injuries (Elliott, Witty, Herrick, & Hoffman, 1991), severe arthritis (Laird, 1992), fibromylagia (Affleck & Tennen, 1996; Tennen & Affleck, 1999), and blindness (Jackson, Taylor, Palmatier, Elliott, & Elliott, 1998). Likewise, Stanton et al. (2000) report that both emotional expression and Hope Scale scores predict perceived health and sense of vigor in women's recovery from breast cancer. Also, these two variables interacted such that the expressive, high-hope women reported less distress and fewer physician visits.

Another important secondary prevention health topic is the endurance of pain stemming from chronic health problems or medical procedures. In three studies using a cold presser task to measure pain tolerance, we have found that the high-hope people endured the pain (i.e., kept hands in ice-cold water) about twice as long the low-hope people (115 vs. 60 sec.; Snyder, Odle, & Hackman, 1999). The high- relative to the low-hopers also: (1) reported experiencing less pain than the low-hopers; (2) produced more strategies for coping with the pain; and (3) reported a much higher likelihood of using those strategies. These high-hopers were evidencing elevated pathways and agency thought, and these reports correlated significantly with longer pain endurances. Adherence to medical regimens also exemplifies secondary prevention. This is a major problem in the health field, with estimates of 50 percent nonadherence across different medical regimens. In a test of the hope and medicine adherence relationship, we found that higher Children's Hope Scale scores related significantly to children's adherence in taking their inhaler medication treatments (for juvenile diabetes; Moon, Snyder, & Rapoff, 2001). In a conceptual replication examining adherence in terms of a person remaining in treatment (rather than taking a medication), higher Hope Scale scores significantly related to staying in a drug treatment program (Seaton & Snyder, 2001). In both studies, the hope and adherence relationships remained when the demographics and quality of life variances were removed.

Outcomes in Psychological Adjustment

Among psychiatric inpatients (Irving, Crenshaw, Snyder, Francis, & Gentry, 1990), higher hope has been associated with more adaptive adjustment patterns as tapped by the Minnesota Multiphasic Personality Inventory. As would be expected, measures of positive and negative affectivity correlate positively and negatively, respectively, with hope. Furthermore, when traced over 28 days, on every day the higher reported state hope was related reliably to larger numbers of positive thoughts and fewer negative thoughts (Snyder, Sympson et al., 1996). Likewise, persons with high- as compared to low-hope have reported: (1) elevated life satisfaction and self-worth, and low depressive feelings (Chang, 1998; Kwon, 2000); (2) more inspiration, energy, and confidence (Snyder, Harris et al., 1991); and (3) more benefits in coping with profound stressors (Affleck & Tennen, 1996; Tennen & Affleck, 1999).

We also have speculated that hope may relate to primary prevention efforts at the larger societal level. For example, when a society sets laws or reward structures that allow the pursuit of goal-directed activities, then citizens should be less likely to become frustrated, angry, and unhappy (Snyder, 1994; Snyder & Feldman, 2000). Three studies cast light on this hypothesis. First, Krauss and Krauss (1968) measured over 20 countries in regard to the degree to which they thwarted the daily goal-pursuit efforts of their citizens. Fewer impediments in societies (and by inference, higher hope) correlated reliably with fewer people committing suicide. Second, higher Hope Scale scores have been related significantly to college students having fewer suicidal ideations (Range & Penton, 1994). Third, in a sample of Vietnam veterans, higher hope was correlated with lower reported frustrations and hostility (Crowson Jr., Frueh, & Snyder, 2001).

Turning to secondary prevention as related to hope and psychological health, high-hopers who encounter an immutable goal blockage are flexible and can find alternative goals. Low-hopers, however, ruminate about their being "stuck" (Michael, 2000) and fantasize (rather magically at times) about escaping, and this passive disengagement makes them feel more trapped.

Upon meeting stressors, high-hopers talk with friends and family (Kwon, in press). Perhaps borne out of their positive early childhood relationships, there is reciprocity, mutuality, and a strong sense of attachment in the relationships of high-hope persons. Related to this point, when looking back on their childhoods, the high- as compared to low-hope people report close ties to caregivers, as well as having caregivers who spent large amounts of time with them (Rieger, 1993). High- relative to low-hope people are far less likely to have lost parents either through divorce or death (Westburg, in press). Higher hope also has been reliably related to: (1) more perceived social support (McNeal, 1997); (2) more social competence (Snyder, Hoza et al., 1997); and (3) more forgiveness of people in general and friends in particular (Tierney, 1995). Likewise, in their interpersonal commerce, high-hope people are interested in their goals *and* the goals of other people (Snyder, Cheavens, & Sympson, 1997). For all of the reasons mentioned in this paragraph, we suggest that people should gravitate toward high-hope individuals.

One last adjustment issue in regard to hope pertains to the "What is the nature of meaning?" question. Snyder (1994) reasoned that people construct life meaning by reflecting about their personal goals and the associated progress in attaining those goals. Following this line of thought, Feldman and Snyder (in press) correlated Hope Scale scores with three measures of meaning, and found very robust correlations in the .70 to .76 range.

Outcomes in Psychotherapy

We have suggested elsewhere that the beneficial changes across various psychotherapy systems reflect clients' acquisition of effective pathways goal-directed thinking, as well as the agency motivation to apply those pathways (Snyder, Ilardi et al., 2000). As but one example of this premise, McNeal (1998) reported that the improvements of children in a family-oriented intervention were mirrored by significant increases in hope (on the Children's Hope Scale).

Psychotherapy outcome research meta-analysis provides a useful means for applying hope theory to psychotherapy. Consider Barker, Funk, and Houston's (1988) meta-analysis. They included only studies in which the positive expectations in the placebo group were the same as those in the active treatment group. By subtracting the no-contact control group outcome effect size from the placebo group outcome effect size, a sheer agency (motivation) effect is left. In a parallel manner, subtracting the placebo effect size from the full treatment outcome effect size produces the pathways-like effect. The accepted approach for measuring magnitudes of change in such meta-analyses is to use standard deviation units reflecting the degree to which one group mean differs from another group mean. Using the aforementioned procedures, the effect sizes in the Barker et al. (1988) meta-analysis were .47 *SD* for agency and .55 *SD* for pathways. Agency alone thus significantly improved outcomes; moreover, by adding pathways, the positive outcomes were augmented by roughly the same magnitude.

Hope theory principles also can be used as a framework for developing successful interventions. In a Klausner et al. (1998) group intervention study, a ten-session series of hope-based group activities lessened the depression of older adults and increased their activity levels significantly more than a reminiscence comparison group therapy. In a pretreatment therapy preparation based on hope theory (Irving et al., 1997), the persons in the pretreatment hope preparation (especially those low in hope) had superior subsequent treatment outcomes than did the people without such pretreatments. Finally, Lopez, Bouwkamp, Edwards, and Teramoto Pediotti (2000) report that a program for promoting hope in junior high students is effective in increasing the students' hope levels.

CONCLUSIONS

We close by commenting on three general approaches for increasing the numbers of "hopeful ones" among us. First, we believe that the number of valued goals in our society presently is too small and delimiting. The present highly valued goals involve physical appearance, intellectual achievement, athletic accomplishments, and money-making. We suggest adding the following goals to this list: (1) caring for others (especially children); (2) conducting basic and applied research; (3) inventing new products; (4) producing durable products; and; (5) building safer environments at home, school, and work. These latter goals yield benefits for large segments of our population (Snyder & Feldman, 2000). The presently valued goals, however, allow only a small percentage of people to "win" at the expense of the large majority. As a counterpoint to this suggestion, it might be argued that we covet our particular goals in spite of how these goals are valued at the societal level. Surely, however, the people who already pursue goals in these five undervalued areas would welcome an endorsement in society more generally, along with the increased remuneration that should accompany the newly elevated status of such work.

Second, in individualistic American society, people often think only about their own goals. Unfortunately, this pursuit of one's goals and a personal sense of uniqueness (Snyder & Fromkin, 1980) often is undertaken without a commensurate concern for the goals of other people. Related to this point, one of the discoveries that we have made about high-hope people is that they, more so than low-hope persons, appear to be interested in their goals and the goals of other people (Snyder, Cheavens, & Sympson, 1997). In the process of increasing the number of valued human goals, as we have described in the previous paragraph, we also would be changing toward an "I win, you win" approach because more goals are rewarded. Additionally, in childrearing, educational, and other arenas, we believe that a crucial and recurring lesson for our offspring is to set "we/me" goals—those goals that meet both the desires of others and the desires of the individual. In a sense, therefore, hopeful thought also will be virtuous and ethical in that it involves a consideration of the welfare of other people and what they want in life.

Third, society needs to rethink the view that the only route to "building better people" rests upon improving their weaknesses. This "fixing weaknesses" approach not only has kept us focused on the negative, but it has hampered the possibilities for flourishing. From the small environs of families to the large arenas of schools and businesses, we should make it more possible for people to participate in activities that match their interests and aptitudes. We are not suggesting that humankind can or should totally ignore its blatant weaknesses, but rather that we would be well advised to spend more of our energies in building on the strengths of people (Buckingham & Clifton, 2001). The "hopeful ones" already seem to know this, because they have constructed their lives so as to accentuate time spent on matters related to their interests and talents. In so doing, they are productive, healthy, and full of joy.

NOTE

For additional information about this or other work related to hope theory, contact C.R. Snyder. 1415 Jayhawk Blvd., Psychology Dept., 340 Fraser Hall, University of Kansas, Lawrence, KS 66045, or e-mail to crsnyder@ku.edu.

REFERENCES

Abramson, L.Y., Seligman, M.E.P., & Teasdale, J.D. (1978). Learned helplessness in humans: Critique and reformulation. *Journal of Abnormal Psychology,* 87, 49–74.

Affleck, G., & Tennen, H. (1996). Construing benefits from adversity: Adaptational significance and dispositional underpinnings. *Journal of Personality,* 64, 899–922.

Anderson, J.R. (1988). *The role of hope in appraisal, goal-setting, expectancy, and coping.* Unpublished doctoral dissertation, University of Kansas, Lawrence.

Averill, J.R., Catlin, G., & Chon, K.K. (1990). *Rules of hope.* New York: Springer-Verlag.

Babyak, M.A., Snyder, C.R., & Yashinobu, L. (1993). Psychometric properties of the Hope Scale: A confirmatory factor analysis. *Journal of Research in Personality,* 27, 154–169.

Bandura, A. (1997). *Self efficacy: The exercise of control.* New York: Freeman.

Barker, S.L., Funk, S.C., & Houston, B.K. (1988). Psychological treatment versus nonspecific factors: A meta-analysis of conditions that engender comparable expectations of improvement. *Clinical Psychology Review,* 8, 579–594.

Barnum, D.D., Snyder, C.R., Rapoff, M.A., Mani, M.M., & Thompson, R. (1998). Hope and social support in the psychological adjustment of pediatric burn survivors and matched controls. *Children's Health Care,* 27, 15–30.

Brown, M., Curry, L.A., Hagstrom, H., & Sandstedt, S. (1999, August). *Female teenage athletes, sport participation, self-esteem, and hope.* Paper presented at the Association for the Advancement of Applied Sport Psychology, Banff, Alberta, Canada.

Brunstein, J.C. (1993). Personal goals and subjective well-being: A longitudinal study. *Journal of Personality and Social Psychology,* 65, 1061–1070.

Buckingham, M., & Clifton, D. (2001). *Now, discover your strengths.* New York: Free Press.

Carver, C.S., & Scheier, M.F. (2000). Optimism, pessimism, and self-regulation. In E.C. Chang (Ed.), *Optimism and pessimism* (pp. 31–52). Washington, DC: American Psychological Association.

Chang, E.C. (1998). Hope, problem-solving ability, and coping in a college student population: Some implications for theory and practice. *Journal of Clinical Psychology,* 54, 953–962.

Clore, G.C. (1994). Why emotions are felt. In P. Ekman & R.J. Davidson (Eds.), *The nature of emotion: Fundamental questions* (pp. 103–111). New York: Oxford University Press.

Craig, K.J.W. (1943). *The nature of explanation.* Cambridge, England: Cambridge University.

Crowson, J.J. Jr., Frueh, C., & Snyder, C.R. (2001). Hostility and hope in combat-related posttraumatic stress disorder: A look back at combat as compared to today. *Cognitive Therapy and Research,* 25, 149–165.

Curry, L.A., Maniar, S.D., Sondag, K.A., & Sandstedt, S. (1999). *An optimal performance academic course for university students and student-athletes.* Unpublished manuscript, University of Montana, Missoula.

Curry, L.A., Snyder, C.R., Cook, D.L., Ruby, B.C., & Rehm, M. (1997). The role of hope in student-athlete academic and sport achievement. *Journal of Personality and Social Psychology,* 73, 1257–1267.

Diekstra, F.F.W. (1995). Depression and suicidal behaviors in adolescence: Sociocultural and time trends. In M. Rutter (Ed), *Psychosocial distur-*

bances in young people: Challenges for prevention (pp. 212–243). New York: Cambridge University Press.

Elliott, T. R., Witty, T. E., Herrick, S., & Hoffman, J. T. (1991). Negotiating reality after physical loss: Hope, depression, and disability. *Journal of Personality and Social Psychology, 61,* 608–613.

Feldman, D. B., & Snyder, C. R. (in press). Hope and meaning in life. *Journal of Social and Clinical Psychology.*

Floyd, R. K., & McDermott, D. (1998, August). *Hope and sexual risk-taking in gay men.* Presented at the American Psychological Association, San Francisco.

Harney, P. (1990). *The Hope Scale: Exploration of construct validity and its influence on health.* Unpublished master's thesis, University of Kansas, Lawrence.

Harris, C. B. (1988). *Hope: Construct definition and the development of an individual differences scale.* Unpublished doctoral dissertation, University of Kansas, Lawrence.

Irving, L. M., Crenshaw, W., Snyder, C. R., Francis, P., & Gentry, G. (1990, May). *Hope and its correlates in a psychiatric setting.* Paper presented at the Midwestern Psychological Association, Chicago.

Irving, L. M., Snyder, C. R., & Crowson Jr., J. J. (1998). Hope and the negotiation of cancer facts by college women. *Journal of Personality, 66,* 195–214.

Irving, L., Snyder, C. R., Gravel, L., Hanke, J., Hilberg, P., & Nelson, N. (1997, April). *Hope and effectiveness of a pre-therapy orientation group for community mental health center clients.* Paper presented at the Western Psychological Association Convention, Seattle.

Jackson, W. T., Taylor, R. E., Palmatier, A. D., Elliott, T. R., & Elliott, J. L. (1998). Negotiating the reality of visual impairment: Hope, coping, and functional ability. *Journal of Clinical Psychology in Medical Settings, 5,* 173–185.

Jacobs, D. G. (Ed.). (1999). *The Harvard Medical School guide to suicide assessment and prevention.* San Francisco: Jossey-Bass.

Klausner, E. J., Clarkin, J. F., Spielman, L., Pupo, C., Abrams, R., & Alexopoulas, G. S. (1998). Late-life depression and functional disability: The role of goal-focused group psychotherapy. *International Journal of Geriatric Psychiatry,13,* 707–716.

Krauss, H. H., & Krauss, B. J. (1968). Cross-cultural study of the thwarting-disorientation theory of suicide. *Journal of Abnormal Psychology, 73,* 352–357.

Kwon, P. (2000). Hope and dysphoria: The moderating role of defense mechanisms. *Journal of Personality, 68,* 199–233.

Kwon, P. (in press). Hope, defense mechanisms, and adjustment: Implications for false hope and defensive hopelessness. *Journal of Personality.*

Laird, S. (1992). *A preliminary investigation into prayer as a coping technique for adult patients with arthritis.* Unpublished doctoral dissertation, University of Kansas, Lawrence.

Langelle, C. (1989). *An assessment of hope in a community sample.* Unpublished master's thesis, University of Kansas, Lawrence.

Lazarus, R. S., Deese, J., & Osler, S. F. (1952). The effects of psychological stress upon performance. *Psychological Bulletin, 49,* 293–317.

Levenson, R. W. (1994). Human emotion: A functionalist view. In P. Ekman & R. J. Davidson (Eds.), *The nature of emotion: Fundamental questions* (pp. 123–126). New York: Oxford University Press.

Lopez, S. J., Bouwkamp, J., Edwards, L. M., & Teramoto Pediotti, J. (2000, October). *Making hope happen via brief interventions.* Presented at the 2nd Positive Psychology Summit, Washington, DC.

Magaletta, P. R., & Oliver, J. M. (1999). The hope construct, will and ways: Their relative relations with self-efficacy, optimism, and general well-being. *Journal of Clinical Psychology, 55,* 539–551.

McDermott, D., & Snyder, C. R. (2000). *The great big book of hope: Help your children achieve their dreams.* Oakland, CA: New Harbinger Publications.

McNeal, L. J. (1997). The effects of perceived non-work social support and hope upon oncology nurses' occupational stress. *Dissertation Abstracts, 58* (4-A):1209.

McNeal, R. E. (1998). Pre- and post-treatment hope in children and adolescents in residential treatment: A further analysis of the effects of the teaching family model. *Dissertation Abstracts, 59* (5-B):2425.

Michael, S. T. (2000). Hope conquers fear: Overcoming anxiety and panic attacks. In C. R. Snyder (Ed.), *Handbook of hope: Theory, measures, and applications* (pp. 355–378). San Diego, CA: Academic Press.

Moon, C., Snyder, C. R., & Rapoff, M. (2001). *The relationship of hope to children's asthma treatment adherence.* Unpublished manuscript, University of Kansas, Lawrence.

Pinker, S. (1997). *How the mind works.* New York: Norton.

Popenhagen, M. P., & Qualley, R. M. (1998). Adolescent suicide: Detection, intervention, and prevention. *Professional School Counseling, 1,* 30–36.

Range, L. M., & Penton, S. R. (1994). Hope, hopelessness, and suicidality in college students. *Psychological Reports, 75,* 456–458.

Rieger, E. (1993). Correlates of adult hope, including high- and low-hope adults' recollection of parents. *Psychology honors thesis,* University of Kansas, Lawrence.

Ruehlman, L. S., & Wolchik, S. A. (1988). Personal goals and interpersonal support and hindrance as factors in psychological distress and well-being. *Journal of Personality and Social Psychology, 55,* 293–301.

Scheier, M. F., & Carver, C. S. (1985). Optimism, coping, and health: Assessment and implications of generalized outcome expectancies. *Health Psychology, 4,* 219–247.

Scheier, M. F., & Carver, C. S. (1987). Dispositional optimism and physical well-being: The influence of generalized outcome expectancies on health. *Journal of Personality, 55,* 169–210.

Scheier, M. F., Carver, C. S., & Bridges, M. W. (1994). Distinguishing optimism from neuroticism (and trait anxiety, self mastery, and self-esteem): A reevaluation of the Life Orientation Test. *Journal of Personality and Social Psychology,* 67, 1063–1078.

Seaton, K., & Snyder, C. R. (2001). *Hope and remaining in a treatment program for drug abuse.* Unpublished manuscript, University of Kansas, Lawrence.

Seligman, M. E. P. (1991). *Learned optimism.* New York: Knopf.

Snyder, C. R. (1994). *The psychology of hope: You can get there from here.* New York: Free Press.

Snyder, C. R. (in press). Hope theory: Rainbows of the mind. *Psychological Inquiry.*

Snyder, C. R., Cheavens, J., & Michael, S. T. (1999). Hoping. In Snyder, C. R. (Ed.), *Coping: The psychology of what works* (pp. 205–231). New York: Oxford University Press.

Snyder, C. R., Cheavens, J., & Sympson, S. C. (1997). Hope: An individual motive for social commerce. *Group Dynamics: Theory, Research, and Practice,* 1, 107–118.

Snyder, C. R., & Feldman, D. B. (2000). Hope for the many: An empowering social agenda. In C. R. Snyder (Ed.), *Handbook of hope: Theory, measures, and applications* (pp. 402–415). San Diego: Academic Press.

Snyder, C. R., Feldman, D. B., Taylor, J. D., Schroeder, L. L., & Adams III, V. (2000). The roles of hopeful thinking in preventing problems and enhancing strengths. *Applied and Preventive Psychology,* 15, 262–295.

Snyder, C. R., & Fromkin, H. L. (1980). *Uniqueness: The human pursuit of difference.* New York: Plenum.

Snyder, C. R., Harris, C., Anderson, J. R., Holleran, S. A., Irving, L. M., Sigmon, S. T., Yoshinobu, L., Gibb, J., Langelle, C., & Harney, P. (1991). The will and the ways: Development and validation of an individual-differences measure of hope. *Journal of Personality and Social Psychology,* 60, 570–585.

Snyder, C. R., Hoza, B., Pelham, W. E., Rapoff, M., Ware, L., Danovsky, M., Highberger, L., Rubinstein, H., & Stahl, K. J. (1997). The development and validation of the Children's Hope Scale. *Journal of Pediatric Psychology,* 22, 399–421.

Snyder, C. R., Ilardi, S. S., Cheavens, J., Michael, S. T., Yamhure, L., & Sympson, S. (2000). The role of hope in cognitive behavior therapies. *Cognitive Therapy and Research,* 24, 747–762.

Snyder, C. R., Lapointe, A. B., Crowson Jr., J. J., & Early, S. (1998). Preferences of high- and low-hope people for self-referential input. *Cognition & Emotion,* 12, 807–823.

Snyder, C. R., McDermott, D., Cook, W., & Rapoff, M. (2002). *Hope for the journey: Helping children through the good times and the bad.* Clinton Corners, NY: Percheron.

Snyder, C. R., Odle, C., & Hackman, J. (1999, August). *Hope as related to perceived severity and tolerance of physical pain.* Paper presented at the American Psychological Association, Boston.

Snyder, C. R., Rand, K., King, E., Feldman, D., & Taylor, J. (in press). "False" hope. *Journal of Clinical Psychology.*

Snyder, C. R., Shorey, H. S., Cheavens, J., Pulvers, K. M., Adams III, V., Wiklund, C. (in press). Hope and academic success in college. *Journal of Educational Psychology.*

Snyder, C. R., Sympson, S. C., Michael, S. T., & Cheavens, J. (2000). The optimism and hope constructs: Variants on a positive expectancy theme. In E. C. Chang (Ed.), *Optimism and pessimism* (pp. 103–124). Washington, DC: American Psychological Association.

Snyder, C. R., Sympson, S. C., Ybasco, F. C., Borders, T. F., Babyak, M. A., & Higgins, R. L. (1996). Development and validation of the State Hope Scale. *Journal of Personality and Social Psychology, 70,* 321–335.

Stanton, A. L., Danoff-Burg, S., Cameron, C., Bishop, M., Collins, C. A., Kirk, S. B., Sworowski, L. A., & Twillman, R. (2000). Emotionally expressive coping predicts psychological and physical adjustment to breast cancer. *Journal of Consulting and Clinical Psychology, 68,* 875–882.

Stotland, E. (1969). *The psychology of hope.* San Francisco: Jossey-Bass.

Tennen, H., & Affleck, G. (1999). Finding benefits in adversity. In C. R. Snyder (Ed.), *Coping: The psychology of what works* (pp. 279–304). New York: Oxford Press.

Tierney, A. M. (1995). Analysis of a new theory of hope and personality as measured by the California Psychological Inventory. *Dissertation Abstracts, 55* (10-B):4616.

Westburg, N. (In press). Hope in older women: The importance of past and current relationship. *Journal of Social and Clinical Psychology.*

Woodbury, C. A. (1999). The relationship of anxiety, locus of control and hope to career indecision of African American students. *Dissertation Abstracts, 59* (11A): 4072.

Chapter 4

FACT OR ARTIFACT: THE RELATIONSHIP OF HOPE TO A CARAVAN OF RESOURCES

Stevan E. Hobfoll, Melissa Briggs-Phillips, and Lisa R. Stines

Hope is clearly related to well-being and health (Yarcheski, Mahon, & Yarcheski, 2001; Magaletta & Oliver, 1999). Numerous studies indicate that persons with a sense of hope are less likely to experience depression (Chang & DeSimone, 2001; Scioli et al., 1997) and better able to withstand the deleterious impact of stressful life circumstances (Obwuegbuzie & Snyder, 2000). Hope has also been linked with better physical health (Carson, Soeken, Shanty, & Terry, 1990) and recovery once a disease is diagnosed (Taylor, 2000). What is less clear is what is embodied in hope. Nor do we mean by this to imply that there are not clear definitions of hope; there are. Instead, in this chapter we set forth the question of whether findings regarding hope are artifactual products of other circumstances and resources that underlie hope, versus whether hope has an independent impact over and above these other circumstances and resources. This question will also lead us to consider different views of hope and how these discrete views may be differentially related to people's overall resource armamentarium.

This is an important question for a number of reasons. First, on the scientific level, we are always interested in whether our constructs have added predictive value over other related constructs. These other constructs may be related, in the sense of being similar, or they may be related in terms of being causally prior. If hope is the byproduct of having lots of extra cash, the extra cash is what is causally related to buying the sports car, not hope. In this case, hope's impact on the sports car purchase was wholly explained by extra cash.

We will explore whether hope is itself related to favorable psychological and health outcomes, or whether hope is a byproduct of underlying circumstances and resources that are the actual active ingredients in obtaining valued goals and positive emotional states. This brings us to a second reason as to why this question is important. Psychology has a long history of ignoring the impact of poverty, race, ethnicity, and gender. Consequently, psychology has been challenged as being not the psychology of the many, but the narrow psychology of white, middle-class men, particularly those of European descent. This is related to hope because it is so easy to see why someone who has everything and has a strong safety net will feel hope. In contrast, it is less clear how hope is sustained for those who are poor, of an ethnic minority group that is subject to racism, of the wrong gender, and without education. The Queen of England is probably hopeful about her financial future; she is the richest woman in the world. An inner-city, financially impoverished, poorly educated, Latina mother with poor English-language skills is less likely to be hopeful about her future. But if she is, is this the same hope possessed by the queen? The literature has, for the most part, ignored this point. It has enormous implications, both scientifically and politically. To the extent we find that hope helps, but what we are referring to is the possession of resources, we are once more blaming the victims for their lack of hope, when it is actually the system that has denied them hope. Indeed, for no other concept may the political, the religious, and the psychological be so interwoven, as hope is what has always been offered as a salve for the poor instead of bread, work, and security in this life.

Researchers have long accepted that hope is a critical component to the process of healing and recovery, whether from physical or mental illness (Obwuegbuzie & Snyder, 2000; Scioli et al., 1997). Less is known, however, about the relationship between hope and various resources. Can one who is without personal and social resources possess hope? Is hope a process that is influenced by additional factors, such as personality characteristics and interpersonal relationships? Current definitions of hope in the psychological domain focus on an individual-centered hope, in which individuals feel they can enact positive outcomes in light of a perceived difficulty or desired goal. Alternatively, for centuries, philosophers and others have conceptualized hope as an existential hope, or a transcending belief that things will work out regardless of circumstances. Resources may be a key distinction between these two types of hope: *individual-*

centered hope assumes that the individual has the personal or social resources required to meet a goal or overcome an obstacle, whereas *existential hope* may be the strength that individuals with few resources call upon to sustain themselves through difficult times. In order to examine hope as a construct, we must first appraise to what extent hope is simply a function of possessing other key resources. To do so, we will examine hope and resources within this hope schematic, exploring individual-centered hope and existential hope. If hope is highly correlated with personal and interpersonal resources such as self-efficacy, problem-solving skills, and social support, it will attest to the idea that hope, in an individual-centered sense, is a resource that exists in assemblage with other resources. Likewise, if hope is correlated with few resources or alternate resources such as spirituality, the evidence will lend credence to the notion of an existential hope. In either case, hope can only be seen as a valuable construct if it is both related to positive outcomes and predicts those outcomes over and above the impact of related resources.

HISTORICAL AND LITERARY VIEWS OF HOPE

Let us first look at some famous adages about hope, as they imply the two hopes that we think emerge in the literature we examine.

"Hope is eternal in the human breast," wrote Alexander Pope. This implies that hope springs forth despite life circumstances. It is a personal resource that people can turn to when all else fails. It is eternal. And when reality fails us, Goethe reminds us that "In all things it is better to hope than to despair. Cicero agrees in his defining of hope, stating, "To the sick, while there is life there is hope." This is the existential hope, the hope of belief.

Contrast this to the English Proverb: "Hope for the best. Prepare for the worst." The message here about hope is quite different. It suggests that hope is a good thing. It implies that hope will lead to staying in the fight, trying harder, remaining goal-directed. However, it suggests that hope will not sustain individuals if problems arise. In such circumstances, hope may even be detrimental, especially if it keeps people from preparing for reality.

Another, less well know aphorism from George Eliot, is "A woman's hopes are woven of sunbeams. A shadow annihilates them." This view of hope is still more pessimistic, or as the pessimist might argue, more realistic. To the extent that hope is not built on realistic skills, resources, and circumstances, it produces a house of cards that comes crashing down the moment reality is faced.

Benjamin Franklin adopted precisely the resources view of hope. For Franklin, "He that lives on hope will die fasting." Similarly, but more directly, Don Marquis wrote, "Every cloud has a silver lining, but it is sometimes difficult to get it to the mint." In these views of hope a utilitarian, one might say cynical, interpretation is offered. Hope is seen as chimerical, at best, and more likely dangerous. It keeps people from judging reality for what it is and addressing that reality with due diligence.

Definitions of Hope

The early understandings and definitions of hope involved simply individuals' positive expectations for successful goal attainment. These positive expectations were discussed as they pertained to general life goals, and very specifically to how they may relate to successful psychotherapy (Cantril, 1964; Frank, 1974; Stotland, 1969). Perhaps Stotland sums it up most simply with his statement that hope is an expectation greater than zero of achieving a goal (p. 2).

Numerous authors have also offered definitions that share this premise of hope being a personal perspective of the future:

> An energized mental state involving feelings of uneasiness or uncertainty and characterized by a cognitive, action-oriented expectation that a positive future goal or outcome is possible. (Haase et al., 1992, p. 143)

> Hope is an anticipation of a future which is good, based on mutuality (relationships with others), a sense of personal competence, coping ability, psychological well-being, purpose and meaning in life and a sense of "the possible." (Miller & Powers, 1988, p. 6)

> Hope...is a subjective state that can influence realities yet to come. (Farran & Popovich, 1990, p. 124)

In this way, these authors define hope as a general expectation that one will experience good outcomes in one's life, and that this positive expectation is a very powerful predictor of behavior, irrespective of effort by self, others, or any other outside force.

Snyder, Irving, and Anderson (1991) expand upon the idea of positive expectations for the future, defining hope as a thinking process that taps a sense of agency, or will, and the awareness of the steps necessary to achieve one's goals. Hope is then defined as a cognitive set that is based on a "reciprocally-derived sense of successful agency (goal-directed determinism) and pathways (planning to meet goals)" (Snyder et al., 1991, p. 571). That is, the will to reach a goal, and the sense that one will be able to successfully generate a plan to get there.

Other definitions of hope include a temporal dimension that conceptualizes hope as containing an element of understanding that the present circumstances are not permanent and are in fact, only temporary. For example, a prominent theorist within the nursing literature (Herth, 1989, 1990, 1991, 1993) summarizes this idea most succinctly. Herth (1989) defines hope as "an energized mental state characterized by an action-oriented, positive expectation that goals and/or needs for self and the future are obtainable and that the present state or situation is temporary" (p. 69).

When we look at leading definitions of hope, they are actually difficult to distinguish either from definitions of optimism or self-efficacy. They are quite starkly not the existential view of hope of literature. They are not the hope that exists when there is nothing left to do than to hope. Statistically, hope has an independent impact on well-being over and above the impact of age, gender, ethnicity, socioeconomic status, other personal and social resources, and "the facts." In other words, hope implies that even against the facts saying that there are long odds against you, you believe that you will ultimately win the race. Winning may be as straightforward as surviving, but whatever it is, the definitions imply that hope has "value added," all other things considered.

CONSERVATION OF RESOURCES THEORY AND HOPE

Conservation of Resources theory (COR) has been presented as a model that aids understanding of the stress process (Hobfoll, 1988, 1989, 1998). COR theory begins with the tenet that people strive to obtain, retain, foster, and protect the things they value. These things they value are called resources. There are many kinds of resources, but one way to subdivide them is into object resources, condition resources, personal resources, and energy resources. Object resources are valued objects that have a physical presence, such as a car, house, clothing, and tools for work. Condition resources are social circumstances and include a good marriage, stable employment, being nested in a supportive network, and tenure. Personal resources include skills (e.g., social aplomb, carpentry skills) and personal attributes (e.g., self-efficacy, optimism). Finally, energy resources are resources that are only resources to the extent they can fuel or catalyze obtaining other resources (e.g., money, credit, knowledge).

People work to obtain, retain, foster, and protect these resources. Also, stress occurs, according to COR theory when resources are (1) threatened with loss, (2) actually lost, or (3) when people fail to gain resources consummate with their resource investment (hence producing a net loss). Although it is not the purpose of this paper to detail all of COR theory, it is important to consider some of the corollaries of COR theory. Principally, COR theory suggests that resources are interwoven. Hence, resources tend to be carried in caravans. The caravan metaphor implies that over life people develop a constellation of resources that they can take with them. Contrariwise, the absence of resources tends to imply the absence of other resources, to the extent that resources appear in constellations.

For hope, this implies that hope is most likely present and helpful to individuals because it is part of their overall caravan of resources. COR theory would predict that hope should have broad overlap with other resources. The caravan begins with being raised in favored social circumstances—this includes money, education, and peace, on one level, and a loving, stable family on another level. Second, it implies that hope will exist in concert with such personal resources as self-esteem, self-efficacy, and optimism. These attributes, already found to be fundamental to well-being and improved stress resistance (Horton & Wallander, 2001) set a high bar for hope, as hope will have to be shown to have added value over and above these other attributes. To the extent hope does not have added value, it can only be said to be a marker for these other traits or some yet undiscovered meta-trait such as developed in BIG 5 research that is seen as underlying other beneficial personal characteristics.

We ask a number of specific questions:

1. To what extent is hope the byproduct of sociodemographic conditions?
2. To what extent is hope just a matter of knowing the odds and that they are, in fact, in your favor?
3. To what extent is hope an artifact of possessing other key personal and social resources?
4. To what extent can hope be seen as having added value over and above favored life circumstances and other key personal and social resources?

SOCIODEMOGRAPHICS IN THE CONTEXT OF INDIVIDUAL-CENTERED AND EXISTENTIAL HOPE

These questions can be first addressed by examining the relationship between hope and sociodemographic markers. Age, gender, education, income, employment, ethnicity, and marital status all impact individuals' life experiences, and thus their access to resources that may affect individual-centered hope. Individuals' sociocultural experiences may lead to oppression and disenfranchisement, or at the other end of the spectrum, privilege and access to financial, emotional, and institutional resources. It is our contention that individual-centered hope may indeed be better understood as a reflection of individuals' possessing resources and other personal characteristics that allow them to have a positive future orientation. It follows that membership in specific demographic categories that allow for access to resources or protection from oppression may contribute to this individual-centered experience of hope.

Conversely, existential hope may be that which people resort to when life circumstances or current resources do not allow for the individual to have a sense of agency or belief in the ability to move toward their future. Perhaps existential hope represents a spiritual, existential or religiously-based sense of trust in fate or higher power that the future will hold something better, irrespective of individual-centered hope. Regardless of whether individual-centered hope and existential hope exist on some sort of continuum or are two distinct constructs, it behooves researchers to be clear when making scientific inquiry into the nature of hope as to what exactly they are discussing.

Age

Bunston, Mings, Mackie, and Jones (1995) sought to develop a model of the determinants of hope using path analysis on data collected from outpatients seeking treatment for ocular melanoma and head and neck cancer. They proposed that sociodemographic variables would have a direct impact on hope, as well as an indirect impact on hope through factors such as coping skills, social support and locus of control. They found age to be directly correlated with hope. Subsequent path analysis indicated that age was also related to hope through the individuals' locus of control and number of concerns, with younger individuals reporting fewer needs and an internal locus of control. These results point to the advantages that youth may offer individuals when facing challenges or adversity in life. Being younger in and of itself is related to positive expectations for the future, but in addition, youth appears to be related to other aspects of life that impact hope, mainly having fewer needs and having an internal, versus external, locus of control. Research, as reviewed later in this chapter, suggests that an internal locus of control is related to higher hope. If youth is related to an internal locus of control, then perhaps advanced age is related to less hope in part because of a decreased sense of personal control.

In a study that explored the relationship between hope, spiritual well-being, and religiousness among women living with breast cancer, Mickley, Soeken, and Belcher (1992), found that being older was related to having less hope. The participants ranged in age from 29–89 years of age, providing a broad sampling of ages. As age increased, the participants' levels of religious well-being, existential well-being, and intrinsic religiousness (internal sense of spirituality) decreased, but their level of extrinsic religiousness (organizational focus) increased. In other words, as the participants aged, they reported increasing use of churches and other external organizations to define their religiousness, at the same time they were reporting less hope. This suggests that as individuals age, the reality of their lives necessitates assistance from others, and less self-reliance. It follows that if individuals report less individual-centered hope as they age, this could be an artifact of our measures assessing some global sense of ability to personally enact events, make decisions, or experience positive feelings about the future in their lives.

In a recent review of the psychological literature on hope, Snyder (2000) concluded that older individuals experience higher levels of depression, which may be a reflection of loss of hope. This loss of hope may be a result of repeated goal blockages that occur. Again, if hope is understood in terms of the individual-centered conceptualization, which places significant emphasis on goal-oriented and directive behavior (Snyder, 2000), then repeated loss and inability to reach a goal might lead to loss of hope, and subsequent depression. In fact, defining hope as achievement, success, or control, as it is often operationalized, may be problematic for elderly people. With their accumulated losses, multiple health problems, and decreasing ability to care for themselves, it may be their sense of achievement, success, and control that deteriorates. However, qualitative research suggests that the elderly, even if terminally ill, describe themselves as experiencing hope (Herth, 1993). Herth (1993) suggests that older adults do maintain hope, but that their goals and dreams are modified to reflect current capabilities and context. Hope may shift from an individual-centered and future goal accomplishment focus to a more existential focus, and this sense of existential hope may be missed in current operationalizations of hope.

Gender

On the whole, research has not indicated that men and women have different levels of hope. Snyder (2000) concluded that "to date, we have not found gender difference in overall hope, or its components—in fact, we have not even produced trends" (Snyder, 2000, p. 21). An interesting commentary follows, in which the author states that what may be missing in data collection is that the hope of achieving goals is the same, but we never ask participants to name their specific goals, thus "the seemingly equal agency and pathways would be in service of vastly disparate goal targets" (Snyder, 2000, p. 21).

However, the conclusion that there are no differences between men and women in their experience of individual-centered or existential hope may be short-sighted. Despite using mixed-sex samples, we found in our review of the literature that investigators almost exclusively collapsed results across gender without first examining any possible differences by sex. We suggest that this is methodologically unsound and future research should explore differences by gender more carefully.

In one study that did compare men and women, women were found to score higher on a survey measure of hope when compared to men in a sample of individuals who were dealing with different forms of cancer (Bunston, Mings, Mackie, & Jones, 1995). Sex was found to be directly related to hope with women reporting more hope. No attempt was made to explore how this difference by sex may be operating. That is, do women have more social connectedness or other related experiences that may have led to higher hope scores? Although this result should be considered in light of the extreme conditions under which people were being asked about their hope for the future (dealing with cancer), it presents an interesting finding that warrants exploration.

Clearly, future research needs to examine gender differences in hope. Following Snyder's (2000) proposal, research needs to examine the goals and pathways being studied in order to determine if men and women are referring to the same targets for which they are hopeful. In this regard, hope might remain constant even as people relinquish their goals. Hence, women in work settings might remain hopeful, but be lowering their target goals, say, due to the glass ceiling in business advancement. In this way, goals may be readjusted to align with reality in order to stabilize hope. This would be a very different conclusion than has been made and would raise the sophistication of the way hope was examined in light of context.

Education, Income, and Employment

Individual-centered hope is clearly related to education. The more education individuals report, the higher their hope scores (Holdcraft &

Williamson, 1991; McGill & Paul, 1993) and the less education individuals report, the lower their hope scores (Mickley, Soeken, & Belcher, 1992).

Two studies focusing on patients with cancer found that education was related to the experience of hope. Hope of recovery from cancer was higher in individuals with higher income, higher occupational status, and more education (Bunston, Mings, Mackie, & Jones, 1995). A study that addressed education about the topic of cancer revealed that the more knowledge college women had about cancer, the more hopeful they were of being able to cope with cancer and survive it (Irving, Snyder, & Crowson, 1998). These results provide evidence to suggest that agency, or belief in the ability to move towards a goal, knowing how, and having the resources to get there may be impacted by education and awareness of resources. Sense of agency may bring hope, but then we return to the question of whether hope is anything more than a sense of agency within the context of knowing what obstacles are likely to be encountered and what resources one has to overcome those challenges.

Income, an important marker of socioeconomic status, has rarely been addressed in the literature on hope. Results of McGill and Paul (1993) suggest that this may indeed be a valuable area to explore. Individuals with cancer reported more concern over money and perceived themselves as less financially secure than individuals without cancer (McGill and Paul, 1993). At the same time, individuals with cancer reported less hope than those without cancer. If individuals with illnesses report that they have less financial security due to the cost of their illness, and that financial security is found to be related to hope, it is probable that research that has not inquired about financial stress may actually not be assessing hope insomuch as the financial strain of the illness.

Snyder (2000) suggested that the relationship between employment and hope warrants attention from researchers. He argued that the necessity of success and satisfaction with employment for fulfillment and happiness has been axiomatic in industrial organization psychology for decades. Evidence suggests that those who maintain employment have more hope and more self-efficacy. In this regard, Foote, Piazza, Holcombe, Paul, and Daffin (1990) explored the relationship between hope, self-esteem, and social support in persons with multiple sclerosis. Employed individuals reported higher hope scores than unemployed individuals. It may be fruitful to explore this further in researching the correlates and predictors of individual-centered and existential hope.

Ethnicity

Little research has attempted to compare cross-cultural or intra-group experiences of hope. The results of Piazza, Holcombe, Foote, Paul, Love, and Daffin (1991) suggest that this might be an oversight. These authors explored the relationship of hope, social support, and self-efficacy in spinal cord injured patients. They found that whites had significantly higher levels of hope than blacks. Upon further examination, they found that 70 percent of blacks, as opposed to 59 percent of whites, were unemployed and 78 percent of blacks were not married compared to 63 percent of whites. These findings suggest that when exploring the difference between racial groups in their experience of hope, as in all group differences research, it is imperative to examine data closely so as to not draw erroneous and misleading conclusions about differences. In this particular instance, Piazza et al. (1991) discovered that perhaps the more important demographic characteristics to consider would be marital and employment status.

An interesting paradox in the hope and hopelessness-depression research is the continued finding that African Americans score higher on scales of depression and hopelessness, but report significantly lower rates of suicide (Beck, Steer, Kovacs & Garrison, 1985). These authors found that one out of 78 African Americans successfully committed suicide (1.8 percent) as opposed to 13 out of 129 whites (10.1 percent). These findings fly in the face of commonly held assumptions that hopelessness is the key component of depression that leads to suicide. Are there cultural experiences that lead to African American individuals learning to cope in the face of adversity without the presence of hope? Have African Americans learned adaptation and coping skills that are unique in response to oppression and the resultant lack of hope? Or is it possible that our current agentic and individual-centered operationalizations of hope have not adequately captured the full array of hope that individuals experience? These findings highlight the importance of continuing to explore the nuances of hope in cross-cultural groups as well as cultural and social factors that may serve as protective factors in African Americans.

Marital Status

Holdcraft and Williamson (1991) found that being single predicted hope for recovery from psychiatric or chemical dependency when assessed at admission. In contrast to these results, less direct evidence suggests that being married may lead one to report more hope. For example, Piazza and colleagues (1991) found that being married was related to perceptions of more social support, and research has suggested that social support is often correlated with hope (Foote et al., 1990; Piazza et al., 1991). It is possible that marital status may be related to hope through social support, although no direct evidence for this relationship exists. In addition, when examining the difference between white and black participants, Piazza and colleagues found that while whites had higher hope, they were also more likely to be married. As is the case for other demographic variables that are related to underlying resource states, there is just too little research to answer these questions. Moreover, even where investigators had the ability to examine how underlying sociodemographic resources are related to hope, they failed to conduct the appropriate analyses in all but a few cases.

PERSONAL RESOURCES AND HOPE

In the next section we examine how hope may be related to personal resources. Again, as in the prior review, our fundamental question is whether hope has a value-added component that is not already explained by other resources. Secondary to this, we ask whether it is individual-centered or existential hope that is being assessed. In other words, is it the "hope springing eternal in the human breast," or a mere positive expectation based on the known facts of the situation?

Self-Esteem and Self-Worth

Hope and self-esteem should be clearly distinguishable constructs. Hope refers to positive expectancy and self-esteem refers to evaluation of self-worth. The two should be correlated, however, in that those with positive self-esteem should see themselves as deserving of positive things happening to them and past successes should build both hope and self-esteem. A number of investigations have examined the relationship of hope to self-esteem and global self-worth. Foote and colleagues (1990) assessed hope and self-esteem in a group of adults with multiple sclerosis. They found that hope was highly correlated with self-esteem ($r = .74$, $p<.001$). Similarly, hope was found to be strongly correlated to self-esteem in a sample of spinal cord injury victims ($r = .91$, $p<.001$) (Piazza et al., 1991). In a study of adolescent burn victims, hope was most highly correlated with global self-worth in both victims and controls ($r = .64$; $p<.01$), suggesting that hope remains, in constellation with other resources, even in adversity (Barnum, Snyder, Rapoff, Mani, & Thompson, 1998).

These studies suggest that self-esteem and individual-centered hope are so highly interrelated that it may in fact be impossible to separate the two constructs. Indeed, with relationships this high, it is questionable that these are separate constructs. When correlations are as high as test-retest reliability, it cannot be said that hope has any value-added addition (Kazdin, 1992) to the construct of self-esteem, or some more basic reflection of inner fortitude. Given the absence of study of how self-esteem is related to more existential hope, the hope that exists when all else fails, it cannot be said that self-esteem replicates what might exist in this more existential view of hope.

Locus of Control and Self-Efficacy

Prior research has hypothesized that locus of control and hope are related, in that those who feel they are in control of their environment will be more likely to have hope. Because it is assumed that the individuals have the resources necessary to implement control of their environment, then by definition locus of control corresponds to an individual-centered hope. Although locus of control may be especially compromised in light of physical illness, studies suggest that locus of control is nonetheless related to having high levels of hope with ill populations. In a study of cancer patients, Bunston, Mings, Mackie, and Jones (1995) found that hope and locus of control were highly correlated. Likewise, an internal locus of control was negatively correlated with hopelessness in a sample of HIV-positive homosexual men, so that those reporting a high internal locus of control also reported lower levels of hopelessness (Rabkin et al., 1990). Hope and self-efficacy were also correlated in a college-student sample assessing general well-being (Magaletta & Oliver, 1999). These studies suggest that locus of control and individual-centered hope are related.

Hunt Raleigh (1992), however, did not find a significant relationship between hope and self-efficacy or locus of control, although this study did not use standardized measures to assess the above constructs. In fact, because Hunt Raleigh focused less on goal-related hope, she may have been assessing the relationship between locus of control and existential hope. Therefore it is possible that her results may reflect the lack of an association between locus of control and existential hope.

The association of hope with locus of control suggests related, but not overlapping constructs. This may be due to the fact that those low in sense of control may derive hope from other sources. Antonovsky (1979) in his sense of coherence construct spoke of other sources of hope that individuals might have. Thus, hope could derive from a sense that significant others have one's best interests at heart, or from belief in a just world. Similarly, individuals could feel that hope is derived from a divine presence who would intercede on their behalf when called upon through prayer. This suggests that hope can be felt even if one cannot exercise direct control over goals. Indeed, by some definitions this is what hope is, that is, what is left when one can no longer exercise control and must nevertheless not lose faith. Instead, the hope that is derived from individuals' direct action may be more of a belief in a positive outcome based on knowing the facts or one's abilities.

Goal Motivation, Problem-Solving Skills, and Coping

Most of the widely accepted definitions of hope in the literature include a goal aspect, whether it is in establishing a goal, creating a means to reach the desired goal, or the motivation to pursue those means (Stotland, 1969; Snyder, 1994). But is an individual only hopeful when he or she is in pursuit of a goal? Do those who are less hopeful demonstrate less motivation to pursue goals? These questions are important in the distinction between individual-centered and existential hope. Goal motivation reflects an individual-centered hope but does not preclude one who is without resources or lacking goals from possessing hope. This simply suggests that those individuals may possess a different type of hope, or existential hope. While the empirical evidence is far from overwhelming, there is evidence of a relationship between goal motivation and levels of hope, wherein those who report more motivation also report higher levels of hope (Cramer, 1998). We suggest that this relationship, however, is specific to individual-centered hope.

Intuitively, one might suspect that hope could be contingent upon the ability to solve life's problems, both mundane and difficult, such that if you are capable of solving a problem, you will be more likely to feel hopeful about the outcome. Likewise, hopelessness might stem from the perception of an inability to solve such problems. Again, this reflects individual-centered hope. Chang (1998) examined the relationship between hope and problem-solving ability among a sample of college students. He found that those students who reported high levels of hope scored higher on a number of problem-solving dimensions including positive problem orientation and rational problem solving. To whatever extent hope is related to problem-solving ability, logic, and reasoning skills, these personal resources may be integral to possessing individual-centered hope.

The association between hope and coping has been widely examined in the literature. Lazarus and Folkman (1985) proposed that hope itself was an important coping strategy, suggesting that the two are tightly interwoven constructs. Empirical evidence supports this notion. In a sample of Vietnam veterans seeking treatment for posttraumatic stress disorder (PTSD), hope was correlated with three approach coping strategies which have been found to be superior to avoidant coping strategies (Irving, Telfer, & Blake, 1997). This is consistent with research with ill children, which found that hope is correlated with active coping, both by children with sickle cell disease and their parents (Kliewer & Lewis, 1995). These results support the argument that individuals with strong repertoires of coping strategies for handling life's difficulties are likely to have high levels of individual-centered hope.

Optimism

Hope and optimism have been defined as separate constructs theoretically (Scheier & Carver, 1985; Snyder, Irving, & Anderson, 1991); however, many studies operationalize the two as similar, if not indistinguishable, constructs. In fact, very few empirical investigations have examined the relationship between hope and optimism. Scioli and colleagues (1997) assessed hope and optimism among college students in a prospective study designed to distinguish between the two. They found that hope and optimism were highly correlated ($r = .46$, $p<.01$). Still, optimism scores accounted for only 16 percent of the variance in hope scores, indicating that they also have unique variance. Similarly, Magaletta and Oliver (1999) found that hope and dispositional optimism were significantly correlated ($r = .55$, $p<.001$), denoting that hope and optimism have strong, overlapping features.

Indeed, with their definitions so close, it raises the question of why the two constructs are not more closely related. What is there in optimism that is not in hope? Given the limited numbers of scales measuring each, it raises the question of whether the difference between the two constructs found in studies might be a product of item sampling. To conduct a test of whether two constructs are separable it is necessary to have multiple measures of each. Then a test of the multi-trait, multi-method (Campbell & Stanley, 1966) can be conducted. Until such tests are done, given their nearly identical definitions, it is not possible to conclude that the constructs are independent. Given that there is so much more empirical support for optimism, it is incumbent on those developing hope constructs and conducting studies of hope to illustrate that it is distinguishable from optimism.

Religiosity

Spirituality has been conceptualized as a resource that may be related to hope. In fact, the presence of spiritual beliefs is often integral to the very definition of hope (Nowotny, 1991). In an examination of spiritual well-being by Carson, Soeken, and Grimm (1988), hope was significantly related to both existential (sense of life purpose and satisfaction) and religious well-being (sense of relationship with God), two components of spiritual well-being. Existentialism and religiosity were also cited as critical aspects to the maintenance of hope in a sample of chronically ill adults (Hunt Raleigh, 1992). Mickley, Soeken, and Belcher (1992) found that spiritual well-being, composed again of existential and religious well-being, accounted for 54.9 percent of the variance in levels of hope. Existential well-being was particularly predictive of levels of hope in that it alone accounted for 53.6 percent of the variance.

Hope and religious well-being were correlated in a sample of elderly women as well (Zorn & Johnson, 1997). Hope was related to spiritual well-being in an examination of adults living with AIDS, in that those who had higher levels of hope also had high levels of spiritual well-being (Carson, Soeken, Shanty, & Terry, 1990). Herth (1993) found that a belief in a power greater than self empowers hope in 92 percent of caregivers for the terminally ill. Spirituality as a personal resource, then, seems to be directly related to existential hope. As in some of the other research we explored, the relationships were so high as to raise questions of independence of concepts in some cases.

Examining across studies, there is considerable evidence that hope is related to possessing other personal resources. Because studies have not examined the issue of value added, it is not clear to what extent hope contributes beyond these other personal resources. Moreover, the critical theoretical test that hope should be a resource that can be relied on in the face of poor odds has not been directly addressed. At this stage it cannot be said that hope is more than the expectation of positive outcomes that is based on people's assessments of their resources in light of the obstacles they are facing.

INTERPERSONAL RESOURCES

Social Support

Social support is an important interpersonal resource that has also been examined in relation to hope. Social support, like optimism, may be related in ways to both individual-centered and existential hope. Barnum and colleagues (1998) found that perceived social support was significantly correlated with hope ($r = .48$, $p<.05$) in a group of adolescent burn victims and their matched controls (Barnum et al., 1998), suggesting that those who have supportive social networks have high hope for the future regardless of illness status. Hope was significantly correlated with social support in victims of spinal cord injuries (Piazza et al., 1991). Likewise, Foote, Piazza, Holcombe, Paul, and Daffin (1990) found that hope was highly related to social support in adults with multiple sclerosis. Herth (1993) found that hope was fostered by the presence of supportive relationships in caregivers of terminally ill people. Family support through time spent together and physical help was related to levels of hope in chronically ill adults (Hunt Raleigh, 1992). In one exception to this trend, hope was not significantly correlated with social support in one sample of cancer patients (Bunston et al., 1995).

Another aspect of social support was examined in a group of adolescents receiving inpatient treatment for substance abuse (Hinds, 1988). She found that adolescents' hopefulness was significantly related to the caring behaviors of nurses at the residential treatment center, thereby implying the broad nature of social support as it relates to hope. Alternatively, hopelessness has been negatively correlated with social support in a sample of HIV-positive men. HIV-positive men who had higher levels of hopelessness also had lower perceived emotional support and lower perceived material support (Rabkin et al., 1990). These findings were replicated when Rabkin, Ferrando, Shu-Hsing, Sewell, & McElhiney (2000) found a correlation of $r = -.81$ ($p<.001$) between hopelessness and social support, such that as hopelessness increases, perception of social support decreases.

Due to the lack of prospectively designed research in this area, the question of causality remains. Does the lack of socially supportive relationships lead to a decrease in levels of hope or do low-hope individuals have fewer of the resources necessary to build and maintain healthy interpersonal relationships? Nonetheless, studies lend credence to the notion that hope is in fact related to possession of resources, in this case social support. The relationship between hope and social support is consistently quite high, but the relationship is so strong in some studies that hope may simply be a reflection of the social support participants have in their lives.

OVERARCHING ISSUES

The Problem of Focus of Measurement

The problems and issues we raise are nowhere made more succinct than by the well-validated Hope scale (Snyder, Harris, Anderson, Holleran et al., 1991). Snyder et al. (1991) see hope as having two underlying components, the perception of agency in meeting goals and the perception of having pathways that allow the attainment of goals. Such a definition, although scientifically acceptable, is the opposite of many classical and romantic definitions of hope. Indeed, referring back to the adage "hope for the best, plan for the worst," there is more plan than hope in Snyder's definition. It is not that this is not hope, but that it is individual, goal-focused hope.

The items of the Hope Scale for agency are as follows:

1. I energetically pursue my goals.
2. My past experiences prepare me well for the future.
3. I've been pretty successful in life.
4. I meet the goals that I set for myself.

The items of the Hope Scale for pathways are:

1. I can think of many ways to get out of a jam.
2. There are lots of ways around any problem.
3. I can think of many ways to get the things in life that are most important to me.
4. Even when others get discouraged, I know I can find a way to solve the problem.

Such items for agency are clearly closely linked with possessing resources and experiencing the past successes that stem from resources. Hope, as it is classically defined as the belief in a positive outcome *against the odds,* would be the extent that such agency is maintained in the face of past failure and long odds, which is not what is encompassed in these items.

Turning to the pathways, there is also potential confounding between the belief in such pathways and having such pathways. Bill Gates, the billionaire, would probably score high on hope pathways. So would Michael Jordan the basketball star. But this is not because they *believe* that pathways are available, they *are* available. Now if you and I were to believe that we have the pathways to beat Michael Jordan, that is hope! These pathways are clearly linked to the objective circumstances at people's disposal.

Nor are we arguing that such items and this scale as a whole are not potentially linked to hope. Rather, it appears that the confounding elements must be situationally considered and controlled for, and only then what remains is hope. Hence, turning to our own work on inner-city women (Ennis, Hobfoll, & Schröder, 2000), among inner-city women who have faced a lifetime of poverty, racism, lack of educational opportunity, dangerous neighborhoods, and health risks, their sense of mastery must consist of a great deal of hope. Said another way, life should have taught them to lose their sense of mastery, but their sense of hope may have helped them sustain a positive outlook despite a lifetime of experiences largely directed at thwarting their positive outlook.

Perhaps this is further clarified by examining a single item of the Hope scale; "I can think of many ways to get out of a jam." If a middle-class college student answers this in the affirmative, it is likely the byproduct of parental support, life circumstances that control challenges to be reasonable and developmentally suitable, financial backing, and a knowledge that justice is available. Our inner-city woman is answering this in the likely absence of a supportive safety net (they are already overburdened and she does not want to be a further burden), past knowledge of many failures in her life and those around her, little or no financial backing, life circumstances that press her with difficult and often impossible challenges that are neither developmentally suitable or fair, and an awareness that justice is often a cruel excuse for exploitation of women like her. The college student is responding to a safe environment filled with safety nets. The inner-city woman is responding with hope.

LIMITATIONS AND CONCLUSIONS

Unfortunately, there are major methodological problems existing in this literature that complicate this review. Foremost, the literature on hope has generally failed to distinguish between these concepts of individual-centered hope and existential hope when operationalizing hope for their investigations. We propose that this distinction is a critical one to make due to the significant associations between a variety of different resources and hope. The evidence presented here suggests that resources can distinguish between individual-centered and existential hope.

Further, the research on hope has focused primarily on ill populations spanning across ages. These findings may not generalize to healthy populations. The role of hope in the context of illness is a critical area for continued work. However, other life circumstances that are particularly challenging are also of interest. The role of hope in the face of traumatic stress, economic crisis, divorce, refugee flight, and war are examples of other important areas for work. Future research should examine hope within this individual-centered and existential framework among healthy individuals who are experiencing highly challenging circumstances.

The process of how hope "performs" is also a critical area deserving of attention. The impact of illness on hope may be twofold, relative to the resources one possesses. In individuals who possess few of the resources examined above, an illness might be the proverbial straw that broke the camel's back. That is, an illness may lead individuals into a hopeless state. Alternatively, in individuals that possess many resources, an illness might engender hope, for example through a newfound reliance on existing social supports (Wheaton, 1985). The relationship between hope and illness should be examined further to ferret out these associations. COR theory may be particularly helpful in this regard as it has guided the study of how resources operate under stress and focused on both resource loss and gain (Hobfoll, 1998). In particular, COR theory predicts resource loss and gain cycles that operate to impact individuals' abilities to adapt and their psychological well-being. This more dynamic picture of stress (Holahan & Moos, 1999, 2000) has been virtually lacking in research on hope.

COR theory would also encourage research on how hope is transformed by circumstances. COR theory suggests that resources are not static, but that they are frequently altered by life challenges. The ability to sustain hope in light of great difficulties, the fleeting nature sometimes of hope that waxes and wanes, and the ultimate loss of hope in some circumstances are important issues. Until such issues are clarified, we will continue to have only a superficial understanding of hope. A construct is more than its correlations with other variables in cross-sectional time. It will be critical for future research to explore these issues.

Regardless of these limitations, the correlations that exist between individual-centered hope, existential hope, and a variety of both personal and interpersonal resources suggest that if you do have resources such as self-esteem, problem-solving skills, and social support you are more likely to possess individual-centered hope. There is a modicum of evidence that those who possess resources such as spirituality will be likely to have existential hope. This said, we still must raise the caution that the high correlations between hope and resources such as social support and self-esteem indicate that we cannot at this time distinguish the construct of hope from the concepts of personal and interpersonal resources. Future research should investigate this distinction that we propose, and the extent to which one is able to maintain hope in spite of a lack of these resources, which are so highly correlated with hope. This is not to suggest that these two types of hope are mutually exclusive; they are not. Rather, the general literature has used a broad definition of hope in theoretical and empirical articles when more specific definitions, such as those suggested in this chapter, may be more useful to delineate the correlates and implications of hope.

REFERENCES

Antonovsky, A. (1979). *Health, stress and coping.* San Francisco: Jossey-Bass.

Barnum, D.D., Snyder, C.R., Rapoff, M.A., Mani, M.M., & Thompson, R. (1998). Hope and social support in the psychological adjustment of children who have survived burn injuries and their matched controls. *Children's Healthcare, 27,* 15–30.

Beck, A.T., Steer, R.A., Kovacs, M., and Garrison, B. (1985). Hopelessness and eventual suicide: A 10-year prospective study of patients hospitalized with suicidal ideation. *American Journal of Psychiatry, 142,* 559–563.

Bunston, T., Mings, D., Mackie, A. & Jones, D. (1995). Facilitating hopefulness: The determinants of hope. *Journal of Psychosocial Oncology, 13,* 79–103.

Campbell, D. T., & Stanley, J. C. (1966). *Experimental and quasi-experimental designs for research.* Chicago: Rand McNally.

Cantril, H. (1964). The human design. *Journal of Individual Psychology, 20,* 129–136.

Carson, V., Soeken, K., & Grimm, P. M. (1988). Hope and its relationship to spiritual well-being. *Journal of Psychology and Theology, 16,* 159–167.

Carson, V., Soeken, K.L., Shanty, J., & Terry, L. (1990). Hope and spiritual well-being: Essentials for living with AIDS. *Perspectives in Psychiatric Care, 26,* 28–34.

Chang, E. C. (1998). Hope, problem-solving ability, and coping in a college student population: Some implications for theory and practice. *Journal of Clinical Psychology, 54,* 953–962.

Chang, E. C., & DeSimone, S. L. (2001). The influence of hope on appraisals, coping, and dysphoria: A test of hope theory. *Journal of Social and Clinical Psychology, 20*(2), 117–129.

Ennis, N., Hobfoll, S., & Schroeder, K. (2000). Money doesn't talk, it swears: How economic stress and resistance resources impact inner-city women's depressive mood. *American Journal of Community Psychology, 28,* 149–173.

Farran, C., & Popovich, J.M. (1990). Hope: A relevant concept for geriatric psychiatry. *Archives of Psychiatric Nursing, 4,* 124–130.

Foote, A. W., Piazza, D., Holcombe, J., Paul, P., & Daffin, P. (1990). Hope, self-esteem and social support in persons with multiple sclerosis. *Journal of neuroscience nursing, 22,* 155–159.

Frank, J. (1974). Common features of psychotherapies and their patients. *Psychotherapy & Psychometrics, 24,* 368–371.

Haase, J., Britt, T., Coward, D., & Leidy, N. (1992). Simultaneous concept analysis of spiritual perspective, hope, acceptance and self-transcendence. *IMAGE: Journal of Nursing Scholarship, 24,* 141–147.

Herth, K. (1989). The relationship between level of hope and level of coping response and other variables in patients with cancer. *Oncology Nursing Forum,* 16, 67–72.

Herth, K. (1990). Fostering hope in terminally-ill people. *Journal of Advanced Nursing,* 15, 1250–1259.

Herth, K. (1991). Development and refinement of an instrument to measure hope. *Scholarly Inquiry for Nursing Practice; An International Journal,* 5, 39–51.

Herth, K. (1993). Hope in the family caregiver of terminally ill people. *Journal of Advanced Nursing,* 18, 538–548.

Herth, K. (1993). Hope in older adults in community and institutional settings. *Issues in Mental Health Nursing,* 14, 139–156.

Hinds, P. S. (1988). The relationship of nurses' caring behaviors with hopefulness and health care outcomes in adolescents. *Archives of Psychiatric Nursing,* 2, 21–29.

Holdcraft, C. & Williamson. C. (1991). Assessment of hope in psychiatric and chemically dependent patients. *Applied Nursing Research,* 4, 129–134.

Horton, T., & Wallander, J. (2001). Hope and social support as resilience factors against psychological distress of mothers who care for children with chronic physical conditions. *Rehabilitation Psychology,* 46, 382–399.

Hunt Raliegh, E. D. (1992). Sources of hope in chronic illness. *Oncology Nursing Forum,* 19, 443–448.

Irving, L. M., Telfer, L., & Blake, D. (1997). Hope, coping, and social support in combat-related posttraumatic stress disorder. *Journal of Traumatic Stress,* 10, 465–479.

Irving, L. M., Snyder, C. R., & Crowson, J. J. Jr. (1998). Hope and coping with cancer by college women. *Journal of Personality,* 66, 195–214.

Kazdin, A. C. (1992). *Research design in clinical psychology* (2nd ed.). New York: MacMillan.

Kliewer, W., & Lewis, H. (1995). Family influences on coping processes in children and adolescents with sickle cell disease. *Journal of Pediatric Psychology,* 20, 511–525.

Lazarus, R., & Folkman, S. (1985). If it changes it must be a process: Study of emotion and coping during three stages of a college examination. *Journal of Personality & Social Psychology,* 48, 150–170.

Magaletta, P., & Oliver, J.M. (1999). The hope construct, will, and ways: Their relations with self-efficacy, optimism, and general well-being. *Journal of Clinical Psychology,* 55, 539–551.

McGill, J., & Paul, P.B. (1993). Functional status and hope in elderly people with and without cancer. *Oncology Nursing Forum,* 20, 1207–1213.

Mickley, J. R., Soeken, K., & Belcher, A. (1992). Spiritual well-being, religiousness and hope among women with breast cancer. *IMAGE: Journal of Nursing Scholarship, 24*, 267–272.

Miller, J. F., & Powers, M. J. (1988). Development of an instrument to measure hope. *Nursing Research, 37*, 6–10.

Nowotny, M. L. (1991). Every tomorrow, a vision of hope. *Journal of Psychosocial Oncology, 9*, 117–126.

Obwuegbuzie, A. J., & Snyder, C. R. (2000). Relations between hope and graduate students' coping strategies for studying and examination-taking. *Psychological Reports, 86*(3), 803–806.

Piazza, D., Holcombe, J., Foote, A., Paul, P., Love, S., & Daffin, P. (1991). Hope, social support, and self-esteem of patients with spinal chord injuries. *Journal of Neuroscience Nursing, 23*, 224–230.

Rabkin, J., Williams, J.B., Neugebeauer, R., & Remien, R.H. (1990). Maintenance of hope in HIV-spectrum homosexual men. *American Journal of Psychiatry, 147*, 1322–1326.

Rabkin, J., Ferrando, S.J., Shu-Hsing, L., Sewell, M., & McElhiney, M. (2000). Psychological effect of HAART: A two-year study. *Psychosomatic Medicine, 64*, 413–422.

Scheier, M., & Carver, C. (1985). Optimism, coping, and health: Assessment and implications of generalized outcome expectancies. *Health Psychology, 4*, 219–247.

Scioli, A., Chamberlin, C.M., Samor, C.M., Lapointe, A.B., Campbell, T., Macleod, A., & McLenon, J. (1997). A prospective study of hope, optimism, and health. *Psychological Reports, 81*, 723–733.

Snyder, C. (1994). *The Psychology of Hope: You can get there from here.* New York: Free Press.

Snyder, C.R., Harris, C., Anderson, J.R., Holleran, S.A., Irving, L.M., Sigmon, S.T., Yoshinobu, L., Gibb, J., Langelle, C., & Harney, P. (1991). The will and the ways: Development and validation of an individual differences measure of hope. *Journal of Personality and Social Psychology, 60*, 570–585.

Snyder, C.R., Irving, L.M., & Anderson, J.R. (1991). Hope and health. In C.R. Snyder and D.R. Forsyth (Eds.), *Handbook of social and clinical psychology: The health perspective.* Elmsford, NY: Pergamon.

Snyder, C.R. (2000). The past and possible futures of hope. *Journal of Social and Clinical Psychology, 19*, 11–28.

Stotland, E. (1969). *The psychology of hope.* San Francisco: Jossey-Boss.

Taylor, J.D. (2000). Confronting breast cancer: Hopes for health. In C.R. Snyder (Ed.), *Handbook of Hope: Theory, Measures, and Applications.* San Diego: Academic Press.

Wheaton, B. (1985). Models for the stress-buffering functions of coping resources. *Journal of Health and Social Behavior, 26*, 352–364.

Yarcheski, A., Mahon, N. E., & Yarcheski, T. J. (2001). Social support and well-being in early adolescents: The role of mediating variables. *Clinical Nursing Research,* 10(2), 163–181.

Zorn, C. R., & Johnson, M. T. (1997). Religious well-being in noninstitutionalized elderly women. *Health Care for Women International,* 18, 209–219.

Chapter 5

THE DOMINANCE OF FEAR OVER HOPE—CAN IT BE CHANGED?

Maria Jarymowicz and Daniel Bar-Tal

Psychology has provided impressive evidence that negative and positive emotions function differently (so-called positive-negative asymmetry, see Peters & Czapinski, 1990; Cacioppo & Gardner, 1999) due to their different origin and neuro-psychological basis (Cacioppo & Berntson, 1994; Damasio, 1994; Ledoux, 1996; Orenstein, 1997). This fundamental difference often leads to the domination of the former over the latter (e. g., Ito, Larsen, Smith, & Cacioppo, 1998). That is, the primary negative emotions such as fear, anger, or disgust, being activated spontaneously, automatically, and on the lower level of the nervous system, tend to override the positive emotions such as hope or pride, which are based on cognitive piecemeal processes, originating in the cortical centers.

This difference is well demonstrated in the functioning of fear and hope in a situation of perceived threat. Fear, which is an automatic emotion based on present and past affective experiences, is processed both unconsciously and consciously, while hope is an emotion based on cognitive activity of deliberate thinking accompanied with positive affective components. In view of this essentially different functioning of fear and hope, we often observe in stressful situations that fear overrides hope and causes distress and misery in the lives of individuals. Taylor (1991) summarized a wide range of evidence suggesting that negative emotions, and especially fear, play a fundamental role in calibrating the psychological system and they often lead to maladjustment and harm. For example, sick individuals are paralyzed by fear when they need to uphold hope in order to cope better with their curable sickness. This phenomenon is well observed in research about animals and human beings, which shows that development and progression of diseases is also influenced by psychological factors such as stress and emotions (Caciopo, Berntson, Sheridan, & McClintock, 2000). Thus, in this line, a series of studies showed that negative emotions such as depression and anxiety have direct influence on the evolvement of coronary heart disease (CHD), essential hypertension (EH) (see Krantz & Manuck, 1984; Troxler, Sprague, Albanese, Fuchs, & Thompson, 1977) and functioning of the immune system (see Cohen & Herbert, 1996).

We do recognize that even in extremely stressful situations, natural automatic mechanisms operate to adapt people successfully to the new conditions and help to achieve psychological comfort (e.g., Czapinski, 1992). However, these processes are more efficient when in one-time events rather than in chronic situations. As a result, in many situations the natural automatic mechanism fails, resulting in fear dominating the person and causing grave consequences, such as shortening his or her lifespan.

In this chapter, we will present an analysis that attempts to answer the question of why fear overrides hope in situations of personal threat and danger, leading to maladaptation. In trying to answer this question we will draw on the recent accumulated knowledge in psychology and neurology. Specifically, the chapter will first describe the nature of emotions, including the different foundations of negative and positive emotions. Second, it will focus on the analysis of fear and hope and present the consequences of their differences. Finally, in the section about implications, primary ideas will be sketched, pointing out the mechanisms that can overcome fear.

THE NATURE OF EMOTIONS

Emotions, as fundamental psycho-physiological reactions to all kinds of stimulation, play a crucial role in human functioning. In essence, human emotions are a multifaceted phenomenon based on unconscious and conscious physiological, affective, cognitive and behavioral processes (Cacioppo & Gardner, 1999, Ekman & Davidson, 1994; Lewis & Haviland, 1993; Zajonc, 1998). They evolved originally for their adaptive functions in dealing with basic external challenges (Johnson-Laird & Oatley, 1992; Mandler, 1975), and as modes of relating to the changing demands of the environment (Damasio, 1994; Lazarus, 1991). In their major role, they decode the meaning of stimulation either unconsciously or consciously. This decoding is based not only on subception or perception, but also on conditioning and memory, which causes individuals to respond with the same emotional reactions when they encounter events perceived as having the same meaning (Christianson, 1992). As a result, sometimes the developed pattern of reactions is irrational and destructive, contributing to the maladaptation of human beings.

The basic processes leading to emotional reaction are biochemical and neurological in nature (Damasio, 2001). Some emotional reactions are thus unconscious, involving automatic processing of information coming from the receptors. Furthermore, these processes directly activate effectors leading to behavior without mediation of cognitive appraisal. Such emotions are spontaneous, fast, uncontrolled, and unintentional (Ekman & Davidson, 1994; Jarymowicz, 1997; LeDoux, 1996). Only in some cases stimulation reaches cortical centers and generates a conscious reaction of feeling (Damasio, 2001).

Conscious processes are connected with people's appraisal of their environment (Frijda, 1986; Lazarus, 1991). These processes are strongly influenced by primary affects, which serve as mediators and as data for processes of feeling, judgment, evaluation, and decision making that may then lead to particular behaviors (Averill, 1980; Carver & Scheier, 1990; Elster, 1999; Frijda, 1986). More specifically, in conscious process, emotions automatically direct our attention to particular cues and information, thus influencing the organization of memory schemas. This process provides differential weight to specific stored knowledge, activates relevant associative networks in memory, influences the order of cognitive processing priorities, and provides an interpretative framework to perceived situations. On this basis we are drawn towards certain objects, situations, individuals, or groups and avoid others (Bower, 1992; Blaney, 1986; Caccioppo & Gardner, 1999; Clore, Schwarz, & Conway, 1994; Isen, 1984; Niedenthal & Kitayama, 1994; Schwarz, 1990; Wyer & Srull, 1989). However, as indicated, only some human emotions are based on the sequence of recognition and understanding (Zajonc, 1980), that is, on an appraisal process related to deliberate thinking, intellectual operations, and evaluations of standards relatively independent of basic affective mechanism (Piaget, 1970, Reykowski, 1989).

The work of LeDoux on fear is especially relevant to the above presented distinction between automatic (unconscious and conscious) and deliberate evaluative processes. He discovered a synaptic link between the thalamus and amygdala, which demonstrated the possible independence of the affective system from the cognitive one. Specifically, he showed that fear may be a derivative of limbic excitations without cortical interference. That is, according to his discovery, an impulse reaches the thalamus and after the initial sensory encoding, excites the amygdala, where the affective decoding takes place. This process is unconscious in its nature and may never reach awareness. Thus, the emotion may not be reflected in feelings or perception and as a result may not require updating of the conscious standards of evaluation (Zajonc, 1980).

On the basis of this discovery, Le Doux made a distinction between two possible roads that transmit impulses eliciting emotions. The first is a *low pathway* of shorter connections between receptors, the central nervous system, and effectors, which links the thalamus and amygdala, producing a primary and purely affective reaction to an external stimulus of which the individual is unaware. The second is a *high pathway,* linking the thalamus and amygdala with the cortex and cortical centers, forming feelings and cognitive aspects of conscious emotional reactions of which the individual is more or less aware. Obviously it should be noted that the above description does not imply that impulses must travel with one of the pathways. In reality, a portion of the stimulation travels in both pathways almost simultaneously. This process does not take place exactly at the same time because the low pathway is shorter and therefore faster. This means that the automatic and unconscious reactions are faster than the conscious ones. Moreover, evidence indicates that the process of feeling, thinking, and reacting is subordinated at least to some extent to the primary affective reaction evoked earlier. The emotional processes are not dominated by primary affect in cases when stimulation either does not have important primary meaning (as evaluated by subcortical structures) and/or emotions are not a result of an external stimulation, but a consequence of cognitive activity such as recalling, analyzing, interpreting, evaluating, planning, and so on. Activation of the amygdala in this case is possible due to projection from the cortical centers with minimal input from the lower centers.

In order to understand the complexity of human emotional functioning, one has to take into consideration not only the distinction between unconscious (subcortical) and conscious (cortical) reactions, but also consider the differentiation between negative and positive emotions reflected in the robust findings about the so-called negative/positive asymmetry (Caciopo & Berntson, 1994; Peters & Czapinski, 1990; Taylor, 1991). Neurobiological evidence suggests different anatomic localization of the negative and positive emotions: the former are linked to the right hemisphere and the latter to the left one (e.g., Ornstein, 1997, Springer & Deutsch, 1998). Of relevance is the fact that the functioning of the right hemisphere is associated with intuitive and holistic information processing, whereas the left hemisphere serves as a basis for specific human capacities such as articulation and analytic thinking. This differential localization seems to be consistent with the psychological findings indicating that many negative emotions, of which fear is one of the most prototypical examples, tend to function in a way specific to the right hemisphere processes, without mediation of analytic conscious appraisal and insight. In contrast, positive emotions such as hope are manifested by the involvement of conscious cognition specific to the left hemisphere processes, which evaluate reality and enable control of primary emotions. This process includes use of abstract ideas and expectations, especially when they do not have a basis in past experiences. Thus, it enables one to consider future states, which do not exist in the psychological repertoire during information processing.

THE PRIMACY OF FEAR

Fear is a primary aversive emotion, which arises in situations of threat and danger to the organism (the individual) and/or to his or her environment (the society), and enables to respond to them adaptively (Cannon, 1927; Gray, 1989; Öhman, 1993; Rachman, 1978). The threats and dangers, which can be detected in present situations or generalized from past experiences, are varied. They can be related specifically to a particular individual (as stimulated by noise, darkness, a dog, or social rejection), or be evoked in collective situations (as for example political persecution, terror attack, or war). Fear, thus, in contrast to anxiety, which is undirected arousal following unspecified perception of danger, is always related to specific objects (Beck, 1978).

Fear constitutes combined physiological and psychological reactions programmed to maximize the probability of surviving in dangerous situations in the most beneficial way. While reactions of fear may be evoked in view of the situation's appraisal through conscious processes, it is to a larger extent activated via automatic programs that allow unconscious reaction processing that deals with danger in a routine way, regardless of intention or thought (LeDoux, 1996). These adaptive mechanisms are based on unconditioned or conditioned stimulus-reaction relations. The latter type can be based on explicit or implicit processes of conditioning (Öhman, Hamm, & Hugdahl, 2000) and both types of conditionings extend the repertoire of objects, attributes, and situations that indicate danger and threat and provide a basis for their further generalization. Fear thus reflects a mechanism of adaptation, which automatically protects homeostasis and life. At the same time, fear may result in irrational and destructive behavior because defensive reactions are not only evoked as a result of cues, which directly imply threat and danger, but also by conditioned stimuli that are non-threatening in their nature (Mowrer, 1960; LeDoux, 1996; Ohman, 1993; Rachman, 1978).

In addition, as demonstrated by Grings and Dawson (1978), fear can be acquired on the basis of perceived information about certain objects, events, people, or situations that are threatening to the person or his or her society (see Rachman, 1977). Once the information about threatening or potentially threatening stimuli is acquired through different modes of learning, it is stored as implicit or explicit memory about emotional situations. Subsequently, both types of memory influence appraisal of a particular situation (Lazarus, 1991). Furthermore, LeDoux (1996) pointed out the functioning of implicit affective memory, which unconsciously arouses reactions of fear in view of a particular cue. This memory is particularly resilient, exhibiting little diminution with the passage of time, and it is independent of descriptive memory (relating to events and facts). Thus, fear can operate as a result of affective experience, independently of reality and is especially powerful when based on implicit memory, which is stronger than explicit memory, because it arouses fear spontaneously and automatically, overcoming cognitive control, rationality, and logic. In fact, fear dominates and controls thinking, because the connections from the limbic (affective system) to the cortex centers (cognitive system) are more numerous than those in the opposite direction from the cognitive system to the emotional system (LeDoux, 1995, 1996; Ohman, 1993). As a result, fear floods consciousness and leads to automatic behavior, preparing the individual for coping with the threatening situation.

In principle, when one encounters the same perceived conditioned or similar stimuli, fear may be retrieved and evoked by both types of memories (Lazarus, 1991; LeDoux, 1996). In this vein it is important to note that memories are never carbon copies of the information provided by learning. Rather, they are biased, modified, or reconstructed on the basis of the absorbed information (Smith, 1998; Wyer & Srull, 1989). This means that fear may be evoked by a wide range of cues and information, much of which initially did not imply either threat or danger.

A prolonged experience of fear leads to a number of observed effects: It sensitizes the organism and the cognitive system to threatening cues, gives priority to processing information about potential threats, extends the associative networks of information about threats, causes overestimation of dangers and threats, facilitates the selective retrieval of information related to fear, increases expectations of threat and dangers, and increases accessibility of procedural knowledge that was effective in coping with the threatening situation in the past (Clore, Schwarz, & Conway, 1994; Gray, 1989; Isen, 1990; Lazarus & Folkman, 1984; LeDoux, 1995, 1996; Öhman, 1993). Once fear is evoked, it limits activation of other mechanisms of regulation, stalls consideration of various alternatives, and is egocentric and maladaptive in situations that require creative and novel solutions for coping. The empirical evidence shows that fear has limiting effects on cognitive processing: it tends to cause adherence to familiar situations and avoidance of risky, uncertain, and novel situations and tends to cause cognitive freezing, which prevents openness to new ideas (Clore, Schwarz, & Conway, 1994; Isen, 1990; Le Doux, 1995, 1996; Ohman, 1993).

Finally, fear motivates defense and protection (such as withdrawal or escape) from events that are perceived to be a threat. When these forms are not efficient, fear may lead to extremely strong aggression against the source of the perceived threat. That is, when in fear, human beings sometimes tend to cope by initiating fight, even when there is little or nothing to be achieved by doing so (Blanchard & Blanchard, 1984; Eibl-Eibesfeldt & Sutterlin, 1990; Lazarus, 1991; Plutchik, 1990).

THE REFLECTIVE NATURE OF HOPE

The emotion of hope arises when a concrete positive goal is expected (Stotland, 1969), such as situations of yearning for relief from negative conditions (Lazarus, 1991). It consists of cognitive elements of visualizing and expecting a goal, conscious appraisal of possible events based on cognitive standards, and affective elements of feeling good about expected pleasant events or outcomes (Staats & Stassen, 1985). The affective component in the case of hope is a secondary one, a consequence of the cognitive elements. According to Snyder (1994, 2000), the affective components of hope have a form of subjective feelings based on goal-directed thinking, which combines goal-directed determination with planning to achieve this goal. Thus, these affective components are complex and may contain positive elements as well as negative ones, since individuals may realize that the achievement of the final goals may involve struggles, costs, and endurance, which may be unpleasant and even painful. Therefore, in our view, hope can be metaphorically depicted as a light at the end of the tunnel. It implies that the affective components, which exist as a result of different cognitive meanings of different aspects of the situation, form a hierarchy but overall are dominated by positive feelings.

As a complex syndrome, hope has not been associated with any specific physiological response leading to specific and concrete forms of behavior. It is based on higher cognitive processing, which requires mental representations of future situations that do not exist. More specifically, it requires setting goals, planning how to achieve them, and use of imagery, creativity, cognitive flexibility, mental exploration of novel situations, and even risk taking (Breznitz, 1986; Clore, Schwarz, & Conway, 1994; Fromm, 1968; Isen, 1990; Lazarus, 1991; Snyder, 1994, 2000).

Hope resembles a state of mind, marked by its disconnection from major reliance on the past by planning, expecting, fantasizing, and so forth—all in a positively valued direction. This state of mind requires development of new "scripts" about future actions. According to Fromm (1968), hope requires conviction about the not yet proven, courage to resist temptation to compromise the vision, and transformation of the present reality in the direction of greater aliveness. Averill, Latlin, and Chon (1990) argued that hope: (a) should refer to an aspiration for achieving a concrete goal that has a likelihood of attainment; (b) should pertain to an aspired goal of vital interest and not of triviality; and (c), should reflect moral values, since people should not hope for socially unacceptable goals.

Individuals differ in their hope orientation in that some have more of a disposition towards hope than others (see Snyder, Harris, Anderson, Holleran, Irving, Sigmon, Yosinobu, Gibb, Langelle, & Harney, 1991). Review of the empirical literature indicates that individuals with high hope orientation are cognitively engaged in more positive events and in fewer negative events than individuals with low hope orientation. The former also spend more time thinking, and were found to perform better on cognitive tasks (Snyder, Sympson, Ybasco, Borders, Babyak, & Higgins, 1996). In addition, individuals with high hope orientation have greater problem-solving abilities, a rational problem-solving style, and less wishful thinking, self-blame, and social withdrawal strategies in comparison to individuals with low hope orientation (Chang, 1998; Snyder, Cheavens, & Michael, 1999).

THE DOMINANCE OF FEAR OVER HOPE

The above presented analysis implies that there are major differences and an asymmetry between functioning out of fear, as a reactive negative affect, and functioning out of hope, as representative of cognitive anticipation and positive affect, and that these different functioning strategies cause the domination of the former over the latter in situations of threat. In view of the above, we will now compare directly between fear and hope.

On the biological level fear operates mainly, and sometimes exclusively, on the basis of the lower centers of the nervous system (i.e., mainly in a limbic system), while hope operates mainly on the basis of the cortical centers. On the level of psychological processes fear can be processed unconsciously, while hope is always based on conscious cognitive activity. In addition, whereas fear is basically activated automatically and without cognitive control, hope is always based on thinking and requires various intellectual skills. Whereas fear is a reaction grounded in perceived threat, often based on the memorized threats of the past, hope has its foundation in anticipation, in the positive imagination of the future, and in goals and programs of actions concerning reality, which do not exist in the present. On the behavioral level fear often leads to defensive and/or aggressive behaviors used in the past, while hope requires conceiving new behaviors to achieve the desired, positively valued goal and attempts to realize it. Finally, we suggest that there are more individual differences with regard to hope than to fear orientation because the latter emotion has universal and phylogenetic basis grounded in primary affect operating regardless of personal will, while the former emotion depends on the individual cognitive skills and activity, which are mostly based on a volitional basis.

The above comparison clearly explains why fear overrides hope. Fear operates fast because the lower pathways through which the stimulus travels from receptors to amygdala and from amygdala to effectors are shorter than the pathways of conscious cognitive processing, including the process of stimulus recognition. The formation of hope involves a complex cognitive process, which requires time and effort. Fear is activated on the basis of a concrete current situation or past, memorized experiences and leads to particular forms of behavior. Hope concerns a situation that does not exist and requires imagination and formation of a program for new forms of behavior. Thus, as determinants of behavior, fear and hope are asymmetrical: Fear has an overcoming power and thus a dominant position. As noted by Cacioppo and Gardner (1999), "Exploratory behavior can provide useful information about an organism's environment, but exploration can also place an organism in proximity to hostile stimuli. Because it is more difficult to reverse the consequences of an injurious or fatal assault than those of an opportunity unpursued, the process of natural selection may also have resulted in the propensity to react more strongly to negative than to positive stimuli" (p. 205).

In sum, fear is an evolutionary safeguard that ensures survival in view of potential threats and dangers encountered by human beings. It is a component of a fundamental mechanism necessary for survival. At the same time, because of classical conditioning or irrational thinking evoked by fear, it leads often to reactions of extremely maladaptive consequences. From a logical point of view, in some situations of threat and danger, hope has important advantages over fear because it provides a rational way of coping. Hope, hence, has to subdue this irrational domination of fear, which is a complex but challenging task.

In view of the abovementioned comparison between fear and hope and the derived conclusion about the dominance of the former, a crucial question should be raised about the possibility of overcoming fear by hope, thus preventing different negative outcomes of individual suffering. The challenge is of great importance in view of the evidence that hope may contribute greatly to the well-being and good adaptation of the human being (Cacioppo et al., 2000). In the realm of health psychology there are consistent data showing that hope and optimism are associated with problem-focused coping and less denial as well as faster rates of physical recovery during hospitalization and an earlier return to normal life following hospital discharge. For example, research by Scheier, Matthews, Owens, Magovern, Lefebvre, Abbot, & Carver (1989) on recovery from artery bypass surgery demonstrated that hope was associated with better coping with the illness and improved surgical outcome. Taylor (2000), summarizing a line of research about breast cancer, noted that women with high hope experience less distress, demonstrate more active and adaptive coping when faced with cancer, find more viable solutions to their problems, and pursue those solutions more energetically than women with low hope.

OVERCOMING FEAR

The presented analysis suggests that although fear functions as an important adaptive mechanism, it also may play a detrimental role in various individual situations. These situations take place especially when hope is needed for adaptation but instead is overridden by fear, causing distress and misery. To understand these situations, we tried to determine why fear overrides hope. However, the presented analysis raises a new question regarding the possibility to overcome fear. This is an important question, which requires serious consideration using knowledge accumulated in psychology. Clinical psychology dealing with patients with anxiety has proposed a number of therapeutic approaches through the years (e.g., Barlow, 1988; Marks, 1987; Meichenbaum & Cameron, 1974). However, we are interested more in an answer, which pertains to non-clinical functioning of human beings on the individual and collective levels. In the final part of this chapter we will outline a number of preliminary ideas that will hopefully be further developed in the near future.

The psychology of hope refers to higher mental processes of anticipation, creative imagination, setting goals, planning, and consideration of alternatives—all of which require openness, creativity, and flexibility, as well as tolerance of uncertainty, which is especially difficult to achieve in a situation of fear. In essence, these processes involve the reflective system of thinking and evaluation, which demands investments of energy, attention, and time. They have to overcome the automatic emergence of fear, which is an evolutionary system with an objective to provide reactions that save time and energy, as a natural preference to maximize outcome with minimum effort. Individuals therefore often act automatically and involuntarily as a natural preference, even when the result may be detrimental. Thus, in order to construct a strong basis for hope that can overcome fear, the basic challenge is to develop skills and abilities for reflexive thinking, of which human beings are capable but not always possess, and a motivational basis to engage in this type of thinking.

Ideas from different lines of studies in psychology can be used as answers to the question about overcoming fear, since they elaborate about the development of abilities, skills, and motives that underlie the evolvement of hope. For example, the development of critical thinking as "reasonable and reflective thinking concerned with what to do or believe" (Norris & Ennis, 1989, p. 3) can provide one direction of ideas. Another direction can be applied from the study of adaptation to conflict situations, which requires learning to manage interpersonal conflicts (Shantz & Hartup, 1992). The immense literature about the development of morality can also provide further ideas (see for example, Kohlberg, 1984; Bebeau, Rest, & Narvaez, 1999). We will focus on a particular approach developed by Polish psychologists. It suggests that motivation to invest energy and time to search for reasonable solutions in a stressful situation can be based on articulated cognitive standards of evaluation (Golab & Reykowski 1985, Reykowski 1989; Jarymowicz, 1999) derived from abstract concepts of right and wrong generated by intellectual operations (Jarymowicz 2001a). These concepts are necessary for understanding and differentiating what is good or bad, since there is a fundamental difference between "to feel what is good or bad" and "to understand what is right and wrong." The former differentiation is based on affective preference, while the latter requires abilities of moral reasoning (Kohlberg, 1984), which are preceded by the development of intellectual skills (Piaget 1970). In other words, we think that it is worthy to distinguish between two systems of evaluation and motivation: (1) the primary system, based on automatic affective reactions, and (2) the reflective system, which is based on intentional intellectual operations (see Jarymowicz, 2001b). Each one has a different neurophysiological basis. The former is mainly connected with subcortical centers and the right hemisphere, while the latter is mainly connected with the cortical centers of the left hemisphere. The latter system is responsible to a large extent for the emergence of hope. Only use of higher mental skills of the cognitive system allows constructing large-scale evaluative dimensions, which are necessary conditions for relative evaluations of keeping distance from self (distance to one's own characteristics, states, and emotions) and taking external perspective in viewing a situation that also allows taking a perspective of others. This system, in contrast to the affective system, enables one to evaluate one's own situation as worse or better in comparison with the situation of others. Moreover, the evaluative dimensions can also be used in judgment of out groups, as well as the in group, when intellectual capacities enable the construction of the concept "we" as an abstract category (such as "we are people"), that leads to the extension and inclusion of social categories (see Jarymowicz, 1994).

The evaluative standards and dimensions facilitate an alternative perception of the stressful situations created by fear. Using them, individuals become sensitive not only to signals of threats, but also to the complexity of the situation and to different perspectives that are involved in it. For instance, in the case of illness, a person is able to collect information about his or her own sickness, compare his or her own situation with other people's sickness, judge his or her own situation on this basis, explore different directions of treatment, select a method of cure, persist in treatment, and maintain optimism during the period of illness.

The above-described standards and dimensions are derived from the system of values that a person develops. The developed values are reflected in beliefs such as ideals or ideology. When these values are internalized, they become a source of motivation and activate the reflective system of thinking. In addition, the standards and dimensions are based on formed heuristics that guide social life. These heuristics, which are acquired as a result of a person's intellectual capacities, behaviors, and experiences, consist of generally desired prescriptions (for example, a desire to be a good person, a healthy person, or a moral one). But in order to have an influence on behavior, these heuristics have to be mentally connected with concrete principles of functioning and their manifestations. Moreover, their direction of influence depends on the personal and/or collective definition of the contents of these prescriptions (for example what does it mean "to be a good person" or "to be moral"). It is essential that these definitions be specific, complex, and inclusive in order for them to lead to the reflective thinking that is required for hoping.

The conception described above identifies particular personal capacities and motivations that are needed for overcoming fear. As already indicated, other conceptions focus on different capacities and motivations that strengthen hope against fear. Our goal was to point out the mechanisms that strengthen hope and allow individuals in need to overcome their destructive fear, which leads to maladaptation.

We realize that the identification of the personal mechanisms that allow us to overcome fear is the second step in the intellectual endeavor, after understating why fear dominates hope. The next step is to specify methods of education and socialization that foster the development of these mechanisms, that is, the necessary personal capacities and motives. This is an immense challenge that has preoccupied human beings for generations. Our goal in this chapter was to argue convincingly that it is up to human beings to overcome their fears in order to live harmoniously and adaptively. Hope is a necessary ingredient for successful coping and adaptation. Individuals will always encounter situations of fear. But the crucial question is whether they will be continuously dominated by it or will succeed to embark on the constructive road of hope. We hope that future research will outline ways that will allow people always to see the light at the end of fear's tunnel, when they fall paralyzed into it.

REFERENCES

Averill, J. R. (1980). A constructivist view of emotion. In R. Plutchik & H. Kellerman (Eds.), *Theories of emotion* (pp. 305–340). New York: Academic Press.

Averill, J. R., Catlin, G., & Catlin, K. K. (1990). *Rules of hope.* New York: Springer-Verlag.

Barlow, D. H. (1988). *Anxiety and its disorders: The nature and treatment of anxiety and panic.* New York: Guilford.

Bebeau, M. J., Rest, J. R., & Narvaez, D. (1999). Beyond the promise: A perspective on research in moral education. *Educational Researcher, 28*(4), 18–25.

Beck, R. C. (1978). *Motivation: Theories and principles.* Englewood Cliffs, NJ: Prentice Hall.

Blanchard, R. J., & Blanchard, D. C. (1984). Affect and aggression: An animal model applied to human behavior. In R. J. Blanchard & D. C. Blanchard (Eds.), *Advances in the study of aggression* (Vol. 1, pp. 1–62). New York: Academic Press.

Blaney, P. H. (1986). Affect and memory: A review. *Psychological Bulletin,* 99, 229–246.

Bower, G. H. (1992). How might emotions affect learning? In S. A. Christianson (Ed.), *The handbook of emotion and memory: Research and theory* (pp. 3–31). Hillsdale, NJ: Lawrence Erlbaum.

Breznitz, S. (1986). The effect of hope on coping with stress. In M. H. Appley & R. Trumbull (Eds.), *Dynamics of stress: Physiological, psychological and social perspectives* (pp. 295–306). New York: Plenum.

Cacioppo, J. T., & Bernston, G. G. (1994). Relationship between attitudes and evaluative space. A critical review, with emphasis on the separability of positive and negative substrates. *Psychological Bulletin,* 115, 401–423.

Cacioppo, J. T., Bernston, G. G., Sheridan, J. F., & McClintock, M. K. (2000). Multilevel integrative analyses of human behavior: Social neuroscience and the complementing nature of social and biological approaches. *Psychological Bulletin,* 126, 829–843.

Cacioppo, J. T., & Gardner, W. L. (1999). Emotion. *Annual Review of Psychology,* 50, 191–214.

Cannon, W. B. (1927). The James-Lange theory of emotions: A critical examination and an alternative theory. *American Journal of Psychology,* 39, 106–124.

Carver, C. S., & Scheier, M. F. (1990). Origins and functions of positive and negative affect: A control-process view. *Psychological Review,* 97, 19–35.

Chang, E. C. (1998). Hope, problem-solving ability, and coping in a college student population: Some implications for theory and practice. *Journal of Clinical Psychology,* 54, 953–962.

Christianson, S. A. (1992). Remembering emotional events: Potential mechanisms. In S. A. Christianson (Ed.), *The handbook of emotion and memory* (pp. 307–340). Hillsdale, NJ: Lawrence Erlbaum.

Clore, G. L, Schwarz, N., & Conway, M. (1994). Affective causes and consequences of social information processing. In R. S. Wyer Jr. & T. K. Srul (Eds.), *Handbook of social cognition* (2nd ed., Vol. 1, pp. 323–417). Hillsdale, NJ: Lawrence Erlbaum.

Cohen, S., & Herbert, T. B. (1996). Health psychology: Psychological factors and physical disease from the perspective of psychoneuroimmunology, *Annual Review of Psychology,* 47, 113–142.

Czapinski, J. (1992). *Psychology of happiness.* Warszawa: Akademos. (in Polish)

Damasio, A. R. (1994). *Descartes' error: Emotion, reason, and the human brain.* New York: Putnam.

Damasio, A. R. (2001). *A neurobiology for emotion and feeling.* Paper presented at the Amsterdam Conference on Feelings and Emotions (June 13–16).

Eibl-Eibesfeldt, I., & Sütterlin, C. (1990). Fear, defense and aggression in animals and man: Some ethological perspectives. In P. F. Brain, S. Parmigiani, R. J. Blanchard, & D. Mainardi (Eds.), *Fear and defense* (pp. 381–408). London: Harwood.

Ekman, P., & Davidson, R. J. (Eds.) (1994). *The nature of emotion: Fundamental question.* New York: Oxford University Press.

Elster, J. (1999). *Alchemies of the mind: Rationality and the emotions.* Cambridge: Cambridge University Press.

Frijda, N. C. (1986). *The emotions.* Cambridge: Cambridge University Press.

Fromm, E. (1968). *The revolution of hope.* New York: Bantam.

Golob, A., & Reykowski, J. (1985). *Studies on development of evaluative standards.* Wroclaw: Ossolineum. (in Polish)

Gray, J. A. (1989). *The psychology of fear and stress* (2nd ed.). Cambridge: Cambridge University Press.

Grings, W. W., & Dawson, M. E. (1978). *Emotions and bodily responses: A psycho-physiological approach.* New York: Academic Press.

Isen, A. M. (1984). Toward understanding the role of affect in cognition. In R.S. Wyer, Jr., & T. K. Srull (Eds.), *Handbook of social cognition* (Vol. 3, pp. 179–236). Hillsdale, NJ: Lawrence Erlbaum.

Isen, A. M. (1990). The influence of positive and negative affect on cognitive organization: Some implications for development. In N. L. Stein, B. Leventhal, & T. Trabasso (Eds.), *Psychological and biological approaches to emotion* (pp. 75–94). Hillsdale, NJ: Lawrence Erlbaum.

Ito, T. A., Larsen, J.T., Smith, N. K., & Cacioppo, J. T. (1998). Negative information weighs more heavily on the brain: The negativity bias in evaluative categorizations. *Journal of Personality and Social Psychology, 75,* 887–900.

Jarymowicz, M. (1994). Different forms of cognitive representations of we and perception of others. In M. Jarymowicz (Ed.), *Beyond the egocentric perception of the self and the external world* (pp.190–212). Warszawa: Wydawnictwo Instytutu Psychologii PAN (in Polish).

Jarymowicz, M. (1997). Questions about the nature of emotions: On unconscious and not spontaneous emotions. *Psychological Journal, 3,* 153–170 (in Polish).

Jarymowicz, M. (1999). On the benefits of research on implicit processing of affective information. *Psychological Studies, 1,* 129–145 (in Polish).

Jarymowicz, M. (2001a). Affective reactions and evaluative judgments. *Polish Psychological Bulletin, 2,* 39–43.

Jarymowicz, M. (Ed.). (2001b). *Between affect and intellect: Empirical studies.* Warszawa: Wydawnictwo Instytutu Psychologii PAN (in Polish).

Johnson-Laird, P. N., & Oatley, K. (1992). Basic emotions, rationality and folk theory. *Cognition and Emotion, 6,* 201–223.

Kohlberg, L. (1984). *The psychology of moral development: Essays on moral development.* (Vol. 2.) San Francisco: Harper & Row.

Krantz, D. S., & Manuck, S. B. (1984). Acute psychophysiologic reactivity and risk of cardiovascular disease: A review and methodological critique. *Psychological Bulletin, 96,* 435–464.

Lazarus, R. S. (1991). *Emotion and adaptation.* New York: Oxford University Press.

Lazarus, R. S., & Folkman, S. (1984). *Stress, appraisal, and coping.* New York: Springer.

LeDoux, J. E. (1995). Emotion: Clues from the brain. *Annual Review of Psychology, 46,* 209–235.

LeDoux, J. E. (1996). *The emotional brain: The mysterious underpinnings of emotional life.* New York: Touchstone.

Lewis, M., & Haviland, J. M. (Eds.) (1993). *Handbook of emotions.* New York: Guilford.

Mandler, G. (1975). *Mind and emotion.* New York: Wiley.

Marks, I. M. (1987). *Fears, phobias and rituals.* New York: Oxford University Press.

Meichenbaum, D., & Cameron, R. (1974). The clinical potential of modifying what clients say to themselves. *Psychotherapy Theory, Research and Practice, 11,* 103–117.

Mowrer, O. H. (1960). *Learning theory and behavior.* New York: John Wiley.

Niedenthal, P. M., & Kitayama, S. (1994). *The heart's eye: Emotional influences in perception and attention.* San Diego, CA: Academic.

Norris, S., & Ennis, R. (1989). *Evaluating critical thinking.* Pacific Grove, CA: Critical Thinking Press and Software.

Öhman, A. (1993). Fear and anxiety as emotional phenomena: Clinical phenomenology evolutionary perspectives, and information-processing mechanisms. In M. Lewis & J. M. Havilland (Eds.), *Handbook of emotions* (pp. 511–536). New York: Guilford.

Öhman, A., Hamm, A., & Hugdahl, K. (2000). Cognition and the automatic nervous system: Orienting, anticipation, and conditioning. In J. Cacioppo, L. G. Tassinary, & G. G. Berntson (Eds.), *Handbook of psychophysiology* (2nd ed., pp. 533–575). New York Cambridge University Press.

Ornstein, R. (1997). *The right mind: Making sense of the hemispheres.* New York: Harcourt Brace.

Peters, G., & Czapinski, J. (1990). Positive-negative asymmetry in evaluations: The distinction between affective and informational negativity effects. *European Review of Social Psychology, 1,* 33–60.

Piaget, J. (1970). Piaget's theory. In P. H. Mussen (Ed.), *Carmichael's handbook of child psychology.* (Vol.1, pp.) New York: Wiley.

Plutchik, R. (1990). Fear and aggression in suicide and violence: A psycho evolutionary perspective. In P. F. Brain, S. Parmigiani, R. J. Blanchard, & D. Mainarcli (Eds.), *Fear and defense* (pp. 359–379). London: Harwood.

Rachman, S. (1977). The conditioning theory of fear acquisition: A critical examination. *Behavior Research and Therapy*, 15, 375–387.

Rachman, S. J. (1978). *Fear and courage*. San Francisco. W.H. Freeman.

Reykowski, J. (1989). Dimensions of development of moral values. In N. Eisenberg, J. Reykowski, & E. Staub (Eds.), *Social and moral values: Individual and societal perspectives* (pp. 23–44). Hillsdale, NJ: Lawrence Erlbaum Associates.

Scheier, M. F., Matthews, K. A., Owens, J. F., Magovern, G. J. Sr., Lefebvre, R. C., Abbot, R. A., & Carver, C. S. (1989). Dispositional optimism and recovery from coronary artery bypass surgery: The beneficial effects on physical and psychological well-being. *Journal of Personality and Social Psychology*, 57, 1024–1040.

Schwarz, N. (1990). Feelings as information: Informational and motivational functions of affective states. In E. T. Higgins & R. M. Sorrentino (Eds.), *Handbook of motivation and cognition: Foundations of social behavior* (Vol. 2, pp. 527–561).

Shantz, C. U., & Hartup, W. W. (Eds.). (1992). *Conflict in child and adolescent development*. Cambridge: Cambridge University Press.

Smith, E. R. (1998). Mental representation and memory. In D. T. Gilbert, S. T. Fiske, & G. Lindzey (Eds.), *The handbook of social psychology* (5th ed., Vol. 1, pp. 391–445). Boston: McGraw Hill.

Snyder, C. R. (1994). *The psychology of hope*. New York: Free Press.

Snyder, C. R. (2000). Hypothesis: There is hope. In C. R. Snyder (Ed.), Handbook of hope: Theory, measures, & applications (pp. 3–21). San Diego: Academic Press.

Snyder, C. R., Cheavens, J., & Michael, S. T. (1999). Hoping. In C. R. Snyder (Ed.), *Coping: The psychology of what works* (pp. 205–231). New York: Oxford University Press.

Snyder, C. R., Harris, C., Anderson, J. R., Holleran, S. A., Irving, L. M., Sigmon, S. T., Yoshinobu, L., Gibb, J., Langell, C., & Harney, P. (1991). The will and the ways: Development and validation of an individual-differences measure of hope. *Journal of Personality and Social Psychology*, 60, 570–585.

Snyder, C. R., Sympson, S. C., Ybasco, F. C., Borders, T. F., Babyak, M. A., & Higgins, R. (1996). Development and validation of the state Hope Scale. *Journal of Personality and Social Psychology*, 70, 321–335.

Springer, S. P., & Deutsch, G. (1998). *Left brain – right brain. Perspectives from cognitive neuroscience* (5th ed.). New York: W. H. Freeman.

Staats, S. R., & Stassen, M. A. (1985). Hope: An affective cognition. *Social Indicators Research*, 17, 235–242.

Stotland, E. (1969). *The psychology of hope*. San Francisco: Jossey-Bass.

Taylor, J. D. (2000). Confronting breast cancer: Hopes for health. In C. R. Snyder (Ed.), *Handbook of hope: Theory, measures and applications* (pp. 355–371). San Diego: Academic Press.

Taylor, S. E. (1991). Asymmetrical effects of positive and negative events: The mobilization-minimization hypothesis. *Psychological Bulletin,* 110, 67–85.

Troxler, D., Sprague, E. A., Albanese, R. A., Fuchs, R., & Thompson, A. J. (1977). The association of the elevated plasma cortisol and early atherosclerosis as demonstrated by coronary angiography. *Atherosclerosis,* 26, 151–162.

Wyer, R. S. Jr., & Srull, T. K. (1989). *Memory and cognition in its social context.* Hillsdale, NJ: Lawrence Erlbaum.

Zajonc, R. B. (1980). Feeling and thinking: Preferences need no inferences. *American Psychologist,* 35, 151–175.

Zajonc, R. B. (1998). Emotions. In D. Gilbert, S. T. Fiske, & G. Lindkzey (Eds.). *The handbook of social psychology* (4th Ed., Vol. 1, pp. 591–632). Boston: McGraw-Hill.

Chapter 6

MAGICAL THINKING AS A WAY OF COPING WITH STRESS

Giora Keinan

Superstition is the poetry of life.
It is inherent in Man's nature;
and when we think it is wholly
eradicated, it takes refuge in the strangest holes
and corners, whence it peeps out all at once.

—Goethe

Recent years have witnessed a growing interest in the effects of psychological stress on cognitive functioning (e.g., Driskell & Salas, 1996; Keinan, Friedland, Kahneman, & Roth, 1999; Mandler, 1993). A review of the literature shows that most of the research and theory in this field has focused on the effects of stress on higher and relatively more complex cognitive processes. For instance, a number of studies have examined the relationship between stress and decision making (e.g., Cannon-Bowers & Salas, 1998; Keinan, 1987), judgment (e.g., Hammond, 2000), or creative problem solving (e.g., Shanteau & Dino, 1993). Much less effort has been directed toward elucidating the potential effects of stress on lower or more "primitive" patterns of thinking.

In this chapter I will discuss the effects of stress on magical thinking, representing lower or relatively simple cognitive processes. In the first part I will clarify the unique characteristics of this mode of thinking. In the second part I will present findings pointing to the influence of stress on superstitious beliefs and magical rituals, as well as theoretical explanations that may account for these effects. Finally, I will present the results of a recent study, which support one of the explanations concerning the nature of the relationships between stress and the behavioral expressions of magical thinking.

DEFINING MAGICAL THINKING

Touching a man with "healing powers" with the intent of improving one's health, destroying the picture of an enemy in order to hurt him, or knocking on wood so as to gain protection against the evil eye are all familiar expressions of magical thinking. This type of thinking has received numerous definitions (e.g., Alcock, 1981, 1995; Nemeroff & Rozin, 2000; Piaget, 1929; Rozin & Nemeroff, 1999). For example, Rozin & Nemeroff (1999) call something "magical or superstitious if it involves human agency (as distinct from religion) and invokes causes inconsistent with current understandings by relevant "experts" (e.g., Western scientists) of how the world operates" (p . 503). A more comprehensive definition was provided by Zusne and Jones (1989), who have defined magical thinking as "a belief that (a) transfer of energy or information between physical systems may take place solely because of their similarity or contiguity in time and space, or (b) that one's thoughts, words, or actions can achieve specific physical effects in a manner not governed by the principles of ordinary transmission of energy or information" (p. 13).

A review of the existing definitions shows that most of them include the idea that magical thinking entails causal attributions or deductions concerning the way the world works and that these attributions do not correspond with the contemporary understanding of science.

The above-mentioned characteristics of magical thinking suggest that superstitions are also rooted in such thinking (see also Jahoda, 1969; Wooley, 1997). Thus, the superstitious belief that entering a room with a right foot forward ensures success in a new job requires causal attributions or deductions that are not supported by known scientific principles or empirical evidence.

In order to further explain the essence of magical thinking, we examine two laws, which were outlined by anthropologists studying traditional cultures (Frazer, 1890/1959; Mauss, 1902/1972; Tylor, 1871/1974), and tested more then 100 years later in Western cultures (Rozin, Millman, & Nemeroff, 1986; Rozin, Markwith, & Mccauley, 1994; Stein & Nemeroff, 1995; Nemeroff & Rozin, 1989; Lindeman & Stark, 1999).

THE LAWS OF SYMPATHETIC MAGIC

The two sympathetic magical laws, which represent according to a number of writers the core of magical thinking (e.g., Nemeroff & Rozin, 2000), are the law of similarity and the law of contagion.

The law of similarity holds that things that resemble one another at a superficial level also share deeper properties. This effect can be summarized as "The image equals the object" (Mauss, 1902/1972) or "like produces like" (Frazer, 1890/1959). A review of the literature provides a number of examples that exemplify this law in traditional cultures (e.g., Frazer, 1890/1959; Meige, 1984). Thus, for example, a "Voodoo Practice" has been documented in African tribes, whereby people who wish to harm their enemies burn or stick pins in a figure representing the enemy (such as a doll). In addition, there have been accounts that the Hua People of New Guinea do not eat red food, as this color is identified with menstrual blood and the vagina (Meige, 1984). However, there is substantial evidence to show that members of Western civilizations also demonstrate various reactions consistent with the law of similarity (e.g., Diamond & Diamond, 1985; Hunt, 1982; Rozin et al, 1986; Rozin, Markwith, & Ross, 1990). For example, Rozin et al. (1986) showed that American students who were asked to throw darts toward pictures of liked and disliked people hit less accurately the pictures of people they liked (e.g., John F. Kennedy), than the ones they disliked (e.g., Adolf Hitler). Another manifestation of the law of similarity in Western culture can be found in Hunt's book "The Seven Keys to Color Healing" (1982). Its readers are advised to drink red drinks because they increase hemoglobin levels.

The second law, the law of contagion, holds that physical contact between one object (the source) and another object (the target), will result in the transfer of some quality (the "essence") from the source to the target.

The transfer of essence creates a continuous connection between the source and the target, as exemplified in Mause's words (1902/1972): "once in contact, always in contact." Contagion can be positive or negative. When it is negative, the target becomes polluted or loses its value. When it is positive, the target becomes clean or acquires a higher value. Research shows that negative contagion is of stronger effect than the positive one (Appandurai, 1981; Nemeroff & Rozin, 1994; Rozin, Nemeroff, Wane, & Sherrod, 1989). Thus, for example, Rozin and his colleagues found that the participants in their experiments showed more contagion effects towards objects (such as clothes) that had been in contact with a disliked or unpleasant person than to objects that had been in contact with liked people or friends. While all participants showed negative contagion effects, only 1/3 showed positive contagion effects (Nemeroff & Rozin, 1994; Rozin, et al, 1989).

Significant evidence for the existence of the contagion effect can be found in relation to food (Beardsworth & Keil, 1992; Marriott, 1968; Meigs, 1984; Rozin, Markwith, & Stoess, 1997; Stein & Nemeroff, 1995) and health (Rozin et al., 1994; Nemeroff, Brinkman, & Woodward, 1994). Evidence shows that the Hua People of Papua believe that young male initiates should eat fast-growing leafy green vegetables, as this would increase their growth rate (Meigs, 1984). Another expression of the law of contagion applying to food can be found among some vegetarians, who claim that eating meat stimulates the animal instinct in human creatures (Beardsworth & Keil, 1992).

Rozin et al.'s study (1994) constitutes an intriguing example as to the existence of the contagion effect in the health domain. These researchers asked the participants in their experiment to report how they would feel if asked to wear a sweater belonging to an AIDS patient, but which he never wore, as opposed to wearing a sweater not owned by this patient, but worn by him once for a day and then washed. They found that the participants preferred to wear the sweater that was not touched by the AIDS patient.

CURRENT PERSPECTIVES ON MAGICAL THINKING

The outlook on magical thinking has undergone substantial changes over the years. It seems that these changes are manifested in the following three themes.

Universalism of Magical Thinking

It was once thought that magical thinking or superstitious behavior is prevalent mainly among primitive tribes (Frazer 1980/1959; Malinowsky, 1954), young children (Freud, 1919/1955, Piaget, 1929) or individuals suffering from certain mental disorders (Klein, 1946/1987; Wilder, 1975). However, today it is believed that magical thinking is universal in nature, and not characteristic only of certain populations or groups (e.g. Cottrell, Winer, & Smith, 1996; Keinan, 2002; Wyse, 1997).

A number of studies show that magical thinking and superstitious behavior is prevalent also among adults in Western cultures, including the educated, intelligent, and mentally healthy (e.g. Blum, 1976; Gallup & Newport, 1991; Gmelch & Felson, 1980). Thus, for example, Gmelch and Felson (1980) reported that 70 percent of the students who participated in their study had engaged in magical rituals. Blum (1976) reported that the percentage of people who held partial or strong beliefs about walking under a ladder was 47 percent, for knocking on wood 41 percent, and for breaking a mirror 41 percent.

A Coexistence of Magical and Scientific Thinking

Relatively early theories concerning the relationships between magical and scientific thinking stated that these are two separate modes of thinking, which cannot coexist. According to this view, the two forms of thinking are two opposing poles on a continuum (e.g., Randall & Desroseir, 1980; Zusne & Jones, 1989). Today most theorists agree that magical thinking can exist alongside scientific thinking (e.g., Subotsky, 1993; Tambiah, 1996). More specifically, the supporters of this view claim that amongst adults living in modern societies, both magical (or primitive) and scientific (or rational) ways of thought can coexist, and they vary as a function of circumstances and of individual differences (Cottrell et al., 1996; Nemeroff & Rozin, 2000; Royalty, 1995).

Thus, for instance, Nemeroff & Rozin (2000) illustrate one way in which different situations provoke the use of different modes of thinking: "When one asks a question in emotional-laden terms—"how worried are you"?—one seems to be accessing an emotional or "gut-level" response system, which follows magical principles, and immanent justice is evoked. In contrast, when one asks a more cognitively/objectively worded question (as in a mathematical probability estimate), more "rational" processes come into play" (p. 13).

Magical Thinking Serving Important Functions

The traditional view of magical thinking pointed mostly to its primitive, sloppy, and irrational nature. However, today there is a growing acceptance of the view that while magical thinking may not adhere to scientific criteria, it may still serve some important functions for human beings (e.g., Griffin, 1988; Nemeroff & Rozin, 2000; Tambiah, 1990; Vyse, 1997).

It seems that the most important function of magical thinking is the enhancement of one's sense of control (Keinan, 1994; Wooley, 1997; Vyse, 1997). Thus, for instance, the belief that entering a new workplace on the right foot will enhance the chances of success in the new job might in itself strengthen the individual's sense of control over the situation.

Other potentially beneficial functions that magical thinking may serve have to do with lowering the level of uncertainty (especially in cases in which information and knowledge are lacking), and with creating meaningful structure, whether in terms of social convention or solutions to existential problems (see Tambiah, 1990).

Finally, in certain cases magical thinking may also enhance hope. This latter point may be noted when individuals perform a magical ritual in order to improve their present condition. For instance, many people put in their pocket a "lucky charm" of some sort before participating in an important contest or a threatening event. This enhances in their mind their chances for success, while providing them with a few moments of hope.

THE EFFECTS OF STRESS ON THE EMERGENCE OF MAGICAL THINKING

A substantial number of authors pointed to the relationship between stress and the emergence of magical thinking (Albas & Albas, 1989; Gmelch & Felson, 1980; Malinowski, 1954; McCann & Stewin, 1984; Padget & Jorgenson, 1982). Thus, for example, Malinowski (1954) found that the Melanesian islanders whom he observed engaged in magical rituals when sailing to the open sea and being exposed to the dangers of sea and weather but not when fishing in closed and safe lagoons. Similarly, Padgett and Jorgenson (1982) found a direct relationship between the emergence of magical thinking and the severity of economic hardship in Germany between the two world wars. Padgett and Jorgenson concluded that "just as the Trobriand islanders surrounded their more dangerous deep sea fishing with superstitions, Germans in the 1920s and 1930s became more superstitious during the times of economic threat" (p. 739). However, the studies cited above were conducted without the use of proper experimental controls, and therefore it is difficult to determine whether the emergence of magical thinking was indeed caused by stress. Moreover, these studies treated magical thinking as a single entity, without attempting to categorize such thinking into several types. Finally, these experiments did not take into account the possibility that certain personality characteristics may serve as moderators between stress and magical thinking.

In a study conducted during the Gulf War (Keinan, 1994), I attempted to address all the aforementioned issues. One hundred and seventy-four Israelis took part in the study. All of them resided during the Gulf War in areas that were either exposed (high stress condition) or not exposed (low stress condition) to Iraqi missile attacks. About three weeks into the war, when it became apparent which cities were in danger and which were relatively safe, we approached inhabitants of the various areas, asking them to complete three types of questionnaires:

1. A questionnaire designed to assess the level of stress experienced by the individual.
2. A questionnaire including three types of items representing different forms of magical thinking, such as:
   a. *Items representing the law of similarity* (for instance: "If, during a missile attack, I had a photograph of Saddam Hussein with me, I would rip it to pieces").
   b. *Items representing the law of contagion* (for instance: "At a time like this, it wouldn't hurt to shake hands with a lucky person").
   c. *Items representing superstitious beliefs* (for instance: "To be on the safe side, it is best to step into the sealed room[1] right foot first").
3. A questionnaire designed to measure tolerance for ambiguity (MacDonald, 1970).

The results showed that people living in areas exposed to Iraqi missile attacks (high stress condition) reported a higher level of stress than people living in areas not exposed to missiles (low stress condition). Furthermore, participants in the high-stress condition expressed more magical beliefs than those in the low-stress condition. Finally, an interaction effect was found between stress and tolerance for ambiguity: the difference between the frequencies of magical thinking exhibited under low- and high-stress conditions was greater in individuals with low tolerance of ambiguity than in those with high tolerance of ambiguity (Figure 6.1 illustrates this interaction).

This pattern of results was obtained for all types of magical thinking, namely, thoughts related to the law of contagion and the law of similarity, as well as to various superstitious beliefs.

The results suggest that psychological stress brings about the various forms of magical thinking and that tolerance for ambiguity serves as a moderator between stress and magical beliefs. This latter finding corresponds with the results shown by Friedland & Keinan (1991), that low-tolerance individuals tend to form more causal attributions under stress than persons with high tolerance.

After presenting empirical evidence showing that stress is responsible for a higher frequency of magical thinking, I will now outline some possible theoretical explanations for these findings.

Figure 6.1
The Interaction between Level of Stress and Tolerance of Ambiguity

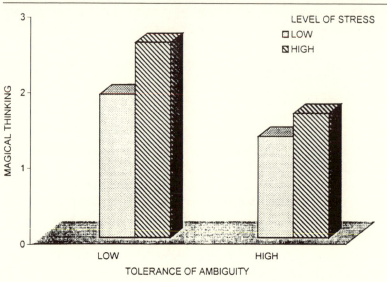

THE EFFECTS OF STRESS ON MAGICAL THINKING: THEORETICAL EXPLANATIONS

The explanations for the findings that psychological stress could foster the occurrence of magical thinking can be derived from three different theoretical approaches.

Psychoanalytically Oriented Explanations

These explanations are based on the psychoanalytic theory and suggest that during development children undergo a stage characterized by magical thinking and that during times of crisis or stress, the remnants of such infantile thinking are likely to reappear in adulthood (e.g., Freud, 1919/ 1955, 1913/1966; Serban, 1982; Werner, 1948). Thus, Freud (1919, 1955) stated that during early development children undergo a phase in which they tend to overestimate their ability to influence the external world and to believe that their thoughts are the causes of events happening about them. He also argued that these phenomena reflect magical thinking, which is a natural outcome of infantile narcissism, and that the remnants of such thinking might emerge when regression occurs as a result of exposure to a threat in adulthood. Similarly, Werner (1948) claimed that during every developmental stage it is possible to regress to an earlier stage when the individual is exposed to a stress-inducing situation. Since during child development there is a stage characterized by magical thinking, Werner hypothesized that adults "under anxiety manifest more magical practice than non-anxious individuals" (Barten & Franklin, 1978, p. 91).

Explanations Based on Information-Processing Models

An additional explanation is derived from information-processing models that deal with the effects of stress on cognitive functioning (e.g., Hamilton, 1982; Mandler, 1993; Wilder, 1993). According to this explanation, when exposed to stress, the individual allocates resources for coping with the stressors and their effects (e.g., Baron, Inman, Kao, & Logan, 1992; Mandler, 1993). Inasmuch as mental control is cognitively effortful (e.g., Gilbert, 1991; Wegner, Shortt, Blake, & Page, 1990) and given that our attention capacity is limited (e.g. Kahneman, 1973; Wickens, 1984), fewer resources can be allocated for the control of cognitive operations. This decrease in the ability to exercise effective control allows expressions of primitive thinking, such as magical beliefs, to surface.

Furthermore, several studies showed that stressed individuals exhibited a higher tendency to form causal attributions (Friedland & Keinan, 1991; Keinan & Sivan, 2001). According to the information-processing models outlined here, it is possible to assert that such a relationship formation enables the person to relate to large units of information instead of to each bit of information separately and, in this way, to leave space in the limited-capacity system for coping with stress. Because magical thinking involves the attribution of causes to unexplained phenomena, one can predict, on the basis of the above, that such thinking will be more prevalent under stress.

The Control-Motivation Explanation

The third explanation is based on the concept of personal control (see Keinan, 1994). There is extensive evidence that stress undermines the individual's perceptions of control (Alloy & Clements, 1992; Lazarus & Folkman, 1984), often leading to increased efforts to maintain or regain such perceptions (e.g., Friedland, Keinan, & Regev, 1992). Resorting to magical thinking, according to this explanation, is one of the ways people may choose to regain or reestablish their sense of control.

In a recently published article (Keinan, 2002), I have suggested that this mode of thinking can promote one's sense of control in several ways. First, it can help individuals understand what is happening in their environment because it provides explanations and reasons for phenomena that are other-wise unfamiliar or inexplicable, thus making their world more understand-able and controllable. Second, by means of superstitious beliefs or magical rituals, individuals may generate solutions that increase their control over the sources of stress. Thus, for example, the belief that putting a lucky charm in one's pocket will improve one's health augments the sense of control over the stressors. Finally, in some situations, magical thinking can create a self-fulfilling prophecy. Thus, the belief that a situation will improve as a result of some magical ritual might augment hope, decrease tension, and improve task performance—all of which may enhance one's sense of control.

The abovementioned explanations have not, to the best of my knowl-edge, been put to empirical testing, apart from the control motivation explanation, the validity of which has been tested by me recently (Keinan, 2002). This research is presented here in short.

THE CONTROL-MOTIVATION EXPLANATION: EMPIRICAL INVESTIGATION

In order to examine the validity of the control-motivation explanation, I chose the desire for control (DC) variable. This variable is a personality disposition that reflects the degree to which people are motivated to con-trol their environment (Burger, 1992; Burger & Cooper, 1979). I reasoned that if the control-motivation explanation is valid, then in high-stress situ-ations that usually impair the sense of control, people with a high need for control would reveal more magical thinking than those with a low need for control. In contrast, in low-stress situations in which there is no threat to the sense of control, the differences in expressions of magical thinking between highs and lows in need for control would be smaller. Conse-quently, I hypothesized that the differences in the frequency of supersti-tious behavior between high DC and low DC individuals would be greater in a high-stress condition than in a low-stress condition.

One hundred and eight students from the faculty of social sciences at Tel Aviv University participated in the study. Half of them were interviewed and filled out several questionnaires under high-stress conditions, namely about half an hour before an examination. The other half were interviewed and filled out questionnaires under low-stress conditions, namely, on a regular school day during which no examinations were held.

The purpose of the interviews, which all the students underwent, was to determine to what extent individuals knock on wood in response to hearing certain questions. Some of the questions included in the interview (target questions) were designed to elicit from the interviewee behavioral expressions of magical thinking (e.g., "Has anyone in your immediate family suffered from lung cancer?"), whereas the remaining questions were designed to conceal the purpose of the study from the interviewee (e.g., "what is the last book you read?").

At the end of the interview each participant was asked to rate how much he or she desired to touch wood. In addition, participants were asked to complete the Desirability of Control scale, which was developed by Burger and Cooper (1979), and to rate the level of stress they experienced during the experiment.

The study employed a 2 (high vs. low level of stress) $\times$ 2 (high vs. low DC groups) factorial design. The dependent variables were the number of times the participants knocked on wood during the interview and the degree of their need to knock, as reported at the end of the interview.

The results confirmed our main hypothesis: it was found that the differences in the frequency of resorting to superstitious behavior between high-DC individuals and low-DC individuals was greater in the high-stress condition than in the low-stress one (Figure 6.2 depicts this interaction).

Figure 6.2
The Interaction between Level of Stress and Desire for Control

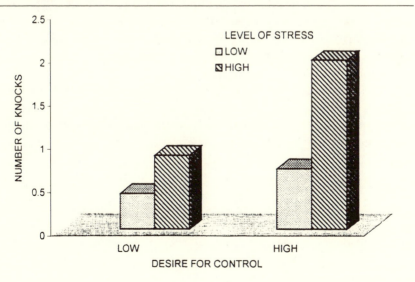

This pattern of results, which was found with regard to both the reported need to engage in superstitious behavior and the frequency of actual superstitious behavior, supports the motivation-control explanation, which posits that stress undermines the individual's sense of control and that resorting to superstitious behavior may provide a means of regaining control.

SUMMARY AND CONCLUSIONS

Magical thinking represents relatively lower cognitive patterns, which do not correspond with the scientific knowledge available today. Nevertheless, this way of thinking is quite prevalent among adults in Western cultures and is often manifested in educated and mentally healthy individuals. This chapter has shown that during stressful times there is a higher tendency to think magically and to resort to superstitious behavior.

It seems that resorting to magical thinking is a way of coping with stress. The findings presented in this chapter suggest that this way of coping portrays the individual's efforts to regain a feeling of control, which has been lowered or undermined as a result of the exposure to stress. However, it should be pointed out that the obtained control is in many cases an illusion, as it is based on the individual's belief that it is in his power to influence events that in reality are uncontrollable.

As mentioned above, the control-motivation explanation is not the only explanation for the rise in frequency of magical thinking due to exposure to stress. There may be other explanations based on psychoanalytic theory and information processes models. However, as far as I know, these possible alternative explanations have not been empirically tested and therefore at this time it is not possible to determine their validity.

To further elucidate the relationship between the emotional state of an individual and the emergence of "primitive" thought, future studies should examine whether superstitious behavior actually reduced the level of stress experienced by individuals and moreover, whether such reduction would be differentially affected by their desire for control.

NOTE

1. The *sealed room* is a room prepared in advance, into which those present in the home gathered during missile attacks in order to defend themselves against chemical warfare.

REFERENCES

Albas, D., & Albas, C. (1989). Modern magic: The case of examinations. *The Sociological Quarterly,* 30(4), 603–613.

Alcock, J. E. (1981). *Parapsychology: Science or magic? A psychological perspective.* Oxford: Pergamon.

Alcock, J. E. (1995). The belief engine. *Skeptical Inquirer,* 19, May/June, 14–18.

Alloy, L. B., & Clements, C. M. (1992). Illusion of control: Invulnerability to negative affect and depressive symptoms after laboratory and natural stressors. *Journal of Abnormal Psychology,* 101(2), 234–245.

Appandurai, A. (1981). Gastro-politics in Hindu South Asia. *American Ethnologist,* 8, 494–511.

Baron, R. S., Inman, M. L., Kao, C. F., & Logan, H. (1992). Negative emotion and superficial social processing. *Motivation and Emotion,* 16, 323–346.

Barten, S. S., & Franklin, M. B. (1978). *Developmental processes: H. Werner's selected writings.* New York: International Universities Press.

Beardsworth, A., & Keil, T. (1992). The vegetarian's option: Varieties, conversions, motives and careers. *Sociological Review,* 40, 253–293.

Blum, S. H. (1976). Some aspects of belief in prevailing superstitions. *Psychological Reports,* 38, 579–582.

Burger, J. M. (1992). *Desire for control.* New York: Plenum Press.

Burger, J. M., & Cooper, H. M. (1979). The desirability of control. *Motivation and Emotion,* 3, 381–393.

Cannon-Bowers, J. A., & Salas, E. (1998). *Making decisions under stress.* Washington, DC: American Psychological Association.

Cottrell, J. E., Winer, G. A., & Smith, M. C. (1996). Beliefs of children and adults about feeling stares of unseen others. *Developmental Psychology,* 32, 50–61.

Diamond, H., & Diamond, M. (1985). *Fit for life.* New York: Warner.

Driskell, J. E., & Salas, E. (1996). *Stress and human performance.* Mahwah, NJ: Erlbaum.

Frazer, J. G. (1959). *The new golden bough: A study in magic and religion.* New York: Macmillan (original work published 1890).

Freud, S. (1955). *The "uncanny."* London: Hogarth Press/Institute of Psychoanalysis (original work published 1919).

Freud, S. (1960). *Totem and taboo: Resemblances between the psychic lives of savages and neurotics.* London: Routledge/Kegan Paul (original work published 1913).

Friedland, N., & Keinan, G. (1991). The effects of stress, ambiguity tolerance, and trait anxiety on the formation of causal relationships. *Journal of Research in Personality,* 25, 88–107.

Friedland, N., Keinan, G., & Regev, Y. (1992). Controlling the uncontrollable: Effects of stress on illusory control. *Journal of Personality and Social Psychology,* 63, 923–931.

Gallup, G. H., & Newport, F. (1991). Belief in paranormal phenomena among adult Americans. *Skeptical Inquirer,* 15, 137–146.

Gilbert, D. T. (1991). How mental systems believe. *American Psychologist,* 46, 107–119.

Gmelch, G., & Felson, R. (1980, December). Can a lucky charm get you through organic chemistry? *Psychology Today,* pp. 75–78.

Griffin, D. R. (1988). *The Reenchantment of Science: Postmodern Proposals.* Albany: State University of New York Press.

Hamilton, V. (1982). Cognition and stress: An information processing model. In L. Goldberger & S. Breznitz (Eds.), *Handbook of Stress: Theoretical and clinical aspects* (pp. 105–120). New York: Free Press.

Hammond, K. R. (2000). *Judgments Under Stress.* New York: Oxford University Press.

Hunt, R. (1982*). The seven keys to color healing.* San Francisco: Harper & Row.

Jahoda, G. (1969). *The psychology of superstition.* New York: Penguin.

Kahneman, D. (1973). *Attention and effort.* Englewood Cliffs, NJ: Prentice-Hall.

Keinan, G. (1987). Decision making under stress: Scanning of alternatives under controllable and uncontrollable threats. *Journal of Personality and Social Psychology,* 52, 639–644.

Keinan, G. (1994). Effects of stress and tolerance of ambiguity on magical thinking. *Journal of Personality and Social Psychology,* 67, 48–55.

Keinan, G. (2002). The effects of stress and desire for control on superstitious behavior. *Personality and Social Psychology Bulletin,* 28(1), 102–108.

Keinan, G., Friedland, N., Kahneman, D., & Roth, D. (1999). The effect of stress on the suppression of erroneous competing responses. *Anxiety, Stress, and Coping,* 12, 455–476.

Keinan, G., & Sivan, D. (2001). The effects of stress and desire for control on the formation of causal attributions. *Journal of Research in Personality,* 35, 127–137.

Klein, M. (1987). Notes on some schizoid mechanisms. In J. Mitchell (Ed.), *The Selected Melanie Klein* (pp. 176–200). New York: Free Press (original work published 1946).

Lazarus, R. S., & Folkman, S. (1984). *Stress, appraisal, and coping.* New York: Springer.

Lindeman, M., & Stark, K. (1999). Pleasure, pursuit of health, or negotiation of identity? Personality correlates of food choice motives among young and middle-aged women. *Appetite,* 33, 141–161.

MacDonald, A. P. (1970). Revised scale for ambiguity tolerance: reliability and validity. *Psychological Reports,* 26, 791–798.

Malinowski, B. (1954). *Magic, science, and religion.* Garden City, NY: Doubleday.

Mandler, G. (1993). Thought, memory, and learning: Effects of emotional stress. In L. Goldberger & S. Breznitz (Eds.), *Handbook of stress: Theoretical and clinical aspects* (pp. 40–55). New York: Free Press.

Marriott, M. (1968). Caste ranking and food transactions: A matrix analysis. In: M. Singer and B. S. Cohn (Eds.), *Structure and Change in Indian Society,* (pp. 133–171). Chicago: Aldine.

Mauss, M. (1972). *A general theory of magic.* New York: Norton. (Original work published 1902).

McCann, S.J.H., & Stewin, L. L. (1984). Environmental threat and parapsychological contributions to the psychological literature. *Journal of Social Psychology,* 122, 227–235.

Meigs, A. S. (1984). *Food, sex, and pollution. A new Guinea religion.* New Brunswick, NJ: Rutgers University Press.

Nemeroff, C., Brinkman, A., & Woodward, C. (1994). Magical cognitions about AIDS in a college population. *AIDS Education and Prevention,* 6, 249–265.

Nemeroff, C., & Rozin, P. (1989). "You are what you eat": Applying the demand-free "impressions" technique to an unacknowledged belief. *Ethos,* 17, 50–69.

Nemeroff, C., & Rozin, P. (1994). The contagion concept in adult thinking in the United States: Transmission of germs and interpersonal influence. *Ethos,* 22, 158–186.

Nemeroff, C., & Rozin, P. (2000). The making of the magical mind. In K. S. Rosengren, C. N. Johnson, & P. L. Harris (Eds.), *Imagining the impossible: Magical, scientific, and religious thinking in children* (pp 1–34). New-York: Cambridge University Press.

Padgett, V. R., & Jorgenson, D. O. (1982). Superstition and economic threat: Germany, 1918–1940. *Personality and Social Psychology Bulletin,* 8, 736–741.

Piaget, J. P. (1929). *The child's conception of the world.* London: Routledge & Kegan Paul.

Randell, T. M., & Desroseir, M. (1980). Measurement of supernatural belief: Sex differences and locus of control. *Journal of Personality Assessment,* 44(1), 493–498.

Royalty, J. (1995). The generalizability of critical thinking: Paranormal beliefs vs. statistical reasoning. *The Journal of Genetic Psychology,* 156(4), 477–488.

Rozin, P., Markwith, M., & McCauley, C. R. (1994). The nature of aversion to indirect contact with another person: AIDS aversion as a composite of aversion to strangers, infection, moral taint and misfortune. *Journal of Abnormal Psychology,* 103, 495–504.

Rozin, P., Markwith, M., & Ross, B. (1990). The sympathetic magical law of similarity, nominal realism, and neglect of negatives in response to negative labels. *Psychological Science,* 1(6), 383–384.

Rozin, P., Markwith, M., & Stoess, C. (1997). Moralization and becoming a vegetarian: The transformation of preferences into values and the recruitment of disgust. *Psychological Science, 8*, 67–73.

Rozin, P., Millman, L., & Nemeroff, C. (1986). Operation of the laws of sympathetic magic in disgust and other domains. *Journal of Personality and Social Psychology, 50*, 703–712.

Rozin, P., & Nemeroff, C. (1999). Magic and superstition. In R. A. Wilson & F. C. Keil (Eds.), *The MIT encyclopedia of the cognitive sciences* (pp. 503–505). Cambridge, MA: The MIT Press.

Rozin, P., Nemeroff, C., Wane, M., & Sherrod, A. (1989). Operation of the sympathetic magical law of contagion in interpersonal attitudes among Americans. *Bulletin of Psychonomic Society, 27*(4), 367–370.

Serban, G. (1982). *The tyranny of magical thinking.* New York: Dutton.

Shanteau, J., & Dino, G. A. (1993). Environmental stressor effects on creativity and decision making. In O. Svenson & J. Maule (Eds.), *Time Pressure and Stress in Human Judgment and Decision Making.* New York: Plenum.

Stein, R. I., & Nemeroff, C. (1995). Moral overtones of food: Judging others by what they eat. *Personality and Social Psychology Bulletin, 21*, 480–490.

Subbotsky, E. V. (1993). *Foundations of the mind: Children's understanding of reality.* Cambridge, MA: Harvard University Press.

Tambiah, S. J. (1990). *Magic, science, religion, and the scope of rationality.* Cambridge, England: Cambridge University Press.

Tylor, E. B. (1974). *Primitive culture: Researches into the development of mythology, philosophy, religion, art and custom.* New York: Gordon Press. (Original work published 1871).

Vyse, S. A. (1997). *Believing in magic: The psychology of superstition.* New York: Oxford University Press.

Wegner, D. M., Shortt, J. W., Blake, A. W. & Page, M. S. (1990). The suppression of exciting thoughts. *Journal of Personality and Social Psychology, 58*, 409–418.

Werner, H. (1948). *Comparative psychology of mental development.* New York: International Universities Press.

Wickens, C. D. (1984). Processing resources in attention. In R. Parasurman & D. R. Davies (Eds.), *Varieties of Attention.* New York: Academic Press.

Wilder, D. A. (1993). The role of anxiety in facilitating stereotypic judgments of out group behavior. In D. M. Mackie and D. L. Hamilton (Eds.), *Affect, cognition, and stereotyping: Interactive processes in group perception* (pp. 87–109). San Diego, CA: Academic Press.

Wilder, J. (1975). The lure of magical thinking. *American Journal of Psychotherapy, 1*, 37–55.

Woolley, J. D. (1997). Thinking about fantasy: Are children fundamentally different thinkers and believers from adults? *Child Development, 68*(6), 991–1011.

Zusne, L., & Jones, W. H. (1989). *Anomalistic psychology: A study of magical thinking* (2nd ed.). Hillsdale, NJ: Erlbaum.

Part II

THREAT AND HOPE IN COPING WITH STRESSFUL LIFE EXPERIENCES

Chapter 7

HOPE AND FANTASY AMONG WOMEN COPING WITH INFERTILITY AND ITS TREATMENTS

Yael Benyamini

Since she had played "house" with her friends, she knew she would be a mother. When she had her first menstrual periods, she was told that this means her body is ready to bear children. For years, she was careful not to, through abstinence or contraception. When she decided to marry, it was because she wanted to share her life with this man and she wanted him to be the father of her children. When they decided to have children, she could imagine her child, and herself as a mother. Failure was not an option for which she was prepared. Yet about one in six couples has experienced infertility, defined as the inability to conceive within one year of regular unprotected intercourse or to bear a child to term, and as many as one in four couples has experienced some problem on their road to bearing a child.

The fantasy was there since the days she played house with her friends; if unfulfilled, it will remain there till she reaches menopause. It is the dominant cultural narrative in most or all traditions and religions and thus it is shared by most women. This fantasy, of her as a mother, holding her own child, does not change. It is passive and static. When this fantasy is not easily fulfilled, women have to build up active, dynamic hope, while coping month after month with the disappointment that follows unsuccessful treatment cycles. In interviews with women undergoing infertility treatments, one of the most frequently mentioned issues is the "emotional roller coaster" they go through, the cycles of hope and despair (e.g., Imeson & McMurray, 1996). Yet, sometimes hope is all they have, and giving it up entails a tremendous loss.

In this chapter I will summarize findings from quantitative and qualitative studies of infertile women, focusing on the nature of hope and fantasy in this situation. The findings will be reviewed in the light of theories and findings from other contexts regarding hope, expectations, wishful thinking, and fantasy. These findings underscore the necessity and the difficulty of maintaining hope while undergoing infertility treatments, and the very thin line between hope and fantasy. Broadening the scope of hope beyond specific hopes of conception is a key ingredient in preserving well-being and quality of life while undergoing infertility treatments and after their conclusion.

This chapter is focused primarily on women, even though many of the studies on which the chapter is based involved both women and men and findings pertaining to both will be presented. Women and men have the same motives for wanting children but they give them different priorities (Newton, Hearn, Yuzpe, & Houle, 1992). Many studies that compared women and men's adjustment to infertility found it to be more stressful for women (see review by Greil, 1997). For example, half of the women, but only 15 percent of the men, in one study reported that infertility is the most upsetting experience in their lives (Freeman, Boxer, Rickels, Tureck, & Mastroianni, 1985). More importantly in the context of this book, hope and fantasy have a unique meaning for *women* pursuing infertility treatments: The motherhood fantasy is the legacy that they have inherited, and it is their self-identity and feelings of self-worth that are more deeply affected by infertility (Blenner, 1990; Sandelowski, Holditch-Davis, & Harris, 1990). They are the ones who actively undergo treatment and are the first to face its success or failure, their dream fulfilled or shattered again.

INFERTILITY AND ITS TREATMENT

Infertility is treated within the health care system although it is not a "disease" in the common use of this term: it is not life-threatening and does not impair physical functioning. In fact, it is not strictly a medical condition, because it does not become apparent until the couple tries to conceive (Sandelowski, Holditch-Davis et al., 1990). When it does become apparent, it is highly threatening, especially since it is usually unexpected: it strikes healthy, young people, who chose to undergo the major transition to parenthood. Instead, they experience a stressful non-event transition (Koropatnick, Daniluk, & Pattinson, 1993), unlike anything they have faced before (Milne, 1988). As a non-event, its beginning and end points are not clearly defined (an important aspect to which I will return). Although not physically debilitating, its emotional impact is comparable to that of serious chronic diseases (Domar, Zuttermeister, & Friedman, 1993). Infertility affects many domains of life—personal, social, work/career, financial, and others (Newton, Sherrard, & Glavac, 1999). Regardless of the source of the problem, female or male, women are always the patients. Nevertheless, it is experienced as a problem of the couple and both partners are greatly affected, as is their relationship (Pasch & Dunkel-Schetter, 1997); even their sexual relationship suffers as it loses its spontaneity (Leiblum, 1993).

Qualitative studies of infertile couples portray a very grim picture of the experience of infertility. These studies are based on in-depth interviews, often conducted at the participants' homes. Interviewees often learn about the studies from ads placed in clinics, support groups, and the media. Thus, they may be a select group of people who are more open to discuss their difficulties and/or are experiencing infertility as a very stressful experience and accordingly feel a greater need to talk about it in a protected setting. Consequently, it is not possible to deduce from these studies whether all couples experience infertility in this way. Indeed, there are some indications that infertility is a life stressor for some of those people some of the time (Jones & Hunter, 1996).

Quantitative studies are often based on questionnaires filled in by consecutive patients attending infertility clinics. Participation rates are typically high. Thus, these studies are based on samples that may be less biased. Similar to the qualitative studies, they report high levels of distress among women undergoing infertility treatments (e.g., Morrow, Thoreson, & Penney, 1995). They also show the great variability in women's reactions to infertility (Dunkel-Schetter & Lobel, 1991). Since distress is to a great extent inherent in the process and inevitable, I propose that underlying the variability among women is their way of maintaining hope and preserving their well-being.

FUTURE OUTLOOKS IN THE CASE OF INFERTILITY: BASIC CONCEPTS

This chapter will focus on three main concepts that represent future outlooks: hope, expectations, and fantasy. In everyday language, when infertile women undergoing treatment talk about their future, these concepts are expressed in similar words. Expectations are more directly tied to the perceived odds of treatment success (researchers typically ask infertile couples to express them in percents). Hope is expressed in statements such as "I tell myself that things will be better next time," or, "I cheer myself on by telling myself that I too will be a mother some day." Positive fantasy refers to the image of success in achieving child-birth, the ultimate goal of infertility treatment. It is apparent in statements such as "I imagine the future, how things will look when the problem is solved" (Benyamini et al., 2002).

Hope and Fantasy

There is a very thin line between hope and fantasy in infertility. Although they sound similar and are positively correlated, hope is associated with greater well-being and fantasy with greater distress (Benyamini et al., 2002; Benyamini, Primor-Horowitz, Shiloh, Gozlan, & Kokia, 2000). Since the fantasy is always there, it seems that women who resort mainly to relying on it are more distressed, while those who manage to actively conjure hope under these stressful conditions are able to maintain their well-being. Oettingen's (1996) distinction between positive expectations and positive fantasies is an appropriate framework for these findings: She defines positive expectations as beliefs about how likely it is that certain events will happen or not, while positive fantasies are daydreams or mental images depicting future events and scenarios. The similarity between the use of the term "fantasy" in this chapter and its use in psychodynamic approaches is not coincidental. This definition of fantasy is congruent with claims that even childless infertile women are likely to have a narrative identity as a mother (Kirkman, 2001) and that the fantasy child exists as a psychologically present though physically absent member of the infertile marriage (Burns, 1987).

In modern personality and social psychology, fantasies have more often been called "wishful thinking." Several coping inventories include a sub-scale of wishful thinking, containing items referring to imagining or dreaming about a desired state, similar to the statement in the previous section (Carver, Scheier, & Weintraub, 1989; Folkman & Lazarus, 1985). In the present context, the term fantasy will be reserved for such images. Wishful thinking will be defined as people's tendency to believe what they wish to be true, a product of normal hypothesis-testing processes, according to Trope, Gervey, & Liberman (1997), and thus more similar to unrealistic positive expectations than to fantasies.

Hope and Positive Expectations

Dufault and Martocchio (1985) proposed two spheres of hope, generalized and particularized, that are both relevant in the present context. Generalized hope is broad and abstract and provides the climate for developing particular hopes. Particularized hope is tied to a specific object. It provides a sense of direction and meaning as it helps people clarify and prioritize what they want to achieve. In the infertility situation, particularized hope refers to the goal of bearing a child, the belief that it is possible, and the need to direct energy towards attaining this goal. Women use it to convey their optimism regarding treatment success.

The extensive literature on particularized hopes, or situated optimism (Armor & Taylor, 1998), shows that people are usually more optimistic in their expectations than is warranted in light of realistic constraints. This phenomenon has been labeled "unrealistic optimism" (Weinstein, 1980) and is sometimes referred to as "positive illusions" (Taylor & Brown, 1988). Reviews of the literature on unrealistic optimism show that these expectations are not entirely out of touch with reality: they are usually only as high as people "can get away with" given the limits set by their physical and social environment (Armor & Taylor, 1998; Taylor & Brown, 1988). Moreover, although people's estimates are overly optimistic in absolute values, they typically show at least some degree of relative accuracy: Those who have a realistically lower chance of success tend to give lower estimates.

In line with these general findings, there have been numerous reports of unrealistic expectations of infertility treatment success (Callan & Hennessey, 1986; Daniels, 1989; de Zoeten, Tymstra, & Alberda, 1987; Kemeter & Fiegl, 1998; Lalos, Lalos, Jacobsson, & von Schoultz, 1985). Couples maintained these unrealistic expectations even when the medical staff have clearly communicated much lower success rates (Johnston, Shaw, & Bird, 1987; Litt, Tennen, Affleck, & Klock, 1992) and in spite of their awareness of the lower numbers provided by the staff (Reading, 1989). Relative accuracy is preserved to a certain extent: Men, but not women, reduced their estimates of success after treatment failure, and, more educated women and men had unrealistic odds but lower than those of less educated people (Achmon, Tadir, Fisch, & Ovadia, 1989).

Actual success rates in infertility treatments are difficult to estimate and depend on the way the estimate is computed and on the population to which it refers; on the average, per treatment cycle, they are quite low (in the order of 10–20 percent) and they decline with additional treatment cycles. For most couples, they are so much lower than the couple's subjective estimates that one wonders whether they should be considered expectations, wishful thinking, or fantasies; the appropriate label differs along the stages of infertility, since actual odds diminish with time.

The Process of Hope

Benzein and Saveman (1998) examined about 100 references with "hope" in the title and identified critical attributes of hope, its antecedents, and its consequences. The most basic of these critical attributes are common to all conceptualizations of hope, from dictionary definitions to theoretical models: Hope is *a positive expectation, oriented to the future.* In addition, hope is *intentional* and *grounded in reality:* one chooses a goal that is uncertain, yet realistically possible. Hope can involve significant others in one's life *(interconnectedness).* It is not a state, but an active process of moving forward (Menninger, 1959, 1963). Even under the most stressful conditions, such as coping with incurable cancer, hope is a dynamic experience (Benzein, Norberg, & Saveman, 2001; Jacoby, 1993). Hope manifests itself when people encounter stressful loss or threat situations in which the temptation to despair is great. It does not serve to deny the gravity of the situation; on the contrary, it allows one to face threat, danger, and pain with awareness and an intention to cope (Jacoby, 1993). The consequences of hope are the abilities of coping, renewal, employing new strategies, gaining peace, an improved quality of life, and physical health (Benzein & Saveman, 1998).

Viewing hope as a dynamic process means that we need to understand how its nature and content change along the stages of infertility. In the most general terms, infertility has been described as a three-stage process: *engagement, immersion,* and *disengagement* (Blenner, 1990). Engagement begins with the initial encounter with infertility and includes the first stages of treatment in which the couple believes the problem will soon resolve. They enter the immersion stage when they begin to realize that it may not be so simple to solve the problem. If unsuccessful over a longer period of time in treatment, they eventually need to disengage from infertility and its treatments. I will now turn to the process of hope in each of these stages.

HOPE ALONG THE STAGES OF INFERTILITY: ENGAGEMENT

Engagement begins after several months of failed attempts to conceive, when women begin to suspect that something might be wrong. Eventually, they decide to seek care. The doctor typically outlines a plan of tests and assessments, which gives the couple a sense of hope (Becker & Nachtigall, 1991). At this point many couples believe they will be pregnant within a few months (Becker & Nachtigall, 1994; Lalos et al., 1985). Hope is taken for granted; the couple is not focused on the future, but on the present and the past, trying to understand what they need to do and why this (unexpected) problem happened to them.

Women often state that they sought care because they wanted to know the cause of their inability to conceive (Becker & Nachtigall, 1991). Looking for a cause to attribute the problem to is a natural thing to do, as frequently reported by patients diagnosed with a variety of health conditions (Benyamini, Leventhal, & Leventhal, 1997). Stress increases the tendency for a causal search as an attempt to regain control by making sense of the situation (Keinan & Sivan, 2001). People often search their past for things they might have done that contributed to their problem. In many health contexts, taking responsibility for the problem could be beneficial: If, for instance, the problem resulted from an unhealthy lifestyle, then acknowledging this provides a feeling of control since a change in lifestyle might prevent recurrence. Searching for the answer to the "why me?" question has also been found to be part of the process of finding meaning in one's misfortune, which helps people cope with their present condition (Taylor, 1983).

In infertility, searching for an answer to the "why me?" question is not necessarily helpful. First, recurrence is not the issue. Second, taking responsibility for the problem typically results in blaming oneself for past behaviors, such as the use of contraceptives, abortions, promiscuity, or substance abuse (Abbey & Halman, 1995; Menning, 1980). Even if any of these factors contributed to the infertility problem, this knowledge does not provide any clues regarding a solution. It can, however, result in a counter-productive process of self-blame (Benyamini et al., 2003). If a specific diagnosis has been made, one spouse may feel guilt (Litt et al., 1992; Mahlstedt, 1985), and the other spouse may secretly resent him or her (Cook, 1987). Even without a clear diagnosis, women often blame themselves. Such feelings of blame and guilt are unspeakable (Demyttenaere et al., 1998), and thus in addition to the internal turmoil, they can cause a rift between the partners, leading to the loss of the main source of support at this time, each other. Third, finding meaning is also not an issue: In the early stages it is out of the question, because couples do not see themselves as "infertile" (and certainly not as "sterile," a taboo word), only as "not yet pregnant" or at the most "experiencing an infertility problem" (Blenner, 1990; Menning, 1980), and thus do not attempt to find meaning in the experience. Even in later stages, infertility is so incomprehensible and traumatic that couples, women in particular, find it difficult to construe any meaning (Greil, Porter, Leitko, & Riscilli, 1989).

There is indirect evidence that women enter the infertility treatment process with a perception that is focused on the responsibility for the problem (male or female) and thus on a past orientation that deals with issues of blame and guilt. Shiloh, Larom and Ben-Rafael (1991) found that infertile women organized their representations of infertility treatments according to the most salient features of the procedures themselves, whereas fertile women organized them according to the source of the problem. Although the data was cross-sectional, they speculated that before they encountered fertility problems, the presently infertile women also perceived infertility treatments mainly through the perspective of the source of the problem. The process in which couples shift from the past orientation of looking for blame and feeling guilt, to the present solution-oriented view and the future view of looking forward to treatment success and engaging in active hope, may be essential to adaptive coping with infertility.

As the engagement stage progresses, couples reach the "hope and determination stage" (Becker & Nachtigall, 1991). They have passed the responsibility on to the doctor, but they may still feel they maintain control by having chosen a good doctor (Abbey & Halman, 1995) and by being good patients who do what they are told to do (Becker & Nachtigall, 1991). They feel that they only need a little bit of patience and they still do not apply the label of "infertility" to themselves: some couples refer only to "the problem" or even state that "there is no problem" (Jones & Hunter, 1996). Their daily life is affected by the demands of the treatment, but since they still perceive it as a temporary problem soon to be solved, its influence is not pervasive. Consequently, they can still manage to comfort themselves with high hopes, despite the fact that the infertility problem arouses anxiety, its unexpectedness causes some distress, and the practical demands of treatment can be burdensome. Hope is crucial at this stage, as in all others, but it is not so difficult to maintain. At this point, the primary manifestation of hope is unrealistically high estimated odds of treatment success.

Why Do Women Form Unrealistically Optimistic Expectations of Treatment Success?

There are several cognitive and motivational explanations for the creation of unrealistic expectations (Armor & Taylor, 1998). First, on the cognitive side, an optimistic assessment of the chances of a favorable outcome is often based on the ease with which a successful scenario can be imagined. Scenarios constructed in order to estimate the probability of a future event are usually oversimplified and focused on success, not on failure (Armor & Taylor, 1998). In infertility, there are no "middle of the road" scenarios, which are possible with other health threats (e.g., partial recovery of functioning following surgery). The "all-or-none" nature of the outcome of infertility treatments leaves room for only two possible scenarios, and the successful one is the easier one to come up with: The fantasy scenario of motherhood is the simplest and most obvious one that comes to mind. The failure scenario was never rehearsed: Most of the participants in the study by Achmon et al. (1989) stated that they have not thought of what they would do if treatment failed. Johnston et al. (1987) suggested that the successful scenario is easily imagined not only because of the way women are socialized, but also because of the greater availability of success stories in the media and in clinics (those that specialize in infertility are often lined with pictures of smiling babies attached to thank you notes).

It is practically impossible to accurately predict the odds of success of a specific couple. Becker and Nachtigall (1991) noted that although uncertainty was inherent in the procedure, and often increased with treatment failures, doctors and patients dealt with it in very different ways. Physicians refer to odds in terms of pregnancy rates in a population of patients. Couples, in contrast, assess the likelihood that they will walk out with a baby. The difference between physicians and couples in point of view, along with the discomfort of talking about the uncertainty, creates a lot of ambiguity in the way odds are conveyed to couples and therefore in the way they are understood (Modell, 1989). Couples form subjective interpretations of their own chances of success. An objectively low estimate, such as 30 percent, could be interpreted by couples as "good" (Blenner, 1990). When told that the chances of success of in-vitro fertilization (IVF) are, for example, 25 percent, such as, one in four couples will bear a child, selective information-processing led many couples to believe that they will be the successful one (Milne, 1988; Modell, 1989). Motivational biases augment the cognitive ones: In general, when people expect an outcome to be favorable, they are more optimistic in their prediction of the time they will finish the task (Buehler, Griffin, & MacDonald, 1997). Confidence in one's chances of success could greatly diminish the anxiety involved in infertility treatments (Abbey, Halman, & Andrews, 1992). Therefore, couples find reasons to discount the significance of failures, e.g., the first cycle was just a trial run (Callan & Hennessey, 1986) and find evidence for "progress" from trial to trial, even when they are all unsuccessful (Sandelowski, Harris, & Holditch-Davis, 1990; Williams, 1988).

The reduction of cognitive dissonance is also an important force that motivates couples to maintain optimistic expectations, as noted by Johnston (1987). Infertile couples, particularly the women, spend vast amounts of physical, emotional, and financial resources in treatment. As one woman put it: "The more sacrifices you make, the more difficult it becomes to quit" (Remennick, 2000, p. 9). Continued belief in the ultimate success of these efforts provides the much needed justification for them. In addition, to the extent that couples share their problem with others, they may feel that they are expected to express optimism: Women often cited remarks from friends telling them that they need to have a positive attitude and not to be anxious (Imeson & McMurray, 1996; Menning, 1980), and, in general there is evidence of a stigma against pessimism (Helweg-Larsen, Sadeghian, & Webb, 2002).

HOPE ALONG THE STAGES OF INFERTILITY: IMMERSION

As time goes on, mounting failures force couples to realize that solving their infertility problem may not be simple and quick. The demanding treatment regimen disrupts daily routines and begins to take its toll on their lives, at least on the women's lives. Feelings of powerlessness and loss of control take over and their distress levels increase accordingly (Stanton, Tennen, Affleck, & Mendola, 1991). They begin to drift away from the fertile world, while idealizing it (Blenner, 1990), yet find themselves struggling with accepting the label of infertility. The approach-avoidance dilemma, swaying from denial to acceptance, is a major dilemma in coping with infertility (Benyamini et al., 2003).

Acceptance of a stressful event is often an essential first step for adaptive coping. Acceptance requires assimilating a new reality while letting go of an old one that is no longer valid (Carver, Scheier, & Pozo, 1992). However, for most infertile couples at this stage, there is no conclusive evidence that the old reality is not valid. They are still undergoing treatment, and the next cycle could be the one in which they will conceive, or the one after that...in which case they will instantly shed the diagnosis and stigma of infertility. This ambiguity about the diagnosis makes it difficult to fully accept it, while reality undermines attempts to fully deny it. Yet even as the balance swings closer to acceptance of the problem, high expectations of treatment success are often maintained (Callan & Hennessey, 1986; Reading, 1989). This is puzzling in light of research showing that people tend to adjust their expectations following failure, even if not in full (Armor & Taylor, 1998), and of findings that these high expectations do not necessarily reduce anxiety among infertile women. Some studies reported less distress among women who perceived their odds as better (Abbey et al., 1992; Reading, 1989), while others reported no correlation between perceived odds and distress (Glover, Hunter, Richards, Katz, & Abel, 1999; Litt et al., 1992). It is possible that optimistic expectations reduce distress up to a certain point in the pursuit of fertility, but as they become less and less realistic, they do not buffer distress anymore. Initial stages of treatment often involve relatively non-invasive medical regimens, such as ovulation-inducing hormones provided in the form of pills or injections. When these fail, couples resort to the more invasive and demanding IVF treatment. Among women who were mostly undergoing preliminary, less invasive treatments, those who reported higher expectations of treatment success also reported lower distress (Benyamini et al., 2000); such expectations were unrelated to distress following IVF failure (Litt et al., 1992).

Seemingly more puzzling are the findings that estimates of likelihood of success have little influence on decisions regarding treatment. The physical and emotional toll in IVF is much greater than in the treatments that precede it. Yet, almost one half of the participants in Reading's (1989) study stated that estimates of success had no influence on their decision to continue treatment. Although they claimed that the probability of treatment success was important in their decision, it was not among the top three factors influencing their decision to undergo treatments such as IVF, and was not the top rated factor for any treatment (Frank, 1990). Even if the chances of success were very low (2 percent), most of the women would still choose IVF (de Zoeten et al., 1987).

Why do infertile women who experience failure after failure still keep their hopes high and opt to continue treatment? Are so many women irrational in continuing to hold overly optimistic expectations in the face of increased risk and a high personal price paid? There are indications that women are not totally unrealistic and irrational. First, they actively test their beliefs and change them: Over time, they lower the level of probability they consider acceptable for trying a treatment (Reading, 1989); they also explain their repeated trials as an attempt to "beat the odds" (Modell, 1989). Second, from their point of view they may be acting very rationally: According to the model of pragmatic hypothesis testing proposed by Trope et al. (1997), they can be viewed as constantly testing the hypothesis that they will have a biological child. There are two possible errors in hypothesis testing: the error of commission, or false acceptance of the hypothesis, and the error of omission, or false rejection of the hypothesis. Trope et al. (1997) proposed that seemingly illogical hypothesis-testing processes are actually very logical if one takes into account the cost of each error. For an infertile couple, if the hypothesis is incorrect, then the price they are paying for false acceptance is the current physical and emotional stress and the future potential risks (e.g. increased chance of ovarian cancer in the future, Rosen et al., 1997). As mentioned above, women give very little weight to this price. In contrast, false rejection would result in the premature end of treatment. The price of this error is unbearable: it means giving up the fantasy, the dream of bearing their own child. There is an additional price that women do everything to avoid: future regret. IVF is considered a "last chance" treatment (Modell, 1989). Women want to at least try it, so that they will not have any regrets later. Anticipated regret is a recurring theme in interviews with infertile women. Many women report a strong need to prove to themselves that they have done everything that could be done in their attempt to conceive (Becker & Nachtigall, 1994; Blenner, 1990, 1992; Daniluk, 1996; de Zoeten et al., 1987; Kirkman & Rosenthal, 1999). This need dwarfs the risk in IVF and other invasive procedures.

It is clear from the above account that letting go of the optimistic expectations is difficult. However, in the immersion stage they cannot be taken for granted anymore—maintaining them is not automatic. Women actively boost them, as one study suggests (Benyamini et al., 2000): Women higher on dispositional optimism were just as realistic about their long-term chances as women lower on optimism. They gave similar estimates of their odds of conceiving within the next one or five years. However, the more optimistic women perceived their odds of success of the coming treatment as significantly higher compared to the less optimistic women. Accordingly, they also reported less distress. Their optimism was not just a "rosy glow" (or they would have rated their long-term odds higher too). They seemed to be carrying out the "work of hope" (Jacoby, 1993)— building up expectations as they get closer to the next treatment. This may help them gather up the energy needed to undergo another demanding cycle of treatment that has no promise of a successful outcome at its end.

The Broadening Scope of Hope in the Immersion Stage

Whether maintaining high expectations is an obvious result of a motivated hypothesis-testing process, or the effortful result of the work of hope in building these expectations, focusing on these expectations contributes to the process of immersion in infertility: Infertility becomes the focus of one's life, taking up time, financial resources, and physical and emotional energy. Distress increases over time (McLaney, Tennen, Affleck, & Fitzgerald, 1995) and quality of life erodes.

Dufult and Martocchio (1985) proposed that when particularized hopes are seriously threatened, generalized hope becomes more evident. This type of hope is not linked to a particular object of hope. It is a general outlook that preserves the meaningfulness of life. When one of the key aspects of the meaningfulness of a young woman's life, future motherhood, is threatened, it is all the more important to broaden the scope of hope to include many areas of life, future parenthood being only one of them. The stressful treatments can easily become overwhelming and impact on all areas of life. An active work of hope is needed in order to continue functioning in other areas as well: This is the key to preserving well-being. If no such work is done, the "default" reaction is increased focusing on infertility and its treatment. If such work is carried out intensively, infertility would still be stressful, but its impact on other areas of life would be minimized. Between these two extremes are moderate amounts of the "work of hope" that somewhat diminish the impact of infertility on one's life. Although both the "work of hope" and its consequences are continuous dimensions, for the ease of presentation I will discuss the two ends of these dimensions and the middle point as three distinct reaction styles. They are described in more detail in the next sections and presented in Figure 7.1, which shows the place of infertility among other domains of life in each of the three styles, and the potential tensions created between infertility and the other domains.

Figure 7.1
Three Styles of Reaction to Infertility

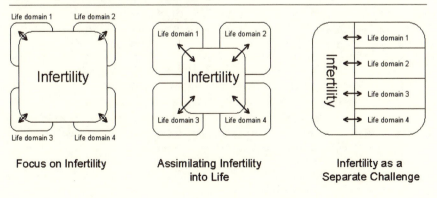

Focus on Infertility   Assimilating Infertility into Life   Infertility as a Separate Challenge

The Focus-on-Infertility Response Style

With time, the impact of infertility on other areas of life steadily rises. Many women find it difficult to invest in their career or work life or to keep up with any personal interests outside of work (Blenner, 1990; Imeson & McMurray, 1996; Milne, 1988). Their lives are "on hold" (Woods, Olshansky, & Draye, 1991). Some of them feel guilty and neglect themselves, believing that they do not "deserve" any rewards at this point. Others reduce their social involvement because they find it difficult to be around women with children (Benyamini et al., 2002; Phipps, 1993). Guilt, blame, or just sheer mounting distress often compromise the one relationship that is most important at this point: their marital relationship (Mahlstedt, 1985; Remennick, 2000). The fantasy is there, leading them to keep pursuing treatment, and although they may keep busy to distract themselves, they are not actively pursuing other life goals.

Women who assigned the greatest importance to having children also reported the greatest fertility stress (Abbey et al., 1992). Since most women who are willing to undergo the stressful infertility procedures probably view having children as important, this finding may actually reflect greater distress among women whose lives are focused mainly on the goal of having a child. This style may be more common among women with lower education and occupational status, who expect parenthood to be a central part of their identity and their main source of personal growth (Newton et al., 1992; van Balen & Trimbos-Kemper, 1995). The same may be true of women who feel great social/cultural pressure to bear children. Remennick (2000), interviewed Israeli women who cope with infertility in the very pronatalist Jewish/Israeli society, and found that many of them felt that they are living their lives in the shadow of infertility: "You become totally obsessed with achieving pregnancy, it becomes your only focus and preoccupation in life" (p. 9). Only educated women are daring and able to challenge the motherhood mandate in pronatalist societies (Kirkman & Rosenthal, 1999; Remennick, 2000).

Paradoxically, the focus-on-infertility style is the easiest route to cope on the day-to-day basis: There is less tension between the demands of infertility and those of other areas of life or other potential identities when those become subordinate to the main goal and potential identity of fertility. They believe that once the fantasy becomes real, all their problems will be solved: the more anxious women in Achmon et al.'s (1989) sample believed that infertility will solve all their problems in life; the infertile identity will be replaced by the parent identity, in which case they will not feel the loss of parts of their other identities. For the time being, their hopes are focused on the fantasy, which serves as their escape. Their high expectations of treatment success may be their way to escape their growing distress. Infertile women who reported high use of escapism were the most distressed (Stanton, Tennen, Affleck, & Mendola, 1992; Terry & Hynes, 1998) while optimistic women used escape less than other women and fared better after treatment failure (Litt et al., 1992).

The Assimilating-Infertility-into-Life Reaction Style

Many women take active measures to limit the impact of infertility on their lives. Women who choose this reaction style maintain the fantasy of motherhood but also actively work to sustain their hope. Although infertility is the central issue with which they are dealing, they make efforts to continue developing their careers, their personal interests, and their social and marital relationships. All these areas are affected by the energy and time that infertility demands, but continuing to invest in them provides sources of satisfaction that restore some of the depleted pool of energy. It is not easy to maintain this style since infertility constantly intrudes into their lives in ways that are difficult to block or minimize. They experience constant tension between the demands of infertility treatments and other demands in their lives. These tensions are symbolized by the arrows in figure 1.

The Infertility-as-a-Separate-Challenge Reaction Style

These women "fight" infertility as if there is nothing else in life, and stand up to all other challenges in their lives as if infertility did not exist. Their hope is broad-based and focused on their quality of life, with future parenthood as one of its aspects. The separation between infertility and other life domains is very demanding and thus difficult to maintain: there is constant tension at the border separating infertility from their other life domains. An analogous pattern, of seemingly contradictory ways of hoping, was found among cancer patients, with constant tension between "hoping for something," that is, hoping even against all hopes, and at the same time "living in hope," that is, maintaining hope through confirmative relationships with others that allow one to live as normally as possible (Benzein et al., 2001). Schmidt (1998) found several coping styles among infertile couples, some of them "open-minded" couples who were in control of their treatment, openly shared their problem and feelings with others, and in the meantime created a life that included parental care for others (e.g., "borrowing" friends' children, foster children, "parenting" pets). These may be the people who view infertility primarily as a challenge rather than a loss (Hansell, Thorn, Prentice-Dunn, & Floyd, 1998).

There is a clear line between this style and denial or avoidance of infertility. Denial means refusal to believe that a stressor exists, or acting as if it were not real (Ben-Zur & Breznitz, 1997). At later stages of treatment, when outright denial is impossible, some women may resort to avoidance: Miller et al. (1998) suggested, on the basis of their findings on avoidance among women undergoing infertility treatment, that the avoidant women may be more likely to drop out or neglect their treatment. This is exactly the opposite of the infertility-as-a-separate-challenge style that characterizes women who are very open and active about coping with infertility. These women do not simply distract themselves by keeping busy, but actively compensate themselves, pamper themselves, and invest in other goals in their life. These actions result in significantly higher levels of well-being, while avoidance results in lower well-being and greater distress (Benyamini et al., 2002).

Evidence for the benefits of this style was reported by Merari, Feldberg, Shitrit, Elizur, and Modan (1996): Women who succeeded in conceiving following IVF treatment, compared with those who did not conceive, were more likely to be working and to have sought alternative methods for solving their problem, such as adoption. Additional indirect support comes from the often documented correlation between age and better adjustment to infertility (McEwan, Costello, & Taylor, 1987; with the exception of the oldest women with "biological clock" anxieties, Koropatnick et al., 1993). These women may have had more years to develop broad interests and accomplish some of their life goals, and thus parenthood is not their only means of ascertaining their identity and self-worth (Newton et al., 1992). Having a self-representation that involves a greater number of roles or identities (i.e., high self-complexity), can buffer against the negative effects of stressful life events (Linville, 1985, 1987), especially if these roles and identities allow one to maintain many independent *positive* self-representations (Morgan & Janoff-Bulman, 1994).

HOPE ALONG THE STAGES OF INFERTILITY: DISENGAGEMENT

Infertility treatments begin with a fantasy that has no question about statistics attached to it. The reality that couples face leads to processes of wishful thinking that yield cognitively and motivationally biased interpretations of their personal odds of success. However, with repeated failure, the grain of truth in the overly optimistic perceived odds becomes smaller and smaller. Eventually, the costs and risks become too high and the chance of success becomes so low that only the fantasy remains. The decision to end treatment is a very difficult one (Braverman, 1996). It is complicated by the fact that there is almost always a slight chance that the next treatment will succeed. Even when doctors try to make it clear that the chances are very slim, they do not entirely rule them out. Some couples conceive spontaneously after quitting treatment; others take a break, return to give it another shot, and succeed. As one woman phrased it: "There is always hope ... you keep on hoping something will happen ... as long as there's hope ... you're not willing to give up" (Gonzalez, 2000, p. 625). Even after abandoning attempts to conceive, applying for adoption, or stating that the infertility crisis has been "resolved," most women interviewed indicated that they would participate in any new reproductive options that would enhance the likelihood of a biological pregnancy (Leiblum, Kemmann, Colburn, Pasquale, & DeLisi, 1987). Thus, until menopause, infertility never has complete closure.

With no clear endpoint, the hypothesis-testing process preserves the fantasy for as long as possible. The ambiguity regarding having reached the "end of the road" explains the difficulty of rejecting the fertility hypothesis and reaching the decision to stop treatment (Remennick, 2000). Women whose lives were focused solely on infertility are in the most difficult situation. The woman interviewed by Remennick (2000) and cited earlier commenting about how infertility became the focus of her life also added: "If you quit, life would lose any sense whatsoever." When they realize that the fantasy may never come true, women whose lives focused on infertility are often devastated and left with a great void that is difficult to fill.

Women who assimilated infertility into their lives but remained involved in other areas may also be devastated, but are more likely to have the emotional resources needed to cope with the tremendous feeling of loss. They have other life domains to which they can turn for self-esteem and satisfaction. Those who kept an active hopeful style of coping with their lives in general and the challenge of infertility as part of it will suffer the least: Giving up the fantasy could still be just as devastating as it is for other women, but they have to cope only with the loss of this potential part of their identity, as they have continued to nurture all other parts throughout the years.

A Final Note on the Three Reaction Styles

The presentation of the three reaction styles is intended to provide a useful terminology. However, one should keep in mind that it is somewhat simplified. First, as mentioned above, the degree to which infertility takes over, or is dealt with as a separate challenge, is a continuous dimension. Second, while some women employ a similar style throughout the infertility experience, others move along this dimension with time. For many women disengagement from infertility is a slow transformation in which they gradually diminish the place of infertility and its treatments in their lives and go back to activities that they have given up. Third, there are additional variations on the theme of future outlook in infertility, such as defensive pessimism, that can co-exist with hope (Sandelowski, Harris et al., 1990).

CONCLUSION: A BROAD CONCEPT OF HOPE AS THE NARRATIVE OF INFERTILITY

People attempt to make sense of their lives and create a coherent life story. Kirkman (2001) noted that "infertile women must deal not only with the blow inflicted by infertility to their sense of self, but also with the difficulties of presenting a simple and coherent life story in the social world." Instead of one coherent story, they must live with three possible scenarios and no control over which of them will come true. One is the "fantasy" scenario that includes a denial of the problem and a belief that this will soon be over. The second is the "wishful thinking and difficulties" scenario, which acknowledges the problem, expects it to be solved, but also acknowledges the difficulties in overcoming it and the possibility that it may take some time. The third is the "failure" scenario, the possibility that the problem will not be resolved and the couple will remain biologically childless. Being able to handle all three scenarios simultaneously, or to alternate among them, is crucial to a realistic but optimistic view of infertility. Hope, in its broader sense that is focused on all life goals, including the quest for a child, can provide the positive mood and energy that is required for dealing with the different future scenarios. Hope can encompass all three scenarios and allow one to create a temporary narrative that is based on this broad concept of hope.

Women who applied for adoption had *higher* hopes of success of the IVF treatment they were undergoing at the same time (Reading, 1989). This suggests that they were able to simultaneously consider scenarios other than the one provided by the fantasy. Even though pondering more than one scenario means that they also have to face the failure scenario, taking steps in more than one direction is one way to regain some of the control lost in the process of being treated for infertility (Lorber & Greenfeld, 1990). These women are able to break down the unattained long-term goal into smaller steps and concentrate on achieving them, a characteristic of high hope people (Snyder, Ilardi, Michael, & Cheavens, 2000). Although the general uncertainty about which scenario will prevail remains, these women are actively translating their hopes into effective steps that will allow them to achieve the best possible quality of life for them.

IMPLICATIONS FOR COUNSELING INFERTILE WOMEN

Many scholars have referred to the resolution of infertility as a process of mourning over the loss of the dream and consequently suggested that it should be treated within a grief or bereavement model. Others have criticized this model, claiming that there is no resolution of infertility, only restitution (Gonzalez, 2000), and that the grief model fails because there is no actual loss (Menning, 1980). When only the fantasy remains, many women experience deep sadness and depression; in contrast with bereavement, this depression is not a stage that can be worked through (Hunt & Monach, 1997). Over time, it becomes chronic sorrow (Unruh & McGrath, 1985).

A broad concept of hope can provide an alternative framework for counseling infertile women. It is not intended to focus solely on the benefits and positive aspects, promoting a "rosy glow" that is unreal, ineffective, and will be perceived by women as insensitive (Stanton et al., 1991). Its primary focus is on reviewing all life goals as worthwhile and encouraging their pursuit as a way to enrich one's life with sources of well-being and satisfaction. It should help remind women that their self-worth is not dependent on parenthood, and that they deserve to be taken care of and to take care of themselves, no less and maybe more than other women.

In order to achieve the maximal benefits from the work of hope, women need to gradually transform hope from a simple belief in a quick solution to their problem to a coping style, a coping task, and a resource for coping (Rustoen, 1995). The cost is the need to add infertility to one's life, not to substitute it for life domains to which they previously devoted their time and energy, and the need to keep in mind simultaneously several contradictory future scenarios.

Counseling is especially important for supporting women and their partners in crossing several "bridges" that await them. The first bridge is the
one from a past orientation to a future one, from a focus on cause and
blame to a focus on the next steps that need to be taken in order to deal
with infertility and other life goals. The second bridge is the one that leads
from denial to acceptance of the problem. Acceptance is part of a realistic
evaluation of the situation and does not preclude hope. It allows one to
devote energy to the active work of hope, from its narrow sense in working up expectations before each treatment cycle, to the broader sense of
continuing to invest in many life domains.

Those who do not conceive or bear a child need to cross the third and last
bridge, the decision to end treatment. They will have to live with the sorrow
and depression that ensue. If their hopes had helped them nurture many life
domains along the way, they will have other sources for self-identity, self-
worth, and well-being. Counseling at this stage is an example of what Omer
and Rosenbaum (1997) proposed: Therapy that is intended to assist clients
to let go of their hope—a "work of despair"—that can be energizing and
liberating. Many couples feel relief after having completely given up the
pursuit of biological parenthood (Daniluk, 1996). They are free now to
build up hopes in other areas of their lives and pursue other goals. Those
who have done this all along are at a better starting point.

SUMMARY

Infertility is a highly stressful condition that threatens the personal and
marital well-being of young couples who experience difficulties in conceiving and bearing a child. The unbridgeable gap between the cultural
mandate of parenthood and the demanding reality and uncertainty of the
treatments invariably creates distress. Women around the world are being
raised with the fantasy of bearing a child and becoming a mother and find
it difficult to deal with obstacles to attaining this goal. Most women form
unrealistically high expectations of treatment success. As time goes by and
treatment failures mount, these expectations are often maintained, although
they become more of a fantasy as they drift further away from reality.

Levels of distress vary among women, but greater variation is seen in
their levels of well-being. Maintaining active hope along the stages of
infertility treatments can promote well-being and quality of life, even if it
does not alleviate the distress. A broad concept of hope can help women
nurture themselves and make progress in other areas, while undergoing

treatment. Such active hope is focused not solely on the goal of parent-hood and on the treatments as the means to achieve this goal, but on goals in diverse domains of life. It is essential to preserving their well-being as they walk the long road to fertility. If, eventually, they do not succeed in conceiving, their dream is shattered, but the broad sense of hope they maintained along the way and the investments they have made in their lives as individuals and couples will serve as resources for disengaging from infertility and regaining control over their lives.

REFERENCES

Abbey, A., & Halman, L. J. (1995). The role of perceived control, attributions, and meaning in members' of infertile couples well-being. *Journal of Social and Clinical Psychology,* 14(3), 271–296.

Abbey, A., Halman, L. J., & Andrews, F. M. (1992). Psychosocial, treatment, and demographic predictors of the stress associated with infertility. *Fertility and Sterility,* 57(1), 122–128.

Achmon, Y., Tadir, Y., Fisch, B., & Ovadia, J. (1989). Emotional characteristics and attitudes of couples during in vitro fertilization treatment. *Harefuah,* 116(4), 189–192.

Armor, D. A., & Taylor, S. E. (1998). Situated optimism: specific outcome expectancies and self-regulation. *Advances in Experimental Social Psychology,* 30, 310–379.

Becker, G., & Nachtigall, R. D. (1991). Ambiguous responsibility in the doctor-patient relationship: The case of infertility. *Social Science and Medicine,* 32(8), 875–885.

Becker, G., & Nachtigall, R. D. (1994). "Born to be a mother": The cultural con-struction of risk in infertility treatment in the U.S. *Social Science and Medicine,* 39(4), 507–518.

Benyamini, Y., Geffen-Bardarian, Y., Gozlan, M., Tabiv, G., Shiloh, S., & Kokia, E. (2003). *Customizing the measurement of coping: The case of women coping with infertility treatments.* Manuscript submitted for publication.

Benyamini, Y., Leventhal, E. A., & Leventhal H. (1997). Attributional processes in health. In A. Baum, C. McManus, S. Newman, J. Weinman, & R. West (Eds.), *Cambridge handbook of psychology, health and medicine.* Cambridge, UK: Cambridge University Press.

Benyamini, Y., Primor-Horowitz, R., Shiloh, S., Gozlan, M., & Kokia, E. (2000). *Between hope and fantasy: The relationship between optimism, expecta-tions and psychological state among women undergoing infertility treat-ments.* Paper presented at the 15th National Conference of the Israeli Organization of Social Work, Tel Aviv, Israel.

Benzein, E., Norberg, A., & Saveman, B.-I. (2001). The meaning of the lived experience of hope in patients with cancer in palliative home care. *Palliative Medicine,* 15, 117–126.

Benzein, E., & Saveman, B.-I. (1998). One step towards the understanding of hope: a concept analysis. *International Journal of Nursing Studies,* 35, 322–329.

Ben-Zur, H., & Breznitz, S. (1997). Denial, anxiety, and information processing. In M. S. Myslobodsky (Ed.), *The mythomanias: the nature of deception and self-deception* (pp. 225–243). Mahwah, New Jersey: Lawrence Erlbaum Associates.

Blenner, J. L. (1990). Passage through infertility treatment: A stage theory. *IMAGE: Journal of Nursing Scholarship,* 22(3), 153–158.

Blenner, J. L. (1992). Stress and mediators: patients' perceptions of infertility treatment. *Nursing Research,* 41(2), 92–97.

Braverman, A. M. (1996). Issues involved in the decision to end infertility treatment: When is enough enough? *In Session: Psychotherapy in Practice,* 2(2), 85–96.

Buehler, R., Griffin, D., & MacDonald, H. (1997). The role of motivated reasoning in optimistic time predictions. *Personality and Social Psychology Bulletin,* 23(3), 238–247.

Burns, L. H. (1987). Infertility as boundary ambiguity: One theoretical perspective. *Family Process,* 26, 359–372.

Callan, V. J., & Hennessey, J. F. (1986). IVF and adoption: the experiences of infertile couples. *Australian Journal of Early Childhood,* 11(4), 32–36.

Carver, C., Scheier, M. F., & Pozo, C. (1992). Conceptualizing the process of coping with health problems. In H. S. Friedman (Ed.), *Hostility, Coping and Health.* Washington, DC: American Psychological Association.

Carver, C., Scheier, M. F., & Weintraub, J. K. (1989). Assessing coping strategies: a theoretically based approach. *Journal of Personality and Social Psychology,* 56(2), 267–283.

Cook, E. P. (1987). Characteristics of the biopsychosocial crisis of infertility. *Journal of Counseling and Development,* 65, 465–470.

Daniels, K. R. (1989). Psychosocial factors for couples awaiting in vitro fertilization. *Social Work in Health Care,* 14(2), 81–98.

Daniluk, J. (1996). When treatment fails: the transition to biological childlessness for infertile women. *Women and Therapy,* 19(2), 81–98.

de Zoeten, M. J., Tymstra, T., & Alberda, A. T. (1987). The waiting list for IVF: The motivations and expectations of women waiting for IVF treatment. *Human Reproduction,* 2(7), 623–626.

Demyttenaere, K., Bonte, L., Gheldof, M., Vervaeke, M., Meuleman, C., Vanderschuerem, D., & D'Hooghe, T. (1998). Coping style and depression level influence outcome in *in vitro* fertilization. *Fertility and Sterility,* 69(6), 1026–1033.

Domar, A.D., Zuttermeister, P.C., & Friedman, R. (1993). The psychological impact of infertility: a comparison with patients with other medical conditions. *Journal of Psychosomatic Obstetrics and Gynecology,* 14(Special Issue), 45–52.

Dufault, K., & Martocchio, B. C. (1985). Hope: Its spheres and dimensions. *Nursing Clinics of North America,* 20(2), 379–391.

Dunkel-Schetter, C., & Lobel, M. (1991). Psychological reactions to infertility. In A.L. Stanton & C. Dunkel-Schetter (Eds.), *Infertility: perspectives from stress and coping research* (pp. 29–57). New York: Plenum Press.

Folkman, S., & Lazarus, R.S. (1985). If it changes it must be a process: A study of emotion and coping during three stages of a college examination. *Journal of Personality and Social Psychology,* 48(1), 150–170.

Frank, D.I. (1990). Factors related to decisions about infertility treatment. *Journal of Obstetric, Gynecological, and Neonatal Nursing,* 19(2), 162–167.

Freeman, E.W., Boxer, A., Rickels, K., Tureck, R.W., & Mastroianni, L.J. (1985). Psychological evaluation and support in a program of in vitro fertilization and embryo transfer. *Fertility and Sterility,* 43(1), 48–53.

Glover, L., Hunter, M., Richards, J.M., Katz, M., & Abel, P. (1999). Development of the fertility adjustment scale. *Fertility and Sterility,* 72(4), 623–628.

Gonzalez, L.O. (2000). Infertility as a transformational process: A framework for psychotherapeutic support of infertile women. *Issues in Mental Health Nursing,* 21, 619–633.

Greil, A.L. (1997). Infertility and psychological distress: A critical review of the literature. *Social Science and Medicine,* 45(11), 1679–1704.

Greil, A.L., Porter, K.L., Leitko, T.A., & Riscilli, C. (1989). Why me?: The idiocies of infertile women and men. *Sociology of Health and Illness,* 11(3), 213–229.

Hansell, P., Thorn, B.E., Prentice-Dunn, S., & Floyd, D. (1998). The relationship of primary appraisals of infertility and other gynecological stressors to coping. *Journal of Clinical Psychology in Medical Settings,* 5(2), 133–145.

Helweg-Larsen, M., Sadeghian, P., & Webb, M.S. (2002). The stigma of being pessimistically biased. *Journal of Social and Clinical Psychology,* 21(1), 92–107.

Hunt, J., & Monach, J.H. (1997). Beyond the bereavement model: the significance of depression for infertility counseling. *Human Reproduction,* 12(Suppl), 188–194.

Imeson, M., & McMurray, A. (1996). Couples' experiences of infertility: a phenomenological study. *Journal of Advanced Nursing,* 24, 1014–1022.

Jacoby, R. (1993). "The miserable hath no other medicine, but only hope": Some conceptual considerations on hope and stress. *Stress Medicine,* 9, 61–69.

Johnston, M., Shaw, R., & Bird, D. (1987). "Test-tube baby" procedures: Stress and judgments under uncertainty. *Psychology and Health,* 1, 25–38.

Jones, S.C., & Hunter, M. (1996). The influence of context and discourse on infertility experience. *Journal of Reproductive and Infant Psychology,* 14, 93–111.

Keinan, G., & Sivan, D. (2001). The effects of stress and desire for control on the formation of causal attributions. *Journal of Research in Personality,* 35(2), 127–137.

Kemeter, P., & Fiegl, J. (1998). Adjusting to life when assisted conception fails. *Human Reproduction,* 13(4), 1099–1105.

Kirkman, M. (2001). Thinking of something to say: Public and private narratives of infertility. *Health Care for Women International,* 22, 523–535.

Kirkman, M., & Rosenthal, D. (1999). Representations of reproductive technology in women's narratives of infertility. *Women & Health,* 29(2), 17–36.

Koropatnick, S., Daniluk, J., & Pattinson, H. A. (1993). Infertility: A non-event transition. *Fertility and Sterility,* 59(1), 163–171.

Lalos, A., Lalos, O., Jacobsson, L., & von Schoultz, B. (1985). Psychological reactions to the medical investigation and surgical treatment of infertility. *Gynecologic and Obstetric Investigation,* 20(4), 209–217.

Leiblum, S. R. (1993). The impact of infertility on sexual and marital satisfaction. *Annual Review of Sex Research,* 4, 99–120.

Leiblum, S. R., Kemmann, E., Colburn, D., Pasquale, S., & DeLisi, A. M. (1987). Unsuccessful in *in vitro* fertilization: a follow-up study. *Journal of In Vitro Fertilization and Embryo Transfer,* 4(1), 46–50.

Linville, P. (1985). Self-complexity and affective extremity: Don't put all of your eggs in one basket. *Social Cognition,* 3, 94–120.

Linville, P. (1987). Self-complexity as a buffer against stress-related illness and depression. *Journal of Personality and Social Psychology,* 52, 663–676.

Litt, M. D., Tennen, H., Affleck, G., & Klock, S. (1992). Coping and cognitive factors in adaptation to in vitro fertilization failure. *Journal of Behavioral Medicine,* 15(2), 171–187.

Lorber, J., & Greenfeld, D. (1990). Couples' experiences with in vitro fertilization: A phenomenological approach. In S. Machiach, Z. Ben-Rafael, N. Laufer, & J. G. Schenker (Eds.), *Advances in assisted reproductive technologies* (pp. 965–971). New York: Plenum.

Mahlstedt, P. P. (1985). The psychological component of infertility. *Fertility and Sterility,* 43(3), 335–346.

McEwan, K. L., Costello, C. G., & Taylor, P. J. (1987). Adjustment to infertility. *Journal of Abnormal Psychology,* 96(2), 108–116.

McLaney, M. A., Tennen, H., Affleck, G., & Fitzgerald, T. (1995). Reactions to impaired fertility: The vicissitudes of primary and secondary control appraisals. *Women's Health: Research on Gender, Behavior, and Policy,* 1(2), 143–159.

Menning, B. E. (1980). The emotional needs of infertile couples. *Fertility and Sterility,* 34(4), 313–319.

Menninger, K. (1959). Hope. *American Journal of Psychiatry,* 116, 481–491.

Menninger, K. (1963). *The vital balance: The vital process in mental health and illness.* New York: Viking.

Merari, D., Feldberg, D., Shitrit, A., Elizur, A., & Modan, B. (1996). Psychosocial characteristics of women undergoing in vitro fertilization: A study of treatment outcome. *Israel Journal of Obstetrics and Gynecology,* 7, 65–72.

Miller, S. M., Mischel, W., Schroeder, C. M., Buzaglo, J. S., Hurley, K., Schreiber, P., & Mandan, C. E. (1998). Intrusive and avoidant ideation among females pursuing infertility treatment. *Psychology and Health,* 13, 847–858.

Milne, B. J. (1988). Couples' experiences with in vitro fertilization. *Journal of Obstetric, Gynecologic, and Neonatal Nursing,* 17(5), 347–352.

Modell, J. (1989). Last Chance Babies: Interpretations of parenthood in an in vitro fertilization program. *Medical Anthropology Quarterly,* 3, 124–138.

Morgan, H., & Janoff-Bulman, R. (1994). Positive and negative self-complexity: Patterns of adjustment following traumatic versus non-traumatic life events. *Journal of Social and Clinical Psychology,* 13, 63–85.

Morrow, K. A., Thoreson, R. W., & Penney, L. L. (1995). Predictors of psychological distress among infertility clinic patients. *Journal of Consulting and Clinical Psychology,* 63(1), 163–167.

Newton, C. R., Hearn, M. T., Yuzpe, A. A., & Houle, M. (1992). Motives for parenthood and response to failed in vitro fertilization: Implications for counseling. *Journal of Assisted Reproduction and Genetics,* 9(1), 24–31.

Newton, C. R., Sherrard, W., & Glavac, I. (1999). The fertility problem inventory: measuring perceived infertility-related stress. *Fertility and Sterility,* 72(1), 54–62.

Oettingen, G. (1996). Positive fantasy and motivation. In P. M. Gollwitzer & J. A. Bargh (Eds.), *The psychology of action: Linking cognition and motivation to behavior* (pp. 236–259). New York: Guilford Press.

Omer, H., & Rosenbaum, R. (1997). Disease of hope and the work of despair. *Psychotherapy,* 34(3), 225–232.

Pasch, L. A., & Dunkel-Schetter, C. (1997). Fertility problems: Complex issues faced by women and couples. In S. J. Gallant, G. P. Keita, & R. Royak-Schaler (Eds.), *Health Care for Women: Psychological, social, and behavioral influences* (pp. 187–201). Washington, DC: American Psychological Association.

Phipps, S. A. A. (1993). A phenomenological study of couples' infertility: Gender influence. *Holistic Nurse Practitioner,* 7(2), 44–56.

Reading, A. E. (1989). Decision making and in vitro fertilization: the influence of emotional state. *Journal of Psychosomatic Obstetrics and Gynecology,* 10, 107–112.

Remennick, L. (2000). Childless in the land of imperative motherhood: Stigma and coping among infertile Israeli women. *Sex Roles,* 43(11/12), 821–842.

Rosen, B., Irvine, J., Ritvo, P., Shapiro, H., Stewart, D., Reynolds, K., Robinson, G., Thomas, J., Neuman, J., & Murphy, J. (1997). The feasibility of assessing women's perceptions of the risks and benefits of fertility drug therapy in relation to ovarian cancer risk. *Fertility and Sterility,* 68(1), 90–94.

Rustoen, T. (1995). Hope and quality of life, two central issues for cancer patients: A theoretical analysis. *Cancer Nursing,* 18(5), 355–361.

Sandelowski, M., Harris, B.G., & Holditch-Davis, D. (1990). Pregnant moments: The process of conception in infertile couples. *Research in Nursing & Health,* 13, 273–282.

Sandelowski, M., Holditch-Davis, D., & Harris, B.G. (1990). Living the life: explanations of infertility. *Sociology of Health and Illness,* 12(2), 195–215.

Schmidt, L. (1998). Infertile couples' assessment of infertility treatment. *Acta Obstetricia et Gynecologica Scandinavica,* 77, 649–653.

Shiloh, S., Larom, S., & Ben-Rafael, Z. (1991). The meaning of treatment for infertility: Cognitive determinants and structure. *Journal of Applied Social Psychology,* 21(10), 855–874.

Snyder, C.R., Ilardi, S., Michael, S.T., & Cheavens, J. (2000). Hope theory: updating a common process for psychological change. In C.R. Snyder & R.E. Ingram (Eds.), *Handbook of psychological change: Psychotherapy processes & practices for the twenty-first century* (pp. 128–153). New York: Wiley.

Stanton, A.L., Tennen, H., Affleck, G., & Mendola, R. (1991). Cognitive appraisal and adjustment to infertility. *Women & Health,* 17(3), 1–15.

Stanton, A.L., Tennen, H., Affleck, G., & Mendola, R. (1992). Coping and adjustment to infertility. *Journal of Social and Clinical Psychology,* 11(1), 1–13.

Taylor, S.E. (1983). Adjustment to threatening events. *American Psychologist,* 38, 1161–1173.

Taylor, S.E., & Brown, J.D. (1988). Illusions and well-being: A social psychological perspective on mental health. *Psychological Bulletin,* 103, 193–210.

Terry, D.J., & Hynes, G.J. (1998). Adjustment to a low-control situation: Reexamining the role of coping responses. *Journal of Personality and Social Psychology,* 74(4), 1078–1092.

Trope, Y., Gervey, B., & Liberman, N. (1997). Wishful thinking from a pragmatic hypothesis testing perspective. In M.S. Myslobodsky (Ed.), *The mythomanias: The nature of deception and self-deception* (pp. 105–131). Mahwah, New Jersey: Lawrence Erlbaum Associates.

Unruh, A.M., & McGrath, P.J. (1985). The psychology of female infertility: Toward a new perspective. *Health Care for Women International,* 6, 369–381.

van Balen, F., & Trimbos-Kemper, T.C.M. (1995). Involuntarily childless couples: Their desire to have children and their motives. *Journal of Psychosomatic Obstetrics and Gynecology,* 16, 137–144.

Weinstein, N.D. (1980). Unrealistic optimism about future life events. *Journal of Personality and Social Psychology,* 39, 806–820.

Williams, L.S. (1988). "It's going to work for me." Responses to failure of IVF. *Birth,* 15(3), 153–156.

Woods, N.F., Olshansky, E.F., & Draye, M.A. (1991). Infertility: Women's experiences. *Health Care for Women International,* 12, 179–190.

Chapter 8

HOPE AND RECOVERY: THE EXPERIENCE OF PRISONERS OF WAR DURING THE ATTRITION WAR[1]

Amia Lieblich

The apparently complete recovery of the Israeli prisoners of war (POWs) from their long incarceration in Egypt during the Attrition War,[2] and their amazing lifestyle as a group of ten men living closely together in prison, are among the most heroic and significant stories circulating in our war-experienced society. Above and beyond their own history, the popularity of this group of prisoners in Israel results from one of their major achievements, namely the translation of Tolkien's book *The Hobbit* (1937). This classic work was translated by the POWs from English to Hebrew and published in Israel after their release (Tolkien, 1977). The translation project epitomized their productive life in prison and symbolized their hope and struggle to return home. In the present chapter, I will tell the story of this group of POWs (for a full description and analysis see Lieblich, 1994), unravel the riddle of their well-being and recovery, and analyze the place and meaning of the translation project within their survival narrative. As will be clarified, hope for their future safe return to their homes and reunion with their families plays a central role in this story, and its maintenance in prison, in spite of hardship and uncertainty, was one of the major elements in the prisoners' physical and psychological coping.

Before expanding on the subject, however, let me emphasize that all the descriptions and conceptualizations in the following pages are based on narratives presented to me in oral form, during interview-conversations that took place 13 years after the POW's liberation. We are dealing, therefore, with subjective accounts, created in the context of my interaction with the men and our joint purpose—that is, to write a book—filtered by memory and forgetting. Each teller's motivation to convey a positive self-image was naturally a major factor in the way the individual stories were narrated.[3] In other words, I am dealing with *reconstructions of the past* rather than with history or reality (see also Spence 1982; Sarbin 1986; Lieblich, Tuval-Mashiach, and Zilber, 1998; Gergen, 1999).

THE STORY OF THE POWs' GROUP: FALL AND REDEMPTION

The following section is mainly descriptive; it presents the collective narrative of the prisoners, as constructed from their individual accounts, in chronological order. The analysis of the material, focusing on the topics of hope and recovery, will be provided in later sections.

The ten Israeli men who later formed the group in the Egyptian prison had all fallen in to captivity between December 1969 and July 1970. The first four were Dan,[4] a 37-year-old reservist, the commander of a military border post on the Suez Canal, who had been severely wounded in the attack preceding his capture; David (19), a parachutist in obligatory service, and Motti B. and Motti C.—two 22-year-old civilians working as military canteen vendors. They were each captured in combat by Egyptian commando units who had penetrated the then-Israeli territory on the western bank of the Suez Canal. The next six captives were all airmen, Israeli Air Force pilots or navigators, whose planes were hit during missions in the Egyptian skies. These men—Rami, Menachem, Yitzhak, Avi, Amos Z., and Amos L.[5]—20 to 31 years old, were captured after parachuting from their planes. One of them, Menachem, was seriously injured during his jump and was hospitalized in Cairo until July 1971, when he joined the POWs' group in prison.[6]

Immediately after being taken captive, each of the men went through a period of interrogations, which lasted from a few weeks to three months. Torture, threats, isolation, and deprivation of basic needs were among the methods used by the Egyptians to make the prisoners talk. At the same time, the POWs developed their individual strategies to avoid pressure and minimize their pain, trying to maintain standards of behavior that they considered appropriate. Yet all the men underwent extreme physical and mental ordeal and experienced moral dilemmas concerning their conduct around concealing or divulging vital military secrets.

Through the period of interrogation the POWs were kept in solitary confinement, sometimes in extremely small, cold, or dark cells. After the termination of the intense stage of interrogation, solitary confinement went on for about three months more. Loneliness, loss of time-space orientation, and immense insecurity characterize this stage, together with continuous physical suffering due to deprivation, and rare hallucinatory states. Gradually, however, most of the men recovered from the initial trauma and found ways to structure the empty time, as for example:

> I made a daily schedule for myself. I didn't want to sleep late and waste my time. I got up at eight o'clock, exercised for about half an hour, jogged a kilometer in my cell, and then dedicated my time to thinking. Every day I made myself concentrate on abstract thoughts for an hour. (Yitzhak, p. 95[7])

> I used to occupy my mind so that I wouldn't go nuts. I found a nail and used it to write on the wall. I made up all kinds of problems, such as planning a business, how I would build a supermarket, how much I needed to invest, what would I gain. (Motti B., p. 80, Heb.)

> I was very proud when finally I learned to stand on my hands. This was an old wish of mine, from the time I was a chubby little fellow. A bell was sounded in prison every two hours, and this was my sign to stand on my hands. At first I had to lean on the wall, and my hands would get sore and tired. Gradually I improved a great deal and managed to stand for a long time without any support. (Rami, p. 92)

The first visits of the Red Cross agents occurred while the men were still in solitary confinement. These were events of tremendous significance in the men's lives at the time. The agents encouraged the POWs, brought them news and letters and sometimes a book, and promised that efforts would be made towards getting all the Israeli prisoners united in a common cell. Their role can be conceived as representatives of the free world outside, as agents of the international law concerning POWs, and as "agents of hope"—a concept to which I will return later.

The next stage of the narrative relates to the prisoners' meeting each other and being gathered in one room—an event that came close in exhilaration, according to some of the narrators, to the day of their liberation. The four POWs captured earlier were gathered first, and lived together for a few weeks. Somewhat later, the five captured airmen were added one by

one to the group in the common room. Menachem, the wounded naviga-
tor, was brought from the hospital several months later.

The process of meeting each other was extremely moving for the men,
and life together seemed to them at the time as a remedy to most of their
misery. This is exemplified in the following quote:

> I kept demanding that they put us all together. Loneliness was terrible for
> me. On the day I was moved, finally, I experienced tremendous joy. I found
> out that the common room was actually very near my solitary cell. When I
> was brought in, they were all there already, except David...It took me some
> time to realize the significance of being together with others in the room.
> Then the stories started to come. (Amos Z., p. 110)

As the group living together grew from four to ten men, the need to
organize their common reality became prominent. Putting together ten
frustrated and anxious men from different backgrounds, with various
needs and moods, in a closed, crowded space might have produced a
catastrophe. Even when physical conditions greatly improved, uncertainty about their future loomed large in the POWs' minds and might have
produced high interpersonal friction. In this group, however, order pre-
vailed over the potential chaos. The first issues that were organized were
very concrete: sharing food and eating together, the use of the single bath-
room, habits of getting up in the morning and having quiet time for sleep
and rest, contacts with the guards and prison authorities, setting priorities
for requests from the Red Cross agents, appropriate dress, appearance,
and such matters. Would such issues be organized and determined by
command, namely the authority of military rank, or by consensus of the
entire group?

In their accounts, which are too long to quote here, the men tried to capture the transition from chaos to structure and routine. This process culminated in the establishment of democratic order in the group, instituting a
"council of ten members," which convened with rotating chairmanship
once a week, on Friday evening after lights out, to discuss problems of the
group and make decisions about its life together. A memorandum of these
weekly meetings was recorded in a notebook, which then became the
"diary of the POWs' group in prison." It is a document that provides a
vivid picture of life in captivity, although some of the entries and names
were coded, to avoid Egyptian interception.

Another important aspect of the group's organization was the study program, which was started about six months after the union. All classes were

taught by the prisoners themselves. Courses were offered mainly in English and mathematics, in two levels, beginners and advanced. The "school" operated every morning, aside from Saturday, holidays, and summer breaks, for the whole duration of the men's captivity.

The social life of the group consisted of many activities, from bridge games to art work of various kinds. Some of the activities were individual, such as painting, knitting, or building models from matches, but most of them were conducted by several men together. On the one hand, the prisoners experienced a great deal of togetherness, even when doing something highly personal like reading a book or writing a letter; on the other hand, individual privacy within the crowded environment was highly respected, and exposure of feelings or intimate matters was rare. While tensions did arise among the men, it seems that the group found constructive means for reducing them and for minimizing fights and confrontations. Subgroups, coalitions, or scape-goating did not develop, in spite of the wide range of personalities. There were, naturally, occasional negative social experiences for some of the men. In their stories, however, they marveled at the lack of aggression or any form of violence within the group.

The leadership of two men, Rami and Menachem, stabilized the interpersonal relations in the group: Menachem by being task-oriented—driving the group to higher standards of living and achievements, and Rami by channeling emotional expressions, becoming a father figure for all, and invoking hope for the future. All in all, the emerging social system resembled a kibbutz and was compared in the men's narratives to a utopia.

The POWs' emotions of longing, fear, or despair, their fantasies regarding escape or release, were rarely displayed in public. They were able and willing, however, to dwell upon them openly in our interviews, thirteen years after their liberation. An example is this confession of Avi:

> The sense of the lost time was the hardest thing to take. I couldn't free myself for a moment from the uncertainty about my future. This soon developed into a fear of dying. I was constantly afraid that I might die the next day. The fact that I had already been imprisoned for three years, and there seemed to be no authority strong enough to release me, aroused in me a deep feeling of anxiety. As a result I believed, for example, that I'd never be a father...it was the same as dying. (p. 191)

The emotional climate in the group was usually mild. An attitude developed whereby when an individual suffered from a bad mood no one questioned its causes or rushed to his rescue. Without words, a quiet support system allowed the man to regain his equilibrium by himself.

The POWs' liberation finally occurred as part of the massive prisoners' exchange between Israel and Egypt after the October 1973 "Yom Kippur War." The return, reception, and reunion with their families were accounted as peak experiences in the ex-POWs' lives, as exemplified in the following quote: "The return was extremely exciting. It's hard to describe it. I was in a kind of euphoria, as if I was walking a meter above the ground, floating" (Amos, p. 230).

The circumstances of the return were, however, far from simple. In addition to the immense personal transition and necessary adaptation, the whole country was under the trauma of the recent war, and some of the returning POWs found out about casualties among their relatives or friends. Each of the men went through individual family and career processes of re-entry into society according to his particular reality and circumstances. All the stories but one seemed to indicate good adjustment. Moreover, the retrospective accounts provided by the men in their narratives implied that their captivity was mostly constructed as a growth and learning experience, which not only had little negative repercussions but effected their lives positively. It taught them about their strength and resilience, educated them, and provided them with friends for life and many social skills. The most dramatic lesson was formulated by Rami, who expressed in the following quote what had become the "group's philosophy":

> I think we took advantage of our conditions in captivity as much as possible…The biggest thing we have learned from captivity is that from every starting point, one has the possibility of climbing up or falling down, and it's a matter of choice which it will be. One may draw something good from any condition, and once you discover that, you can be happy or unhappy with what you've got. I give credit to the guys for discovering this truth when they were in such difficult situation as imprisonment, at the very bottom. (p. 261)

REDEMPTION IN CAPTIVITY—EXPLANATORY FACTORS

It goes without saying that the accounts of the POWs of their captivity included numerous traumatic episodes, difficult emotions, and painful moments. Had I not heard this side of the story, I would have found it highly incredible. Yet the striking other side of the story, namely its positive aspects and implications, was much more elaborated in the men's stories and deserves an explanation. Indeed, whether I asked them directly or not, most of the interviewed men provided several answers to the basic riddles of their story: How come the difficult, wasted years were not constructed purely as such, and what contributed to the POWs' psychological well-being during and after their captivity?

One answer should be ruled out immediately, namely that the objective conditions of imprisonment in Egypt provided a relatively comfortable environment for the POWs. Without going in detail into comparisons of various conditions of POWs in different countries, in different periods, I have three arguments against this claim:

1. Notwithstanding later conditions, there is no doubt that the first stages of captivity—sudden capture, torture, interrogation, and isolation—were traumatic for all the men and could have left a lasting aftermath.

2. Whatever the comforts provided to the men in their common cell in prison, for example their own cooking facility, a courtyard, or a wealth of books and materials for their study groups and hobbies, they were still incarcerated against their will, for an unknown duration, in crowded quarters. They were continuously deprived of their freedom and contacts with their loved ones, and this in itself is a highly stressful condition.

3. Much of the "comfort" obtained by the men resulted from their own efforts, initiatives, and wisdom in running the group. Therefore, using "comfort" as a factor is only begging the question about the *source* of these initiatives, which has to be searched in the realm of subjectivity or psychology.

Regarding psychological factors, these can be roughly divided into individual versus social factors.[8] First among the individual resources for successful adaptation and survival is the men's personal background: many of them originated from highly selective military units, and the airmen were also specifically trained for the eventuality of falling into captivity. Next comes a list of what is usually called defense mechanisms: among them rationalization (of the inevitability of being captured, of conduct under interrogation), dissociation (of the tough reality from the self), and splitting or suppression (of memories that are too painful to bear at present). Finally, coping mechanisms such as invoking empowering memories and ideas, release of pain and tension by crying, creating a routine to alleviate insecurity, and mainly distraction by a variety of activities.

Once the group assembled in the common cell, many aspects of the group's characteristics and lifestyle could be conceived as contributions to the well-being of the group's members, among them adherence to certain values, stable leadership, and the social climate within the group.

Specific values were advocated, reinforced, and became highly significant for the group as a whole:

- Patriotism, in seeing themselves as representatives of the state of Israel, and the Israeli Defense Force.
- The value of democracy or the kibbutz tradition,[9] as manifested in the organizational structure of the Friday night assembly meetings.
- An existential world view, advocating the "here and now" principle, the responsibility of individuals for their mental situation and the motivation for personal growth under all circumstances.

The prominence of these values enabled the men to make sense or attribute meanings to their lot as prisoners of war, a process that is known to be highly advantageous for survival in extreme situations (Frankl, 1959).

In addition to the strong value orientation, and the norms and practices derived from them, the group was blessed with a stable and well-balanced leadership. The influence of its two leaders was enormous in providing personal models for coping, in channeling emotional expressions and potential violence, and in keeping the individual prisoners busy in routines of chores, studies, hobbies, games, and celebrations (of birthdays, Jewish holidays, etc.).

The special social climate cultivated in the group under this leadership was, in my opinion, one of the major contributions to the men's well-being in the common room. This was well expressed by Rami:

> In some unplanned, unconscious manner, we never pried into each other's intimate world. When someone got a letter, he would climb up one of the high beds to read it alone. Nobody asked him, what's in your letter? In a group of ten very different men, we didn't allow ourselves to build closer relationships among us; somehow we felt that we would not be able to cope with the commitments and problems resulting from such intimacy. (p. 174)

All these factors together, in both the individual and the group spheres, appear to have remained in the men's memory, and/or were reconstructed in their narratives as major themes in the stories of their coping with their long captivity.

HOPE, SURVIVAL, AND RECOVERY

In the framework of this chapter, however, I would like to emphasize the significance of hope and its maintenance during captivity as one of the major mechanisms for survival and recovery. I suggest that the term *hope* means, in the present context, maintaining a positive view of the future, or building a mental bridge between the difficult present and the bright future. Moreover, I propose that to be effective, hope should be moderate: not too high to risk disappointment, or too low to cause depression and despair. Hope can be aroused by the self, and/or by others, who may be termed "hope agents." The art of keeping hope alive seems to have thrived in the prisoners' group, as will be demonstrated below.

During the first stages of solitary captivity, the prisoners had to suffice with hope as aroused by the self, in many cases against the Egyptian captors or interrogators, who tried to "kill" hope. The first hopeful idea, quoted by most of the narrators, was that: "In a short while I will be rescued by the IDF," followed by a similar idea: "Israel will not let me remain in captivity, I will be returned home very shortly." When they were first imprisoned the POWs mobilized relevant memories to reinforce these hopes—about pilots who were rescued heroically out of enemy territory, or about the brief duration of captivity in former cases of Israeli POWs. As the time went on, and the difficult stage of torture and interrogation lasted beyond these expectations, the broader hopeful idea was formed that "Israel, IDF, and my family are doing everything they can to liberate me, but it is a tough process and may take some time." This was indeed the major hope-idea that had been sustained throughout the years of captivity, as expressed succinctly by Amos L.: "We had the whole country behind us, and we had hope" (p. 188).

It is well documented in the men's stories how the Egyptians attacked these hopes, first and foremost by telling the new POW that nobody knew he was alive, or, rather—that "in Israel they are certain you are dead." Avi, for example, recalled the following:

> On the way [from where he parachuted to the first interrogation in the intelligence center, A.L.] I heard my name in the news, in Arabic naturally, and I realized that they had been announcing my capture. This served me very well later on, because it was clear that people knew I was alive, in the hands of the Egyptians, in spite of the fact that the interrogators often tried to create a completely different impression. (pp. 49–50)

Sustaining hope was sometimes aided by bringing up in one's imagination powerful significant others, who inspired the prisoner during the hardest times.

> During the interrogations, I sensed that visualizing my family made me weaker, because I missed them so badly, and I was sad to be causing them

all this worry. So I taught myself never to think about them, except for my father, who was a strong man and his presence inspired me. (Avi, p. 221, Heb.)

Above all else, the men kept their hopes alive by building mental images of their good future, and especially the moment of return. This fantasy was expressed in many variations during the interviews, as for example:

> I kept building a colorful picture of my future return. I would see how we'd be welcome by everybody at the airport, how I'd meet my grown daughters...I was determined to go back to my profession [as a pilot]. (Yitzhak, p. 183)[10]

As the interrogations faded off, and the prisoners were left to their own devices in isolation, with complete uncertainty about what might happen to them next, the shifting moods of hope versus despair colored their days. This is when external agents of hope became immensely significant. The Red Cross agents in Egypt, two European men, who visited the prisoners in their captivity, played a major role in reinforcing and sustaining the POWs' hopes. The mere hope to receive a Red Cross visit was one of the positive experiences for the prisoners, especially during their solitude. The following quote demonstrates the multiple role of the Red Cross agents, being a bridge to the free world outside, to the family back home, as well as to the other Israeli POWs in prison. They symbolized sanity and the promise for better conditions, and most of all—the hope for a safe return home as soon as possible.

> A handsome, tall man came smiling into my cell. This was Beausart. I believe it was the end of August. He brought me a small parcel, with chocolate, nuts and the Bible in Hebrew. He also gave me a special postcard and told me to write home a few words...I asked for a doctor. I asked him how many Israelis had been captured and he winked but refrained from answering...I was extremely happy to see him. It was a proof that people outside knew I was alive. I assumed that after his visit the Egyptians wouldn't dare continue their threats [of killing him, A.L.] and torture. (Yitzhak, pp. 93–94)

The Red Cross agents reassured the prisoners that every possible national and international means and channels were mobilized to bring about their liberation. In the meantime, they promised to effect the very desired situation of getting all the Israeli POWs joined in a common room in prison. As told by David:

Mr. Beausart couldn't believe I had no books, and he went to one of the other POWs and returned with a Bible. It was from Dan. The nicest thing was that he told me to climb to the window and then indicated the common room of the other Israelis. (p. 90)

This, however, proved to be a case of setting high hopes, in fact too high, for immediate changes, as David continued in his account: "It was a hard time. The interrogations were less frequent, I had more free time, and I suffered from loneliness, especially since I knew that the others were all together already" (p. 90).

Another quote, taken from the story of Amos Z., whose wife was pregnant with their first child when he fell into captivity, demonstrates the role of the Red Cross agents in promising fast return: "They asked me, when is your daughter due to be born? In October? Well, by then you'll be home for sure" (Amos, p. 186).

The Red Cross agents continued in their multiple functions for the joined group as well. In later stages, their functions included also assisting the prisoners to obtain a wide range of improvements in their conditions, from leaving the courtyard open at all times, to deliveries of books, special food, and various study materials from Israel. They also used to meet the family members in Israel and provide reports about the situation of their dear ones. Even when the men became frustrated with the long months and years of waiting for their liberation, and the continuous Egyptian threat that they would not be exchanged for anything, the Red Cross agents remained a steady source of hope that things could, and would, change. As in therapy, personal attachment to the hope-agent developed, and when the time came for Mr. Beausart to be replaced by another agent, the men experienced a devastating sense of being let down or deserted.

After the group of prisoners had been gathered in the common cell, and as it established its way of life and social organization in captivity, the agents of hope now included the group's leaders, especially Rami, whose life-philosophy will be further elaborated below. In addition, each of the men was occasionally a speaker for hope in specific conversations and interactions. This was, in my view, one of the major advantages of being together. *Morale* was one of the more general terms used for hope in the military parlance of the POWs. To have *high morale* meant being optimistic and hopeful about the *future,* as well as leading daily life on a high standard at *present,* for example a certain dress code, getting up on time, physical appearance, cleanliness of the room, eating and speaking politely, attending classes, and so forth. The following quotations demonstrate the mechanisms of keeping hope alive for oneself and each other, as narrated in the POWs' accounts, starting with Rami:

> I had a famous saying: "In two months we will be out of here." Why in two months? There was always an answer: "In two months it will be Passover," for example. I used to explain to the men that "two months" was a fictitious period of time. It wasn't too long, so that we wouldn't despair, and yet it wasn't too short, so that we couldn't just sit packed and ready to leave. If it was "in two months" we had enough time to go about our business... I never dealt with the problem of how much longer I would be held by the Egyptians. I always tried to plan ahead for the next two months. (p. 175)

This can be conceived as constructing a bridge towards the goal, which resides somewhere in the not-too-far-away future, or establishing what I defined above as a moderate hope. The power of this idea can be evaluated by its impact, in other words by the fact that it became a common wisdom of the group, expressed directly in all the men's narratives, as for example: "One cannot live with complete uncertainty about the time [of return, A.L.]. Rami's solution was to behave as if we'd soon be released, say in two months" (Amos Z., p. 186).

Avi also related to this idea, making a distinction between the first and second stage of his captivity. About the first stage, in which he was totally isolated, he said: "For a long time I clung to the sense of transience in captivity, as if my release was close, and I avoided organizing myself for a long stay" (p. 190).

While telling about his later adjustment, in the common cell, he speaks in plural voice: "In the second stage of our confinement, we used to imagine a month or two months of future captivity. We'd get up in the morning and say: In two months we'll be back home" (p. 191).

This was of course some sort of a make-believe game, as admitted by Amos L: "We didn't permit ourselves to look forward to a certain liberation date in order not to be disappointed" (p. 188).

Other manners of interpersonal support were also used, although less elaborated than the "two months' formula." For example: "When ten men live together, whenever one loses heart, the others support him" (Rami, p. 175). Or: "We were all depressed when Beausart, the Red Cross agent whom we had all liked so much, was replaced... Somehow we came out of it. I think it was during The New Year. I gave the men a pep talk, and it helped" (Rami, p. 176).

As I suggested above, it might have been psychologically dangerous to hope for very unlikely developments. In case of the POWs, this refers mainly to the idea or fantasy of escape. While the men cultivated their hopes for being returned "legally" through international influence, diplomacy, or prisoners' exchange, they simultaneously tried to abate hopes of a miraculous escape from jail. There were rare references to escape plans in the men's narratives, even in answer to my direct questions about it. Only one man, Motti C., spoke at length about escape plans. Most of his "plans" seemed to me child-like and far from realistic, and I understood that they were not taken seriously by the others, probably because the group leaders did not approve of them—as I suggested—in order to prevent great disappointment and despair.

> I had a complete plan. There was one guard who used to leave his clothes—rags, really—in our cell. I planned to put them on and walk out. I had asked the pilots about an airfield nearby, and they had even instructed me how to fly a plane... I could hijack a plane... I would have managed to escape and was willing to be the leader, but the guys put all kinds of obstacles in my way... One plan was to dig a tunnel under our shower. The floor tiles were loose, and I saw sand underneath... I heard later that in Israel they had some plans to come to our rescue.... (p. 194)

A more mature perspective is the following:

> We discussed the possibility [of escape, A.L.] and analyzed the odds. We believed that it was possible to get out of prison, but we estimated that we might be stuck in Cairo, and even if we reached the Canal, we wouldn't have means to cross it... We reached the conclusion that it wasn't feasible. (Amos, Z. p. 186)

Another POW recalled that the idea of escape was rejected because the men concluded that they had to escape together, or else the remaining prisoners would pay dearly for their friends' freedom. Escaping together was, however, impossible since Dan was hardly able to walk on his feet. In another context, one of the men told me about a letter he wrote to his wife that caused some alarm, because the "silly Egyptians" (who censored all correspondence) believed it contained a coded escape plan, while any person in his right mind would know that it was impossible, even for Israeli supermen. To sum up, it is clear from the accounts that the dominant attitude of the prisoners was to sustain the moderate hope of being released in two months, rather than the wild hope of being rescued or escaping. My suggestion is that this management of hope was one of the most significant mechanisms in the prisoners' coping and adaptation.

TRANSLATING *THE HOBBIT*

Reading was a major activity for all the prisoners of the group. Books were sent in parcels by their families as well as the IDF authorities, and the POWs' private library grew in size, and reached, towards the end of their stay, about 3,000 volumes. Several men told me that reading was extremely rewarding in prison. It allowed the individual to escape from his dire state and live outside through the plots and adventures of the heroes. Yet, according to the POWs' accounts, reading used to be a *collective* activity in prison. As one read quietly, he stopped to share some passages with his friends. Books that were enjoyed by one were passed on to other readers in the group, and discussions of the books' plots and meanings frequently took place. This was a significant part of the men's self-education in captivity.

Most of the volumes received by the men were in Hebrew. However, since Yitzhak was a native English speaker, his family sent him books in English as well. During the second year of their captivity, as the men had already organized their life into a stable routine, Yitzhak got Tolkien's *The Hobbit* from his brother. Yitzhak read this English classic with immense pleasure and tried to share the story and its great sense of humor with his friends. For that purpose he started to translate orally into Hebrew sections of the book. This spontaneous act led the airmen to the idea to translate the whole book systematically, a project that occupied the group for many months.

Two points should be made about the translation project: The translation of *The Hobbit* was extremely challenging and ambitious. The language of Tolkien in his books is famous for its originality. The book has many puns, as well as poems and riddles in rhyme, which require high skills from the translator. Many terms for imaginary creatures and places do not exist in any form in Hebrew. Yet, the men met the challenge of this project, and the quality of their translation enabled its commercial publication after their release.

Only some of the POWs, all of them airmen, had enough linguistic and literary abilities to undertake the translation. However, the group managed to include everybody in the project. Difficult passages and terms were brought up to the entire group for their advice and suggestions. Some of the men were employed in making copies (all this was done in handwriting, naturally!) of the work for further editing and saving for the future.

The selection of *The Hobbit* for the group's major project, and the fact that it was the only book translated during their captivity (although they had many other books in English, including the remaining books by

Tolkien), seems to me like one of the riddles of the book itself. I am certain that this was not accidental. A translation is a very intimate common journey of an involved translator and the book he or she works on. When the rare event occurs that a translation is undertaken and sustained by a *group* of individuals, this involvement encompasses the group as a whole. Its "journey" of reowning the story and rewriting the text becomes a rare kind of group experience. Why then *The Hobbit?*

Reading *The Hobbit* once more after my research with the POWs was completed, I was able to discern many aspects in the story of *The Hobbit* that must have been significant for the men in captivity. Without encumbering this chapter with quotes from this classical book, I may point to the main aspects that could make *The Hobbit* such a special story for the POWs.

The plot of *The Hobbit* is about a group of fourteen dwarves who long for their long-abandoned faraway land and treasures, now ruled by a fierce dragon. Advised by Gandalf the wizard, they approach Mr. Bilbo Baggins the hobbit—a small, polite, home-loving creature—and more-or-less force him to accompany them on their dangerous trip, in the role of a "burglar." This starts a long adventure in "Wilderland," in which the group of dwarves—obviously the good guys, although not always nice—encounters many terrible dangers and is captured more than once by a variety of horrible creatures—the bad guys. As the story unfolds, we hear again and again about the "good and just" being overcome by "the evil." Thus, the dwarves and their burglar are captured, interrogated, tortured, and isolated in dark tunnels and caves—events and descriptions that undoubtedly aroused much identification of the prisoners-readers.

There are many smart and successful escapes in this story, which could probably be envied by these readers, or seen as fantasies of wish fulfillment (e.g. the fantasy of becoming invisible). At the end, after all kinds of struggle and suffering, the dwarves regain their kingdom—in other words return home. The kind hobbit also returns home eventually, going back to his dwelling, his comfortable "hole in the ground" somewhere in the West. As implied by the subtitle of the book—"There and Back Again"—the theme of the return is its major message. The various "returns" are described as peak experiences, as moments of extreme elation. There is no need to elaborate the significance of this fulfilled fantasy of "the return" for the prisoners, whose return seemed to be delayed further and further in time.

More than the thematic similarity, *The Hobbit* is a story about a very cohesive and loyal group of creatures, who treat each other with utmost consideration, loyalty, and solidarity. The transformation of Bilbo's character and identity, his emergence as a brave and resourceful leader is one of the most interesting plot lines in the story. Upon his return home, he is not the weak, comfort-seeking individual who started on the quest. This plot line conveys a message of the hidden inner resources in each creature, and the possible transformation by ordeal. The "happy ending" of this story is presented also as a matter of some religious or mystical intervention, which when coupled with the individual's effort may bring about the realization of one's fantasies. This idea is the theme of the last conversation in the book, which takes place between Bilbo and Gandalf:

> "Then the prophecies of the old songs have turned out to be true, after a fashion!" said Bilbo. "Of course!" said Gendalf. "And why should not they prove true? Surely you don't disbelieve the prophecies, because you had a hand in bringing them about yourself? You don't really suppose, do you, that all our adventures and escapes were managed by mere luck, just for your sole benefit? You are a very fine person, Mr. Baggins, and I am very fond of you; but you are only quite a little fellow in a wide world, after all!" (p. 285)

With these words in mind, it is clear that the book could indeed be read as a prophecy about the POWs' redemption, and as such—that it was a significant hope agent in their lives. This could explain and justify the sustained efforts that led to the completion of the translation project.

It is interesting to note that hope as such is rarely discussed in the plot. The various creatures exhibit great determination and dedication to their goal, which is probably based on the hope to obtain it. When they are hungry, they hope to be invited for a meal, when they are lost in darkness, they hope to find a source of light. More than anything, however, they hope to win their just cause and succeed in their mission. But they speak much more about fear or treasures, while the term "hope" is somehow avoided, (like the term "God"?) perhaps because it shouldn't be used too lightly.

One of the few sections in which I found direct reference to hope is when the group faces its most difficult ordeal—escape from suffocation in the dragon's Underworld. And this is how Tolkien tells it: [One of the dwarfs says:]

> "Let us try the door," he said. "I must feel the wind on my face soon or die"...We are trapped they groaned. "This is the end. We shall die here." But somehow, just when the dwarves were almost despairing, Bilbo felt a strange lightening of the heart, as if a heavy weight had gone from under his waistcoat. "Come, come", he said. "While there is life there is hope!" as my father used to say. (p. 222)

Hope is the essence of life is what Tolkien said so clearly, and I feel that the sentence, or rather the sentiment and belief behind it, is what made this book so dear to the POWs.

IN CLOSING

In a recent paper, McAdams and Bowman (2001) make a distinction between self-narratives of *redemption* and *contamination*. In the first kind of narrative, emotionally negative situations are transformed into positive outcomes, so that bad scenes or the narrator are redeemed by the manner in which the story is constructed. In McAdams and Bowman's words, "If there is to be redemption, there must first be pain" (p. 3 of ms). A similar idea was expressed by Jung many years earlier, when he talked about the individual and cultural power of "transformation tales" or the "archetype of re-birth" (Jung 1936/1959). According to McAdams and Bowman, a reverse movement is depicted in contamination sequences, in which a positive or good experience is spoiled, ruined, or contaminated by a negative or bad outcome. The collective story of the Israeli POWs clearly belongs to the redemption type; in the long run, the trauma of falling into captivity, of torture, isolation, and interrogation was constructed as a challenge and an opportunity, rather than a personal disaster.

It is perhaps the sense of hope that can turn negative circumstances and stories into positive ones, of redemption. The place of hope in the lives of the POWs of this study was very central, and its voice steady and clear: There is no sense to despair, we will be out of here. My understanding is that this hope experience was mainly a manner of constructing time: trying to remain in the present, convincing oneself that the future in prison will not be longer than two months, yet making a mental bridge in time towards the final return and redemption. Keeping this hope moderate, rather than wild or extreme, is one expression of the group's wisdom which is quite hard to verbalize. Due to this, when the day of liberation finally arrived, these ten men were psychologically sane, and as prepared as one can imagine for adult life as free individuals.

NOTES

1. This chapter is based on a study conducted in 1987–1989, and published by Lieblich in Hebrew in 1989, and in English, 1994. I am deeply thankful to the prisoners and their wives for sharing their stories with me.

2. The War of Attrition between Israel and Egypt took place between June 1967, right after the Six Days War, and August 1970, when a cease-fire agreement was signed (Schiff and Haber, 1976). The POWs whose personal history is the topic of the present paper (and the original study) were taken captive in 1970, and returned to Israel in November 1973, after the Yom Kippur War.

3. In my original study, however, some documents were used to provide additional perspectives on the oral accounts. I was given the men's diary in captivity (see p. 170 in this chapter), which recorded the POWs' weekly Friday night group meetings. I also received some of the private letters sent by the men to their families, and the Red Cross reports to the families. With all their historical value, the importance of these documents—from my perspective—is secondary to the oral reports procured in the individual interviews, which portray the adult perspective of the experience of captivity and its meaning within the context of the tellers' autobiographies.

4. Dan Avidan, the oldest member of the group, suffered continuously from his leg wounds, which had never been fully treated by the Egyptians, till he passed away in 1999. After his release from captivity he changed his career and became a social worker. This paper is dedicated to his memory.

5. With the tellers' agreement, their real first names are used in the story. In the English version of the book (1994), the name of Amos L. was replaced by Amnon, and Motti B. by Benny, to avoid confusion.

6. To be precise, there was another wounded POW—Yehezkel Dori—who spent the first few months with the group and was released to be medically treated in Israel. His departure occurred before the group organized and developed its life style, and therefore he was not included among the interviewed men.

7. Most of the quotes (and reference to page numbers) are from the English version of the book, *Seasons of Captivity,* 1994. Since the Hebrew version (1989) included more material than the English one, some quotes appear as free translation from the Hebrew book, and are marked "Heb."

8. For a full discussion of the individual and group mechanisms of coping, see Lieblich, 1994, pp. 317–334.

9. Although the kibbutz population in Israel consisted at the time of about 3 percent of the total Jewish population, two out of the ten POWs were kibbutz members, and four more had been raised or educated in the kibbutz.

10. It may be interesting to inform the reader that 27 years after liberation, Yitzhak is still an experimental pilot in one of the largest aviation firms in the United States.

REFERENCES

Frankl, V. (1959). *Man's search for meaning.* New York: Beacon Press.
Gergen, K.J. (1999). *An invitation to social construction.* London: Sage.

Jung, C. G. (1959). The archetypes and the collective unconscious. In *Collected works,* Vol. 9, Part I. Princeton Univ. Press (First German edition in 1936).

Lieblich, A. (1989). *Only the Birds—the story of Israeli POWs in Egypt.* Tel Aviv: Schocken. (Hebrew).

Lieblich, A. (1994). *Seasons of Captivity.* New York: University of New York Press.

Lieblich, A., Tuval Mashiach, R., & Zilber, T. (1998). *Narrative research: Reading analysis and interpretation.* Thousand Oaks, California: Sage.

McAdams, D.P., & Bowman, P.J. (2001). Narrating life's turning points: Redemption and contamination. In D.P. McAdams, R. Josselson, & A. Lieblich (Eds.), *Turns In The Road: Narrative Studies Of Lives In Transition* (pp. 3–34). Washington, DC: APA Books.

Schiff, Z, and Haber, E. (1976). *Israel, Army and Defense—A Dictionary.* Tel Aviv: Zmora, Bitan, Modan. (Hebrew).

Sarbin, T.R. (Ed.). (1986). *Narrative psychology: The storied nature of human conduct.* New York: Praeger.

Spence, D. P. (1982). *Narrative truth and historical truth: Meaning and interpretation in psychoanalysis.* New York: Norton.

Tolkien, J.R.R. (1937). *The Hobbit.* London: Allen and George Unwin Ltd. (Reference to pages in this chapter are from the paperback edition, London: HarperCollins Publishers, 1993).

Tolkien, J.R.R. (1977). *The Hobbit.* Tel Aviv: Zmora, Bitan, Modan. (Hebrew).

Chapter 9

THREAT AND HOPE IN COPING WITH CANCER FOR HEALTH CARE PROFESSIONALS

Ronna F. Jevne and Cheryl L. Nekolaichuk

INTRODUCTION

With rare exception, the most dreaded words a person can hear are "You have cancer." The most dreaded message, spoken or unspoken, that can accompany these words is "There is no hope." Cancer patients want to hear, "Where there is life there is hope. Miracles do happen." They want to hear that there are exceptions and that statistics are not the only issue. If things look bad, then they want assurances that loved ones and health professionals care. Patients want to sense everything possible will be done. They understand that they can hope even when the chances of recovery are slim. They want those in their world to help them hope, if not for cure, then for something.

When the diagnosis of cancer is entered onto a chart, the patient enters into a time and place of uncertainty. In all likelihood the onset may have been silent, or at least obscure. The prognosis, even if it is positive, is knowingly subject to individual variability. The treatment, even if it is minor, will mean interruptions and disruptions to one's life. The pursuit of cure is often elusive; the experience of recurrence is stressful. Hope allows patients to co-habit with uncertainty throughout the process.

When the long distance call came from Dr. H.' s office requesting that I be present when he spoke to my dad, I knew our first hope, the hope for no cancer, had vanished. The blockage that had prompted the investigations announced the dreaded cancer. He had complained of the hardness in his abdomen for months. An unwellness had crept into his being. Day to day vitality seeped from him, yet he colluded in unspoken avoidance. At 84, he wrestled with what was aging and what was illness.

We turned our hope to the obviously required surgery, grateful it was an option. The hope for a surgeon of preference in a hospital of compassion was negotiated. The hope to avoid a teaching hospital with its lengthy waits, invasive and impersonal protocols, was fulfilled.

Within a day, the little hopes emerged. The hope that his roommate would cease his constant irrelevant chatter. The hope that the intravenous would be easily inserted. The hope that dad could handle his life long needle phobia. The hope for a compassionate surgeon. The hope that nothing would propel us into unnecessary premature despair.

The nurses pronounced his name correctly. The physician shook his hand. As a farmer there were only three fingers on that hand but the two men met with a firm grasp. Their eyes exchanged trust. Both knew the seriousness. Neither overemphasized it.

The teaching video describing his surgery was loud enough he could hear it. His few questions were answered directly. The option of having a family member accompany him to the surgical suite fulfilled his unspoken hope not to be alone.

The surgeon came directly to the room to speak with me following the surgery. Dad had done well despite his age. The cancer was somewhat more advanced than expected. They had had to take part of the abdominal wall but he was reasonably confident that he had gotten it. Dad was stable.

The hope for near normalcy in our own lives was fulfilled. We shared sitting with dad during daylight hours, offering the small blessings of extra nursing care. A hand held in recognition. A forehead wiped. An analgesic requested. The hope to be out of pain dominated the first few days. The hope for no complications was fulfilled.

It was tougher than Dad anticipated. He was weaker than he had ever been. He hurt more than was endurable. The first glimmer of the man we knew was his smile at graduating from intravenous to a popsicle. He slipped to a frail 119 pounds. Would he ever regain his strength? Would we ever have the dad we knew back? In the crevasses of our souls lurked the question, did they get it all?

In lieu of flowers we had placed a disposable camera at his bedside. Over the days we had snapped the occasional record of the events. Weeks and months later they served as a reference point for moments when he felt he hadn't come far enough, fast enough. Hope was made visible with this concrete record of the passing of time. And with time and the hopeful nature he is prone to, he enjoys his days fully again and with deepened gratitude. He has raised the question recently whether he should build a new home.

How might this situation have been different had this been a younger man? Had there been no family support? Had the surgeon been aloof or negative? Had the patient been of another culture? Had the nursing staff been overextended? Had the cancer been inoperable? Had the outcome been less positive? Hope is a function of a multitude of factors.

What then is this thing called hope? How important is it in the recovery and management of illness? How does it shift over the trajectory of a condition? How do caregivers know how hopeful a person is? What, if any, obligations do health care professionals and lay caregivers have for enhancing it? How can it be strengthened? How is it dashed? Can it be learned?

The purpose of this chapter is to provide an overview of the role of hope in coping with a cancer diagnosis. Three key questions will be addressed:

- What is the nature of hope, particularly in the context of cancer?
- What are the challenges in understanding and applying hope in the clinical setting?
- What strategies might be helpful for the assessment, maintenance, and enhancement of hope in cancer patients?

The remainder of the chapter is divided into four parts. The first section provides an overview of the concept of hope, particularly within the cancer setting. The second section focuses on the challenges of studying and applying hope in clinical practice. The third section highlights specific assessment and intervention strategies for the clinical setting. The final section summarizes the key points within this chapter, highlighting a clinical model for the cancer context.

WHAT IS THE NATURE OF HOPE?

The Nature of Hope

When discussing a phenomenon, it is customary to have a consensual definition. As yet, a universal definition of hope does not exist. Hope has been defined in terms of future possibility (Fromm, 1968; Lynch, 1965; Menninger, 1959; Vaillot, 1970), transcendency (Marcel, 1951/1962); an inner state (Herth, 1993; Miller & Powers, 1988; Thompson, 1994), goal directedness (Frank, 1968; Snyder, Irving, & Anderson, 1991; Stotland, 1969), a multidimensional dynamic life force (Dufault & Martocchio, 1985) and an experience of personal spirit, risk, and authentic caring (Nekolaichuk, Jevne, & Maguire, 1999). In other words, its descriptions have spanned *soul* and *goal, being* and *doing, process* and *outcome, state* and *trait.*

To integrate these many dimensions, Farran, Herth, and Popovich (1995) suggested that hope could be expressed as a way of feeling (affectively), thinking (cognitively) and behaving (behaviorally). They described four central attributes of hope: an experiential process (the pain of hope), a spiritual transcendent process (the soul of hope), a rational process (the mind of hope) and a relational process (the heart of hope).

Jevne (1994) suggests that "Whether hope is viewed as a human need, a biological life force, a mental perspective or an external pull to transcend self, it is capable of changing individual lives. It enables individuals to envision a future in which they are willing to participate" (p.8). Without hope, the professional is impotent to influence adjustment or recovery. In other words, "Hope is a phenomenon closely linked with man's adaptive powers and with meaningful human life" (Dufault, 1981, p. 5). Hope is indeed a need of those facing challenges.

The Nature of Hope in Health Care

The powerful influence of hope is well recognized in the health care field. More than forty years ago, Karl Menninger (1959) implored his medical colleagues to intentionally integrate hope in clinical practice. The words in his presidential address to the American Psychiatric Association still resonate with us today: "Are we not duty bound to speak up as scientists, not about a new rocket or a new fuel or a new bomb or a new gas, but about this ancient but rediscovered truth, the validity of hope in human development" (p. 491)?

Since Menninger's landmark presidential address, a body of research focusing on hope and illness has gradually developed. Early studies focused on hopelessness, as opposed to hope (Farran et al., 1995). Initial interest established a clear link between hopelessness, depression and suicidal ideation (Beck, Steer, Kovacs, & Garrison, 1985; Beck, Weissman, Lester, & Trexler, 1974). This initial focus has gradually shifted to an interest in the power of hope.

Recent health studies suggest that hope may be linked to positive health outcomes, including coping (Elliot, Witty, Herrick, & Hoffman, 1991; Herth, 1989), quality of life (Staats, 1991) and healing (Cousins, 1989; Udelman & Udelman, 1985, 1991). In relation to coping, hope has been described as an antecedent to coping (Weisman, 1979), as a coping strategy (Korner, 1970) and as an outcome of effective coping (Miller, 1983; Schneider, 1980). The underlying mechanisms for these connections remain unclear. Within the field of psychoneuroimmunology, some researchers have demonstrated a link between stress and an alteration of the immune system (Bonneau, Kiecolt-Glaser, & Glaser, 1990; Kiecolt-Glaser & Glaser, 1995, 1999). Others have begun to explore the impact of hope upon the immune system (Udelman & Udelman, 1985, 1991).

The Nature of Hope in the Cancer Experience

Given the positive link between hope and health, what then might be the role of hope within the context of a life-threatening illness such as cancer? The diagnosis of cancer strikes an initial fear in the minds and hearts of most people. Cancer patients often experience a fluctuating illness course, characterized by profound uncertainty, loss of control, chronicity, and changes in energy and body functions. They also may experience a sense of collapsed time, as they wrestle with the reality of their own mortality. Accompanying this unpredictable course, patients' hopes may wax and wane, with some patients placing less emphasis on a futuristic hope.

To better understand these experiences, researchers have explored the relationship between hope and cancer from many perspectives. Studies have spanned the illness spectrum, ranging from newly diagnosed, to recurrence, to end stage disease. In a review of the hope and cancer literature, Farran et al. (1995) described three major research themes: (a) relationship between hope/hopelessness and disease variables (e.g. uncertainty, phase of illness, treatment setting, information needs, physical symptoms); (b) relationship between hope/hopelessness and demographic variables such as coping styles, age, and education; and (c) impact of hope on health outcomes such as psychosocial adjustment and physical function. In this review, they suggested that hope was not significantly affected by factors such as age or gender. They did suggest, however, that there may be a relationship between hope and treatment settings, coping styles, physical health, and information sharing.

Some studies have focused on the professional caregivers' role in the cancer patients' experience of hope. These studies have ranged from communication issues, including the breaking of bad news, (Links & Kramer, 1994; Sardell & Trierweiler, 1993) to the development of hope-enhancing strategies for patients. Other studies have attempted to understand patient experiences of hope from the patients' (Flemming, 1997) or health care providers' (Benzein & Saveman, 1998; Owen, 1989) perspectives.

THE CHALLENGES OF UNDERSTANDING AND APPLYING HOPE IN PRACTICE

The complex, intangible nature of hope presents many challenges. The experience of hope has both a universal and an intensely personal dimension. Although it is an inherent human quality, it is also uniquely configured. No two people experience hope in the same way, especially within the context of a life-threatening illness. The lack of a consensual definition has resulted in a diversity of definitions and models. Its elusive intangible qualities make it difficult to capture the experience in words. There is no shared language for hope, as it crosses contexts and disciplines. Many of the existing hope assessment and intervention frameworks were not developed specifically for cancer patients. Ethical concerns about the appropriate use of hope in practice need to be addressed.

The breadth and variation of understandings of hope reported in the literature can all be observed in the clinical setting. Patients know the enticement of possibility in the pain of uncertainty. Many know the mystery of believing against seemingly insurmountable odds. Others lean more to the rational assessments based on visible evidence. Yet others are nourished and sustained through a difficult time by valued relationships. The need for conceptual clarity or purity is rarely a need of the patient. For patients, hope is a lived experience. It is known by its absence as profoundly as by its presence. It is an essential thread woven into the fabric of living with illness. It cannot be x-rayed or injected but a day without it is very difficult. Whatever our conceptual framework, patients routinely make statements about hope. *I don't know what to hope for any more. She gave me hope. There's no hope. Why did he have to take away my hope?*

Max Van Manen (1990) suggests that people experience their world in terms of lived space, lived body, lived time and lived human relations (p. 101). People speak about being in a good or bad space. The body houses the sensations that act as evidence that a person is feeling good. Vivid descriptions of fragrances, sounds, images, and textures are often included in recollections of hopeful memories. The substance of lived time is found in a person's lived history (p. 104). The nature and level of hope that people experience is a function of their life story. Each person has a different combination of people and events that influence her or his capacity to look toward the future with positive expectancy. Hence, the unique aspects of an individual's hope. A common template for understanding or a universal protocol for intervention may be inappropriate for hope.

The relational component of hope is illustrated by a Norwegian study, which found cancer patients who lived alone had lower hope than those who did not (Rustoen & Wiklund, 2000). The desire for a hope-enhancing relationship with health care professionals is further demonstrated in a study of 248 urban cancer patients who reported wanting help finding hope (Moadel et al., 1999).

How then might we *ethically* and *intentionally* assess and use hope to assist patients? Assuming hope is a *lived experience,* people, with assistance, can search internally and externally for enhancers of hope. Hoping becomes a behavior of searching the past, present and, in some cases, future for possibility.

A major challenge in understanding and applying hope in practice is to select a perspective that is congruent with the goals of patients and professional caregivers. Thinking of hope as an orientation—a way of searching past, present and future experience—assists in understanding vast differences in people's hope without privileging the hope of any one party involved. Using this perspective as a foundation, we have premised our views on assessment and intervention on the following assumptions:

- Hope has value and addressing hope in the context of cancer is appropriate.
- No consensual definition exists and perhaps one is not necessary. Clinically, it is useful to think of hope as a confident yet uncertain expectation of achieving a future good (Dufault & Martocchio, 1985, p. 380), recognizing that some cancer patients may place less emphasis on a futuristic hope. Hope is a search behavior for possibility, rather than knowledge of probability. As such, hope does not necessarily reflect logic or problem-solving processes.
- There is a hoping self. Each person has a personal and unique DNA of hope based on her or his lived experience embodied through the senses.
- Hope can be intentionally accessed, learned, and repaired.
- Assessment and intervention are closely intertwined, dynamic, and continuous processes. This close interconnection suggests a recursive relationship between assessment and intervention. Both are a form of the other. As health care professionals come to understand (assessment), they are more able to be positive participants in the individual's experience (intervention).

ASSESSMENT AND INTERVENTION STRATEGIES

Assessing Hope

How do I know how hopeful a person is? What do I need to know to better understand this person's experience of hope? These questions perplex clinicians and researchers alike, in their quest to understand the role of hope in the cancer patient's experience. Efforts towards answering the first question have resulted in a number of instruments that measure a person's level of hope. Although these instruments require further psychometric development (Farran et al., 1995), they have contributed to the quantitative representation of hope. Addressing the second question is more challenging, as a person's experience of hope may be inherently invisible and intensely unique. The lack of well-validated procedures that capture the qualitative, dynamic nature of the hope experience impedes our understanding of this complex construct from both the individual and interpersonal perspectives.

In an attempt to answer these two questions, a variety of approaches have been developed. These include the development of assessment frameworks (Farran et al., 1995; Farran, Wilken, & Popovich, 1992; Nekolaichuk & Bruera, 1998; Penrod & Morse, 1997), interview guides (Jevne, 1991; Mayers, 1992); and hope instruments (Erickson, Post, & Paige, 1975; Gottschalk, 1974; Herth, 1991, 1992; Hinds & Gattuso, 1991; Miller & Powers, 1988; Nowotny, 1989; Obayuwana et al., 1982; Plummer, 1988; Snyder, 1994; Stoner & Keampfer, 1985), with subsequent adaptations for clinical assessment (Holdcraft & Williamson, 1991; Nowotny, 1991). In spite of these efforts, the development of assessment measures and techniques remains in its infancy (Farran et al., 1995).

Different conceptual models of hope offer different possibilities for assessing hope. We present two for consideration: (a) a qualitatively derived model of hope (Dufault & Martocchio, 1985); and (b) a model that attempts to capture the qualitative experience of hope (Nekolaichuk, Jevne, & Maguire, 1999).

Dufault and Martocchio's (1985) Hope Model

Dufault and Martocchio (1985) described two different kinds of hopes: particularized hopes and generalized hopes. Particularized hopes are hopes that are directed towards specific goals. In contrast, generalized hopes represent an intangible inner experience of hope that is not connected to any specific goal or object. For cancer patients, particularized hopes vary depending upon the patients' place along the cancer trajectory. These expressed hopes may include a hope for a cure, hope for pain relief, hope to complete a specific task before dying, or a hope for a peaceful death. It is common for some patients to concurrently hold what may appear as two opposing hopes, such as hope for a cure and hope for a peaceful death. This may be distressing for professional caregivers, who may interpret this desire to hold on to a hope for a cure as denial.

Patients, however, are very good at prioritizing their hopes. It is important to listen to the descriptive words that they attach to their hopes, acknowledging the range (and depth) of their hopes. One elderly patient who was forced to stop traveling due to a progression of his disease described his hope to travel as a forlorn hope. Another palliative patient who expressed a hope for peace in the world described that particular hope as a big hope. Yet another patient who hung onto a hope for a cure, despite being told that her cancer was incurable, suggested that it may not be a very realistic hope, but that miracles do happen. For a patient who believed in life after death, her hope to be united with God was her ultimate hope. The nature and direction of patients' hopes may change over time, from being directed towards themselves to hopes in the future for their families, their country, and the world.

In addition to these targeted hopes, patients also have the capacity to experience hope at a deep, inner, or spiritual level. This experience, which is often invisible, reflects a way of being in the world, a general orientation to life. Regardless of the hopelessness of the situation, there is always hope for the person.

Nekolaichuk et al.'s (1999) Experience of Hope Model

To capture the inner, qualitative experience of hope, Nekolaichuk et al. (1999) developed a model of hope based on the personal experiences of 550 people. The sample consisted of three sub-samples: people who were illness-free, people with chronic or life-threatening illness, many of whom had cancer, and nurses. Using factor analytic procedures, three distinct yet interconnected dimensions of the hope experience were identified: *personal spirit, risk,* and *authentic caring. Personal spirit* was a predominant personal dimension, characterized by a core theme of meaning. *Risk,* a situational dimension, was primarily represented by a core theme of uncertainty. *Authentic caring,* a relational dimension, was characterized by the complementary themes of credibility and caring.

This model suggests that people experience hope primarily as a holistic, inner experience, in which meaning plays a fundamental role *(personal spirit)*. Many people with cancer are challenged to find new meaning in their lives after being diagnosed with a life-threatening illness, regardless of their prognosis. Their search for meaning represents a hopeful orientation, as they struggle to make sense of living with cancer. Many people with cancer also experience a profound loss of predictability and control, which is an inherent component of the hope experience *(risk)*. Re-establishing a sense of control in some aspects of a person's life may enhance a person's willingness to risk or may help deal with the uncertainty in other domains *(risk)*. The relational dimension of hope *(authentic caring)* reinforces the need for credible, caring relationships within the cancer experience. Comfort and caring alone may not be sufficient for experiencing hope within relationships. Many people with cancer are searching for relationships with professional caregivers, for example, who are honest and credible, in addition to being caring.

Based on this model, assessment frameworks for clinical practice (Nekolaichuk, 1999) and terminally ill patients (Nekolaichuk & Bruera, 1998) have been developed. An assessment framework adapted for cancer patients appears in Table 9.1.

Table 9.1
Hope Assessment Framework for Cancer Patients (adapted from Nekolaichuk, 1999; Nekolaichuk & Bruera, 1998)

Theme	Questions for the Clinician	Questions for the Patient
Personal Spirit	• What is meaningful for this person?	• How have you been able to take stock of your life? • What has been meaningful to you in the past? • What is meaningful to you now?
Risk	• What is this person's tolerance for uncertainty?	• How have you dealt with uncertain times in the past? • How have you been able to handle the uncertainty of having cancer? • How, if at all, has your view of time changed?
Authentic Caring	• Who cares about this person? About whom (what) does this person care?	• Who cares about you? • Who (what) do you care about?

Intervention

Although there is recognition that hope is an essential thread that runs through the cancer experience, hope has not been a conscious focus of psychological interventions. Most of the scholarly work in the field of hope has focused on developing a conceptual understanding of hope and/or translating such understandings into assessment measures of hope. Articles are beginning to appear that suggest (a) that the health care provider has an ethical obligation to support hope (Butow, Dunn, & Tattersall, 1997; Kodish & Post, 1995) and (b) that there are strategies that assist in this effort (Herth, 1990; Jevne, 1991, 1993, 2000; Jevne & Miller, 1999; Koopmeiners et al., 1997; Miller, 1989; Rustoen & Hanestad, 1998; Rustoen, Wiklund, Hanestad, & Moum, 1998).

Most of these proposed strategies were derived clinically and rely heavily on the relational aspects of hope. Miller (1989) points towards a neglected area of research when she states, "The importance of hope is accepted. However, despite wide acceptance, the domains of hope and how persons maintain hope while confronting adversity are not well-known" (p. 23).

Discussion of the need for caregivers to examine their own hope is beyond the scope of this chapter. However, hope work is not something that professionals do to patients. Both the health care provider and patient are key to harnessing the power of hope (Edey, Jevne, & Westra, 1998; Manrique, 1984; Snyder, 1995). Snyder maintains that when professionals evaluate their own level of hope, they are evaluating their ability to be effective helpers. Professionals must find a way of sustaining a hopeful orientation in the presence of those who don't comply with treatment, don't get well, won't take advice, and don't convey a sense of appreciation.

Despite concern about false hope, few if any professionals would deny the benefits of hope in the every day life of cancer patients. Normally, however, hope operates as a silent factor in practice, playing a subordinate role to discussion of problems related to cancer, which if resolved, are likely to result in hope. In other words, hope is thought of as an *outcome*.

Edey and Jevne (2003) suggest that the challenge for professionals when encountering less hopeful people is to find the hope and to coax it out of hiding. *A hopeful framework* is a step in that direction. This perspective implies reflection or dialogue by the health care professional(s) on such questions as: What is the best possible outcome for this situation? What in this is a threat to hope? In this situation, to what degree do I understand the hope of the patient and my own hope? What do I know about hope that would be helpful in this situation? At this level, hope itself does not enter directly into the conversation with the patient.

Hope-focused practice takes a further step and involves the intentional use of strategies to make hope visible to all parties. The overall goal of hope-focused practice is to make hope visible and broaden the perspective of patients whose options have been limited by feelings of hopelessness or diminished hope (Yeasting, Jevne, & Edey, 1998). It is not necessarily to solve problems. Therefore, it becomes necessary to learn about the patient's hope. Based on their lived experience, patients will vary widely as to what enhances or dashes their sense of hope. Clearly, the inspiring of hope is not a simple task.

A process by which professionals can learn to inquire about and convey hope is in ongoing development at The Hope Foundation of Alberta, a center for hope research (Edey, Jevne, & Westra, 1998). These understandings were derived from people with chronic illnesses, including but not exclusively cancer patients. They are described as patients who, in their efforts to cope with illness, had experienced the hopelessness of filling out forms, talking to receptionists when they wanted doctors, waiting months for appointments with specialists, receiving diagnoses, and being told to accept their illness. They had personal collections of self-help books. They had taken medication, been helped by medication, been overwhelmed by side effects, changed medication, and developed allergies. They had fought for disability benefits and declared themselves unemployable in order to qualify for government programs. Theirs were complicated lives, lives with many features that challenge and diminish hope (Edey et al., 1998, p. 6).

The following hope-focused strategies reflect a combination of tacit knowledge gathered from years of experience in the oncology setting, systematic interviewing of many chronically ill patients (Jevne, Williamson, & Stechynsky, 1999) and a thematic analysis of an extensive literature base. The recurring themes emerging from these sources have been organized into the Seven C's: *caring, communication, committing, coping, creating, community, and celebrating.* The first two C's represent the interpersonal experience of hope, while the remaining five C's encompass hope work. Admittedly, at this point, much of what is known is still tacit knowledge, as yet untested by conventional science, perhaps not even conducive to traditional paradigms of inquiry.

Caring

It has been said that suffering is the mother of hope (Alves, 1969, p. 120). Unlike positive thinking, hope does not deny the experience of suffering.

Rather it allows patients to cohabit with it. Suffering is often not specific to the patient's condition, but an assault on his or her life, on a person's sense of self. Suffering, like hope, is ultimately a personal matter. Like hope, it is unique to the person and his/her interpretation of the events of life.

Very small gestures of caring can enhance hope and reduce suffering— a reassuring word, a smile, a quiet extra moment, a hearty laugh. Disturbing, however, is the awareness that equally small insensitivities assault hope by undermining the trust established by caring. A brusque word, a broken promise, a tactlessly communicated diagnosis, an uninvited physical intrusion—all erode hope. Indiscriminate language in particular is lethal to hope.

Health care professionals may find it helpful to ask a number of questions about caring. What is caring? What does it look like in practice? What is the nature of the caring to which I am committed? Creating a personal credo of caring deepens a commitment to the tasks of caring. An example of a personal credo, written by one of the authors while working in a cancer setting, appears in Figure 9.1.

Communication

One's sense of self is a narrative phenomenon (Stivers, 1993). Greenhalgh and Hurwitz (1998) propose there is a value to hearing patients' symptoms by means of their story. Yet, Nichols (1995) suggests, listening is so basic that we take it for granted. Unfortunately, most of us think of ourselves as better listeners than we really are (p. 11). The temptation to judge or advise is common. Patients often simply want to be heard. They are not asking caregivers to solve something.

The easiest way to draw hope out of a story is to ask questions that focus directly on hope. *Hope-focused* communication uses language to specifically explore and enhance hope. Questions that focus on hope are distinctive and somewhat unusual in that they generally include the word hope or one of its derivatives. Listeners who ask hope-focused questions can begin to understand the patient's story and motivation in the context of hope.

Hope-focused questions can span a variety of contexts: initial expectations; individual differences; the current state of hope; and the client's lived experience of hope, including the hope history and current representations of hope. It is also possible to strengthen hope, using language that encourages the patient to think about a new perspective. The language of *when* (implying that a person's stated problem will be solved), *options,* and *I believe* introduce these ideas. The language of *I believe* clearly states that the listener has hope, which the patient can borrow. Lenders of hope must

Figure 9.1
A Personal Credo of Caring

I have a dream--a vision of how caring could be. Of how being ill didn't mean fear and loneliness--didn't mean long days of anxiety. That it could mean coming to an institution that cared--not just one person caring--not just an individual nurse, a unique doctor, a gentle orderly. Where a whole institution of caring people understood that nothing is as therapeutic as recognizing the pain, not only the physical pain.

I have a vision that doctors would talk compassionately. That families would talk openly. That patients could talk freely. That death could be something to be faced, not feared. That joy could surface in our sadness. That tears could give way to laughter and anger to tenderness.

I have a vision that care-givers would share a strength--a strength that comes only from a common purpose. That comes from belonging to a community--a community of people who believe--who believe that caring makes a difference. That custodians matter as much as physicians, that volunteers have a place beside nurses, that letters and titles matter less than kindness.

That line-ups are no more. That people are cared for before paper. That voices convey caring before directions. That waiting rooms reflect hope rather than convenience. That death means knowing a lot of people care. That there will be no physical pain and no aloneness.

(Jevne, 1991, p. 172)

have hope to lend. They need to find ways to express their own hope and be willing to accept the risk that their predictions may be proven wrong. A guide to hope-focused questions and statements appears in Table 9.2.

Table 9.2
A Guide to Hope-Focused Questions

Theme	Hope-Focused Questions
Hope in the context of initial expectations	• What hope brought you here today? • What are you hoping will happen as a result of our getting together? • How would we know if you had more hope? • What do you hope could happen?
Individual differences in hope	• With regard to this situation, how do you think your hope is like/different from others? • Who would have hopes most similar to yours? most different? • What is unique about your hope? • How has your hope changed over time?
Current State Of Hope	• On a scale of 1 to 10, with 1 being a very small amount, can you tell me how hopeful you are now (at this moment/during this time of your life)? How do you account for this number? Why isn't it higher? Why isn't it lower? • When you think of your circumstances, what is it that most threatens your hope? • If your hope has been influenced by someone recently, who would that be? • If I wanted to understand your hope during this time, what would I need to know about you?

Table 9.2 (continued)

Theme	Hope-Focused Questions
The hope history	• For you has hope tended to be friend or foe? • Has hope been a constant in your life? At what points was it at its strongest? At what points at its lowest? • How hopeful a person would others describe you? • How do you account for the hope that you have?
Representations and sensory recollections of hope	• If you woke up hearing the most hopeful sound in the world, what sound would you be hearing? • If a smell could bring hope to your mind, what would that fragrance be? • If a picture hanging beside your bed could remind you of hope when you wake in the morning, what would that picture be? Why? • What item would you carry in your pocket or purse if you wanted to have something close at hand to remind you of hope? Why would you choose that item?
The language of hope and change	• What is the smallest change that could increase your hope? • What would a hopeful person do in your circumstances? • How would you be different if you were more hopeful? • What changes in your actions or behaviour would send a message to others that you had become more hopeful?

Table 9.2 (continued)

Theme	Hope-Focused Questions
The language of *"when"*	• When you are finished treatment • When you find a remedy for the pain • When this difficult time passes • When you connect with a doctor whose opinion you trust
The language of *options*	• What is the worst possible outcome of this situation? • What is the best possible outcome of this situation? • Who might have information, which would be helpful to us in better understanding this situation? • Whose example would you follow if you decided to behave in a hopeful manner?
The language of *"I believe"*	• I believe that things will improve. • I believe you can do this even though it may be difficult. I believe this because I know about some difficult things you have already done. • I believe you will find some way of coping with this disease, but experience tells me it will probably take some time. • I believe you will find a way to cope with the pain, but experience tells me that you may have to try a number of approaches before you can decide which one will be the best.

Commitment

How committed are you to working with me on this challenge? If commitment is low, then the patient is unlikely to intentionally implement strategies for strengthening and maintaining hope. It may be necessary to spend time building a relationship with the patient and doing the explorations that enhance commitment. Commitment may be derived from unfinished goals, important relationships, or a seemingly invincible spirit. Conscious commitment includes an agreement that hope is important and that it will be intentionally monitored in the process of cancer treatment. The characteristics of hope are discussed and often reading is assigned. It is emphasized that it is normal to have hope come and go at times. Once commitment is established, such activities as keeping a hope thermometer, writing in a hope journal, or attending a support group may allow people to monitor their commitment over time (Jevne, 2000).

Coping

Hoping and coping are intricately intertwined. In clinical conversations, patients are clear that hoping is different than coping. In day to day clinical work, caregivers observe that both are necessary and neither sufficient. Patients have appreciated reference to them as the "ping" twins—hoping and coping. A useful clinical approach is to think of hoping and coping within a two-dimensional matrix. Hoping and coping are represented along two continuums or axes, ranging from low to high, that intersect in the middle forming four separate quadrants: *high hoping–high coping, high hoping–low coping, high coping–low hoping* and *low coping–low hoping*. Each quadrant represents different hoping and coping characteristics. For example, people with *high hoping–high coping* levels will resolve problems effectively and look toward the best possible future. People with *high coping–low hoping* levels will be flat. They will describe themselves as doing fine. They are managing. Just dying on the inside. Jevne, Nekolaichuk, and Williamson (1998) describe a model for counseling cancer patients that is based on a coping model. Effective use of resources, quality decision-making, and deliberate action characterize the coping response.

Creating

Patients create or select representations of hope that trigger the experience through the senses. Many patients appreciate encouragement to intentionally make their hope visible in some way. Examples of such efforts have included a hope collage, a hope quilt, a hope journal, a hopeful ritual, a hope symbol, hope music, hope images and/or the preparation of a hope kit (Jevne, 1995). A specific example would be a cancer patient who decided to photograph things that strengthened his hope. During hospitalizations he kept the photographs on his bedside table. Staff at a family medicine training clinic took this aspect of hope one step further and had the entire clinic redesigned to be a more hopeful environment (Ross, 2001). Entire intervention programs for cancer patients designed around the importance of the creative arts have begun to appear.

Community

A feeling of belonging to a group of people who care and/or who share common challenges strengthens hope. Specific cancer support group experiences are not for everyone. However, having the opportunity to be with other people who are comfortable talking about similar issues is helpful to many. Some groups who share a common cancer have found community by taking on specific and somewhat unrelated challenges, which require their collective strength. One example is the formation of rowing (Dragon Boat) teams, where women with breast cancer experience community and a common vision. Others find strength in being part of sports, music, or faith-based groups. At a Hope Retreat, participants are asked to draw a group mandala to remind themselves of the sense of community developed over a five day in-residence exploration and experience of hope (Jevne, 2001).

Celebrating

Hopeful people *celebrate* life. They learn to accept a rhythm of life that ebbs and flows between success and failure, stability and uncertainty, freedom and captivity. They are able to see small gifts in each day. Small steps on the journey matter, as well as the more distant eventual hopeful outcome. People vary widely in how they express their sense of celebration and appreciation of life. Some patients report celebrating illness-related milestones, such as completing chemotherapy or the anniversaries of being cancer free. Others, with or without the status of being cured, consciously celebrate life by creating non-illness related rituals, such as a public renewal of their marriage vows.

These seven themes of hope-focused strategies (i.e. the Seven C's) can be integrated with Nekolaichuk et al's (1999) experience of hope model to develop a hope assessment and intervention framework for cancer patients (see Table 9.3).

SYNTHESIS AND CONCLUSIONS

The diagnosis of a life-threatening illness, such as cancer, casts a shadow over the normalcy of life. Regardless of the prognosis, cancer catapults patients and their families onto a path of uncertainty, fear and potentially despair. Patients, family members and health care professionals alike struggle to make sense of this sudden intrusion on life.

Along the cancer journey, hope serves as a welcomed companion to temper the uncertainty and ward off the fear. Despite the lack of a consen-

Table 9.3
A Hope Assessment and Intervention Framework for Cancer Patients

ORIENTATION	ASSESSMENT	INTERVENTION
Personal	*Personal Spirit*	3 S's • soul • suffering • story
Interpersonal	Authentic Caring	7 C's • caring • communication
Situational (Hope Work)	Risk	• committing • coping • creating • community • celebrating

sual definition, patients and health care providers recognize the therapeutic value of hope in the clinical setting. Researchers have corroborated these clinical observations, through the development of a growing body of research focusing on the positive effects of hope within the cancer context.

There are a number of challenges in the development of effective assessment and intervention strategies. These include the elusive, intangible nature of the hope concept; the ability to understand the uniqueness of the hope experience; the lack of a consensual definition; the lack of appropriate assessment and intervention frameworks for cancer patients; and the need to address ethical concerns.

Regardless of perspectives and challenges, assumptions about hope need to be made to be effective in clinical practice. These assumptions assist in the selection of assessment and intervention frameworks that are congruent with patients' and professional caregivers' goals. Based on the assumptions presented in this chapter, we believe that assessment and intervention strategies need to be uniquely configured for each person.

Ultimately, effective clinical frameworks need to integrate conceptual understandings, clinical issues, and methodological concerns with a heightened ethical sensitivity. An integrative model for understanding, assessing, and enhancing hope in clinical practice appears in Figure 9.2. This model highlights the need for professional caregivers to address a number of key questions. What assumptions about hope do I have as a pro-

Figure 9.2
An Integrative Model for Understanding, Assessing, and Enhancing Hope in Cancer Patients

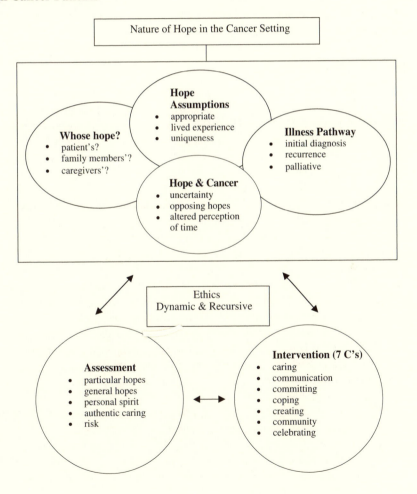

fessional caregiver? Whose hope needs to be assessed and enhanced? The patient's? The family member's? My own? How far along the illness pathway is this patient? How has the experience of a life-threatening illness impacted this patient's hopes? How might my hopes, as a professional caregiver, influence the hopes of my patients? These key questions represent a base for the development of specific hope-focused assessment and intervention strategies.

Despite many medical advances, cancer continues to pose a serious threat to an individual's physical, psychological, and spiritual well-being. Coping strategies, though effective, are not sufficient to master this life-threatening force. Hope, in all of its configurations, provides a comfort and catalyst for embracing life, regardless of the odds. The professional caregiver's intentional integration of hope-focused assessment and intervention strategies within clinical practice helps patients live out the reality that where there is life there is hope!

REFERENCES

Alves, R. (1969). *A theology of human hope.* Washington: Corpus Books.

Beck, A. T., Steer, R. A., Kovacs, M., & Garrison, B. (1985). Hopelessness and eventual suicide: A 10-year prospective study of patients hospitalized with suicidal ideation. *American Journal of Psychiatry,* 142, 559–563.

Beck, A. T., Weissman, A., Lester, D., & Trexler, L. (1974). The measurement of pessimism: The hopelessness scale. *Journal of Consulting and Clinical Psychology,* 42(6), 861–865.

Benzein, E., & Saveman, B. (1998). Nurses' perception of hope in patients with cancer: A palliative care perspective. *Cancer Nursing,* 21, 10–16.

Bonneau, R. H., Kiecolt-Glaser, J. K., & Glaser, R. (1990). Stress-induced modulation of the immune response. *Annals of the New York Academy of Sciences,* 594, 253–269.

Butow, P. N., Dunn, S. M., & Tattersall, M.H.N. (1997). Denial, misinformation, and the assault of truth. In R. K. Portenoy and E. Bruera (Eds.). *Topics in Palliative Care,* Vol. 1 (pp. 263–278). New York: Oxford University Press.

Cousins, N. (1989). *Head first: The biology of hope.* New York: E. P. Dutton.

Dufault, K. (1981). *Hope of elderly persons with cancer.* Unpublished doctoral dissertation, Case Western Reserve University, Cleveland.

Dufault, K., & Martocchio, B.C. (1985). Hope: Its spheres and dimensions. *Nursing Clinics of North America,* 20(2), 379–391.

Edey, W., & Jevne, R. (2003). *Hope, illness and counseling practice: Making hope visible.* Canadian Journal of Counseling, 37(1), 44–51.

Edey, W., Jevne, R., & Westra, K. (1998). *Key elements of hope-focused counseling: The art of making hope visible* (Experiments in Hope Monograph No. 4). Edmonton, Alberta: The Hope Foundation of Alberta.

Elliott, T. R., Witty, T. E., Herrick, S., & Hoffman, J. T. (1991). Negotiating reality after physical loss: Hope, depression and disability. *Journal of Personality and Social Psychology*, 61, 608–613.

Erickson, E., Post, R., & Paige, A. (1975). Hope as a psychiatric variable. *Journal of Clinical Psychology*, 31, 324–330.

Farran, C. J., Herth, K. A., & Popovich, J. M. (1995). *Hope and hopelessness: Critical clinical constructs.* Newbury Park, CA: Sage.

Farran, C. J., Wilken, C. S., & Popovich, J. M. (1992). Clinical assessment of hope. *Issues in Mental Health Nursing*, 13, 129–138.

Flemming, K. (1997). The meaning of hope to palliative care cancer patients. *International Journal of Palliative Nursing*, 3, 14–18.

Frank, J. (1968). The role of hope in psychotherapy. *International Journal of Psychiatry*, 5(5), 383–395.

Fromm, E. (1968). *The revolution of hope—Toward a humanized technology.* New York: Harper & Row.

Gottschalk, L. (1974). A hope scale applicable to verbal samples. *Archives of General Psychiatry*, 30, 779–785.

Greenhalgh, T. and & Hurwitz, B. (1998). *Narrative based medicine: Dialogue and discourse in clinical practice.* London: BMJ Books, BMA House.

Herth, K. A. (1989). The relationship between level of hope and level of coping response and other variables in patients with cancer. *Oncology Nursing Forum*, 16(1), 67–72.

Herth, K. (1990). Fostering hope in terminally-ill people. *Journal of Advanced Nursing*, 15, 1250–1259.

Herth, K. (1991). Development and refinement of an instrument to measure hope. *Scholarly Inquiry for Nursing Practice: An International Journal*, 5(1), 39–51.

Herth, K. (1992). Abbreviated instrument to measure hope: Development and psychometric evaluation. *Journal of Advanced Nursing*, 17, 1251–1259.

Herth, K. A. (1993). Hope in the family caregiver of terminally ill people. *Journal of Advanced Nursing*, 18, 538–548.

Hinds, P., & Gattuso, J. (1991). Measuring hopefulness in adolescents. *Journal of Pediatric Oncology Nursing*, 8(2), 92–94.

Holdcraft, C., & Williamson, C. (1991). Assessment of hope in psychiatric and chemically dependent patients. *Applied Nursing Research*, 4(3),129–134.

Jevne, R. F. (1991). *It all begins with hope: Patients, caregivers & the bereaved speak out.* San Diego, CA: LuraMedia, Inc.

Jevne, R. F. (1993). Enhancing hope in the chronically ill. *Humane Medicine*, 9(2), 121–130.

Jevne, R. (1994). *The voice of hope: Heard across the heart of life.* San Diego, CA: Lura Media, p. 8.

Jevne, R. (1995). The hope kit: First aid for uncertainty. *Hope Newsletter,* 4(6), 3.

Jevne, R. (2000). *Hoping coping and moping: Handling life when illness makes it tough.* Los Angeles: Health Information Press.

Jevne, R. (2001). *A hope retreat.* Unpublished manuscript.

Jevne, R., & Miller, J. (1999). *Finding hope: Seeing the world in a brighter light.* Fort Wayne, Indiana: Willowgreen Press.

Jevne, R., Nekolaichuk, C., & Williamson, H. (1998). A model for counseling cancer patients. *Canadian Journal of Counseling, 32* (3), 213–229.

Jevne, R., Williamson, H., & Stechynsky, A. (1999). *Minerva dialogues: Hope and chronic conditions* (Experiments in Hope Monograph #5). Edmonton, Alberta: The Hope Foundation of Alberta.

Kiecolt-Glaser, J.K., & Glaser, R. (1995). Psychoneuroimmunology and health consequences: Data and shared mechanisms. *Psychosomatic Medicine, 57,* 269–274.

Kiecolt-Glaser, J.K., & Glaser, R. (1999). Psychoneuroimmunology and cancer: Fact or fiction? *European Journal of Cancer, 35,* 1603–1607.

Kodish, E., & Post, S.G. (1995). Oncology and hope. *Journal of Clinical Oncology, 13*(7), 1817–1822.

Koopmeiners, L., Post-White, J., Gutknecht, S., Ceronsky, C., Nickelson, K., Drew, D., Watrud Mackey, K., & Kreitzer, M.J. (1997). How do healthcare professionals contribute to hope in patients with cancer? *Oncology Nursing Forum, 24,* 1507–1513.

Korner, I. (1970). Hope as a method of coping. *Journal of Consulting and Clinical Psychology, 34*(2), 134–139.

Links, M., & Kramer, J. (1994). Breaking bad news: Realistic versus unrealistic hopes. *Supportive Care Cancer, 2,* 91–93.

Lynch, W. (1965). *Images of hope: Imagination as healer of the hopeless.* New York: New American Library.

Manrique, J. (1984). Hope as a means of therapy in the work of Karen Horney. *The American Journal of Psychoanalysis, 44*(3), 301–310.

Marcel, G. (1962). *Homo viator: Introduction to a metaphysics of hope* (E. Crauford, Trans.). New York: Harper and Row. (Original work published in 1951.)

Mayers, K.S. (1992). Hope in a geriatric psychiatric hospital population: Results of a structured interview. *American Journal of Alzheimer's Care & Related Disorders & Research, 7*(6), 3–8.

Menninger, K. (1959). The academic lecture: Hope. *The American Journal of Psychiatry, 116,* 481–491.

Miller, J. (1983). Inspiring hope. In J. Miller (Ed.). *Coping with Chronic Illness* (pp. 287–299). Philadelphia: F.A. Davis.

Miller, J.F. (1989). Hope-inspiring strategies of the critically ill. *Applied Nursing Research, 2*(1), 23–29.

Miller, J.F., & Powers, M.J. (1988). Development of an instrument to measure hope. *Nursing Research, 37*(1), 6–10.

Moadel, A., Morgan, C., Fatone, A., Grennan, J., Laruffa, G., Skummy, A., & Dutcher, J. (1999). Seeing meaning and hope: Self-reported spiritual and existential needs among an ethnically-diverse cancer patient population. *Journal of Psychosocial Oncology,* 8(5), 378–85.

Nekolaichuk, C. L. (1999). The meaning of hope in health and illness. *Bioethics Forum,* 15(1), 14–20.

Nekolaichuk, C. L., & Bruera, E. (1998). On the nature of hope in palliative care. *Journal of Palliative Care,* 14, 36–42.

Nekolaichuk, C. L., Jevne, R. F., & Maguire, T. O. (1999). Structuring the meaning of hope in health and illness. *Social Science & Medicine,* 48, 591–605.

Nichols, M. P. (1995). *The lost art of listening.* New York: The Guilford Press.

Nowotny, M. L. (1989). Assessment of hope in patients with cancer: Development of an instrument. *Oncology Nursing Forum,* 16(1), 57–61.

Nowotny, M. L. (1991). Every tomorrow, a vision of hope. *Journal of Psychosocial Oncology,* 9(3), 117–126.

Obayuwana, A., Collings, J., Carter, A., Rao, M., Mathura, C., & Wilson, S. (1982). Hope Index Scale: An instrument for the objective assessment of hope. *Journal of the National Medical Association,* 74(38), 761–765.

Owen, D. C. (1989). Nurses' perspectives on the meaning of hope in patients with cancer: A qualitative study. *Oncology Nursing Forum,* 16(1), 75–79.

Penrod, J., & Morse, J. M. (1997). Strategies for assessing and fostering hope: The hope assessment guide. *Oncology Nursing Forum,* 24, 1055–1063.

Plummer, E. M. (1988). Measurement of hope in the elderly institutionalized person. *Journal of the New York State Nurses Association,* 19(3), 8–11.

Ross, F. (2001). Creating a place of hope. *Health and Healing,* Winter, 26–28.

Rustoen, T., & Hanestand, B. R. (1998). Nursing intervention to increase hope in cancer patients. *Journal of Clinical Nursing,* 7, 19–27.

Rustoen, T., & Wiklund, I. (2000). Hope in newly diagnosed patients with cancer. *Cancer Nursing,* 23(3), 214–219.

Rustoen, T., Wiklund, I., Hanestad, B. R., & Moum, T. (1998). Nursing intervention to increase hope and quality of life in newly diagnosed cancer patients. *Cancer Nursing,* 21, 235–245.

Sardell, A. N., & Trierweiler, S. J. (1993). Disclosing the cancer diagnosis: Procedures that influence patient hopefulness. *Cancer,* 72, 3355–3365.

Schneider, J. S. (1980). Hopelessness and helplessness. *Journal of Psychiatric Nursing and Mental Health Services,* 18(3), 12–21.

Snyder, C. R. (1994). *The psychology of hope.* New York: The Free Press.

Snyder, C. R. (1995). Conceptualizing, measuring, and nurturing hope. *Journal of Counseling & Development,* 73, 355–360.

Snyder, C. R., Irving, L. M., & Anderson, J. R. (1991). Hope and health. In C. R. Snyder & D. R. Forsyth (Eds.). *Handbook of Social and Clinical Psychology: The Health Perspective* (pp. 285–305). Elmsford, NY: Pergamon Press.

Staats, S. (1991). Quality of life and affect in older persons: Hope, time frames, and training effects. *Current Psychology: Research and Review,* 10(1&2), 21–30.

Stivers, C. (1993). Reflections on the role of personal narrative in social science. *Journal of Women in Culture and Society,* 18(2), 408–425.

Stoner, M.H., & Keampfer, S.H. (1985). Recalled life expectancy information, phase of illness and hope in cancer patients. *Research in Nursing and Health,* 8, 269–274.

Stotland, E. (1969). *The psychology of hope.* San Francisco: Jossey-Bass.

Thompson, M. (1994). Nurturing hope: A vital ingredient in nursing. *Journal of Cancer Nursing,* 11(4), 10, 12–17.

Udelman, D.L., & Udelman, H.D. (1991). Affects, neurotransmitters, and immunocompetence. *Stress Medicine,* 7, 159–162.

Udelman, H.D., & Udelman, D.L. (1985). Hope as a factor in remission of illness. *Stress Medicine,* 1, 291–294.

Vaillot, M.C. (1970). Hope: The restoration of being. *American Journal of Nursing,* 70(2), 268–273.

Van Manen, M. (1990). *Researching lived experience: Human science for an action sensitive pedagogy.* London, ON: The Althouse Press.

Weisman, A.D. (1979). *Coping with cancer.* New York: McGraw-Hill.

Yeasting, K., Jevne, R., & Edey, W. (1998, June). *Hope in motion: A counseling perspective.* Poster session presented at the annual meeting of the Canadian Psychological Association (CPA), Ottawa, Canada.

Chapter 10

VULNERABILITY AND RESILIENCE INTERTWINED: A REVIEW OF RESEARCH ON HOLOCAUST SURVIVORS

Dov Shmotkin

The study of Holocaust survivors has presented an array of unsettled dilemmas concerning victimization and survivorship in the course and the aftermath of extreme trauma (Suedfeld, 2000). In addition to the horrors of a human-made industry of death, the mass extermination of Jews in Europe during World War II inflicted on its victims hate-driven persecutions and atrocities, systematic degradation, physical torment and starvation, disruption of individuality and self-identity, the loss of the entirety of former life, and a total collapse of fundamental human values (Cohen, 1988; Eitinger & Major, 1993). Depicted as "conditions of maximum adversity" (Levav, 1998), this trauma has posed compelling questions about the limits of human suffering and endurance.

Several decades had passed before public opinion and professional circles were ripe to fully appreciate the ordeal that Holocaust survivors went through (Nadler, 2001; Solomon, 1995). This historical process led to unfortunate omissions in the treatment as well as the study of survivors in earlier years. Presently, 60 years after their traumatization, the remaining survivors face old age. Their physical and mental status fuses together long-term aftereffects of the trauma and ongoing aging processes. It is evident, however, that most survivors have managed to lead a normal, productive life. Thus, their study provides a valuable opportunity to shed light on the processes by which trauma-inflicted damages coincide with resourceful coping along large portions of the life course.

In this chapter I review empirical investigations of Holocaust survivors. I elaborate with more detail on some of my recent studies when they provide further understanding of conceptual and methodological issues. According to the main conclusion emerging from these investigations, the sequelae of extreme trauma should be understood in joint terms of vulnerability and resilience, emphasizing variability rather than uniformity in coping potentials. As explicated, such an integrative view bears both theoretical and methodological implications for the future study of trauma survivors.

RESEARCH ON HOLOCAUST SURVIVORS: AN OVERVIEW

Studies of Holocaust survivors have demonstrated a host of physical and mental disturbances lasting decades after World War II (see reviews by Dasberg, 1987; Eitinger & Major, 1993; Levav, 1998; Sadovoy, 1997). The sequelae of the trauma were observable particularly among survivors diagnosed or treated in clinical settings and were characterized as "the concentration camp syndrome" or "the survivor syndrome" (Chodoff, 1963; Eitinger, 1964; Krystal, 1968; Niederland, 1968). The major symptoms included among these interrelated syndromes are chronic anxiety and depression, physiological dysfunctions, impaired cognitive functioning, anhedonia, guilt, and difficulties in self-image and social relations. Since the 1980s, the diagnosis of posttraumatic stress disorder (PTSD; American Psychiatric Association, 1994) has increasingly served clinicians in evaluating Holocaust survivors (Kuch & Cox, 1992; Marmar & Horowitz, 1988; Yehuda, Schmeidler, Siever, Binder-Brynes, & Elkin, 1997). PTSD includes three major clusters of symptoms: reexperiencing of the trauma as in intrusive recollections, avoidance of stimuli and emotions that might be associated with the trauma and hyperarousal that often involves anxiety manifestations. The psychological disturbances of PTSD involve certain biological mechanisms as well (Yehuda, 2002).

Most of the psychological publications about Holocaust survivors have highlighted pathological conceptions of dysfunction and intrapsychic dynamics, mainly because the investigators approached survivors via clinics and health care providers (Lomranz, 1995). This orientation is indispensable for understanding the clinical repercussions of trauma and for meeting the urgent needs of survivors at risk. In the last three decades, however, there has been a growing interest in community-based, nonclinical populations of Holocaust survivors who endure their long-lasting plight while living an apparently normal life. A large number of such community-oriented studies found more emotional distress and psychological difficulties among survivors as compared to controls (Antonovsky, Maoz, Dowty, & Wijsenbeek, 1971; Carmil & Carel, 1986; Eaton, Sigal, & Weinfeld, 1982; Fenig & Levav, 1991; Levav & Abramson, 1984; Nadler & Ben-Shushan, 1989). There were also other findings showing that survivors were not necessarily impaired in their psychological adaptation (Harel, Kahana, & Kahana, 1988; Leon, Butcher, Kleinman, Goldberg, & Almagor, 1981; Shanan, 1989; Weinfeld, Sigal, & Eaton, 1981). Some studies even found survivors to be better-off in specific aspects of coping, social adjustment, and hope (Carmil & Breznitz, 1991; Harel, Kahana, & Kahana, 1993; Shanan, 1989).

Several studies addressed the subjective well-being of Holocaust survivors. This concept refers to the individual's overall evaluation of life and serves as a crude indicator of mental health in positive terms such as life satisfaction and happiness (Diener, 2000; Shmotkin, 1998). While Holocaust survivors reported a lower subjective well-being than that of comparison respondents in certain studies (Antonovsky et al., 1971; Harel et al., 1988; Harel et al., 1993), their reports did not differ from those of the comparisons in other studies (Carmil & Carel, 1986; Landau & Litwin, 2000; Leon et al., 1981). In a comprehensive study that included an array of subjective well-being measures and a number of comparison groups, Shmotkin and Lomranz (1998) found that survivors were lower in subjective well-being than comparisons mainly on gerontological measures designed to specifically address older populations (such as the Philadelphia Geriatric Center Morale Scale, Lawton, 1975).

The inconsistency of findings across community-based empirical studies appears also in the comparison of survivors who were incarcerated in concentration camps with survivors who were not. Certain studies revealed, in line with a prior expectation, that camp survivors were psychologically worse-off than non-camp survivors (Fenig & Levav, 1991; Robinson et al., 1990; Robinson, Rapaport-Bar-Sever, & Rapaport, 1994), but other studies failed to reveal such differences (Leon et al., 1981; Yehuda et al., 1997) or found mixed results (Lev-Wiesel & Amir, 2000).

The relatively few controlled studies relating to the physical health of Holocaust survivors have not presented a consistent picture either. There are findings indicating lower self-ratings of physical health as well as greater health problems among survivors (Antonovsky et al., 1971; Harel et al., 1988; Landau & Litwin, 2000; Yaari, Eisenberg, Adler, & Birkhan, 1999). Nevertheless, certain studies of large community samples did not find differences between survivors and controls in various medical parameters (e.g., blood cholesterol, blood glucose, hypertension) as well as in psychosomatic complaints (Aviram, Silverberg & Carel, 1987; Carmil & Carel, 1986).

In sum, controlled studies of community samples have shown a great deal of evidence that mental and physical health problems among Holocaust survivors may last for decades after the trauma. However, this evidence is not consistently confirmed in the literature. It appears, then, that a proper characterization of the survivor population requires a comprehensive view, integrating the aftereffects of extreme traumatization in terms of both vulnerability and resilience outcomes. As will be elaborated later, posttraumatic effects undergo a dynamic process during which they are continuously modulated by developmental trajectories over time.

DYNAMICS OF VULNERABILITY AND RESILIENCE AMONG SURVIVORS

Holocaust Survivors and Aging: New and Renewed Threats

In examining the long-term effects of the Holocaust, one should consider the possibility that the past trauma may be reactivated or aggravated later in life (Kahana, 1992). Indeed, the lack of longitudinal data on Holocaust survivors acutely obstructs any scrutiny of the transformations that the traumatic experiences have undergone from early life to older age. Nevertheless, there is a body of observations in clinical and social work that the trauma can be resensitized by the aging processes. Such processes may normally include illness, frailty, dependency, social isolation, institutionalization, loss of significant others such as spouses and siblings, and facing one's own death. These conditions may bear similarity to traumatic memories of the Holocaust and thus renew threatening experiences that overburden the survivors' adaptation to old age (Brandler, 2000; Danieli, 1981; Harel, 1995; Safford, 1995; Steinitz, 1982).

Due to their heightened sensitivity to the normal processes of aging, older Holocaust survivors may exhibit particular difficulties in coping with exceptional stress. For instance, the Gulf War, in which the Israeli population underwent actual missile attacks accompanied by the threat of poisonous gas, had a significantly more distressful impact on older Holocaust survivors in Israel than on control groups (Robinson et al., 1994; Solomon & Prager, 1992). In another example, cancer was found to involve stronger distress and less adaptive coping among Holocaust survivors suffering from the disease than among cancer patients who had not gone through the Holocaust (Baider, Peretz, & Kaplan-De-Nour, 1992, 1993).

The vulnerability of aging Holocaust survivors may be intensified in the face of the particular developmental tasks of old age. Most pertinent to these tasks is Erikson's (1982) conception of integrity, defined as the sense of coherence and wholeness about one's life while facing finitude. According to Butler (1975), integrity is normally achieved through a life-review process, where older people reminisce about their past and revise its interpretation. Integrity involves a congruent self-narrative, in which older people seek resolution for unsettled issues of the past as well as a meaningful expression of one's unity and identity (Cohler, 1982; McAdams, 1990). These psychological imperatives of late life may be particularly weighty for elderly Holocaust survivors. Their self-integration and self-reconciliation may be hampered by unresolved complications of the trauma, such as emotional agitation and splits, unfinished mourning, guilt, humiliation, and rage (Krystal, 1981, 1991).

These psychodynamic considerations have not been empirically examined in controlled studies. However, a hint of the difficulty of aging Holocaust survivors to formulate an integrative outlook on their life is provided in Shmotkin and Lomranz's (1998) study, where survivors differed from nonvictims in aging-related themes of well-being, notably by the former's lower ability to regard one's past life in congruence with one's self and present expectations.

A Large-Scale View of Very Old Holocaust Survivors: Overall Resilience, Specific Vulnerabilities

In a comprehensive investigation, Shmotkin, Blumstein, and Modan (in press) addressed long-term traumatic effects among 126 Holocaust survivors who had been drawn from a nationally representative sample of the older (aged 75–94) Jewish population in Israel. Their study included two comparative groups of European descent that had immigrated to Israel either before or after the Holocaust, and employed a broad-spectrum assessment of health-related and psychosocial domains. After controlling for socio-demographic variables (age, gender, education, marital status, and income), the results indicated that Holocaust survivors fared significantly worse than pre-war immigrants in certain domains, the former group showing more cumulative life-event distress (indicated by more traumatic events along the life course), a lower level of lifestyle activity (indicated by less frequent everyday activities such as using the mass media and entertaining), and weaker social support (indicated by less availability of somebody to help in emergency). No significant differences were found between these two groups on a variety of other measures that indicated the domains of physical health (e.g., number of diseases), subjective health (e.g., self-rated health), physical functioning (e.g., activities of daily life), health behavior (e.g., taking care of own health), mental health (e.g., ever suffering from a mental disease), cognitive functioning (e.g., memory) and the number of people providing social support. Also intriguing was the lack of significant differences between the survivors and the comparison post-war immigrants, except for the former group's report of more traumatic events in life.

This study suggests that in most areas of life, old survivors do not differ from their counterparts. A similar pattern also emerged in Landau and Litwin's (2000) study on Holocaust survivors of similar age (75+), sampled in the community. They found relatively few significant differences between survivors and controls on various measures of personal resources and vulnerability. However, the survivors in their study did present specific impairments in important outcomes such as PTSD prevalence (among men) and health difficulties (among women).

Very old Holocaust survivors represent the dialectics of leading resilient yet fragile lives. Their very success sustaining life in such an advanced age demonstrates strong capabilities of survival (Perls, 1995). Consisting of "surviving survivors" (Shanan, 1989), the reported non-clinical samples did not include feebler survivors who were too disabled, whether physically or mentally, to be interviewed at the same age or had already passed away in younger age. Nevertheless, there are specific vulnerabilities that make these very old survivors distinguishable from comparable people of similar age and background. Relying on cross-sectional comparisons, we cannot determine whether such vulnerabilities have lingered for many years or rather pertain to this stage of late life. Inspection of the major weaknesses of the survivors in Shmotkin et al.'s (2003) study reveals that they relate to issues of experiencing life as more traumatic in general (life-event distress), vitality and capability to enjoy life (lifestyle activity), and the threat of helplessness (availability of help in emergency). While depressive symptoms revealed only a borderline effect in this study, it is feasible that depressive tendencies among the survivors were masked by compelling high rates of depression in the entire representative sample of the Israeli elderly (Ruskin et al., 1996).

The Survivors' Cumulative Experience Since the Trauma: Loss versus Gain Spirals

Research of the general population confirms the long-lasting effect of traumatic life events, particularly in young age, on subsequent distress and psychopathology (Kessler, Gillis-Light, Magee, Kendler, & Eaves, 1997; Wheaton, Roszell, & Hall, 1997). It appears, however, that cumulative adversity since the focal trauma also has a strong impact on the current mental health status of trauma survivors (Turner & Lloyd, 1995). As elaborated by Singer, Ryff, Carr, and Magee (1998; see also Ryff, Singer, Love, & Essex, 1998), both positive and negative events along the life course generate numerous pathways of cumulative effects on individuals' well-being, thus leading people with mental suffering in the past (e.g., depression) into variations of resilience or vulnerability in the present. Thus, cumulative life events should be conceived as incremental, long-term forces that may yield, in terms of Hobfoll's (1989, 1991) theory, either gain or loss spirals: while a gain spiral restitutes and enhances the individuals' resources, a loss spiral perpetuates the debilitation and depletion of these resources.

Very few studies have addressed cumulative life experiences among Holocaust survivors. Kahana, Harel, & Kahana (1988) found that cumulative life crises of survivors related to lower subjective well-being. Another study by Yehuda et al. (1997) found that the perceived lifetime stress was associated with greater PTSD symptoms of avoidance, particularly emotional detachment and foreshortened future, though it was less related to intrusive and hyperarousal symptoms. In further examination of these associations, Yehuda et al. (1995) demonstrated that cumulative lifetime trauma had a unique contribution to the severity of symptoms among Holocaust survivors, although it could not account for these symptoms entirely.

In Shmotkin et al.'s (2003) study, cumulative life-event distress proved to be a major discriminator between survivors and comparisons. The survivors enumerated more traumatic events, which they considered as highly influential along their lives. However, this cross-sectional finding may confusingly reflect both an earlier process, whereby the focal trauma subsequently led to continued vulnerability and anguish in the survivors' lives, or a later process, whereby the trauma colors the retrospective view of the survivors on their lives. Interestingly, the enumeration of happy events along life did not differentiate the survivors from the comparisons, possibly indicating the greater impact of loss, compared to gain, on people's resource balance (Hobfoll, 1991).

The Time Perspective of the Survivors: Is the Trauma Past or Present?

The experience of time plays an important role in regulating human functioning throughout the life span (Gorman & Wessman, 1977). Apart from other aspects of psychological time, the concept of time perspective refers to the evaluations and the relative emphases that people attach to their temporal coordinates of past, present, and future (Zimbardo & Boyd, 1999). The conception of these time zones in one's life is important for understanding processes of coping, well-being, and aging (Shmotkin, 1991; Shmotkin & Eyal, 2003).

There is both clinical and empirical evidence suggesting incongruities in the time perspective of trauma survivors at large (Holman & Silver, 1998; Terr, 1983) and Holocaust survivors in particular (Krystal, 1981; Lomranz, Shmotkin, Zechovoy, & Rosenberg, 1985). These difficulties may be expressed in either an avoidance of, or overemphasis on, one's past history, a failure to integrate the traumatic experience with the subsequent survivorship and rehabilitation, and a general disruption in the sense of continuity across the life continuum.

The role of time perspective emerged in the study of Shmotkin and Bar-ilan (2003), which extensively analyzed medical records and interview data of 38 Holocaust survivor patients who were either hospitalized or under ambulatory care. The results showed two distinct factors of expressions by which the survivors related to their Holocaust experience. In one factor, labeled Holocaust-as-Present, the trauma is conceived as actually continuing in present life, thus sustaining perceptions of existential threats, persecution and instability. Survivors high on this factor may manifest inappropriate reactions (e.g., preparing oneself for another Holocaust) or misinterpretation of current reality (e.g., undue somatization). This factor is positively correlated with mental symptoms and the number of medical diagnoses.

In contrast, in the other factor, labeled Holocaust-as-Past, the trauma is conceived as a demarcated past event that ended long ago. This involves a relative freedom from intrusion of traumatic memories and related emotional remnants into the present life. Survivors high on this factor focus instead on the social and personal implications of being presently a survivor (e.g., bearing a stigma, handling the consequences of past deprivations). The Holocaust-as-Past factor is associated with fewer mental symptoms and a lower number of medical diagnoses. Intriguingly, however, those high on Holocaust-as-Past are more likely to be rated by their physician as high on danger to life, perhaps because a serious disease made them enter into the medical setting in the first place.

These two expression factors represent differential time perspectives, which serve as modes of coping with the traumatic experience. While Holocaust-as-Present maintains an approach of sensitization and enmeshment with regard to the trauma, Holocaust-as-Past provides a greater extent of repression and distance, which alleviate the emotional involvement with that trauma. Notably, survivors opting for Holocaust-as-Past do not get rid of their plight: rather, they continue to deal with the present implications of their survivorship. Although they appear to employ the more adaptive strategy, their strategy may have its costs. Like repressors in general, they complain less and claim to be healthy, yet their health may take a toll in physiological vulnerability and susceptibility to disease (Schwartz & Kline, 1995; Shedler et al., 1993). Thus, they may tend to be in a higher risk when a serious disease breaks out.

Who Is Actually a Survivor? The Dynamics of a Definition

So far I have referred to "Holocaust survivors" as a group that appears delineated in a host of studies. Usually, this group consists of Jews who lived during World War II in countries that were, at the time, occupied or dominated by the Nazi regime. This biographical fact was sufficient to make these people targets for an official policy of persecution and, in most cases, extermination. Thus, the mere report of living under Nazi rule customarily defines people as survivors, although it is evident that these people actually underwent diverse kinds and levels of traumatic experiences.

In Shmotkin et al.'s (in press) study, the survivor group was determined by factual criteria (the participants reported they had actually been during 1939–1945 in European countries occupied or dominated by the Nazi regime and immigrated to Israel after World War II), as well as by a subjective criterion (the participants answered "Yes" to the question "Do you define yourself as a Holocaust survivor?"). As mentioned above, the survivor group differed little from one of the two comparison groups, namely the post-war immigrants that were of European descent as well but did not define themselves as survivors. An inspection of data relating to these post-war immigrants reveals that most of their life histories were nevertheless affected in one way or another by the Holocaust. Thus, more than half of them actually stayed in Nazi-occupied or

-dominated countries (e.g., former Soviet Union, Romania, Bulgaria, France) and many of them had migrated one or several times before immigrating to Israel, either under the threat of Nazism before the war or as refugees and evacuees during the war. Those who stayed under Nazi or pro-Nazi rule probably managed the dangers of persecution in various ways such as serving in a required field of work or living in conditions of secrecy. It appears, then, that these people, even if not formally considered survivors, did undergo Holocaust-related experiences such as migrations, deportation, separation from families, economic hardship, or otherwise stressful or traumatic conditions. It is also possible that some of the participants in this group were ambiguous or indecisive regarding their survivorship—a phenomenon also known from the literature. Thus, Yehuda et al. (1997) indicate that Holocaust survivors who were not in concentration camps often feel "spared" or "lucky" in comparison to camp survivors, and thus may often decline to identify themselves as Holocaust survivors.

As already noted, the survivors in Shmotkin et al.'s study differed mainly from the comparison group of European-born Jews that had immigrated before World War II to pre-state Israel. This is a group that serves as the only control in most other studies on Israeli Holocaust survivors (an equivalent group of pre-war immigrants serves in studies of survivors in North America). While pre-war immigrants usually represent highly adapted and vigorous people, part of them cannot be considered free from Holocaust-related experiences. Thus, Shmotkin and Lomranz (1998) delineated a special group of pre-war immigrants who had come to pre-state Israel in young age, mostly as adolescents, with their parents staying in Europe and eventually being killed in the Holocaust. This group proved relatively vulnerable compared to other comparison groups. Thus, although not being considered survivors themselves, these Holocaust-inflicted orphans constituted a special category that had not been properly identified in prior research.

In sum, the definition of Holocaust survivors is far more complicated than the way it is usually handled in the extant literature. Recent studies have started to draw attention to the plight of various groups that are not considered Holocaust survivors, either because they did not live under Nazi rule or declined to define themselves as survivors for any reason. These groups, however, experienced a variety of Holocaust-related afflictions, and thus may have been exposed to the delicate interplay of vulnerability and resilience in ways similar to those of recognized survivors.

RESEARCH ON HOLOCAUST SURVIVORS: IMPLICATIONS

Widening the View of Resilience

Clinical diagnosticians and therapists have documented the vast damage and the ceaseless anguish caused to Holocaust survivors along their life after the trauma. Apart from this clinically approached survivor group, community studies suggest that most survivors constitute a non-clinical population and usually lead a normal life. At the same time, however, these survivors do bear unhealed wounds of their trauma, often in various forms of sub-clinical impairments. This review draws attention to the dialectics of vulnerability and resilience among such survivors.

While vulnerability among trauma survivors has been readily conceived in terms of disturbed functions and abnormal manifestations, resilience appears more evasive for detection and evaluation. Indeed, several authors have argued that the inclination to concentrate on psychopathologically oriented constructs may obstruct attempts to reach the fully dynamic picture of weaknesses and strengths among the survivors (Berger, 1988; Marcus & Rosenberg, 1988; Lomranz, 1995). It is warranted, therefore, to specify the multifaceted appearances of resilience.

On a first level, survival itself is an achievement of overcoming a socially abnormal reality (Lifton, 1993). For many survivors, this probably required an enormous self-mobilization of strengths in inconceivable conditions. Encountering social attitudes of suspicion, disbelief, and stigmatization in the immediate years after World War II (Nadler, 2001), Holocaust survivors often found it difficult to incorporate this personal triumph into their self-perceived worth and identity.

Another major achievement of most survivors is their success aligning themselves with the normative requirements of life in their society. Surprisingly, researchers often failed to appreciate the real significance of "no significant differences" they found between Holocaust survivors and control groups on various functioning measures. In fact, this lack of differences attests to a compelling resilience on the part of the survivors, who started their self-rehabilitation from a point of an entirely devastated life.

A central aspect of resilience relates to the ability of many survivors to formulate new meanings in life. A most pertinent example is Victor Frankl (1963), a survivor of the Nazi concentration camps, whose widely known theory of logotherapy derived from the vital role of meaning in the psychological recovery of people surviving extreme traumatization. More recently, models of posttraumatic growth (Calhoun & Tedeschi, 1998;

Tedeschi, Park, & Calhoun, 1998) have elaborated the ways in which the coping with trauma may be transformed into further insights and enrichment in one's perceptions of self, interpersonal relationships, and philosophy of life. In this vein, a large number of Holocaust survivors have succeeded in finding a profoundly positive meaning in bearing witness to the Holocaust so that its historic lesson is properly learned and remembered, in raising a family, which ensures their victory over an evil and deadly fate, in building flourishing careers, which benefit society at large, and in dedicating themselves to social causes and cherished values (Helmreich, 1992; Shantall, 1999).

In line with the foregoing discussion, several authors have strongly argued for a balanced view of Holocaust survivors, whose functional impairments and mental suffering do not exclude simultaneous achievements of restorative adjustment and successful coping (Berger, 1988; Harel et al., 1993; Kahana & Kahana, 1998; Robinson et al., 1990; Shmotkin & Lomranz, 1998; Sigal & Weinfeld, 1989). Indeed, this co-residence of contradictory vectors may lead survivors to develop a "paradoxical self" (Lomranz, 1995) or a "serial self" (Laufer, 1988), which reflect the complexity of combining extremes of adversity and advantage into a coherent framework.

Appreciating the Diversity of Overcoming the Trauma

As specified earlier in this chapter, the research on Holocaust survivors has suggested certain factors that may be particularly relevant to this population in regulating the balance between vulnerability and resilience. Thus, reconciliation with one's aging may prove an essential factor of this kind because aging is not favorable to the containment of past trauma. In very old age, the maintenance of vitality through continuous activity may become of special importance for promoting resilience. Also mentioned as influential factors were the spirals of cumulative life-event experience, the time perspective in which the trauma is perceived, and the self-defined identity as survivor. This list is clearly selective but sufficient to exemplify how objective (e.g., aging processes) and subjective (e.g., psychological time) factors may join together in determining diverse combinations of vulnerability-resilience with regard to the trauma. As shown in some of the cited studies, such combinations may be detected only via a wide-spectrum assessment of the survivors' physical and mental functioning. It is well observed that traumatized people may present both functional and dysfunctional behaviors in independent, but also in related, domains of life (Lyons, 1991).

There are obviously many other factors that await clarifications as to how they may generate human variability in the context of extreme trauma. Two most fundamental examples are the survivor's gender and the survivor's age when the trauma took place.

The impact of gender is definitely not settled in the studies on Holocaust survivors. For example, Landau and Litwin (2000) suggest that gender differences in late life (e.g., a higher proportion of widowhood among women) may affect gender proportions in survivor samples (increasing the relative number of men). Their study, as specified above, found completely different patterns of posttraumatic effects among men and women. In other studies of Holocaust survivors, there were findings of women having more emotional distress than men (Carmil & Carel, 1986; Levav & Abramson, 1984), as well as the opposite (Nadler & Ben-Shushan, 1989). Many studies refrained from any gender comparisons (or adjusted for gender effects) and two sampled only women (Antonovsky et al., 1971; Fenig & Levav, 1991). In view of the general literature on gender differences in reaction to trauma (women tending to exhibit greater vulnerability, e.g., Wolfe & Kimerling, 1997), we should expect further clarifications about gender-based diversity following the Holocaust trauma.

Regarding the impact of age at the trauma, we also face different messages. On the one hand, there is a vast psychodynamic literature suggesting that extreme trauma in the formative years of early life may disrupt subsequent psychological development in most profound and often irreversible ways. On the other hand, there are various reports of astonishing recovery and adaptability of traumatized children in the Holocaust (Dasberg, 2001; Krell, 1985; Sigal & Weinfeld, 2001; Valent, 1998). Although this chapter has cited more studies on older survivors who endured the Holocaust as late adolescents and young adults, the issue of child survivors will certainly become central when they soon become the only survivor population remaining alive. Conceptually, it is urgently needed to adopt an integrative life-span approach to the study of survivors in order to understand the effects of both early and late developmental processes on the diverse modes of coping with the trauma (Lomranz, 1995; Kahana & Kahana, 1998).

Handling Prevalent Methodological Flaws

Evidently, much of the inconsistency in the body of research on Holocaust survivors stems from abundant methodological problems. Notably, empirical studies constitute only a small fraction of the psychological publications on Holocaust survivors. Most of the empirical studies are methodologically flawed in various ways, such as employing very small samples of survivors, questionable procedures of sampling, inappropriate comparison groups or the complete lack of them, and a failure to properly report the background characteristics of the participants (for reviews of this subject, see Harel et al., 1993; Lomranz, 1995; Solkoff, 1992). The accumulation of these omissions over more than five decades indeed introduces many questions and doubts in relation to the available data on Holocaust survivors.

The sampling of trauma survivors and their comparison with suitable control groups have posed difficult challenges for trauma researchers in general (Kulka & Schlenger, 1993). Recent findings have shed some light on the implications of different sampling procedures for the study of Holocaust survivors. Thus, Shmotkin and Lomranz (1998) found differences between study participants that were purposely sampled as Holocaust survivors (as by membership lists of relevant community organizations or by personal acquaintance networks) and study participants that were incidentally sampled for research unrelated to the Holocaust (and identified by a questionnaire item that queried about their survivorship status). The results showed that the former had a remarkably higher level of subjective well-being (mainly positive affect) than the latter. It might be that the higher survivorship salience in the former group paradoxically ameliorated the traumatic strains by providing the survivors with a meaningful identity, supportive affiliations, and cathartic opportunities to bear witness. This finding means that the Holocaust survivors who are more accessible to the researchers and the public may not accurately represent the many survivors who stay "hidden" in the larger population. While the drawing of Holocaust survivors from nationally representative samples remains rare (Carmil & Breznitz, 1991; Shmotkin et al., 2003), it is imperative that researchers be fully attentive to the implications of different sampling strategies for an accurate characterization of distinct survivor subgroups.

Besides the few studies that distinguished between different samples of Holocaust survivors (e.g., Kahana et al., 1988; Nadler & Ben-Shushan, 1989; Shmotkin & Lomranz, 1998), there are even fewer studies that employed more than one control group (Shmotkin et al., 2003; Shmotkin & Lomranz, 1998). As explicated above, the possible complications in defining survivors bear the implication that the employment of a single control group is no longer adequate. In fact, the term "control group" should be replaced by "comparison group" because Jews of

European descent, who shared the same cohort and socio-demographic background with the survivors, actually represent varying experiences, whether direct or indirect, of Holocaust-related afflictions.

CONCLUSION

The extant body of research on Holocaust survivors is highly perplexing unless one looks for a refined differentiation rather than an overgeneralization. While the mixed picture raises doubts about the methodological soundness of some research designs in this area, it certainly points to the variability in human potentials of overcoming most extreme adversity. Approaching its last phases, the research on Holocaust survivors should be explicit in its contributions to the understanding of trauma at large. A contribution of this kind is to highlight the perpetual dialectics of vulnerability and resilience, thus reflecting the universal dilemma of trauma survivors: bridging the gap between the traumatic and the posttraumatic spheres of life. Eventually, the relative predominance of vulnerability and resilience signals the extent to which the survivors find it possible to settle their agony and to come to terms with life.

REFERENCES

American Psychiatric Association (1994). *Diagnostic and Statistical Manual of Mental Disorders* (DSM, 4th ed.). Washington, DC: Author.

Antonovsky, A., Maoz, B., Dowty, N., & Wijsenbeek, H. (1971). Twenty-five years later: A limited study of the sequelae of the concentration camp experience. *Social Psychiatry, 6*, 186–193.

Aviram, A., Silverberg, D. S., & Carel, R. S. (1987). Hypertension in European immigrants to Israel—the possible effect of the Holocaust. *Israel Journal of Medical Sciences, 23*, 257–263.

Baider, L., Peretz, T., & Kaplan-De-Nour, A. (1992). Effect of the Holocaust on coping with cancer. *Social Science and Medicine, 34*, 11–15.

Baider, L., Peretz, T., & Kaplan-De-Nour, A. (1993). Holocaust cancer patients: A comparative study. *Psychiatry, 56*, 349–355.

Berger, L. (1988). The long-term psychological consequences of the Holocaust on the survivors and their offspring. In R. L. Braham (Ed.), *The psychological perspectives of the Holocaust and its aftermath* (pp. 175–221). New York: City University of New York and Columbia University Press.

Brandler, S. (2000). Understanding aged Holocaust survivors. *Families in Society, 81*, 66–75.

Butler, R. N. (1975). *Why survive? Being old in America.* New York: Harper & Row.

Calhoun, L. G., & Tedeschi, R. G. (1998). Beyond recovery from trauma: Implications for clinical practice and research. *Journal of Social Issues,* 54, 357–371.

Carmil, D., & Breznitz, S. (1991). Personal trauma and world view—Are extremely stressful experiences related to political attitudes, religious beliefs, and future orientation? *Journal of Traumatic Stress,* 4, 393–405.

Carmil, D., & Carel, R. S. (1986). Emotional distress and satisfaction in life among Holocaust survivors—A community study of survivors and controls. *Psychological Medicine,* 16, 141–149.

Chodoff, P. (1963). Late effects of the concentration camp syndrome. *Archives of General Psychiatry,* 8, 323–333.

Cohen, E. A. (1988). *Human behavior in the concentration camp* (M. H. Braaksma, Trans.). London: Free Association Books.

Cohler, B. J. (1982). Personal narrative and life course. In P. B. Baltes & O. G. Brim Jr. (Eds.), *Life-span development and behavior* (Vol. 4, pp. 205–241). New York: Academic Press.

Danieli, Y. (1981). On the achievement of integration in aging survivors of the Nazi Holocaust. *Journal of Geriatric Psychiatry,* 14, 191–210.

Dasberg, H. (1987). Psychological distress and Holocaust survivors and offspring in Israel, forty years later: A review. *Israel Journal of Psychiatry and Related Sciences,* 24, 243–256.

Dasberg, H. (2001). Adult child survivor syndrome: On deprived childhoods of aging Holocaust survivors. *Israel Journal of Psychiatry and Related Sciences,* 38, 13–26.

Diener, E. (2000). Subjective well-being: The science of happiness and a proposal for a national index. *American Psychologist,* 55, 34–43.

Eaton, W. W., Sigal, J. J., & Weinfeld, M. (1982). Impairment in Holocaust survivors after 33 years: Data from an unbiased community sample. *American Journal of Psychiatry,* 139, 773–777.

Eitinger, L. (1964). *Concentration camp survivors in Norway and Israel.* Oslo: Oslo University Press.

Eitinger, L., & Major, E. F. (1993). Stress of the Holocaust. In L. Goldberger & S. Breznitz (Eds.), *Handbook of stress: Theoretical and clinical aspects* (2nd ed., pp. 617–640). New York: Free Press.

Erikson, E. H. (1982). *The life cycle completed: A review.* New York: Norton.

Fenig, S., & Levav, I. (1991). Demoralization and social supports among Holocaust survivors. *Journal of Nervous and Mental Disease,* 179, 167–172.

Frankl, V. (1963). *Man's search for meaning: An introduction to logotherapy.* New York: Pocket Books.

Gorman, B. S., & Wessman, A. E. (Eds.). (1977). *The personal experience of time.* New York: Plenum.

Harel, Z. (1995). Serving Holocaust survivors and survivor families. *Marriage and Family Review,* 21, 29–49.

Harel, Z., Kahana, B., & Kahana, E. (1988). Psychological well-being among Holocaust survivors and immigrants in Israel. *Journal of Traumatic Stress,* 1, 413–429.

Harel, Z., Kahana, B., & Kahana, E. (1993). Social resources and the mental health of aging Nazi Holocaust survivors and immigrants. In J. P. Wilson & B. Raphael (Eds.), *International handbook of traumatic stress syndromes* (pp. 241–252). New York: Plenum.

Helmreich, W. B. (1992). *Against all odds: Holocaust survivors and the successful lives they made in America.* New York: Simon & Schuster.

Hobfoll, S. E. (1989). Conservation of resources: A new attempt at conceptualizing stress. *American Psychologist,* 44, 513–524.

Hobfoll, S. E. (1991). Traumatic stress: A theory based on rapid loss of resources. *Anxiety Research,* 4, 187–197.

Holman, E. A., & Silver, R. C. (1998). Getting "stuck" in the past: Temporal orientation and coping with trauma. *Journal of Personality and Social Psychology,* 74, 1146–1163.

Kahana, B. (1992). Late-life adaptation in the aftermath of extreme stress. In M. L. Wykle, E. Kahana, & J. Kowal (Eds.), *Stress and health among the elderly* (pp. 151–171). New York: Springer.

Kahana, B., Harel, Z., & Kahana, E. (1988). Predictors of psychological well-being among survivors of the Holocaust. In J. P. Wilson, Z. Harel, & B. Kahana (Eds.), *Human adaptation to extreme stress: From Holocaust to Vietnam* (pp. 171–192). New York: Plenum.

Kahana, B., & Kahana, E. (1998). Toward a temporal-spatial model of cumulative life stress: Placing late-life stress effects in a life-course perspective. In J. Lomranz (Ed.), *Handbook of aging and mental health: An integrative approach* (pp. 153–178). New York: Plenum.

Kessler, R. C., Gillis-Light, J., Magee, W. J., Kendler, K. S. & Eaves, L. J. (1997). Childhood adversity and adult psychopathology. In I. H. Gotlib & B. Wheaton (Eds.), *Stress and adversity over the life course: Trajectories and turning points* (pp. 29–49). Cambridge, England: Cambridge University Press.

Krell, R. (1985). Child survivors of the Holocaust: 40 years later. *Journal of the American Academy of Child Psychiatry,* 24, 378–380.

Krystal, H. (Ed.). (1968). *Massive psychic trauma.* New York: International Universities Press.

Krystal, H. (1981). The aging survivor of the Holocaust: Integration and self-healing in posttraumatic states. *Journal of Geriatric Psychiatry,* 14, 165–189.

Krystal, H. (1991). Integration and self-healing in post-traumatic states: A ten-year retrospective. *American Imago,* 48, 93–118.

Kuch, K., & Cox, B. J. (1992). Symptoms of PTSD in 124 survivors of the Holocaust. *American Journal of Psychiatry,* 149, 337–340.

Kulka, R. A., & Schlenger, W. E. (1993). Survey research and field designs for the study of posttraumatic stress disorder. In J. P. Wilson & B. Raphael (Eds.),

International handbook of traumatic stress syndromes (pp. 145–155). New York: Plenum.

Landau, R., & Litwin, H. (2000). The effects of extreme early stress in very old age. *Journal of Traumatic Stress, 13,* 473–487.

Laufer, R. S. (1988). The serial self: War trauma, identity, and adult development. In J. P. Wilson, Z. Harel, & B. Kahana (Eds.), *Human adaptation to extreme stress: From Holocaust to Vietnam* (pp. 33–53). New York: Plenum.

Lawton, M. P. (1975). The Philadelphia Geriatric Center Morale Scale: A revision. *Journal of Gerontology, 30,* 85–89.

Leon, G. R., Butcher, J. N., Kleinman, M., Goldberg, A., & Almagor, M. (1981). Survivors of the Holocaust and their children: Current status and adjustment. *Journal of Personality and Social Psychology, 41,* 503–516.

Levav, I. (1998). Individuals under conditions of maximum adversity: The Holocaust. In B. P. Dohrenwend (Ed.), *Adversity, stress, and psychopathology* (pp. 13–33). New York: Oxford University Press.

Levav, I., & Abramson, J. H. (1984). Emotional distress among concentration camp survivors—A community study in Jerusalem. *Psychological Medicine, 14,* 215–218.

Lev-Wiesel, R., & Amir, M. (2000). Posttraumatic stress disorder symptoms, psychological distress, personal resources, and quality of life in four groups of Holocaust child survivors. *Family Process, 39,* 445–459.

Lifton, R. J. (1993). From Hiroshima to the Nazi doctors: The evolution of psycho formative approaches to understanding traumatic stress syndromes. In J. P. Wilson & B. Raphael (Eds.), *International handbook of traumatic stress syndromes* (pp. 11–23). New York: Plenum.

Lomranz, J. (1995). Endurance and living: Long-term effects of the Holocaust. In S. E. Hobfoll & M. W. de Vries (Eds.), *Extreme stress and communities: Impact and intervention* (pp. 325–352). Dordrecht, the Netherlands: Kluwer.

Lomranz, J., Shmotkin, D., Zechovoy, A., & Rosenberg, E. (1985). Time orientation in Nazi concentration camp survivors: Forty years after. *American Journal of Orthopsychiatry, 55,* 230–236.

Lyons, J. A. (1991). Strategies for assessing the potential for positive adjustment following trauma. *Journal of Traumatic Stress, 4,* 93–111.

Marcus, P., & Rosenberg, A. (1988). A philosophical critique of the "survivor syndrome" and some implications for treatment. In R. L. Braham (Ed.), *The psychological perspectives of the Holocaust and its aftermath* (pp. 53–78). New York: City University of New York and Columbia University Press.

Marmar, C. R., & Horowitz, M. J. (1988). Diagnosis and phase-oriented treatment of post-traumatic stress disorder. In J. P. Wilson, Z. Harel, & B. Kahana (Eds.), *Human adaptation to extreme stress: From Holocaust to Vietnam* (pp. 81–103). New York: Plenum.

McAdams, D. P. (1990). Unity and purpose in human lives: The emergence of identity as a life story. In A. I. Rabin, R. A. Zucker, R. A. Emmons, & S.

Frank (Eds.), *Studying persons and lives* (pp. 148–200). New York: Springer.

Nadler, A. (2001). The victim and the psychologist: Changing perceptions of Israeli Holocaust survivors by the mental health community in the past 50 years. *History of Psychology, 4,* 159–181.

Nadler, A., & Ben-Shushan, D. (1989). Forty years later: Long-term consequences of massive traumatization as manifested by Holocaust survivors from the city and the kibbutz. *Journal of Consulting and Clinical Psychology, 57,* 287–293.

Niederland, W.G. (1968). Clinical observations of the "survivor syndrome." *International Journal of Psychoanalysis, 49,* 313–315.

Perls, T.T. (1995). The influence of demographic selection upon the oldest old. *Journal of Geriatric Psychiatry, 28,* 33–56.

Robinson, S., Hemmendinger, J., Netanel, R., Rapaport, M., Zilberman, L., & Gal, A. (1994). Retraumatization of Holocaust survivors during the Gulf War and SCUD missile attacks on Israel. *British Journal of Medical Psychology, 67,* 353–362.

Robinson, S., Rapaport, J., Durst, R., Rapaport, M., Rosca, P., Metzer, S., & Zilberman, L. (1990). The late effects of Nazi persecution among elderly Holocaust survivors. *Acta Psychiatrica Scandinavica, 82,* 311–315.

Robinson, S., Rapaport-Bar-Sever, M., & Rapaport, J. (1994). The present state of people who survived the Holocaust as children. *Acta Psychiatrica Scandinavica, 89,* 242–245.

Ruskin, P.E., Blumstein, Z., Walter-Ginzburg, A., Fuchs, Z., Lusky, A., Novikov, I., & Modan, B. (1996). Depressive symptoms among community-dwelling oldest-old residents in Israel. *American Journal of Geriatric Psychiatry, 4,* 208–217.

Ryff, C.D., Singer, B., Love, G.D., & Essex, M.J. (1998). Resilience in adulthood and later life: Defining features and dynamic processes. In J. Lomranz (Ed.), *Handbook of aging and mental health: An integrative approach* (pp. 69–99). New York: Plenum.

Sadovoy, J. (1997). A review of the late-life effects of prior psychological trauma. *American Journal of Geriatric Psychiatry, 5,* 287–301.

Safford, F. (1995). Aging stressors for Holocaust survivors and their families. *Journal of Gerontological Social Work, 24,* 131–153.

Schwartz, G.E., & Kline, J.P. (1995). Repression, emotional disclosure, and health: Theoretical, empirical, and clinical considerations. In J.W. Pennebaker (Ed.), *Emotion, disclosure, and health* (pp. 177–193). Washington, DC: American Psychological Association.

Shanan, J. (1989). Surviving the survivors: Late personality development of Jewish Holocaust survivors. *International Journal of Mental Health, 17,* 42–71.

Shantall, T. (1999). The experience of meaning in suffering among Holocaust survivors. *Journal of Humanistic Psychology, 39,* 96–124.

Shedler, J., Mayman, M., & Manis, M. (1993). The illusion of mental health. *American Psychologist,* 48, 1117–1131.

Shmotkin, D. (1991). The role of time orientation in life satisfaction across the life-span. *Journal of Gerontology: Psychological Sciences,* 46, 243–250.

Shmotkin, D. (1998). Declarative and differential aspects of subjective well-being and implications for mental health in later life. In J. Lomranz (Ed.), *Handbook of aging and mental health: An integrative approach* (pp. 15–43). New York: Plenum.

Shmotkin, D, & Barilan, Y. M. (2003). Expressions of Holocaust experience and their relationship to mental symptoms and physical morbidity among Holocaust survivor patients. *Journal of Behavioral Medicine,* 25, 115–134.

Shmotkin, D., Blumstein, T., & Modan, B. (2003). Tracing long-term effects of early trauma: A broad-scope view of Holocaust survivors in late life. *Journal of Consulting and Clinical Psychology,* 71, 223–234.

Shmotkin, D., & Eyal, N. (2003). Psychological time in later life: Implications for counseling. *Journal of Counseling and Development,* 81, 259–267.

Shmotkin, D., & Lomranz, J. (1998). Subjective well-being among Holocaust survivors: An examination of overlooked differentiations. *Journal of Personality and Social Psychology,* 75, 141–155.

Sigal, J. J., & Weinfeld, M. (1989). Trama and rebirth: Intergenerational effects of the Holocaust. New York: Praeger.

Sigal, J.J., & Weinfeld, M. (2001). Do children cope better than adults with potentially traumatic stress? A 40-year follow-up of Holocaust survivors. *Psychiatry,* 64, 69–80.

Singer, B., Ryff, C.D., Carr, D., & Magee, W.J. (1998). Linking life histories and mental health: A person-centered strategy. *Sociological Methodology,* 28, 1–51.

Solkoff, N. (1992). Children of survivors of the Nazi Holocaust: A critical review of the literature. *American Journal of Orthopsychiatry,* 62, 342–358.

Solomon, Z. (1995). From denial to recognition: Attitudes toward Holocaust survivors from World War II to the present. *Journal of Traumatic Stress,* 8, 215–228.

Solomon, Z., & Prager, E. (1992). Elderly Israeli Holocaust survivors during the Persian Gulf War: A study of psychological stress. *American Journal of Psychiatry,* 149, 1707–1710.

Steinitz, L. Y. (1982). Psycho-social effects of the Holocaust on aging survivors and their families. *Journal of Gerontological Social Work,* 4, 145–152.

Suedfeld, P. (2000). Reverberations of the Holocaust fifty years later: Psychology's contributions to understanding persecution and genocide. *Canadian Psychology,* 41, 1–9.

Tedeschi, R.G., Park, C.L., & Calhoun, L.G. (1998). *Posttraumatic growth: Positive changes in the aftermath of crisis.* Mahwah, NJ: Lawrence Erlbaum.

Terr, L. C. (1983). Time sense following psychic trauma: A clinical study of ten adults and twenty children. *American Journal of Orthopsychiatry,* 53, 244–261.

Turner, R. J., & Lloyd, D. A. (1995). Lifetime traumas and mental health: The significance of cumulative adversity. *Journal of Health and Social Behavior,* 36, 360–376.

Valent, P. (1998). Child survivors: A review. In J. S. Kastenberg & C. Kahn (Eds.), *Children surviving persecution: An international study of trauma and healing* (pp. 109–123). Westport, CT: Praeger.

Weinfeld, M., Sigal, J. J., & Eaton, W. W. (1981). Long-term effects of the Holocaust on selected social attitudes and behaviors of survivors: A cautionary note. *Social Forces,* 60, 1–19.

Wheaton, B., Roszell, P., & Hall, K. (1997). The impact of twenty childhood and adult traumatic stressors on the risk of psychiatric disorder. In I. H. Gotlib & B. Wheaton (Eds.), *Stress and adversity over the life course: Trajectories and turning points* (pp. 50–72). Cambridge, England: Cambridge University Press.

Wolfe, J., & Kimerling, R. (1997). Gender issues in the assessment of posttraumatic stress disorder. In J. P. Wilson & T. M. Keane (Eds.), *Assessing psychological trauma and PTSD* (pp. 192–238). New York: Guilford.

Yaari, A., Eisenberg, E., Adler, R., & Birkhan, J. (1999). Chronic pain in Holocaust survivors. *Journal of Pain and Symptom Management,* 17, 181–187.

Yehuda, R. (2002). Post-traumatic stress disorder. *The New England Journal of Medicine,* 346, 108–114.

Yehuda, R., Kahana, B., Schmeidler, J., Southwick, S. M., Wilson, S., & Giller, E. L. (1995). Impact of cumulative lifetime trauma and recent stress on current posttraumatic stress disorder symptoms in Holocaust survivors. *American Journal of Psychiatry,* 152, 1815–1818.

Yehuda, R., Schmeidler, J., Siever, L. J., Binder-Brynes, K., & Elkin, A. (1997). Individual differences in posttraumatic stress disorder symptom profiles in Holocaust survivors in concentration camps or in hiding. *Journal of Traumatic Stress,* 10, 453–463.

Zimbardo, P. G., & Boyd, J. N. (1999). Putting time in perspective: A valid, reliable individual-differences metric. *Journal of Personality and Social Psychology,* 77, 1271–1288.

Chapter 11

AFRICAN AMERICANS' HOPE AND COPING WITH RACISM STRESSORS

Virgil H. Adams III, Kevin L. Rand, Kristin Kahle, C. R. Snyder, Carla Berg, Elisa A. King, and Alicia Rodriguez-Hanley

HOPE THEORY

In hope theory, hope is defined as the perceived capacity to produce pathways to desired goals (called pathways thinking), along with the motivation to initiate and sustain movement toward those goals (called agency thinking) (Snyder, 1994a). The three components of goals, pathways, and agency are essential for understanding human action sequences. Let's examine each more closely.

Goals are the targets of mental action sequences. Such goals may be positive or negative, and they can be short- or long-term in duration. Positive (or approach) goals focus on either obtaining a novel outcome, sustaining a present goal, or furthering a current goal (Snyder, 2002a). Negative (or avoidance) goals involve the forestalling or delaying of a negative event. Vivid and clearly specified goals, along with goals that stretch previous levels of attainment, are more characteristic of high- as compared to low-hope people.

Whereas goals are the targets of behavior sequences, pathways thinking reflects the perceived capacity to find effective routes for desired goals (Snyder, 1994b). This pathways thought may activate already known skills, or it may initiate the acquisition of new skills. High-hope individuals tend to be decisive and confident that they can find effective routes (Snyder, LaPointe, Crowson Jr., & Early, 1998). These high-hope individuals also evaluate and refine their plans as necessary, and find alternative routes when encountering blockages (Snyder, Cheavens, & Michael,

1999). Thus, pathways thinking constantly evolves, and high- as compared to low-hope individuals more readily alter their routes so as to maximize the effectiveness of their goal pursuits. It also should be noted that pathways thinking reflects the perception of capabilities, although the actual capabilities are implicated when pathways thought is put into action.

Agency thought is the motivating force that initiates and sustains movement along the routes to goals (Snyder, Harris, et al., 1991). Through agency, individuals produce the mental energy for goal attainment, with thoughts such as "I can" and "I will not be stopped" (Snyder, Harris et al., 1991). Individuals with high levels of agency also will readily apply their motivation to alternative goal routes when blockages are encountered (Snyder, 2002a). As we observed in regard to pathways thinking, *agency thought reflects the perception about one's motivation* to use pathways. These perceptions, in turn, are translated into actual usage.

At this point, we need to introduce the concepts of stress and emotion. Within hope theory, stress(ors) are defined as the blockages that are encountered in the pursuit of goals. Likewise, emotions are experienced as feedback about perceived success in the goal-seeking sequence (Snyder, 2002a). Specifically, positive emotions are posited to reflect the perception of successful goal attainment, whereas negative emotions reflect the perception of impeded progress. Research supports these postulates in that perceived goal-pursuit progress drives the subsequently experienced emotions (Snyder, Sympson et al., 1996).

Because high- as compared to low-hope people tend to be more successful in their goal pursuits, they experience more positive emotions. Furthermore, the high hopers generally react to stressors (i.e., goal blockages) by initiating the appropriate, goal-directed coping responses. In this way, hope enhances well-being (Diener, 1984; Emmons, 1986).

In summary, hope is an active cognitive process in which pathways and agency thoughts are interactively translated into actions that move individuals toward goal attainment. Additionally, stressors are encountered as blockages to goals, and emotions provide feedback to people throughout their goal-seeking efforts.

HOPE AMONG AFRICAN AMERICANS

The history of African Americans is intriguing in that the group has gone from slavery to legalized separation to "equal" status. As such, one would expect that a population encountering so many hardships would be lacking in hope. In actuality, however, there is some evidence that the opposite appears to be the case for African Americans. In a study of college students, for example, African Americans were higher in hope than their Caucasian counterparts (Munoz-Dunbar, 1996). Nevertheless, African Americans have encountered numerous obstacles in their lives, and it is not surprising that they often fare poorly relative to their Caucasian counterparts on many objective indices of well-being—shorter life spans and higher rates of heart disease, stroke, cancer, cirrhosis, and diabetes (Minino & Smith, 2001).

In a series of studies conducted by Adams and colleagues (Adams, 2002; Adams & Jackson, 2000; Adams & Nelson, 2001), hope consistently has been found to play an important role in the subjective well-being (as measured by life satisfaction) reported by African Americans. Adams and Jackson (2000), for example, conducted a panel analysis of three age cohorts based on data from the National Survey of Black Americans (Jackson & Gurin, 1987). Hope was measured by two items that tapped the conceptualization of hope by Snyder and colleagues (1991). More specifically, pathways was measured by an item that assessed whether respondents perceived that their plans would work, and agency was measured by an item that assessed respondents' perceived motivation about attaining their life goals. The results suggested that a connection existed between higher hope and increased satisfaction for all three cohorts, although the mechanisms of hope differed somewhat in each age cohort.

In another survey study, Adams and Nelson (2001) examined life satisfaction among African American fathers. They found that hope accounted for variance beyond that attributable to parental strain, self-esteem, and perceptions of how well these fathers provided for their families. In other words, higher hope uniquely predicted these fathers' perceptions of being able to provide for their families. Adams (2002) also reports similar findings in recent work examining African American mothers. More specifically, hope accounted for variance in the reported life satisfaction of African American mothers even after considering income, marital status, concerns about finances, social support, perception of family care, self-esteem, identity, and family help.

Overall, in commenting on this set of findings, Adams (2001) has noted that African Americans draw on hope as a way of remaining resilient in the face of adversity. As such, hope appears to be tied intimately to the active and adaptive coping mechanisms in several different samples of African Americans.

Through hopeful thinking, minorities such as African Americans can gain new insights into their goal attainment activities. Importantly, high- as compared to low-hope African Americans appear to be better able to deal with the blockages to their goal attainments (i.e., stressors). We believe that these blockages are part of the harsh realities associated with living in a race-conscious society. Indeed, one of the leading obstacles is that which stems from the discrimination and prejudice related to racism.

RACISM STRESSORS

Racism has been defined as "an individual's prejudicial attitudes and discriminatory behavior toward people of a given race, or institutional practices (even if not motivated by prejudice) that subordinate people of a given race" (Myers, 2002, p. 330). Although racism as directed toward African Americans has received the most attention (Bowen-Reid & Harrell, 2002), it is important to keep in mind that all U.S. minority groups experience some degree of racism (Sydell & Nelson, 2000).

The more blatant forms of racism have given way in contemporary American society to what Pettigrew and Martin (1987) have called "modern racism," which manifests four basic characteristics. These include: (a) a rejection of stereotypes and blatant prejudice (e.g., because it is no longer acceptable to be a bold-faced bigot, racism is masked in more subtle forms); (b) opposition to racial change for ostensibly non-racial reasons (e.g., opposition to affirmative action programs); (c) group-based self-interest and subjective threat (e.g., "this is not about me as an individual, but it is that my group is being subjected to reverse prejudice"); and (d) individualistic conceptions of opportunity in America (e.g., "it is best to pull yourself up by your bootstraps; if you don't succeed, it is not because of prejudice, but rather because you're not working hard enough") (Pettigrew & Martin, 1987). In a nutshell, Pettigrew and Martin reason that a *widely held but inaccurate belief* is that contemporary American society has a level playing field where anyone with the desire can succeed. Accordingly, those who hold this "level playing field" view fail to realize that minorities in general, and African Americans in particular, experience a different reality.

Yet another component of modern racism is worthy of note. Namely, there must be direct evidence of a comparison group in order to demonstrate that racism exists. For example, to prove that a restaurant was being racist when it compelled African American patrons to pay before receiving their meals, there had to be a comparison group of Caucasian patrons who did *not* have to pay before eating. Thus, the current legal perspective has shifted the burden of proof to the very African Americans who are the victims of the racism.

As noted earlier, African Americans all too often have experienced the racism stressor. Many researchers have emphasized how racism and prejudice are omnipresent and chronic stressors for African Americans (Burke, 1984; Essed, 1990; Feagin & Sikes, 1994; Fernando, 1984; Smith, 1985; Utsey & Ponterotto, 1996; Utsey, Ponterotto, Reynolds, & Cancelli, 2000; White & Parham, 1990). Essed described the chronicity of racism as follows: "to live with the threat of racism means planning, almost everyday of one's life, how to avoid or defend oneself against discrimination" (p. 260; cited in Utsey & Ponterotto, 1996).

The stress associated with racism has been implicated in the development of depression (Burke, 1984), antisocial behavior (Simpson & Yinger, 1985), lowered self-esteem (Broman, 1997; Fernando, 1984), lower levels of happiness and life satisfaction (Jackson et al., 1996), and poor academic performance (Gougis, 1986). In addition, frequent encounters with racism have been linked with stress-related health problems such as hypertension and cardiovascular disease (Jackson et al., 1996; Krieger & Sidney, 1996; Smith, 1985). Indeed, some researchers (e.g., Abernethy, 1995; Priest, 1991) have suggested that the stress from such racism is so debilitating that it is one of the major reasons that African Americans seek psychotherapy.

Understanding the stressful effects of racism, however, is not achieved simply by knowing the amount of exposure to prejudice. According to Clark, Anderson, Clark, and Williams' (1999) biopsychosocial model of racism as a stressor, exposure to racism results in exaggerated psychological and physical responses among African Americans. These responses are moderated, however, by factors such as physical constitution, sociodemographic factors, psychological and behavioral factors, and coping responses. For example, exposure to racism seems to be exacerbated by psychological characteristics such as the Type A behavior pattern, cynical hostility, neuroticism, low self-esteem, hardiness, perceived control, and anger expression (Clark et al., 1999). Given these latter factors, it logically follows that a cognitive variable such as hope would be a crucial moderator of the racism and the well-being relationship among African Americans.

We hypothesize that the role of hope in the coping process can depend on the type of racism that is experienced (i.e., institutional versus individual). When dealing with institutional racism, we believe that the high- as compared to low-hope individual will more readily activate group level responses. When dealing with individual racism, hope would serve as a mediator between the perception of racism and well-being. That is to say, when encountering racism perpetuated by an individual, having high levels of hope should facilitate more adaptive responding such that the racism stressor is less likely to undermine one's level of well-being. Under such circumstances of individual racism, one cannot control the acts of the perpetrator, but having higher hope can change how one responds so as to lessen the impact of the racist perpetrator.

There are three broad reasons for examining hope and stress among African Americans. First, the stressors experienced by minorities are unique; most majority group members don't face the deleterious effects of prejudice. Second, minority groups have particular coping strategies for dealing with various stressors. Although these strategies also are used by the members of the majority (i.e., Caucasian) populations as well, their effects on well-being differ between minorities and Caucasians. For minorities, we contend that coping strategies not only must enhance well-being, but they also must protect well-being from threats. For instance, Taylor, Jackson, and Chatters (1997) have noted that many African American parents teach their children that they are both Black and American. Such early education about the duality of identity prepares their children for potential incidents of racism and prejudice. Furthermore, such identity inoculation prevents (or lessens the likelihood of) children from internalizing racism's inherently prejudicial negative messages. Third, research has shown that certain factors protect against the deleterious effects of stress (Clark et al., 1999). Moreover, these protective factors differ significantly from the protective factors of Caucasians (such as the example of identity presented earlier). Because most theory and research either has been dedicated to Caucasian populations or has assumed that the information gathered on Caucasians generalizes to all groups, it is important to examine what is known about stressors in minority groups, along with the effects of such stressors on their physical and psychological well-being.

Minorities in the United States encounter stress that is tied expressly to their status as minorities. Although this may not be true for all U.S. minorities, it holds for too many. Minorities currently comprise 25% of the U.S. population. The U.S. Census Bureau (2000) recognizes African Americans or Blacks, Native Americans (including Aleuts and Eskimo), and Asian/ Pacific Islanders, and one national origin group (Hispanic/Latino) as minority groups. As is the case with many other industrialized countries, however, the United States is changing rapidly. On this point, it has been estimated that the next 50 years will see the percentage of minorities rise to nearly 48% (U.S. Census Bureau, 2000).

The changing U.S. demographic composition makes it imperative that we better understand our discrimination perceptions and any related prejudices. More importantly, we need to understand how these processes affect the perceived stressors and subsequent coping activities of African Americans.

Our focus is on African Americans because the available research has focused on this minority population. In this regard, research consistently has shown that African Americans disproportionately are exposed to both chronic and acute environmental stressors (James, 1993; Outlaw, 1993; Thompson, 1996). The three reasons for this are that African Americans: (a) are more likely than the general population to be affected by racism and prejudice (see Coll et al., 1996); (b) are more likely than the general population to be exposed to and be victims of violence; and (c) have high proportions who are living in poverty conditions. This elevated stress exposure has multiple negative effects on the psychological and physical health of African Americans. In particular, the psychological problems in African American children include social skills deficits, acting out, shyness, and anxious behaviors (McCabe et al., 1999).

AFRICAN AMERICAN COPING STRATEGIES

Outlaw (1993) modified the popular stress and coping model of Lazarus and Folkman (1984) so that it would apply to African Americans who were dealing with racism-related stressors. Similar to Caucasians, African Americans engage in primary and secondary appraisal of environmental stressors. When the stressor is racism, however, Outlaw contends that African Americans would never make a benign positive or an irrelevant primary appraisal. Instead, she theorizes that African Americans accurately will perceive racism as a threat, loss or harm, or a challenge.

Once racism is appraised in the environment, African Americans begin to implement coping strategies. Plummer and Slane (1996) made three observations about these coping efforts of African Americans to racism: (a) they use less active coping; (b) confrontative coping behaviors become necessary; and (c) coping options are restricted. In general, it appears that African Americans use significantly more active *and* passive coping strategies than Caucasians. Plummer and Slane inferred from these findings that racism requires that African Americans use the full range of coping behaviors.

It also is important to note that different forms of racism result in different forms of coping. According to Utsey et al. (2000), the three forms of racism are individual (or personal), institutional, and cultural. Individual racism is particularly deleterious to coping. For example, although African American women generally prefer to seek social support as a coping strategy, when encountering individual racism they tend to rely on avoidance coping (Utsey et al., 2000). In fact, avoidance often can be a common African American response to individualistic racism because confrontation involves too much energy investment (Feagin, 1991). Use of avoidance has important implications for the well-being of African Americans, however, because avoidant coping consistently has been linked to maladjustment in general (Snyder & Pulvers, 2001), as well as to lowered self-esteem and life satisfaction among African Americans (Utsey et al., 2000).

Avoidant coping in racism situations is understandable given that minority groups tend to perceive their stressors as uncontrollable (Stein & Nyamathi, 1999). Active coping and problem-focused coping only become likely when individuals perceive that they have some control over their stressors (Carver, Scheier, & Weintrab, 1989; Gulick, 1995; Terry, 1994). For example, minority fathers of unplanned pregnancies report feeling extreme stress and a sense of powerlessness in their coping efforts (Clinton & Kelber, 1993). This "fatherhood" issue is very important in the African American community because as many as 69% of African American children (as compared to 26% for Caucasians) are born to single mothers (U.S. Census Bureau, 2001).

When we consider the negative health outcomes that have been associated with stressors, it becomes evident that the viability of minority populations within the United States (and around the world) will be dependent on their ability to find adaptive ways of dealing with stress. We suggest that hopeful thinking will be extremely useful in both understanding and increasing these coping efforts.

INCREASING HOPE AMONG AFRICAN AMERICANS

Hope theory suggests that a basic approach to increasing hope is to reduce the actual goal blockages. Because our thesis in this chapter is that racism represents an enormous goal blockage, a first step in increasing the hope of African Americans is to decrease racism in America. This is something that everyone—African Americans, Caucasians, Hispanics, and so on—should work on. By leveling the proverbial playing field, the considerable talents of African Americans and other minorities can be nurtured for the benefit of all citizens (Lopez, Gariglietti, McDermott, Shermin, Floyd, Rand, & Snyder, 2000; Snyder & Feldman, 2000).

Until we eliminate racism from our society, and even once we have (because African Americans will face the "normal" life stressors faced by Caucasians), it will be crucial for African American children to be taught how to think hopefully. This job of teaching hopeful thinking begins in the home by parents (Snyder, Tran, Schroeder, Adams, & Laub, 2000) and must be reinforced in schools by teachers (Snyder, 2002; Snyder & Shorey, in press) and school counselors (Snyder, Feldman, Shorey, & Rand, 2002).

Adult African Americans also could profit by learning to think hopefully. It already has been shown that African Americans' well-being is related to elevated hope (Adams & Jackson, 2000; Adams & Nelson, 2001). Accordingly, the next step is to increase the hope of African American adults in general, and of African American males in particular.

Increasing the hope of African American children can be accomplished in several ways. First, African American children must be taught how to think hopefully. We would hasten to note that these same lessons for imparting hope apply to children whatever their racial backgrounds may be. In this regard, we espouse the tenets of hope theory as they pertain to nurturing hope throughout childhood (for reviews, see McDermott & Snyder, 2000; Snyder, 1994; Snyder, McDermott, Cook, & Rapoff, 2002; Snyder, Tran, et al., 2000). When asked to look back on their childhoods, high- as compared with low-hope adults consistently note that their caregivers spent large amounts of time in mentoring them (Snyder, 1994a). Therefore, African American children need to have adult "coaches" (neighbors, aunts or uncles, coaches, teachers) who invest large amounts of time with them. For example, in the absence of blood relatives for African Americans, their "fictive kin" can provide this necessary time and loving care (George & Swyther, 1988). This sense of community support is important for African American children, and to accomplish this the adults in their local communities must share in mentoring them.

African Americans, as is the case for other children, spend too much time in front of televisions. Children watching television is the antithesis of learning hopeful thinking—instead it teaches passivity. More active interactions are needed to engender children's hopeful thinking. Thus, adults need to read to children, and conversely, children need to read to adults. Additionally, whatever the exact nature of the activity, our point is that it is important to do things with children. Adults are modeling hope to African American children just by spending time with them.

The three components of hopeful thinking in hope theory offer specific ways for teaching African American children to think hopefully. Let's begin with goals, which are the anchors of hopeful thought. African American children need to learn to set clear goals; such goals have the added advantage of enabling children to see that they have made progress. Borrowing from what has been observed in high-hope children, a child profits most by setting a goal that is slightly higher than that attained previously (called stretch goals). Furthermore, it helps to teach children to be concerned with their own goals, but also to care about the goals of other children.

The next component in hope theory is to be able to find workable pathways to reach desired goals. As such, caregivers need to work with African American children to make plans. Crucial to such lessons is learning how to break a long-term goal down into small sub-steps. Thus, African American children can be taught positive mental scripts about how to go step-by-step in order to reach their goals. Also, it helps to coach the child about what she or he might do if a given pathway is blocked. African American children need to be facile at finding alternate ways to get what they want.

The final component in hope theory involves teaching the African American children to motivate themselves to use the routes that they have come up with to reach their goals. Being willing to expend strong efforts is a big part of remaining hopeful. Likewise, African American children will profit by learning that roadblocks are part of life, and that they obviously will encounter these at times. Related to this point, children profit when they learn to view such impediments as challenges rather than the preludes to failures.

By being taught these specific strategies to become more facile at setting goals, finding routes to goals, and motivating oneself, children learn to think of themselves as having the capacity to do these things in the future. Thus, it is not just the skills per se that engender hope, but perhaps more importantly for sustaining hopeful thinking, African American children should perceive that they can find ways to do these things in the future.

Second, there needs to be a concerted effort by agencies and organizations that provide services within the African American community (both formal social service agencies as well as informal organizations such as churches and other social organizations). These social institutions are in position (i.e., by having significant contact) to disseminate information about hopeful thinking.

Third, it is imperative that we inform community leaders about the many benefits of hopeful thinking. These individuals often are viewed as the pillars of the African American community and, as such, they are in a position to increase the awareness of other community members. If hopeful thinking is to become widespread within the African American community, it is these leaders who can provide the valuable conduits.

Fourth, we must be cognizant that goals may vary by age cohort and social-economic status. In this regard, we already know from research conducted by Adams and Jackson (2000) that predictors of well-being change in different age cohorts. Similarly, the goals or desired life outcomes also may change as the cohort ages. Awareness of the differences in need will enable leaders and teachers of hope to better serve clients and students. As Clark et al. (1999) have noted, African Americans who have reached middle-class status still face racism, although it is of a more subtle or covert nature. As we noted earlier, there may be different roles for hope based on the form of racism encountered. This is an important empirical question that warrants future research attention.

There also needs to be more intervention research aimed at teaching hopeful thinking to Americans in general, and African Americans in particular. On this point, we must not assume that what has worked for Caucasians will automatically generalize to African Americans and other groups. Future research should also consider whether or not there are gender differences among African Americans in terms of hopefulness. To date, there have been no observed gender differences in hope among Caucasian Americans (Snyder, 2000).

In conclusion, although African Americans have faced a barrage of stressors associated with racism, their maintaining high levels of hope have buoyed their coping efforts. African American parents must understand the importance of imparting hopeful thinking so as to prepare their children for a world where they may not always be treated as equals. Our strongly held view is that we must embrace hopeful thinking as the world community, and American society in particular, increasingly treats all citizens with the same high respect.

NOTE

For further information about hope as applied to various populations, contact the senior author, c/o Psychology Dept., California State University, Channel Islands, Camarillo, CA 93012, or email to virgil.adams@csuci.edu. For information about hope theory, contact C.R. Snyder, c/o Psychology Dept., 1415 Jayhawk Blvd., University of Kansas, Lawrence, Kansas, 66045, or email to crsnyder@ku.edu.

REFERENCES

Abernethy, A.D. (1995). Managing racial anger: A critical skill in cultural competence. *Journal of Multicultural Counseling and Development, 23,* 96–102.

Adams III, V. (2002). *Changes in African American mothers' hope and life satisfaction between 1980 and 1992.* Unpublished manuscript, Department of Psychology, University of Kansas, Lawrence.

Adams III, V., & Jackson, J.S. (2000). The contribution of hope to the quality of life among aging African Americans: 1980–1992. *International Journal of Aging and Human Development, 50* (4), 279–295.

Adams III, V., & Nelson, J. (2001). Hope, happiness, and African American fathers: Changes between 1980 and 1992. *African American Research Perspectives, 7* (1), 148–156.

Bowen-Reid, T.L., & Harrell, J.P. (2002). Racist experiences and health outcomes: An examination of spirituality as a buffer. *Journal of Black Psychology, 28*(1): 18–36.

Broman, C.L. (1997). Race-related factors and life satisfaction among African Americans. *Journal of Black Psychology, 23,* 36–49.

Burke, A.W. (1984). Is racism a causatory component in mental illness? *The International Journal of Social Psychiatry, 30,* 1–3.

Carver, C.S., Scheier, M.F., & Weintraub, J.K. (1989). Assessing coping strategies: A theoretically based approach. *Journal of Personality and Social Psychology, 56,* 267–283.

Clark, R., Anderson N. B., Clark, V.R., & Williams, D.R. (1999). Racism as a stressor for African Americans. *American Psychologist, 54,* 805–816.

Clinton, J.F., & Kelber, S.T. (1993). Stress and coping in fathers of newborns: Comparisons of planned vs. unplanned pregnancy. *International Journal of Nursing Studies, 30,* 437–443.

Coll, C.G., Lamberty, G., Jenkins, R., McAdoo, H.P., Crnic, K., Wasik, B.H., & Garcia, H.V. (1996). An integrative model for the study of developmental competencies in minority children. *Child Development, 67,* 1891–1914.

Diener, E. (1984). Subjective well-being. *Psychological Bulletin, 95,* 542–575.

Emmons, R.A. (1986). Personal strivings: An approach to personality and subjective well-being. *Journal of Personality and Social Psychology, 51,* 1058–1068.

Essed, P. (1990). *Everyday racism: Reports from women of two cultures.* Claremont, CA: Hunter House.

Feagin, J.R. (1991). The continuing significance of race: Anti black discrimination in public places. *American Sociological Review,* 56, 101–116.

Feagin, J.R., & Sikes, M.P. (1994). *Living with racism: The black middle-class experience.* Boston: Beacon Press.

Fernando, S. (1984). Racism as a cause of depression. *The International Journal of Social Psychiatry,* 30, 41–49.

George, L.K., & Swyther, L.P. (1988). Support groups for caregivers of memory impaired elderly: Easing caregiver burden. In L.A. Bond & B.M. Wagner (Eds.), Families in transition: Primary prevention programs that work. *Primary prevention of psychopathology* (Vol. 11, pp. 309–331). Thousand Oaks, CA: Sage.

Gougis, R.A. (1986). The effects of prejudice and stress on the academic performance of Black-Americans. In U. Neisser (Ed.), *The school achievement of minority children: New perspectives* (pp. 145–158). Hillsdale: Erlbaum.

Gulick, E.E. (1995). Coping among spouses or significant others of persons with multiple sclerosis. *Nursing Research,* 44, 220–225.

Jackson, J.S., Brown, T.N., Williams, D.R., Torres, M., Sellers, S.L., & Brown, K. (1996). Racism and the physical and mental health status of African Americans: A thirteen year national panel study. *Ethnicity and Disease,* 6, 132–147.

Jackson, J.S., & Gurin, G. (1987). *National survey of black Americans, 1979–1980* [machine-readable data file]. 1st ICPSR ed. Ann Arbor, Mich.: Inter-university Consortium for Political and Social Research.

James, S.A. (1993). Racial and ethnic differences in infant mortality and low birth weight: A psychosocial critique. *Annals of Epidemiology,* 3, 130–136.

Krieger, N., & Sidney, S. (1996). Racial discrimination and blood pressure: The CARDIA study of young black and white adults. *American Journal of Public Health,* 86, 1370–1378.

Lazarus, R.S., & Folkman, S. (1984). *Stress, appraisal, and coping.* New York: Springer.

Lopez, S.J., Gariglietti, K.P., McDermott, D., Sherwin, E., Floyd, R.K., Rand, K., & Snyder, C.R. (2000). Hope for the evolution of diversity: On leveling the "field of dreams." In C.R. Snyder (Ed.), *Handbook of hope: Theory, measures, and applications* (pp. 223–242). San Diego, CA: Academic Press.

McCabe, K.M., Clark, R., & Barnett, D. (1999). Family protective factors among African American youth. *Journal of Clinical Child Psychology,* 28, 137–150.

McDermott, D., & Snyder, C.R. (2000). *The great big children's hope book.* Oakland, CA: New Harbinger.

Minino, A.M., & Smith, B.L. (2001). Deaths: Preliminary Data for 2000. *National Vital Statistics Reports,* Vol. 49 (12).

Munoz-Dunbar, R. (1996). *Hope among minority college students.* Unpublished master's thesis, University of Kansas, Lawrence.

Myers, D. G. (2002). *Social psychology* (7th ed.). New York: McGraw-Hill.

Outlaw, F. H. (1993). Stress and coping: The influence of racism on the cognitive appraisal processing of African Americans. *Issues in Mental Health Nursing,* 14, 399–409.

Pettigrew, T. F., & Martin, J. (1987). Shaping the organizational context for black American inclusion. *Journal of Social Issues,* 43(1): 41–78.

Plummer, D. L., & Slane, S. (1996). Patterns of coping in racially stressful situations. *Journal of Black Psychology,* 22, 302–315.

Priest, R. (1991). Racism and prejudice as negative impacts on African American clients in therapy. *Journal of Counseling & Development,* 70, 213–215.

Simpson, G. E., & Yinger, J. M. (1985). *Racial and cultural minorities: An analysis of prejudice and discrimination* (5th ed.). New York: Plenum Press.

Smith, E. M. J. (1985). Ethnic minorities: Life stress, social support, and mental health issues. *The Counseling Psychologist,* 13, 537–579.

Snyder, C. R., (Ed.) (1994a). *The psychology of hope: You can get there from here.* New York: The Free Press.

Snyder, C. R. (1994b). Hope and optimism. In V. S. Ramachandren (Ed.), *Encyclopedia of human behavior* (Vol. 2) (pp. 535–542). San Diego, CA: Academic Press.

Snyder, C. R. (2002a). Hope theory: Rainbows in the mind. *Psychological Inquiry,* 13(4), 249–275.

Snyder, C. R. (2002b). Hope for teaching and vice versa. *Shutz Distinguished Teaching Award monograph.* University of Kansas, Lawrence.

Snyder, C. R., Cheavens, J., & Michael, S. T. (1999). Hoping. In Snyder, C. R. (Ed.), *Coping: The psychology of what works* (pp. 205–231). New York: Oxford University Press.

Snyder, C. R., & Feldman, D. (2000). Hope for the many: An empowering social agenda. In C. R. Snyder (Ed.), *Handbook of hope: Theory, measures, and applications* (pp. 389–412). San Diego, CA: Academic Press.

Snyder, C. R., Feldman, D., Shorey, H., & Rand, K. (2002). Hopeful choices: A school counselor's guide to hope theory. *Professional School Counseling,* 5(5), 298–307.

Snyder, C. R., Harris, C., Anderson, J. R., Holleran, S. A., Irving, L. M., Sigmon, S. T., Yoshinobu, L., Gibb, J., Langelle, C., & Harney, P. (1991). The will and the ways: Development and validation of an individual-differences measure of hope. *Journal of Personality and Social Psychology,* 60, 570–585.

Snyder, C. R., LaPointe, A. B., Crowson Jr., J. J., & Early, S. (1998). Preferences of high- and low- hope people for self-referential input. *Cognition & Emotion,* 12, 807–823.

Snyder, C. R., McDermott, D., Cook, W., & Rapoff, M. (2002). *Hope for the journey: Helping children through good times and bad.* Clinton Corners, NY: Percheron.

Snyder, C. R., & Pulver, K. (2001). Copers coping with stress: Two against one. In C.R. Snyder & S. Lopez (Eds.), *Handbook of positive psychology.* New York: Oxford University Press.

Snyder, C. R., & Shorey, H. (in press). Hope in the classroom: The role of positive psychology in academic achievement and psychology curriculum. *Psychology Teacher Network.*

Snyder, C. R., Sympson, S. C., Ybasco, F. C., Borders, T. F., Babyyak, M. A., & Higgins, R. L. (1996). Development and validation of the State Hope Scale. *Journal of Personality and Social Psychology,* 70, 321–335.

Snyder, C. R., Tran, T., Schroeder, L. L., Pulvers, K. M. Adams III, V. & Laub, L. (2000). Teaching children the hope recipe: Setting goals, finding routes to those goals, and getting motivated. *Today's Youth,* 4, 46–50.

Stien, J. A., & Nyamathi, A. (1999). Gender differences in relationships among stress, coping, and health risk behaviors in impoverished, minority populations. *Personality and Individual Differences,* 26(1): 141–157.

Sydell, E. J., & Nelson, E. S. (2000). Modern racism on campus: A survey of attitudes and perceptions. *Social Science Journal,* 37(4): 627–635.

Taylor, R. J., Jackson, J. S., & Chatters, L. M. (1997). *Family life in black America.* Thousand Oaks, CA: Sage.

Terry, D. J. (1994). Determinants of coping: The role of stable and situational factors. *Journal of Personality and Social Psychology,* 66, 895–910.

Thompson, V. L. S. (1996). Perceived experiences of racism as stressful life events. *Community Mental Health Journal,* 32, 223–233.

U.S. Census Bureau (2000). *Population Projections Program, Population Division, Washington, D.C.* Internet Release Date: January 13, 2000.

U.S. Census Bureau (2001). *Profiles of general demographic characteristics, Population Division, Washington, D.C.* Release Date: May, 2001.

Utsey, S. O., & Ponterotto, J. G. (1996). Development and validation of the Index of Race-Related Stress (IRRS). *Journal of Counseling Psychology,* 43, 490–501.

Utsey, S. O., Ponterotto, J. G., Reynolds, A. L., & Cancelli, A. A. (2000). Racial discrimination, coping, life satisfaction, and self-esteem among African Americans. *Journal of Counseling and Development,* 78, 72–78.

White, J. L., & Parham, T. A. (1990). *The psychology of Blacks: An African American perspective* (2nd ed.). New Jersey: Prentice Hall.

Chapter 12

FROM HOPELESS FUTURE TO FUTURELESS HOPE: TEMPORALITY AMONG THE AGED

Haim Hazan

INTRODUCTION

The concept and rhetoric of gerotranscendence is gaining increasing ground as a fashionable currency in contemporary gerontological literature (Tornstam, 1997a,b, 1999). This trend could be attributed to a growing interest in spirituality in general and in religion in particular, as a response to processes of secularization and their corresponding rejection of symbolic immortalization (Lifton, 1983). Old age is deemed as the last frontier (Fontana, 1976) separating the living from the dead, and as such constitutes a taboo zone not to be inhabited by those wishing to advance along the set trail of modern life. Future orientation is enabled and restricted by the structural conditions encoded in the project of modernity, and thus socially sustained hope is reserved for those marked and assignated as legitimate actors on the stage of progress and achievement. The category of the old is excluded from that playground of modernity and hence is robbed of any claim for prospective planning and amelioratory expectations.

However, adherence to modernity is not an exclusive option for living, and deconstruction rather than construction could be entertained as a source for fostering a mode of existence unfettered by imperatives and insignia of forwardness. Such a transformation in reality orientation could be accomplished through the introduction of a shift in temporality from the linear to the cyclical without resorting to a transcendental fabrication of the world. This turn becomes plausible through the reframing of the linguistic articulation of patterns of time.

The cultural terms within which such change is facilitated are to be found in the properties of the late or post-modern era as applied to the position of the old in today's global society. Fluidity of identities, transnationalism, alternative life styles, and virtual communication contribute to the demarginalization of the old and to the awakening of the public sphere to hushed voices and squashed options (Blaikie, 1999; Featherstone, 1995). Heightened self-awareness and reflexivity among the old sketch out "a fresh map of life" in later years (Laslett, 1989) and encourage new lives for old people.

BASIC CONCEPTS

- It is difficult to think in terms of a human being who has been brought up with a set of concepts—some of them very deeply embedded—and it is not easy to think that if you have changed, these would be exchanged for other ones. But, I think what is universal is that these things are evolved in order, initially, just to survive. Obviously, it is not just survival in a physical sense, but being able to work with others and to derive some satisfaction in your life. These are the tests as to whether your particular constructs are right or wrong. The first thing that hits you, no doubt, is that you started with a set of concepts which carry you along during your active life, professional life and so on. But no, faced with changed circumstances, you start being unhappy in one form or another, eventually suffering from other more severe problems. And it is then you obviously have to adjust if you want to survive—and sometimes literally survive because people do die very often early in the day and give up. You have to adjust your concepts—the ones that govern your behavior to the new circumstances, and that does require a lot of hard thinking of the highest order.

- The thing to remember is that you have to continue to test and continually question things. It's the difference between taking everything for granted when you get to a situation where somehow your actions do not provide the desired effects. Our ability to reflect is not an automatic ability to consider things, to weigh up the factors and to make a decision.

- I think it is not just the reflexivity. There is also a sense of creativity which arises without any input from the outside. You reflect on new ideas and as a result you change your concepts. You have to change your language. Provided you do that in an orderly fashion, there is no basic problem.

The interlocutors are members of the University of the Third Age (U3A) in Cambridge, England; the setting is an informal discussion and the gaze is a rather pensive, somewhat detached look at life and its essentials (Hazan 1996). A few lessons could be drawn from the spirit of that exchange and a number of challenges to the anthropological endeavor to study the old could be posited.

Elderly people, being their own ethnographers, deconstruct and demystify their own lives. Awareness of this process might cast a critical doubt on some commonly shared assumptions regarding the properties of our knowledge about aging in particular and the hermeneutics of social communication in general. Do we superimpose our implicitly linear sequential notions of "narrative," "life story," and "life review" on people whose concept of life is, to use V. Turner's terms, "antistructural" or liminal—a state of consciousness where chronological ordering ceases to operate in a conventional manner? That doubt prompts the first part of this paper and will set the scene for problematizing the issue of communicating with the old, as both an epistemological dilemma and a cultural testing ground.

This will lead us to the second and main part of the argument where the call by our Cambridge speakers to alter concepts and language is to be addressed and formulated in socio-anthropological constructs. In some respects the gist of that challenge is the subversive observation made by members of that group to the effect that culture, former identity, and life story do not necessarily inform selfhood in old age. What might be seen as an apparent contradiction in terms—selfhood devoid of self or person, stripped of persona—becomes a trigger for the development of a heuristic discourse pertaining to the plausibility of that seeming paradox and offering a model for its resolution.

In conclusion we shall return to the deconstruction process in light of yet another plea of our elderly constructors. This is the recurrent unequivocal proclamation that the project of growing old is all about survival. The question posed by Butler (1975) of "Why Survive?" is replaced by the quest for ways and means of how to survive. It will be argued that the structural position of old age in modern society, the functional stratagems employed by elderly people, and the expressive manifestations articulated and uttered by them, set the boundaries of that category, furnish its discourse, and generate practices of communication among its incumbents. Three sets of concepts are to be interlocked in an attempt to propose a model of comprehending communication among the aged: otherness and strangeness, metonymic and metaphoric, and temporality and atemporality. I would like to argue that texts of identity such as elicited life stories and allured narratives of the self-writing-selves are merely partial representations of reconstructed lives, and not necessarily weighty ones at that.

At the outset of the following, a word of exhortation and lowering of expectations must be voiced. The discussion takes a cue from a multitude of studies but is committed to none. Rather, I subscribe to an adductive exploratory method of explication. To that end I shall merely touch upon a few ethnographic studies, while the brunt of the argument is borne by piecing together a medley of theoretical deliberations and framing the mosaic within a social constructivist view of aging.

ASSUMPTIONS IN QUESTION

The underlying assumption of our analysis is the otherness of old age, both as a social construct and as an object of inquiry. Let me begin then with a number of anthropological observations as to the understanding of the old as the "other."

Anthropological authority has traditionally stemmed from the craft of presenting the voice of the "other" to, and into, academic discourse. This authority, textual or otherwise, has been challenged from various directions (see Ruby, 1982; Clifford, 1983; Clifford & Marcus, 1986; Sanjek, 1990). The object of anthropology as a translation of cultural codes has been described by Asad (1986: 161) as "not the historical situated speech (that is the task of the folklorist or the linguist) but "culture," and to translate culture the anthropologist must first read and then inscribe the implicit meanings that lie beneath/within/beyond situated speech." It is the ultimate accomplishment of translation through the unraveling of hidden agendas that justifies and constitutes the research method of participant observation developed by anthropologists to obtain knowledge of the "other" by the "other." However, Asad continues to criticize that rather commonly invoked model of ethnography as translation, whose apparent "neutrality" is enmeshed in global power inequalities of post-colonialism, modernization, capitalism, and cultural hegemony. There are persistently "strong" and "weak" languages, he acutely observes, and the vast majority of ethnographies are written in strong language. Moreover, "cultures" are not coherent languages or texts, but are themselves composed of many conflicting discourses.

The anthropology of aging adds further dimensions to this criticism. Here, the gulf between the two protagonists of the research—the anthropologist and the "other"—is such that "othering," namely entering the other's world and viewing it from within, becomes frankly impossible. Unlike other ethnographic situations, the human condition of old age is inimitable and unprecedented in the course of one's life. The aging-imputed experience of facing impending death, counting one's losses and reviewing life, distance the elderly from the "non-old," whose own experience is fraught with such reckonings.

The epistemological lacuna inherent in all ethnography looms larger in the case of old age. One conceivable solution for such a predicament could be offered by the aged themselves. The anthropologist, whose questionable knowledge regarding the state of being old does not allow for a credible translation of the language of aging into an anthropological twang, can enlist the help of elderly persons in spelling out the principles of their own language. Putting the elderly in a position of vicarious anthropologists is not tantamount to the traditional role of the informant, where the right of reflexive conceptualization becomes the reserved privilege of the anthropologist once the roles are reversed and former hearer (field-ethnographer) becomes speaker (anthropological author) while former speakers (informants) become spoken texts. If the argument put forward by some anthropologists that peer-group communication in old age produces new norms and novel meanings (Keith, 1980) is valid, then elderly persons could be regarded as commentators of that unknown, old-age peculiar cultural edifice. This challenge, which must be met in order to ascertain the validity of any endeavor to make aging audible, might be taken by elderly students of old age whose reflexive faculties can do justice to the nature of their experience, hence transmitting it to the domain of the non-old.

Attempts at anthropological decipherment of the "exotic" world of the aged are numerous. If V. Turner's (1978) dictum that the role of the ethnographer is "to exoticize the familiar and to familiarize the exotic" is to be considered a guideline for researchers, then the anthropologist is not only a translator of the language of folk-models to the language of analytic construction, but also vice-versa. He or she must invest resources other than academic to be able to straddle the two universes of researcher and researchee. This investment could be personal and subjective, by way of empathy and identification, reserved and guarded to subscribe to the accepted codex of scientific investigation, or strictly striving for objectivity premised on the belief in human universals, which bridge the gap between the "native" and his student. Any of these methods ought to grapple with the dilemmas posed by trying to understand aging as a phenomenon verging on incomprehensibility, hence transmuting it from the realm of the unknown to that of the unknowable.

The scope of fundamental issues embedded in the study of aging encompasses some of the most intriguing dilemmas looming on the horizons of our understanding. Many of those are eclipsed by convention and camouflaged by our own defenses. The introduction of aging as a source of knowledge, infusing and illuminating such topics, might prove to be an intellectual boon, but also an analytic bane. Deprived of conceptual frames to befit the phenomenon at hand (see Fabian, 1983) and denied, by virtue of age discrepancy, of the opportunity to share the experience of aging with the "native," the anthropologist of old age is methodologically at a loss.

To illustrate this point, and before explicating its possible solution (adumbrated earlier), let me briefly enumerate some seemingly unanswerable questions broached by touching upon the concept of aging:

1. How to represent identity and cultural presence without their attributed insignia, namely socially allocated roles, which, in the case of elderly people, are usually stripped off. Concepts of mobility, status, and stratification are analytically erroneous in a state where social rewards and sanctions are divorced from procedures of exchange, mutuality, and cumulativity.

2. How to think of that subject in the anthropologically sacrosanct holistic fashion, when so many aspects of being old are diverse, compartmentalized, and do not inform one another. Body is disengaged from mind and the physical does not answer to the mental, and vice versa (de Beauvoir, 1975). The aging self is split between its ageless properties and its rapidly dramatically changing circumstances. Inner life is no longer furnished by external appearance (Neugarten, 1976) and the composite self consisting of the subjective "I" and the social "me" (Mead, 1934) is rendered divisible. Hence, the tacit cultural assumption sustained by anthropologists regarding the unity of the self does not withstand the scrutiny of the encounter with elderly people.

3. How to relate to persons whose course of social mobility has come to an end, and hence their yardsticks for assessing and constructing reality are fundamentally different from those held by the still socially mobile researcher. Furthermore, this is not just a question of socially endorsed rewards and progress along the life cycle, since it draws on significant transformations in conceptions of time, space, and meaning.

    Such changes may account for an unredeemable and irreversible breech of communication between the world of the anthropologist and that of the informants. Understanding the other under such conditions could be about comprehending impertinent matters while overlooking the hub of the phenomenon under study. Thus an illusion of knowledge could be mistaken for knowledge.

4. How to reconcile the obvious universal properties of the process of aging with cultural diversity and personal idiosyncrasies. Is aging a

unique state to be understood within its own terms or is it a random multitude of commonly labeled, culturally dependent phenomena? The former assumption leaves the researcher without tools whereas the latter robs her or him of the justification to be engaged in the study of aging in the first place.

5. How to conduct meaningful communication with people whose language is edified upon long-life experience and is fraught with material belonging to other cohorts and generations. Furthermore, how can an anthropologist expect to cope with universes of relevance completely alien to his or her own experience? If we add to that the government of stereotypical images, which rules our view of the old, and the sometimes technical difficulties in making sense of the verbal utterances of elderly people, we might be facing a multifaceted blockage in communication.

6. Finally, how can a researcher, who is often in the midst of a career and whose life is presumably not coming to a close, "go native" and stand alongside a researchee at the brink of the most inexplicable human state—that of death. This mixed sense of awe and fascination is both a drive and a deterrent for anthropologists who consider the world of the aged as a viable field of study. This obviously draws them near to the limits of their understanding of the old, but first and foremost of themselves.

If only a few of these caveats are valid, it could be cautiously suggested that the anthropologist of aging should be looking not only for richer and unbiased material, but mainly for the basic faculties with which the elderly themselves construct and express their world. This implies that elderly persons may develop special facilities to structure their unique experience. Succinctly stated, it claims that the central problem confronted by elderly persons is not the issue of role relinquishment, functioning, or the stereotypes and cultural images in which they find themselves entrapped. The key problem, from which the current issues emerge and against which they reverberate, is that aged people exist in a world of disordered and disjointed time, space, and selfhood. It is a world shot through with paradox, the crux of which is the irreconcilable gulf between old people as people sharing and inhabiting the same world as their contemporaries on the one hand, and the cultural assignation of a special universe for the category of the old, on the other (Hazan, 1994). The emergent selfhood of old age is begotten by that incongruity, and its resulting code of practice of the elderly towards them is manifested in the evolution of a dual mode of representing experience. We shall now examine some of the terms and forces that engender that condition.

MULTIPLE SELVES

Anthropological wisdom has it that effect rather than cause, function rather than motive, constitute the subject of its inquiry. Selfhood, therefore, to the scant extent that it has been studied, is invariably construed in terms of cultural conditioning and changing circumstances (Carrithers, Collins, & Lukes, 1985). This socially relative view turns the anthropologists' gaze to performative practices and their observed contexts, sometimes to the exclusion of past formative forces. In its extreme, the self is thus accounted for within the framework of the ethnographic present inhabited by both researcher and researchee (Crapanzano, 1980).

These assumptions are gravely challenged when the discipline focused its attention on the life span and on the sense that people make of their lifelong experiences. Recording personal accounts recounted by elderly people, anthropologists found it necessary to shift their theoretical thrust from the "here and now" to the "there and then." This methodical diversion required some reconsideration of epistemological underpinning, of which the most significant was the abandonment of contextual principles in favor of universal premises as to the psychological needs of humans in general and old people in particular. Concepts such as "life-career" (Myerhoff & Simic, 1978), "continuity," and the "ageless self" (Kaufman, 1986) were formulated to enable anthropologists to encompass the entirety of one's life story and to offer a theoretically cogent interpretation of its reconstruction in old age. The more momentum that trend has gathered, the more anthropologists applied themselves to such psychologically informed perspectives (Langness & Frank, 1981). The paradox generated by their vein of research in anthropological thought was only too evident. Two conceptions of self were simultaneously invoked—one that is situationally anchored and pragmatically engineered, while the other is culture bound and psychologically driven. The former is a self of practical reasoning and existence, whereas the latter is a self of meaning-seeking and existentialism (Cohen 1974). The decision that self is predominant depends largely upon conceptual references just as much as on field data.

The coexistence of these two selves presents no novelty, neither for psychological theory nor for anthropological discourse. However, rarely has it been suggested that these two modes of personhood could be completely separate from each other and, indeed, may be mutually exclusive as alternative modus operandi.

Empirically, this notion of irreconcilable split between practical reasoning and the quest for meaning was sparked off in the course of an anthropological fieldwork I conducted on a self-help organization of elderly people in Cambridge, England. It was among the members of the University of the Third Age that I detected a twofold behavioral pattern consisting of practical management of daily living on the one hand, and what might be termed a metaphysical expression of reality, on the other. The two states were kept as separate worlds and it was only through an unintentional coincidence that I was able to learn about the dire consequences of their fusion. The description of that incident will provide the rationale for the argument to follow.

Members of the University set up their own research committee to investigate matters of importance to the elderly residents of Cambridge. One of the topics on their agenda was the cost of funerals and the nature of the service administered by funeral directors. Having conducted a meticulously designed inquiry into all the factors involved, and having interviewed a sizable number of respondents, the committee decided to enhance their knowledge of burial arrangements by inviting a guest speaker—a Ph.D. student, who had made a study of that subject. After a hair-raising presentation concerning the gruesome abuse of the dead by undertakers and about the corrupt system surrounding it, the funeral project was, as they put it, "buried." It would appear that turning the ultimate reality into a practical issue could not withstand the encroachment of death as a forbidden taboo zone. Here, the unintended merger between the two selves brought to a halt the attempt at playing brinkmanship with death. Evidently further and more conclusive material has to be adduced to corroborate this argument, but for the purpose of this heuristic exercise, suffice it to say that the conscious endeavor by members to distance the two selves from each other to avoid any polluting overlap is a theme running throughout the entire ethnography.

Many questions could be posed with regard to that separation. I would like to confine the discussion to the socio-cultural terms that structure these two selves and to their implications to the understanding of the reality of being old in post-industrial society. The assumption, controversial though as it is, that guides this approach is that selves are generated, engineered, and sustained through socio-cultural processes (Rose, 1990). It is maintained that the choice and employment of adaptive strategies, such as the double self (Lifton, 1986), is induced by structural conditioning no less than by the quintessential properties of the individual. With these premises in mind, the following is set to offer a sociological discourse aimed at eliciting a model of modes of articulating experience in later life as produced and constructed by the position of the category known as "growing old" or as "the third age" in late modern society. My theoretical stance draws on schools of thought interweaving social knowledge, cultural codes, and structure of power (Foucault, 1980). It will be shown how macro-social forces prescribing the imagery of the life span construct the micro interactional fabric of organizing everyday experience by the elderly occupying that symbolic space of "the third age." The management of late life's incongruities and stresses is to be explained in terms of the handling of resources and constraints embedded in that culturally predesignated age territory.

AUDIBILITY AND VISIBILITY

Knowledge about the old is invariably produced and disseminated by the non-old. It involves all individuals who, by mere virtue of their chronological age, are discarded into the gray territory of the "Limbo" (Hazan, 1980). It is, indeed, the unavoidable, but nevertheless avoided association between death and the old that endows the latter with taboo-like attributes (Hazan, 1994). The category of the old as a culturally constructed whole delineates a symbolic space where reciprocal relationships turn into dependency, and hence standards of everyday communication and information cease to apply (Hockey & James, 1993). Denied of many social resources, the old are also deprived of the means to negotiate terms with others—their voice.

Society mutes the voice of the old by applying various methods of screening, so that what is heard on the receiving end of that distorted line is inevitably selective to befit social interests and expectations. The portrayal of aged persons as victims of crime, social abuse, poverty, family neglect, and medical maltreatment articulates a common language about aging that only attests to its medicalization, victimization, marginalization, infantilization, and stigmatization. In a word, aging is made into a social problem that presupposes and predestines the image of the aging self.

Examples of the subjugating discourse of old age are abundant. Preassumptions as to the pejorative pathological nature of aging, for example, play a major part in medicalizing almost all forms of communication concerning the old. Since diagnosis of geriatrically-related syndromes is not always decidedly clinched and hence may rest within a gray scientific area, the range of superimposed medical labels pertaining to aging is almost infinite. It is more often than not that a common interest of both the physician and custodians formulate the condition of the old in medically intelligible terms so that supervisory measures can be applied. The old person is expected to comply with a set of tests purporting to evaluate her or his cognitive capacities and designed to establish adaptive properties. Failure to meet such standards by appropriately demonstrated aptitudes results in the classification of the subject as incompetent and thus in need of care and attention. In other words, the old person is deemed disoriented, maladjusted, and incoherent unless proven otherwise. Consequently, any information produced by an old person about herself or himself, unless congruous with the construction of reality of the non-old, is liable to be discredited. Hence, repetitious locutions uttered by elderly persons, adherence to maxims and aphorisms, a-chronological accounts of life histories, inconsistent speech-acts, profuse recourse to reminiscences or alternatively dead silence—all serve as testimonies to "garbled talk," "disorientation," and "senility." It has been shown that supposedly neutral speech cues, such as slow rate of speech, bad pronunciation, and other age markers, lead hearers to draw downgrading stereotypical inferences such as "doddery," "vague," "frail," and "upset."

The reduction of the old into corporeal attributes not only restricts the language about the aging self to physiological determinants, but also introduces a split within the Western culture "paradigm" of the indivisibility of body and soul (Featherstone & Hepworth, 1990). It confines the old to a category of social treatment such as medicine or the social welfare system, where bodies are separated from selves (Zola, 1982). It is intriguing to observe that protest against the social abandonment of the old often invokes the "invisibility" (e.g., Myerhoff, 1982) of the elderly as an insignia of such avoidance. However, the condition of the elderly put under the social gaze is one of over-visibility, as the old in fact exist only as long as they are seen. Indeed, it is the separation of bodies from selves which makes the aged only too visible. The old, the patient, and the dependant all share the over-visibility of a subject objectified and a person-cum-persona. This adaptation-oriented perspective robbed social gerontologists of some of the most central templates of thinking about the aging self. The result is a theoretical impasse.

Socio-cultural research into the experience of aging has formulated its frustrations by contriving concepts and theories that attest to the aborted attempt to make sense of old age in conventional socio-anthropological terms. In fact, the very phrasing of these concepts is a self-evident admission of that failure. They all revert to nomenclature and hypotheses that negate rather than explain the subject at hand. Thus the elderly have been sociologically declared to be "roleless" (Burgess, 1950), "deculturized" (Anderson, 1972), in a state of "no exit" (Marshall, 1979), "anomie" (Fontana, 1976), "disengaged" (Cumming & Henry, 1961), and symbolically "invisible" (Myerhoff, 1978). To rectify this conceptual myopia, a multitude of alternative constructs has been proposed, none of which stem from the self-expressed world of the aged, and all draw on social models designed not by but for the aged, and indeed for the non-aged. Hence activity, continuity, life-span development, and cultural themes (Clark & Anderson, 1967; Kaufman, 1981) were enlisted as key explanatory forms. The assumption that old age is a mere socio-logical extension of the other ages of humanity reigns supreme in the various modes and models of understanding aging, while elderly people are denied the otherwise common intellectual right to present their own worldview to the middle-aged scientific community studying them.

"Old age" is represented by and to middle-aged society through the so-called "mask of aging." The aging self is masked, concealed behind specular stereotypes, objectified through medical and gerontological discourses. The elderly self-presentation in public, often made to conform to its social image, further reinforces that image. Featherstone and Hepworth's (1991) important concept of the "mask of aging" recapitulates similar conceptualizations already suggested in the sociology of aging (e.g., Hazan, 1994; Gubrium, 1994). It proposes that the image of the elderly is part of the scopic regimes of modernity whose other inmates are the sick (most recently and blatantly, the HIV/AIDS patients), the insane, the primitive, and ultimately the "other" in all of its embodiments. The sociology of aging, itself a powerful image-maker, is part of that scopic regime too. It is part of the ocular centrism of contemporary society and sociology, which gives prominence to the image and privileges of sight over sound. The ocular-centric gaze of the sociology of aging, even when self-reflexive, has tended to emphasize the visual: either the hyper-visibility of the "mask" of aging or its complementary opposite, namely the elderly social "invisibility" (e.g., Eckert, 1980; Myerhoff, 1982; Unruh, 1983; Hazan, 2000).

Masking is often a repressive act. Woodward (1991), for example, argues that repression of aging is connected to the visible oppression of old people in our society. Following Germain Greer's (1991) contention, in her recent book, *The Change,* that old age generates angst, Woodward proposes that aging is not only seen as a general catastrophe but is also particularly associated with women, reflecting a Western "gerontophobia" from the aging body, regarded as bad, and split off from the youthful body, regarded as good. While the image of the elderly should be deconstructed and unmasked, the attempt may prove self-defeating. Invoking both hyper-visibility and invisibility as a banner against ageism may be self-subversive, as it carries the risk of inadvertently strengthening that which it seeks to criticize. Conjuring up images, even in a critical manner, already reproduces them. To avoid that double bind, this chapter suggests another metaphorical venue into the aging self: not (in)visibility, but (in)audibility. We here make an attempt to lend an ear to the voices of the old as a possible means of evading the tyranny of the mirror-hall of images. Where then are the social languages about the aging self and of the aging self or selves?

LANGUAGES OF OLD AGE

Our argument is that any constitution of self is bound up by age categorization, and hence a transition within the age set spells a redefinition of the social self (Bernardi, 1985; Kertzer & Keith, 1984). Age groups are constituted through cultural anticipations, echoed in the various metaphors related in each and every society to the "seasons of man's life" (Levinson et al., 1978). Such a social span of control demands different discursive frames of reference for "hearing," "discussing," "explaining," and ultimately "understanding" the various age groups defined. These discourses, in turn, often become part of their subjects' repertoire, internalized into forms of articulation that characterize the symbolic exchange practiced among members of the age group and between that group and others.

"Old age," I argue, is a symbolic category defined primarily by middle age and mainly through two discursive systems, or "languages," termed here the literal and the metaphysical. These two discursive formulations of "old age" respectively imply two socially-reified views of the life-span: the "life cycle" and the "life course." These are seen here as being primarily mechanisms of normative control rather than free alternatives open for individual choice.

Literal language is the quest for a complete identification between words and things, concepts and objects, signifier and signified. Metaphysical language is the expression of the ideal, the thing in itself rather than its representation. Both literal and metaphysical languages derive from a common origin—metonymical thinking. This is a self-contained system of communication as well as a state of mind where there is no division between signified and signifier and hence no representations are possible (Leach, 1976). Metonymical thought, such as myth and philosophy, possesses attributes of a-temporality and a-contextuality beyond the "here" and "now." Conversely, non-literal language is the articulation of reality by means of interconnecting separate semantic zones. This production of meaning is symbolic by nature, practical by function, and metaphorical by aesthetic conventions. The two linguistic modes are simultaneously present in everyday life while their relative prevalence alters from one situation or context to another. In the case of the social discourse of old age, it will be argued that the predominant mode is the metonymical, while the metaphorical, being the core language of middle age, is absent from the construction of late life. It should be noted that an important difference between the mode of articulation, one that is responsible for the discourse of infantalization of the old (Hockey & James, 1993; Meyerowitz 1984), is that metaphorical-pragmatic language spells rationality, causality and logic, whereas metonymic-mythical language is presumed a-rational, illogical, and essentially incomprehensible. This difference has far-reaching repercussions on the construction of vindicating the dependency and ineptness imputed to the old.

Let me first discuss how middle age uses literal language in order to define old age. It has already been pointed out at the outset of this chapter how mass media, welfare criteria, and social stereotypes provide programs of talking about the old that are further validated by selectively-induced expressions uttered by elderly people. The old person is further expected to comply with a set of tests purporting to question and evaluate her or his cognitive capacities and designed to establish adaptive properties and measure "life satisfaction" (Gubrium & Lynott, 1983).

Old age and childhood are prescribed with structurally similar social positions through the use of literal language. In childhood, this is the language of socialization, which only gradually develops into nonliteral forms such as irony and metaphor (Winner, 1990; see also Astington, 1991; Trevarthen & Logotheri, 1989). Story-telling whose moral is emphasized is presumably shared by both children and the elderly. As in the case of nursery rhymes, folktales, and legends, the elderly stories are viewed as "plotted prose with an explicit moral" (Mergler & Goldstein, 1983, p. 186) which is based on common narratives, idioms, and proverbial vocabularies (Koch, 1977; Blythe, 1979; Coupland & Coupland, 1991; Myerhoff, 1978). The elderly "deculturated" (Anderson, 1972) discourse of "life-reviewing" and "reminiscence" can be regarded as symmetrical to childhood's socializing discourse of nursery tales and "secret-sharing" (Katriel, 1991). Both share a master narrative based on literality, metonymy, self-referentiality, and myth-like qualities (see also Searle, 1979 on literal meaning). Some psycho-linguists even ventured to state that this "literal talk" is a result of deficiencies in working memory and linguistic competence (Kemper, 1988). The literal, found both in childhood and in later life, thus presents itself as an extremity—as either a point of entrance, a marker of socialization, or as a point of departure, a sign of deculturation.

In contrast to youth and old age, middle age (as conceived of and constituted by its own occupants) dictates other constraints and social prescriptions. The ideal type of mid-life is concerned with effectiveness and objective information, the aligning of desires and capabilities in everyday domains such as work, love, and family life (Hepworth & Featherstone, 1982). This demands a pragmatic disposition, an outward-oriented, objective frame of reference, which is furthermore capable of metaphorically—i.e., nonliterally—interconnecting the various life-worlds (e.g., professional, familial, consumerist, political etc.) of middle age. Such pragmatic, metaphorical, "better-equipped" disposition, once defined, can be used to separate and distinguish middle age from both childhood and old age.

Besides the more commonly used, abovementioned practices of the literal discourse that account for both childhood and old age, as well as make both categories accountable to the social order of middle age, there is yet another language that is part of the "discourse of aging." This language is, by and large, reserved for designating old age. It is a metaphysical language, which has become the interpreting framework for discussing and authorizing the so-called "aging self." "Ego integrity" (Erikson, 1982) and "the ageless self" (Kaufman, 1986) are two such idealized, metaphysical cultural paradigms revealing more of middle age's expectations and fears than of the actual phenomenology of aging. The trope of the old is dually occupied by the literally-speaking, "confused," bed-ridden and house-bound elderly, as well as the aging, metaphysically-speaking "blind prophet," It is dually constituted by the archetypal "scheming hag" as well as by the literal stereotype of the "dear old thing" (Cool & McCabe, 1983).

Metaphysical interpretation is often evoked by proponents of "old age style." Woodward (1980), for example, who studied the late poems of Eliot, Pound, Stevens, and Williams, argues that aging positions the poet to see "the whole of the system." In Cohen-Shalev's (1992, p. 297) account of the late style of novelists as well as artists, it is defined as "a tendency to strip down artifice." "The relative lack of distinction between fact and fantasy, autobiography and invention, prose and poetry," he claims (ibid.), "does not result in a harmonious resolution of these opposites, but rather in a coexistence that seems to transcend logical thought categories." Viewing the elderly as incorporating the ability to "see the whole system" and "to strip down (social) artifice" is part of the metaphysical discourse of marginalization, which endows aging not only with the prescriptions of liminality, but also with the powers of estrangement. It is the unavoidable, but nevertheless avoided association between death and the old that credits the latter with such a metaphysical language.

LINGUISTIC PROPERTIES

The three different age-related languages (literal, metaphysical, and the metaphoric-pragmatic) can now be superimposed onto one's path of life. The dominant model found in the final stage of life in effect defines it as either a course or a cycle. Life course is an image of the linear progression of the self through the life span beginning with the literal language of fairy tales, legends, and non-negotiable social perceptions, continuing with a metaphorical-pragmatic articulation of reality, and ending up with a generative process governed by metaphysical wisdom. The conception of the life cycle starts at the literal, proceeds to the metaphorical, and reverts to the literal in old age. That image of the "life cycle" is very similar to the one proposed by B. S. Turner (1987: 123). It represents childhood and old age as homologous in terms of social liminality and disengagement, or what Turner calls lack of reciprocity, which is (according to him) the basis for social prestige.

Turner's narrative, therefore, belongs to the "life cycle" type, in which youth and old age are symmetrically constructed through the literal language. "Because the child and the elderly share a number of common social characteristics (such as the absence of work), and they are often described in the same pejorative and stigmatizing fashion" (Turner, 1987: 123). Childhood and old age, socialization and deculturation, irresponsibility and disengagement, are all the outcomes of social regulation. The dominance of literal language in those two extremes of the life cycle—childhood and old age—can also be seen as such an outcome. It is more of a socially prescribed language than an inherent part of these groups. "To speak literally" can serve as a normative control mechanism in its own right, mainly as it obliterates the need to decode the speaker's idiosyncratic, nonliteral intentions. Literal language is, therefore, the key to what Hockey and James (1993) call, in a very similar manner, the discourse of infantilization: the cultural pervasiveness of metaphors of childhood within the discourses surrounding aging and dependency...has become "naturalized." It is seen as somehow inevitable, as the way things are. Through this culturally constructed model of dependency, many of those in old age and others who are infantilized—the chronically sick or disabled, for example—may be made to take a conceptual position alongside children on the margins of society (ibid., p. 13).

The metaphysical language is in purpose no different from the literal. Through it, the nomadic aging self in late modern society is masked, muted, dubbed, and ultimately defined as the metaphysical object of "pilgrimage through life." Giddens (1991) argues that the postmodern blurring of age structure is closely linked to the rejection of the pre-destination narrative of identity that dominated Western thought for a long time. In his words (ibid., p. 14): "Self-identity for us [in the late modern age] forms a trajectory across different institutional settings of modernity over the duree of what used to be called the 'life cycle,' a term which applies more accurately to non-modern contexts than to modern ones. Modernity is a post-traditional order, in which the question, 'How shall I live?' has to be answered in day-to-day decisions about how to behave, what to wear, and what to eat—and many other things—as well as interpreted within the temporal unfolding of self-identity."

Bauman (1992) distinguishes between two symbolic types of "identity seekers": The postmodernist nomads and the Protestant (modernist) "pilgrims through life." The former wander between unconnected places, have no pre-set itinerary, and hence only momentary identities, "for today," until-further-notice identities. Predestination has been replaced, in their case, with uncertainty. The "pilgrims" have their destination pre-selected (by religion, society, gender, class, origin, etc.) and guide their life according to a "life-project," crystallizing a single core-identity throughout this "path of life." The "nomads" can be said to move further in the life span, while "pilgrims" either "progress" in the "life course" or continue along the "life cycle." Western adult society, postmodernist and all, by and large still considers its elderly according to the second narrative—that of pilgrimage.

Literal and metaphysical, in the case of the elderly, are two sides of the same coin, or in other words, a matter of interpretation. "The language of the elder is perhaps simply all language made plain," argue Mergler and Schleifer (1985); but "speaking plainly" can be both literal and metaphysical.

There is an ambiguity inherent in the aging situation of simultaneously possessing a sense of self and otherness about oneself, a situation emanating from the split between the quintessential "I" and the socially accountable "me." Furthermore, it is because of that complete split in the life-worlds of the elderly, that metaphor—being a symbolic vehicle designed to connect different worlds by means of some analogy (Davidson, 1979)—becomes impossible. It is only within such a split, for example, that "habit" can be understood as both a (literal) weary repetition and a (metaphysical) crystallization in which "the past is brought to life again, the future anticipated" (de Beauvoir, 1975, p. 696). Literal or metaphysical interpretation, in the case of both childhood and old age, does not hinge on the speaker's own intention, but rather on some collective knowledge, a socially shared record of images and stereotypes. This disciplinary convention is crucial in the case of the old. Where autobiography is too idiosyncratic and relationships are built on non-reactive networks (i.e., "social worlds," see Unruh, 1983), nonliteral personal meaning is hardly communicable. The literal and the metaphysical, therefore, befit the discourse of aging as both a social measure of normative control and a form of talk. It enables one to understand one's words without having to decipher, in the process, one's world. The old speaker's world is hence too often muffled by the discourse of aging.

THE TIME OF OLD AGE LANGUAGE

The structural comparison drawn between childhood and old age points to yet another aspect of the specific age group under study. It should be noted that the members of the U3A distinctly referred to themselves as belonging not to the category of "old age" but to a category they called "third age." They even created an academic organization to stand as evidence to the existence of such a "third age." This category is defined as preceding "old age," but still as different from it. One member of the group reflected on the subject by saying "I wonder whether it has occurred to anybody else here that we are a very curious group, but then again we are not really old. We may say that we are ante-aged."

But what is "ante-aged?" It was, in the eyes of members, a social buffer zone between past upward careers and social integration on the one hand, and the prospects of disengagement and deterioration on the other. Following the "life cycle" symmetry, I argue that the age group that is symmetrical to that "third age" is, in effect, adolescence. "Third age" (or the "young old" as Neugarten (1976) dubbed it), one might say, is the "adolescence of old age." "Ante-age" is symmetrical to "post-childhood" (note that the life-cycle symmetry is of a reverse type—which is one of the reflections of the socially-prescribed character of that paradigm). Moreover, third age and adolescence share a number of social characteristics. First and foremost, they are considered as betwixt and between—already out of their former age category, but still not part of the next category. This sense of "half-baked" categories depicts them as being caught up in ambiguity and crisis. Most significantly, these characteristics lend these age categories a social license to experiment—with values, norms, social conduct, and personal behavior. I believe that their (perhaps unconscious) identification with those characteristics underpinned the creation of a "third age" by the members of the U3A, and indeed by aging people involved in the movement all around the world. It was this sense of ambiguity and crisis, as well as the urge to experiment with new frames-of-mind, that confers on this category special cultural properties.

With the dissolution of the discourse of metaphorical language, the literal/metaphysical, on the one hand, and the non-literal on the other, become totally incongruent and mutually exclusive. Whereas usually these languages are interwoven and mixed, in old age they become differentiated.

The young elderly entering old age occupy a social territory where social self, as defined by modes of articulating experience, is still undetermined and open to experimentation. However, the leeway for maneuvering narrows down behavioral options and, as shown in the case of the funerals projects, it might disappear altogether. By internalizing the social discourses of aging, elderly people are subjected to no-win situations. They either hold on to codes of pragmatic practices and expose themselves to external sanctioning such as ridicule, inconsideration, abuse, and confinement, or conversely, if succumbing to loss of power and control, they restrict their communication with others to the literal and the metaphysical. Whichever adaptive mechanism is chosen, the authentic sense of selfhood is masked behind it. The student of old age is, therefore, forced to deliberate between two optional epistemologies: accepting the idea of one, incoherent though it might be, self disguised behind inconsistent and at times contradictory behavioral presentations; or submitting to the notion of "a homeless mind" (Berger, Berger, & Kellner, 1973), multiple selves or doubling (Lifton, 1986), which exonerates one from the assumptions of masking at the price of challenging the very concept of selfhood. The choice of a mode of interpreting the nature of adaptive stratagems correspondingly constitutes the type of communication devices employed to comprehend the old, respond to their assumed needs, and avoid the situation of the old and the non-old being divided by a supposedly common language.

REFLECTIONS

Let us now return to the outset of the chapter where the challenge of a reconstructed old age was posed by the elderly members of the U3A. Our analysis suggests that, to the extent that such new concepts are formulated, this reconstitution of experience is enabled by the position allocated to the category of the old by the prevailing ethos of middle age. This set of values embedded in an institutional framework of secularization, bureaucracy, and linearity, designates the old as its absolute opposite and hence as the ultimate other. The concept of the old, owing to its nearness to the unknown and presumably unknowable zone of death, is rendered a signifier without a corresponding signified. Its physical presence in the midst of midlife makes it even more salient in its strangeness (Bauman 1990). The liminal properties of that category, which places it at the brink of both middle age and death, endow it with the fluidity and nomadism of the Simmelian stranger (Simmel, 1950), alongside the unique, albeit ubiquitous image of the foreigner or stranger conjured up by Beck and Kattago (1996) as a phantom of late modernity. In that respect, the new "reflexive modernity" described by Beck and Kattago (ibid.) as a self-subversive condition emanating from blurred boundaries and nebulous identities, and leading to "unintentional often unseen questioning of the self, personal change and self overcoming" (Beck & Kattago, 1996: 387).

The atomistic individualization implied by this argument, if applied to the category of the old, prompts its occupants to stake a claim for exclusive self-knowledge, unshared by others, and to constitute their subjectivity not as strangers, but as socially legitimate operators of two separate software systems of selfhood. This split existence that optimizes pragmatic survival without compromising meaning and identity also helps obliterate the position of the old as a stranger (Dowd, 1986). Splicing selfhood into the practical and the essential renders the former familiar with the hegemoneous world of mid-life (Hazan & Raz, 1997), hence a sense of "us" is created, while the latter becomes the unknown "other," alien to and removed from any recognized codes of cultural representation. Thus the old can resort to the language of middle age without polluting and risking it with the self-referent language of being old.

As long as the two languages do not inform each other, they can operate independently. The metaphorical-instrumental communicates intelligible familiarity and apparent coherence in the form of practical conduct as well as situationally anchored life reviews and plotted narratives (Gubrium, 1994). At the same time it keeps at bay the ominous presence of the inexplicable language of utter otherness known only to the old. That language encapsulates existence within an ageless myth-like self-sustaining cycle. On the verge of life, playing brinkmanship with undeniable terminality and constructed immortality, hope becomes a fleeting concept contingent upon the elderly power to keep the two options apart.

REFERENCES

Anderson, B. (1972). The Process of Deculturation—Its Dynamics among United States Aged. *Anthropological Quarterly* 45: 209–216.

Asad, T. (1986). The Concept of Cultural Translation in British Social Anthropology. In J. Clifford & G. Marcus (eds.), *Writing Culture: The Poetics and Politics of Ethnography*. Berkeley: University of California Press.

Astington, J. (1991). Narrative and the Child's Theory of Mind. In B. Britton & A. Pellegrini (eds.), *Narrative Thought and Narrative Language*. Hillsdale, NJ: Lawrence Erlbaum Associates.

Bauman, Z. (1990). *Thinking Sociologically*. Oxford: Blackwell.

Bauman, Z. (1992). *Mortality and Immortality and Other Life Strategies*. Cambridge: Polity Press.

Beck, U. and S. Kattago (1996). How Neighbors Become Jews: The Political Construction of the Stranger in an Age of Reflexive Modernity. *Constellations. An International Journal of Critical and Democratic Theory* 2(3): 378–396.

Berger, P., B. Berger, & H. Kellner (1973). *The Homeless Mind*. Random House: Vintage.

Bernardi, B. (1985). *Age Class Systems: Social Institutions and Politics Based on Age*. Cambridge: Cambridge University Press.

Blaikie, A. (1999). *Aging and Popular Culture*. Cambridge: Cambridge University Press.

Blythe, R. (1979). *The View in Winter*. New York: Harcourt Brace Janovitz.

Burgess, E. (1950). Personal and Social Adjustment in Old Age. In M. Derber (ed.) *The Aged and Society*. Champaign, Illinois: Industrial Relations Research Association, pp. 138–156.

Butler, R. (1975). *Why Survive: Being Old in America*. New York: Harper and Row.

Carrithers, M., S. Collins, & S. Lukes (eds.) (1985). *The Category of the Person*. Cambridge: Cambridge University Press.

Clark, M., & B.G. Anderson (1967). *Culture and Aging*. Springfield, IL: Charles Thomas.

Clifford, J. (1983). On Ethnographic Authority. *Representations* 1 (2):118–146.

Clifford, J., & G. E. Marcus (eds.) (1986). *Writing Culture: The Poetics and Politics of Ethnography*. Berkeley: University of California Press.

Cohen, A. (1974). *Two Dimensional Man*. London: Routledge and Kegan Paul.

Cohen-Shalev, A. (1992). Self and Style: The Development of Artistic Expression from Youth through Midlife to Old Age in the Works of Henrik Ibsen. *Journal of Aging Studies* 6(3): 289–301.

Cool, L., & J. McCabe (1983). The "Scheming Hag" and the "Dear Old Thing": The Anthropology of Aging Women. In J. Sokolovsky (ed.) *Growing Old in Different Societies*. Belmont: Wadsworth, pp. 56–71.

Coupland, J., & N. Coupland. (1991). Formulating Age: Dimensions of Age Identity in Elderly Talk. *Discourse Process* 14: 87–106.

Crapanzano, V. (1980). *Tuhami: Portrait of a Moroccan.* Chicago: University of Chicago Press.

Cumming, E., & W. Henry. (1961). *Growing Old: The Process of Disengagement.* New York: Basic Books.

Davidson, D. (1979). On Metaphor. In S. Sachs (ed.) *On Metaphor.* Chicago: University of Chicago Press.

de Beauvoir, S. (1975). *The Coming of Age.* A Warner Communications.

Dowd, J. J. (1986). The Old Person as Stranger. In V.W. Marshall (ed.) *Later Life: The Social Psychology of Aging.* Beverly Hills: Sage, pp. 147–190.

Eckert, J. K. (1980). *The Unseen Elderly.* San Diego: Campanile Press.

Erikson, E. (1982). *The Life Cycle Completed.* NY: Norton.

Fabian, J. (1983). *Time and the Other: How Anthropology Makes its Object.* New York: Columbia University Press.

Featherstone, M., & M. Hepworth. (1990). Images of Ageing. In J. Bond & P. G. Coleman (eds.) *Ageing in Society: An Introduction to Social Gerontology.* London: Sage.

Featherstone, M., & M. Hepworth. (1991). The Mask of Ageing and the Post-Modern Life Course. In M. Featherstone, M. Hepworth & B. Turner (eds.) *The Body: Social Process and Cultural Theory.* London: Sage, pp. 370–89.

Featherstone, M. (1995). "Post-Bodies, Aging and Virtual Reality." In M. Featherstone & A. Wernick (eds.) *Images of Aging.* London, Routledge, pp. 227–244.

Fontana, A. (1976). *The Last Frontier.* Beverly Hills, CA.: Sage.

Foucault, M. (1980). *Power/Knowledge: Selected Interviews and Other Writings.* Brighton: The Harvester Press.

Giddens, A. (1991). *Modernity and Self-Identity: Self and Society in the Late Modern Age.* Cambridge: Polity Press.

Greer, G. (1991). *The Change: Women, Ageing and Menopause.* London: Hamish Hamilton.

Gubrium, J. (1994). *Speaking of Lives.* New York: Aldine de Gruyter.

Gubrium, J. F., & R. S. Lynott (1983). Rethinking Life Satisfaction. *Human Organization* 42: 30–38.

Hazan, H. (1980). *The Limbo People: A Study of the Constitution of the Time Universe Among the Aged.* London: Routledge & Kegan Paul.

Hazan, H. (1994). *Old Age: Construction and Deconstruction.* Cambridge: Cambridge University Press.

Hazan, H. (1996). *From First Principles: An Experiment in Aging.* Westport, CT: Bergin & Garvey.

Hazan, H. (2000). Terms of Visibility: Eldercare in an Aging Nation State—The Israeli Case. *Journal of Family Issues* 21(6):733–750.

Hazan, H., & A. Raz (1997). How Middle Age Writes Old Age in Postmodern. *Semiotica,* 113(3/4): 257–276.

Hepworth, M., & M. Featherstone (1982). Surviving Middle Age. Oxford: Blackwell.

Hockey, J., & A. James (1993). *Growing Up and Growing Old: Ageing and Dependency in the Life Course.* London: Sage.

Katriel, T. (1991). Sodot: Secret Sharing as a Social Form among Israeli Children. In T. Katriel (ed.), *Communal Webs.* Albany: SUNY Press, pp. 183–197.

Kaufman, S. F. (1986). *The Ageless Self: Sources of Meaning in Late Life.* Madison: University of Wisconsin Press.

Kaufman, S. R. (1981). Cultural Components of Identity in Old Age. *Ethos* 9(1): 51–87.

Kemper, S. (1988). Geriatric Psycholinguistics: Syntactic Limitations of Oral and Written Language. In L. Light & D. Burke (eds.), *Language, Memory and Aging.* Cambridge: Cambridge University Press, pp. 58–76.

Kertzer, D. & J. Keith (eds.) (1984). *Age and Anthropological Theory.* Ithaca: Cornell University Press.

Koch, K. (1977). *I Never Told Anybody: Teaching Poetry Writing in a Nursing Home.* New York: Random House.

Langness, L. L., & G. Frank (1981). *Lives: An Anthropological Approach to Biography.* Novato: Chandler & Sharp.

Laslett, P. (1989). *A Fresh Map of Life: The Emergence of the Third Age.* London: Weidenfeld Nicolson.

Leach, E. (1976). *Culture and Communication.* Cambridge University Press.

Levinson, D., C. Darrow, E. Klein, M. Levinsons, & B. McKee (1978). *The Seasons of Man's Life.* New York: Knopf.

Lifton, R. (1983). *The Broken Connection.* New York: Basic Books.

Lifton, R. (1986). *The Nazi Doctors.* New York: Basic Books.

Marshall, V. W. (1979). No Exit: A Symbolic Interactionist Perspective on Aging. *International Journal of Aging and Human Development* 9: 345–358.

Mead, G. H. (1934). *Mind, Self and Society.* Chicago: University of Chicago Press.

Mergler, N., & M. Goldstein. (1983). Why Are There Old People? Senescence as Biological and Cultural Preparedness for the Transmission of Information. *Semiotica* 54(1/2):177–199.

Mergler, N., & R. Schleifer. (1985). The Plan Sense of Things: Violence and the Discourse of the Aged. *Semiotica* 54(1/2): 177–99.

Meyerowitz, J. (1984). The Adult Child and the Childlike Adult. *Daedalus* 113(3): 19–48.

Myerhoff, B. (1978). *Number Our Days.* New York: Dutton.

Myerhoff, B. (1982). Life History Among the Elderly: Performance Visibility and Remembering. In J. Ruby (ed.) *A Crack in the Mirror: Reflexive Perspectives in Anthropology.* Philadelphia: University of Pennsylvania Press.

Myerhoff, B., & A. Simic (eds.) (1978). *Life's Career—Aging: Cultural Variations on Growing Old.* Beverly Hills, CA: Sage.

Neugarten B. L. (1976). The Future and the Young Old. *The Gerontologist* 15: 4–9.

Rose, N. (1990). *Governing the Soul: The Shaping of the Private Self.* London: Routledge.

Ruby, J. (ed.) (1982). *A Crack in the Mirror: Reflexive Perspectives in Anthropology.* Philadelphia: University of Pennsylvania Press.

Sanjek, R. (1990). On Ethnographic Validity. In R. Sanjek (ed.) *Fieldnotes.* Ithaca, NY: Cornell University Press, pp. 385–419.

Searle, J. (ed.) (1979). *Expressions and Meaning.* Cambridge: Cambridge University Press.

Simmel, G. (1950). The Stranger. In Kurt H. Wolff (ed.) *The Sociology of Georg Simmel.* New York: The Free Press of Glencoe, pp. 402–408.

Tornstam, L. (1997a). Life Crisis and Gerotranscendence. *Journal of Aging and Identity* 7: 117—131.

Tornstam, L. (1997b). Gerotranscendence: The Contemplative Dimension of Aging. *Journal of Aging Studies* 11: 143–154.

Tornstam, L. (1999). Gerotranscendence and the Functions of Reminiscence. *Journal of Aging Studies* 4: 155–166.

Trevarthen, C., & K. Logotheri (1989). Child in Society, and Society in Children: The Nature of Basic Trust. In S. Howell & R. Willis (eds.) *Societies at Peace: Anthropological Perspectives.* London: Routledge.

Turner, B. S. (1987). Aging, Dying and Death. In B. S. Turner (ed.), *Medical Power and Social Knowledge.* Newbury Park: Sage, pp. 11–31.

Turner, V. (1978). Foreword. In B. Myerhoff, *Number Our Days.* New York: Dutton.

Unruh, D. (1983). *Invisible Life: The Social Worlds of the Aged.* Beverly Hills, CA: Sage.

Winner, E. (1990). *The Point of Words: Children's Understanding of Metaphor and Irony.* Cambridge, MA: Harvard University Press.

Woodward, K. (1980). *At Last, the Real Distinguished Thing: The Late Poetry of Eliot, Pound, Stevens and Williams.* Columbus: Ohio State University Press.

Woodward, K. (1991). *Aging and Its Discontents.* Bloomington: Indiana University Press.

Zola, I. K. (1982). *Missing Pieces.* Philadelphia: Temple University Press.

Part III

INTERVENTIONS

Chapter 13

CULTIVATING THE SEEDS OF HOPE

Albert Pesso

INTRODUCTION

Abuse and the trauma that follows it are topics of high current interest. We read about it and hear of it everywhere. Children are abused by their parents, their teachers, and others who would ordinarily be expected to be earnestly concerned with their care. Wives are abused by their husbands, and husbands by their wives. And now, in this insane period when acts of terrorism have become common, ordinary citizens, tourists, and innocent bystanders are beaten, held as hostages, and often murdered (Pesso, 1991, p. 169).

The experience of trauma often leaves victims feeling hopeless in the present and despairing as they confront a meaningless future. It is common in the treatment of abuse/trauma to attend to the wounded aspect of victims and to create a safe atmosphere within which they can learn to return to the outside world with a modicum of calm and control. This is as it should be. However, there are other issues pertaining to the trauma victim's distrust of their own inner world that may be overlooked in typical therapeutic processes, resulting in unrelieved suffering even after years of treatment. In this chapter I will pay special attention to those unattended topics and explain how Pesso Boyden System Psychomotor (PBSP) theories and techniques can help those victims recover more rapidly and more fully. PBSP is a body-based psychotherapy co-founded in 1961 by myself and my wife, Diane Boyden-Pesso (see Howe, 1991).

To begin with, I will look at the anatomy of hope and despair. Later, I will look at the psychological impact of trauma and especially at the role played by automatic body responses to trauma in the diminishment of hope and loss of self-control when the feeling of alarm is extreme. I will describe in detail the application of PBSP theories and techniques regarding body-ego limits, which innate responses to trauma appear to drastically disrupt. I will also discuss other standard PBSP techniques we use with trauma victims to confirm the dignity and validity of their existence. Then I will describe the special therapeutic setting called the Possibility Sphere, which is the arena we create in PBSP to conduct therapy. Following that I will briefly review the theories, techniques, and procedures we use to create a new, satisfying, symbolic, synthetic history for clients. This new history enables clients to face the vicissitudes of life without sinking into despair as it helps them discover, cultivate, and sustain the emotional resources necessary to fulfill what they hopefully, yet realistically, have envisioned for their future.

The Anatomy of Hope

Hope is the natural state of human existence. Our genetic heritage is the source of the wellspring of hope, for it fosters the expectation that there will be a good end coming, that there will be light at the end of the tunnel, and that we will manage to experience sufficient safety and pleasure during our lifetime to warrant going on living, for, after all, hasn't life progressed with greater and greater success and complexity since the beginning of time? Hope is primarily a felt body-state and not only a state of mind (Damasio, 1994, 1999). The felt state of hope is first established in an infant's *physical* relationship with its mother who pays attention to the bodily satisfaction of its needs. Thus the feeling of hope is reinforced and becomes an expectation about the future as the mother regularly and reliably satisfies those basic needs when they arise (Erikson, 1964; Stern, 1986).

What are the underlying mental processes that give rise to the possibility of experiencing hope? First, one must have a clear notion of the flow of time that includes experiencing the present. Second, one must have the ability at a later time to consciously recall that present experience as a memory of events that have passed by. This is the past. Finally, one must all the while be able to conjure up memories in an inner theater of the mind where one can imaginatively and creatively elaborate upon and project those memories into the not-yet-present time, which is called the future. Memories are not to be thought of as only representing recollections of past thoughts and experiences, but more importantly, as Edelman has written, they are "representations of interactions." Likewise, the inner theater of the mind encompasses not only the "mind's eye," but also the "mind's body." Thus, in that inner theater of the mind those remembered interactive representations can be interiorly "seen" and "felt."

In that inner theater of imagination, using soul-satisfying memories of life-validating interactive events as a base, one can inertly practice experiencing interactive events of what one would desire to have happen *before* it happens. It is precisely this ability that constitutes hope. Antonio Damasio, in his book, "The Feeling of What Happens" (1999), calls this process of inner practice "making a memory of the future." By making a memory of the future, one can practice today what one would like to have happen in some future tomorrow by using the memory of that practice as a template/model for what will actually happen when that future comes.

Thus, in order to have hope, one must have a plentiful supply of memories of past interactive satisfactions upon which to base future anticipations of interactive satisfactions. With such a history one can enter the future with hope and confidence, supported by memories of life-validating events that were confirming of one's true being. In PBSP we use this knowledge about memory and its effect on future expectations to provide clients with body-based experiences—cast in the hypothetical past—to create new symbolic memories that support having hope in the future.

People with a history replete with interactive satisfactions of basic developmental needs come naturally to the conclusion that there is love and caring in the world and that there is a future of pleasurable connectedness to look forward to (Erikson, 1964). They are able to live contentedly in the present, fully certain that they will experience pleasure and satisfaction in the future.

It is this deeply engrained hope that sustains us in times of adversity. If one has been fortunate enough during their maturational years to have it sufficiently reinforced and well-registered in their personal memories, they will be able to continue functioning productively, sustained by realistic hope, regardless of outer stress (McFarlane & van der Kolk, 1996). If one has not, we can provide its symbolic equivalent in PBSP sessions (Cooper, 1996).

The Anatomy of Despair

Those who experience constant despair also have a clear notion of the flow of time that includes experiencing the present, the past, and future. They too are able to conjure up memories in an inner theater of the mind where they can elaborate upon those memories of the past and project those memories into the future. Those who live in despair, however, do not have an interior, treasured store-house of optimistic expectation. In contrast, they have memories of significant, life-conditioning interactive events that have denied the validity of their being.

The above storehouse of optimistic expectation can be damaged or destroyed in anyone who has faced life-threatening events of terror, abuse, and trauma. It is even more likely in those who have also lacked the history of satisfactions of basic developmental needs. They have to have been treated not as a human self with wondrous capabilities, but as a thing, an object, a commodity to be used by others. They have to have experienced the uselessness of their attempts to control the outer world. They have to have had an early history where all their needs and choices were nullified or denied. This results in their images of a future full of frustration and their expectations of satisfaction nullified.

The major damage in all traumatic shocks is to that part of the self that is conscious, has identity, a sense of autonomy, a sense of mastery of the self and others, a sense of meaning, a sense of the future, and a sense of hope. Trauma causes tremendous losses to these senses and leaves the fragment remains of the self in despair.

THE PSYCHOLOGICAL/METAPHORIC IMPACT OF TRAUMA

Trauma/abuse figuratively pierces the personal boundaries of the self and breaks the encircling bands of victims' interactively crafted egos, which had heretofore enabled them to manage and control the dual domains of the inside and outside worlds. The traumatic event itself can be experienced as rape, for it thrusts a powerful, unwanted experience at the victim, without his or her consent. The ego is thereby severely damaged as abusers do whatever they want with the victim. The ego, which throughout one's lifetime constantly increases mastery of the self and surroundings, suffers a great shock, for the trauma gives it no part in what will come in to one's body or consciousness. Ordinary ego capacities are reduced, resulting in intermittent feelings of loss of control, loss of language, loss of consciousness, loss of identity, loss of meaning, loss of ability to discriminate between the inner and outer words, fantasy and reality, dream and wakefulness, and other bi-polar distinctions (Pesso, 1991a, pp. 170–173).

As trauma is extremely life threatening, it produces highly charged survival reactions, which figuratively raise the internal temperature to a dangerously high degree. This condition leaves the inner soul without boundaries and gives rise to unbearable but surprisingly addictive, experientially omnipotent, levels of feeling (see Pesso, 1991a, pp. 180–186). The victim's interior feels chaotic and seemingly without order and purpose. This may be so because until now victims may have never been fully in touch with the power of those innate forces. Their life histories may simply not have prepared them for that amount of reactivity. As these feelings may have had insufficient interaction or contact with any ego-constructing figures such as parents or appropriate caregivers during their upbringing, they have remained unknown. The result is that there may have never been a place made for that level of primitive emotions in their self-construct. They may not have had the help of having names given to those powers. Naming defines forces, describes their functions, and gives them dimension. Not doing so leaves them outside the realm of the cognitive part of the self. Thus, those powers are reacted to as if foreign.

Having also lost control of their inner world, which now appears strange, unfamiliar, mysterious, and without dimension, victims tend to distrust their own core emotional processes, for it appears to them that it is their core itself that is the source of those now uncontrollable, spewing, chaotic forces. Thus, they try to distance themselves from their own bodies and whatever other interior regions they fear might harbor and release those threatening energies. This leads to coping strategies of dissociation, passivity, or frantic external action. Unlinked from their core, they become even more uncertain as to who they are, and what their true identity is (van der Kolk, 1996). Thus, they become terrified and wary, not only of the *outside* world—the original source of the threat—but also (and sometimes even more so) of their own *inner* world. This is evidence that their weakened ego is in great distress and jeopardy.

Instinctive Repertoire to Threat

Threat-aroused impulses have the potential to have a powerful, almost irresistible, effect on our emotional states, producing survival reactions evolutionarily geared to provide us with behaviors that will result in the continuity of our existence: keeping alive (Ledoux, 1996, pp. 138–178; Ekman, 1973). That is one of the two primary goals of our genetic heritage. The other is keeping the species alive. We have built-in systems and tendencies laid down in us by evolution with the aim of making sure there is a continuity of existence beyond our immediate generation (Gazzaniga, 2002). In other words, replication of the species is the main aim of sexuality.

The instinctive terms are clear and simple: when danger appears, freeze, flee, fight, appease (Ledoux, 1996, pp.128–137). How clever of our genes to note and make use of the fact that offering love can sometimes result in surviving a life-threatening encounter. When the danger is simple enough—and one's ego strong enough—all goes as one's genes predict and the problem is well attended to. According to each given situation, one can hide, run away, fight off the threat, or offer love and receptivity to the threatening person and all's well that ends well.

When held in check by the ego, our psyches can present us with the livable stuff of complex, varied, external, and internal reality. When that membrane of containment and differentiation, the ego, is stripped off, pierced, or shattered by unbearable trauma or abuse, those energies are no longer felt on the individual, human, living dimension. Though this is clearly a metaphor, the energies in our psyches react like—and feel similar to—cosmic events. It is a personal, psychological holocaust that is the equivalent of a nuclear explosion and a nuclear meltdown combined. The nuclear forces of polar opposites in the core expand/explode/open without the restraining, containing, discriminating, and modifying effects of the surrounding band of the encircling ego. Order and complex states are no longer experienceable and atomic, psychic forces are unleashed in their simplest, primeval, uncontrollable level. Primordial expanding, exploding forces and their opposite engulfing, receptive, swallowing forces are set loose and the outer world seems on the verge of being destroyed by one's self, or hell-bent on plummeting into one's self—incinerating the boundaries between inside and outside. Thus, traumatized clients feel both the unbound forces of exploding fury and the capacity for boundless receptivity awakened inside themselves and they become terrified and helpless in the face of their seeming uncontrollability.

It takes a lot of power to meet those forces in the therapy session, and that is why body action and touch are absolutely necessary to deal with them. It requires great strength and enduring, consistent physical effort to tame those forces so that the primacy of the executive ego can be re-established.

We are better or worse for having those powers and capacities within us depending on the level of discrimination afforded by our egos, which when healthy, can screen and differentiate between appropriate or inappropriate entrances of the outer world. It is our ego that filters and modifies the intake process, just as it does the outgo process. When our egos are shattered, people don't feel so much like a well-contained human being serene in the integration of polarities, but as if they were oscillating wildly between the open vulnerability of endless space and its corollary, a black hole sucking in everything in its vicinity, like a hellish explosive force able to demolish anything it comes in contact with. The unbound primal psyche can feel as if it can both explode and implode if there is nothing to hold its immense forces in check. Power erupts and gaping chasms of vulnerability (openness) are present—destroying everything by force or capable of drawing everything outside, inside, without end. The personal, experiential level of terror this produces seems infinite and without dimension. Cataclysmic, chaotic action or frozen, powerless paralysis can ensue.

How can we repair the intra-psychic damage caused by traumatic events and heal the shattered ego? How can we resurrect the primacy of the fully integrated, conscious, worthy, sovereign, autonomous self? How can we help trauma victims to reawaken hope? In the remainder of this chapter, we will discuss PBSP interventions, which help traumatized clients find hope and order in their lives once again.

The Ego and the Body

Having explained how the shock of trauma overrides the ego, we need now to touch on PBSP theory's view on the ego and its relationship with the body. As I have said, in trauma, the ego is endangered both by the outside and inside worlds, and when this happens hope is destroyed and despair is triggered (van der Kolk, 1996). PBSP technique is based on our theories about how the ego was created and can be repaired. In order to understand our approach to treating trauma and the restoration of hope, it is necessary to first understand our theory about the ego, which I will now explain.

Think of the soul as a biological entity that has not yet accumulated a personal history but has within it the history of all successful life processes pushing forward to live/survive in the present and to thrive in the future. A newly living soul could be described as a nuclear, organismic center of being that is fresh, naked, and having no present knowledge of a self with an inside and no present experience of an outside world. Though the core is genetically pre-organized, the outer membrane surrounding that center is only constructed through contact with the outside world. The organism itself, as it develops and matures in interactions with that outside world, becomes a living record of its encounters with it. In other words, the ego is literally created through interactions. It is in those encounters with the outside world that its actual, as well as its metaphoric/psychological skins are woven. The psychological skin, which can also be thought of as an ego membrane, can be described as the interactive interface between the inner and outer worlds. It is an interface in that one side of the membrane faces in and from that standpoint is able to regulate and modify what is coming out. The other side of the membrane faces out and from that standpoint is able to filter, regulate, and modify what is coming in. Thus, the interactive interface is able to filter, regulate, and modify what is coming out of the self as well as what is coming in. It can regulate behavior (output) as well as perception (intake). The soul, now with an interactively woven skin, can evolve into a conscious, inward and forward-looking, self-directing, human being.

From birth onward, through every developmental phase of life, loving, meaningful interactions, first with parental figures and then with the rest of the life-supporting outside world, lay the foundation for the development of those interactive/containing membranes that become the building blocks of hopeful, healthy egos. In contrast, if one has had frustrating, negative, and meaningless interactions with the overseers of their rearing and later, similarly negative relationships with figures in the outside world, memories of those life-conditioning, interactive events become the building blocks of despairing, unhealthy egos (see Pesso, 1973, pp. 121–154).

Another way to say it is that the soul is a given, but the skin of the soul—the ego—is constructed in interactions with the outside world. The combination of the soul and the ego comprises the self. A true, hopeful self results when the soul's interaction with the world sufficiently matches the genetic expectations coiled in its DNA. A false, despairing self occurs when the soul's interactions with the outside are combined with an ego that has been fashioned in a way not congruent with the needs, true dimensions, and characteristics of the soul.

Development of the ego is not only a cognitive process. Prior to the existence of a psychological ego, there is a body ego that is created by sensorimotor, kinesthetic interactions with parents and other early caregivers (Stern, 1986). Motor activity in satisfying, life-validating interactions is essential for maturing individuals to learn how to cope, not only with the outer world but also with the nuclear, core resources in their inner world during childhood. That is precisely why the body has to be involved in the healing (and further development) of the ego following traumatic events. Familiarity and control of those previously out-of-control forces need to be re-experienced and re-integrated on the sensorimotor, kinesthetic level and not merely on a cognitive rational level. In order to deal with the damage caused by trauma to the body ego and to create the deeper levels of healing necessary for trauma victims to over-come despair and replace it with hope, it is clear that body-based thera-peutic interventions are absolutely essential.

THE PBSP SETTING

Before we can discuss how we in PBSP help trauma victims reconstruct their lives and regain their lost hope, we need to first explain the main ele-ments of PBSP. The key elements we will touch upon are the Possibility Sphere, the notion of Accommodation, the notion of a Structure and the notion of making a New Memory and describe the steps leading to the ful-fillment of the self. In this brief explanation of PBSP techniques we'll begin by describing the PBSP concept of the Possibility Sphere, because this is how we conceptualize the psychological space within which the therapy takes place.

The Possibility Sphere

The possibility sphere is a psychological, welcoming, expansive space, which we metaphorically extend to the client as part of the therapeutic relationship. The reason we call it the possibility sphere is that it is a sur-round that is so flexible and so full of "yeses" to the soul that it gives the unspoken message, "Yes, all that is within you is possible to come into being, life is possible, life is good. You can feel hope that nothing in you has to die in order for you to live. None of your potentiality, your possibil-ity as a person, has to die, and those parts of you that you felt you had to abandon may still come alive." It's very much a "yes" to life, and implicit in it is a belief that life is good, so it is an optimistic view. It transmits the message that the energy the client is born with is essentially good. The possibility sphere offers an environment that implicitly says "yes" to the energy that's in the soul.

The possibility sphere is connected to the notion of the need for interac-tion and for counter shape. It's a sphere that is so open and so full of non-shape that it has all shapes in it. The possibility sphere contains all possible counter shapes to whatever shape is coming out of the person at any given time. Thus, the possibility sphere, by its very nature, prepares the ground for trauma victims to become familiar with and accepting of the positive, interactive, healthy ego-building satisfactions that will be experienced later in structures (Pesso, 1991b).

Accommodation

Accommodation is a technique used in PBSP to provide clients with the kinds of interactive responses that "match" or "counter shape" the "shapes" or physical forms of each emotion the clients express in their individual work (called a "structure"), in the group. Since the PBSP process includes motoric/bodily expression, emotions are not only spoken about but also acted upon (see Pesso, 1969, pp. 159–185). For instance, if clients express fear in its physical form, and either run for safety or curl up in a ball (shapes)—they know they can ask one of the group members to role-play a "protection figure" or a "safety-giving figure" who would supply the wished for physical responses (counter shapes) of a haven to be run to. The role-players represent figures who, in the hypothetical past created in the structure, would offer the safety of their own body as a protective shield to be securely wrapped around them, when the client would have felt vulnerable and would have curled up into a ball in the past.

In PBSP, all physical reactions that might and do emerge as sensations and impulses in the body are met with the archaically wished for and internally anticipated outcomes via the accommodation process. Counter shaping, or matching the expressed emotion, gives it a place in the ego, allowing newly discovered emotions to be expressed and consciously experienced by the client. The client is the arbiter and decider of the aptness and correctness of the counter shapes that are offered. Nothing is done in an interaction that is not acceptable to the client or requested by him or her. This supports the clients' mastery and control throughout the process, that is, their consciousness and their pilot.

THE PBSP PROCESS

Structure

When I describe the work of "structures" in PBSP it will become clear that what we do is "stage" a piece of "new" history in the Possibility Sphere, where we make, not a *memory of the future* in order to have hope, but a *memory of a hypothetical past*. It is memories of the past that people internally call upon to make preparations for the future (Schacter, 1996; Rose, 1993). Trauma clients have experienced severe deficits of life-satisfying interactions. With structures we help them enrich the database of their actual histories with healing "symbolic interactive events." In structures they have a powerful sensorimotor experience with role-players representing kinship figures that their genes had prepared them to anticipate in their lives. Instead of having only an *interior theater* where the practice of the future takes place, structures provide a sensory motor, *external theater* to provide sensorimotor, kinesthetic experiences out of which new representations of interactions will be made. This provides them with a well-stocked bank leading to hope because these new memories are abundant with pleasurable and satisfying "felt" memories (Lea, 1997).

A "structure" is the name given to the approximately 50-minute time-limited segment of the therapy session where each client in turn is given the opportunity to be fully in charge of the creation of his or her new memory. The rest of the group is then available to accommodate or role-play, when requested by the client who is having the "structure."

The structure begins with "micro-tracking" the client's present consciousness with the understanding that present consciousness is made up of the client's present *affect* and its concomitant bodily responses to what is presently felt, plus the client's *thoughts* and attitudes about what he or she is seeing and feeling at the moment. It is a given in PBSP that *present consciousness* is mostly driven and influenced by *past memories* (Schacter, 1996; Rose, 1993). This fact becomes abundantly clear when past memories associated with the review of the present immediately come to mind and at once affect the client's body and emotional state at that moment.

When a significant event of the past arises during the micro-tracking process—in which the client is now able to recognize what has negatively influenced his or her present situation—that past event can then be played out in the group assisted by group members' role-play. This gives the client the opportunity to discover what had been felt or experienced in the past. For now, having a structure with the freedom given in the possibility sphere, they have the opportunity to physically, as well as verbally, express whatever comes to body or mind. This part of the "structure" allows the client to process unexpressed emotions and discover, with greater consciousness, the implications of that past event's impact on his or her present state. However, this expression and insight are only the first steps of the structure.

Making New Memories

Processing the past, grieving about the losses experienced, and gaining insight is not enough. In Pesso Boyden System Psychomotor (PBSP) we take the bold step to create new symbolic memories to offset the debilitating effects of past, deficit-ridden, personal histories.

The heart of this part of the work consists of creating a "counter-event" that is staged and controlled by the client. This is framed as if it too had taken place in the past, but this time with more satisfying interactions provided by "ideal figures" who, had they been in the client's past, would have provided what was necessary to assist them in developing their full capacities. Their interactions are staged to offset the toxic effects of the actual event with the original figures. This "antidote" event is organized and configured to provide the client with a new piece of "synthetic, symbolic memory" as if it had happened at a requisite age and with the appropriate kinship relationship that would have been optimal for that client's maturational development. Though indeed we are creating a symbolic fantasy, these role-players do not represent magical, spiritual, or non-human figures. The "ideal figures" parental behaviors are based on the genetic/evolutionary human capacities we are born to anticipate from parents in the real world.

As I noted above, people with a history replete with interactive satisfactions of basic developmental needs come to the conclusion that life has meaning, that there is love and caring in the world, that there is a future of pleasurable connectedness to look forward to (Erikson, 1964). Thus, with the help of these kinds of structures, they are able to live contentedly in the present, fully certain that they will experience pleasure and satisfaction in the future.

Steps Leading to Fulfillment of the Self

These new memories are not randomly supplied but conform to fundamental ideas regarding the maturation process leading to optimal maturational states. Thus, PBSP structures attend to what we see as the necessary steps that would result in optimal living and generativity. For a complete review of those steps see Pesso (1997).

We need to:

1. Satisfy the basic developmental needs for:
   - Place
   - Nurture
   - Support
   - Protection
   - Limits
2. Integrate and unify the polarities of our biological and psychological being:
   - Sperm/Egg—own and comfortably identify with mother's and father's antecedents and gene pool.

- Neurological—integrate and have good communication between left hemisphere and right hemisphere.
- Sensorimotor—be comfortable and skillful in all combinations of perception and action.
- Behavioral—have an easy acceptance and comfortable use of all body apertures involved in "putting-out" and "taking-in."
- Symbolic—at ease with one's metaphoric androgyny of combined "maleness/femaleness"(Animus and Anima) while able to identify with one's biological gender.

3. Develop our consciousness—increase subjectivity/objectivity, with a well-developed interior world of images and concepts combined with a strong sense of individual identity and ego.

4. Develop our "pilot"—have a strong, active, self-organizing, self-initiating center, akin to taking our rightful place as the "president" of our own "united states of consciousness."

5. Realize our personal uniqueness and potentiality—come to maturity, ripen, and bring the precious fruit of our existence to the world.

Structures are basically geared to provide the client with experiences that should have taken place in the past and would have provided the satisfaction of fundamental life needs. The pleasure that is experienced when such satisfactions symbolically take place in a structure provides the experiential basis that makes it possible for the client to have hope in the future. It is our understanding that given a personal history where the above tasks have been successfully attended to either in actual history or in structure-created "symbolic memory," a client would be more able to contend successfully with the vicissitudes of the real world and especially with the consequences of traumatic events. However, when working with traumatized clients, structures are especially focused on what would help them experience, integrate, and find limits for the unruly emotions released by the trauma.

Cultivating the Seeds of Hope by Offering Limits to Unbounded Receptivity and Aggression

The following is about a client who had a history of incest with her father. The story below is a compilation of several structures done over a period of time but presented in the form of a single structure.

The client began to remember the sexual contacts with her father. She started to feel sick and felt that she would throw up. I understood that reaction as having too much feeling in her body, more than she could handle. This is an example of her ego being disrupted. She was one of those people who learned how to leave her body and now we could see why, because if she felt what was in there it would be too much. Whenever there is such an overload, I know that the route out is to have the person use the energy in their body very strongly and then to have that action that comes out of the body be in contact with supporting or containing figures who provide counter-shaping pressure and resistance to the action as a way to help them handle it. Without those outside people to contact them when they have those feelings, they might feel as if their egos would explode from the force of the feelings inside and that they then might go crazy. The physical contact and pressure from the outside contacting people is experienced like a healing seal or cover over the hole torn in their fragile egos.

So I suggested she select some people to role-play just such contact-containing figures so she could process that energy. The contact figures, who were females, gently put their arms around her as she sat on the floor with her arms around her knees and then I suggested that she tightened the muscles around the areas of tension in her body. She began to tremble. The contact figures held her more securely and she began to cry, saying she was very frightened. I understood that she was frightened not only because she remembered how helpless she felt when her father abused her but that she might also be frightened of the feelings that it brought up in her that she did not understand. It could be fear of the inside as well as the outside. In those instances, the contact figures are usually asked to say, or are needed to say things like, "We can help you handle how scared you are." This gives license to the feelings, giving them a name and making them handleable as the containing figures are there as an outer surface to hold them together.

The client, in the arms of the protective figures, felt free to touch even deeper levels of fear and terror. Suddenly, she clasped her neck, which had cramped with pain. That is a common reaction when people feel very vulnerable. At those moments some part of the body, frequently the neck, becomes very hard, as a kind of alternative to one's own softness that has made one feel so defenseless. I asked her to exaggerate the tension in her neck and in doing so her head pressed backward. That action needed to be contacted with and one of the containing figures, with her approval, placed her hands around the base of her head and the client, using the force created by the contracted muscles, pushed her head backwards into her hands.

This kind of intervention is provided to meet the counterforce that the client calls up in the attempt to balance the too vulnerable feelings. It is important that when this hard reaction to their soft feelings surfaces, it is not met with limits. Limits are that special intervention that stops an action from being completed (see Pesso, 1991c). In this case limits are not required, but a more subtle amount of resistance is offered, with just the right amount of pressure. This allows the clients to continue to move their body in whatever direction they wish it to go, but they have to work harder to make it happen. This intervention demonstrates to the clients that their strength and force is effective. The words that the accommodators might be asked to say in connection with it are, "You're strong, you can have an effect on me," or other words that would give a similar message of validating the client's attempts at increasing the amount of power they have available in their bodies. This validation of that increase of strength has the paradoxical effect of giving the clients the license and safety to go deeper into their vulnerable feelings. Hope has arisen that it could be safe to be vulnerable again.

From that interaction, the client, with great force, pushed her hips forward and with the contact figures giving counter pressure on her hip bones, the client's thighs and pelvis shook violently.

She said something like "That is so sexual," sat back on her heels and began to pound on her thighs. Quickly the containing figures restrained her from hitting her legs and in a flash she began to aim her fists toward her face, which it appeared she would attempt to smash. She seemed to be in a fit of self hate, guilt, and shame for having sexual feelings in her body and would destroy those parts of herself that had those feelings. The limiting figures, with her agreement (I must say that nothing is allowed to happen without the client's agreement) say to her, "We will not let you hurt yourself." Then, when they are clearly ready for her attempts, the client feels free to release all the pent-up self hate and disgust she has about her own sexual feelings. Clients at this juncture struggle greatly but it is always a relief for them to find that no matter how hard they try they will be limited from doing damage to themselves.

The guilt that she feels at such moments is enormous. She blames herself for her own predicament. The fact that she just found herself feeling sexual seems proof to her that it was her fault that the abuse occurred. She would kill the offending parts of herself; "If thine eye offend thee pluck it out." She would pluck out her sexual feelings in her guilty thighs and smash the sexual feelings out of her head.

But when this self-hate and guilt is limited it can quickly turn to hatred and murder directed toward the person who made all those unwanted feelings happen. That too must be expressed, but in a form where it is clear that there would not be allowance for literal murder.

When those feeling of self-hate shift to become hatred of the person who brought those feelings out in her, the client chose to have a negative father enrolled so that she could vent her fury at him. The negative father role-player accommodated as if struck when she directed her blows at him. It was satisfying to the client to see her negative father in pain. She wanted to punish him for what he had done to her.

"I'll really kill him now" she said. If she had not been limited she might become frightened that nothing would stop her from carrying out her murderous intentions. At such moments the containing figures can say, "It's all right to be so angry at him, but we won't let you literally kill him. We can handle your anger and we can help you handle it." Their firm limiting action is concrete proof of that. This allowed her to fully express all the hatred and rage she felt for him. She lunged toward him and punched in his direction and kicked toward him, venting all the suppressed hostility.

But she didn't stay with anger for long. Shortly, she was remembering how much she loved her father; how he had been the adored daddy for her in her childhood and now she could not bear to think of him being hurt. That aroused a great sadness and loss in her, for she remembered how hurt and confused she was the day he first approached her sexually. It was like the end of her world.

Paradoxically, during the process of expressing this sadness and grief, right in the middle of her crying and all the shaking and convulsive feelings that came with it, she noted that her thighs were trembling and that there was another tension in her belly and lower back. When I asked her to exaggerate the tension and to see what movement came of it, it made her legs shake in a way that they oscillated between opening and closing. Before carrying out the appropriate intervention to limit this erotic receptive feeling I explained some of the theoretical notions about it to her. This was helpful to her and permitted her greater freedom to move under the force of those impulses.

The limiting figures, and it is important that in this case they be female and not male, otherwise it might feel like she was submitting to male strength, wrapped their arms around her knees so that no matter how hard she might try to open her legs she would not be able to do so. It is a paradoxical thing. Here is a person who has been abused and who wants more than anything to close herself up to keep from being abused, and she finds that a part of herself that she is not in conscious control of, intends to move in a way that is quite the opposite. Now that external figures are doing the closing, she can attend totally to the impulse to open her legs, and that releases an enormous amount of energy. There is a great struggle, and not only does she fight to separate them, but her hips thrust forward repeatedly and when she makes the sounds that the effort brings, it surprises her. She says, "Those are the sounds that he made when he was doing it." Now the emotions connected to that event are entirely conscious and she can find some of the same feelings in herself. Although it at first makes her ashamed, she finds that she can continue to make the movement and the sounds and is relieved that she can own those sexual feelings in herself but still while she is kept from separating her legs. If in the sexual contact a client had included some conscious sexual excitement and a wish to have incestuous relations, the ideal limiting figures could say something like this, "It is OK that you might want to have sex with your father but we won't let you literally do it." There is relief when limiting figures succeed in getting that omnipotent feeling of receptive sexuality and vulnerability under control. After the limits, she feels that her body is more her own and she relaxes in a way she has not been able to do before. This is another increase in the possibility of hope, now that her own interior, unruly, unconscious responses to the incestuous events are having more body-ego as well as psychological-ego control.

She takes some time now to review and examine her emotional state and remarks that the room looks different, lighter, and her body feels softer and less tense. She looks over to where the negative father was and begins to remember her real father again and how she used to adore him. Feelings of love well up in her and she begins to cry. She is filled with tenderness and begins to stroke the floor in front of her as she remembers and speaks about how wonderful she thought he was.

She then asked a group member to role-play the loved aspect of her real father. This second figure is spatially placed to be entirely separate from the negative aspect of the father and represents only the part of her real father that she loved. This polarization allows her tender feelings to be expressed toward the loved aspect of her father without ambivalence. In the event that she might begin to be angry again, those feelings would be directed toward the negative father.

At this moment, she is not feeling sexual, furious, or guilty. Instead, she is suffused with the tender feelings of the unexpressed love she had felt for him in her childhood, feelings which she could no longer express after the incest began.

The male group member role-playing the loved aspect is asked to sit closer. She is still being held by the contact figures around her. As she looks at him, her body begins to tremble again and they do their encircling function to help her to contain her vulnerability as she feels the love for him. This is reassuring, for without it those feelings might get out of control. In a way it is omnipotent tenderness. Their holding can include their saying, "We can help you handle how much you love him." For her love feelings are also somewhat out of body-ego control.

As she reaches her hand to touch him she becomes frightened by the force of her feelings and other containing figures are enrolled to hold onto her wrists as she reaches toward her father's face and hair. They exert a little counter pressure, giving just enough resistance so that the effort is not stopped completely. That is why they are called resistance figures, not to represent her resistance, but to give her enough external resistance so that she does not get paralyzed by her own ambivalence about touching him. Those resistance figures make it just possible for the tender feelings to be expressed without getting out of control.

This intervention enables her to give vent to all the tenderness she feels inside without being overwhelmed. It is very touching to see that moment and to note the open, happy, hopeful expression on her face.

The structure has brought her to a place where she is more able to face and control the forces that had been ignited within her by the incest. Now she needs to have an alternative, symbolic experience with parental figures who would have supplied her with the kind of childhood interactions that would have permitted her to become her adult self with greater mastery of her inner and outer worlds and with a sense of safety, comfort, and hope as she anticipates the future.

Here is how she uses the ideal parents in her structure. She chooses two group members, male and female, to represent the ideal father and ideal mother. They are instructed to sit side by side, entirely opposite to the original situation where the parents were not close at all. She said something about still not believing that they liked each other or had sex together and I asked her if it would be okay if I provided her with what I have found is a kind of classic image of parental intimacy. I described it to her and when she agreed I instructed the ideal parents to embrace each other and look into each other's eyes. This made her face light up. She said she had never seen her real parents so close and that it was wonderful to imagine her ideal parents being so intimate. The ideal father would say, "I would never be sexual with you, I would only be sexual with your mother." It was a great relief for her. It made her feel free like a child and now she felt she could have a mother again. She began to cry and climbed into her ideal mother's lap like a little child, experiencing what she hadn't felt in her actual childhood, being loved and protected by a mother who was only a mother and not a competitor.

This work has brought her to a place where her nuclear forces of power and vulnerability need no longer be totally suppressed and are less likely to bring her to a place where she is in dread of imminent meltdown. She has expressed the emotions in her body in a way that she can feel more control over them. They have been seen, touched, named, and given boundaries and are thereby ego-wrapped. She is more of one piece. The integrity of her body and the feelings in it have been recognized in a respectful setting and given a place. The establishment of these new memories can become the basis for hope in the future.

SUMMARY

This ends my overview of the ideas and methods used by PBSP therapists to help trauma victims move from despair to hope. Structures are designed to help clients review past, life-determining situations in the possibility sphere and then reconstruct those events with appropriate ideal kinship figures in interactions that support and confirm gene-based expectations of success in surviving and thriving. This is achieved with the help of new, healing, memory-building symbolic events that take place in the therapy room and are seen with the client's real eyes and felt in the client's real body. They are then placed, with the aid of the mind's eye and the mind's body, in the appropriate storage space in the brain where real old memories are kept and can later be accessed. The traumatized clients construct the kinds of interactions their sorely taxed egos are "starved" for. The end result is a hopeful, more optimistic person with an ego-structure more able to regulate and control both the inner and outer domains.

Though the therapeutic process is by its nature "symbolic," the client's experience is anything but artificial. When the wished-for interactions are seen with the client's real eyes and felt with the client's real body, the impact on the client is dramatic. Those real feelings of expansion and realization are what make the new memory so memorable and so believable. The new memory is not an abstract construct; it is a felt experience of great power. What makes it symbolic is that the client shifts the locus of the storage of that memory from a short term "happening right now" location, to a long term "it happened when I was a child" location. This shift in time, age, and place is what gives the structure the power of long-term memory.

The look of relief, the relaxation of tense muscles and rigid postures, the tears of grief at knowing what was missed, the heartfelt expressions of warmth and gratitude to the figures in their structure, the look of happiness and hope as their demeanor shifts from a gloomy interior focus to a smiling, sunny, outward-looking expression—one can only feel awe in the presence of a soul, stretching and flowering, safe and unthreatened, shining in all its glory. It is my hope that the materials presented here will help trauma victims to return more rapidly to a life of hope with plentiful quantities of pleasure, satisfaction, meaning, and connectedness.

REFERENCES

Cooper, D. (1996). PBSP as the practical resolution: Combining insights from a 1995 interview with Albert Pesso and Diane Boyden-Pesso, and the works of Jurgen Habermas, Michael Walzer, and selected post-modern feminist writers. August 29th–30th. *Proceedings of the Third International Conference of Pesso-Boyden Systems Psychomotor therapy.* http://www.pbsp.com/cooper.htm

Damasio, A. (1994). *Descartes' Error: Emotion, Reason, and the Human Brain* (Chapter 7, pp. 127–164). New York: Putnam.

Damasio, A. (1999). *The Feeling of What Happens: Body and Emotion in the Making of Consciousness* (Chapters 2, 9, pp. 33–81 & pp. 277–295). Orlando, FL: Harcourt Brace.

Ekman, P. (Ed.) (1973). *Darwin and Facial Expression: A Century of Research in Review.* New York, London: Academic Press.

Erikson, E. (1964). *Childhood and Society.* Homburger, 1964; reprinted 1993, New York: Norton.

Gazzaniga, M., Ivry, R. and Mangun, G. (2002). *Cognitive Neuroscience, Second Edition.* New York: Norton.

Howe, L. (1991). Origins and history of Pesso system/psychomotor therapy. In A. Pesso & J. Crandell, Eds. *Moving Psychotherapy: Theory and Application of Pesso System/Psychomotor Therapy* (pp 3–32). Cambridge, MA: Brookline Books. Also http://www.pbsp.com/lhowint1.htm

Lea, R. (1997). *Neuroscience, PBSP Psychomotor, and the Re-invention of Talk Therapy.* Copyright by Robert Lea, Ed.D. http://www.pbsp.com/reinvent.htm.

Ledoux, J. (1996). *The Emotional Brain: The Mysterious Underpinnings of Emotional Life.* New York: Simon & Schuster.

McFarlane, A., & van der Kolk, B. (1996). Trauma and its challenge to society. In: B. van der Kolk, A. McFarlane, and L. Weisaeth (eds.). *Traumatic stress* (pp. 24–46). New York: Guilford Press.

Pesso, A. (1969). *Movement in Psychotherapy* (pp. ix–xii). New York: New York University Press.

Pesso, A. (1973). *Experience in Action.* New York: New York University Press.

Pesso, A., (1991a). Abuse. In A. Pesso & J. Crandell, Eds. *Moving Psychotherapy: Theory and Application of Pesso System/Psychomotor Therapy* (pp. 169–188). Cambridge, MA: Brookline Books.

Pesso, A. (1991b). Ego development in the possibility sphere. In A. Pesso & J. Crandell, Eds. *Moving Psychotherapy: Theory and Application of Pesso System/Psychomotor Therapy* (pp. 51–63). Cambridge, MA: Brookline Books.

Pesso, A. (1991c). Ego function and Pesso system/psychomotor therapy. In A. Pesso & J. Crandell, Eds. *Moving Psychotherapy: Theory and Application of Pesso System/Psychomotor Therapy* (pp. 41–49). Cambridge, MA: Brookline Books.

Pesso, A., & Wassenaar, H., (1991). The relationship between PS/P and a neurobiological model. In A. Pesso & J. Crandell, Eds. *Moving Psychotherapy: Theory and Application of Pesso System/Psychomotor Therapy* (pp. 33–40). Cambridge, MA: Brookline Books.

Pesso, A. (1995). The realization of hope: Anticipations and interactions between inner worlds and outer worlds and the realization of hope. *Journal of Communication and Cognition,* Vol. 28, No. 2/3.

Rose, S. (1993). *The Making of Memory: From Molecules to Mind.* New York: Anchor Books.

Schacter, D. (1996). *Searching for Memory: The Brain, the Mind, and the Past.* New York: HarperCollins.

Stern, D. (1986). *The Interpersonal World of the Infant.* New York: Basic Books.

van der Kolk, B. (1996). The Black Hole of Trauma. In B. van der Kolk, A. McFarlane, and L. Weisaeth (eds.). *Traumatic Stress* (pp. 24–46). New York: Guilford Press.

Chapter 14

THE NEVERENDING STORY: A MODEL FOR THE "WORK OF HOPE"

Rebecca Jacoby

In recent years, interest in the subject of hope and its positive influence on human coping has been kindled by reports of people who have survived extremely trying conditions, such as war and concentration camps (Frankl, 1963; Birenbaum, 1983; Pisar, 1981), natural disasters (Ghinsberg, 1985; Henderson & Bostock, 1977) and severe handicap and illness (Alsop, 1976; Amiel, 1979; Cousins, 1979; Sacks, 1986). These testimonies have paved the way to more serious attempts at defining, explaining, and exploring the nature of hope, its sources, and its effects. During the last 20 years the field of psychology (cognitive psychology in particular), has been developing the concept of hope both on a theoretical and empirical level. This trend in psychology represents a shift of interest from the pathogenesis approach, which focuses on the negative effects of stress, to the salutogenesis approach, which emphasizes positive personality variables and coping strategies that aid in coping with stress.

While the understanding of the concept at the theoretical level and the development of assessment tools are of great importance, it is no less important to understand how hope really works, in order to utilize its potential for fostering processes of coping and in therapy.

What is hope? Emotion? Cognition? Coping mechanism? Or maybe all of the above? There is a consensus that hope is related to the future and has a positive aspect. However, as we all know, the experience of hope is above all subjective and therefore, difficult to define, quantify, or measure.

In this chapter, I shall discuss two approaches dealing with the concept of hope: the dynamic and the cognitive-behavioral. Thereafter, I shall present my own conceptualization, trying to integrate these two approaches using a developmental angle, existential ideas, and clinical experience. Finally, I will demonstrate the "never-ending story" as a model for the "work of hope" in psychotherapy.

THE DYNAMIC APPROACH

The dynamic theories that dealt with the concept of hope and its role in developmental and coping processes are based primarily on clinical observations and subjective impressions. They focused on the definition of the concept on a theoretical–philosophical level (Boris, 1976; French, 1952; Menninger, 1959), on the role of hope in psychotherapy (Frank, 1968; Searles, 1979; Mitchell, 1993; Kanwall, 1997), recovery processes (Freud, 1953), and in doctor–patient relationships (Menninger, 1959).

Freud (1953) related to hope in the context of physical diseases:

> Our interest is most particularly engaged by the mental state of expectation, which puts in motion a number of mental forces that have the greatest influence on the onset and cure of physical diseases. Fearful expectation is certainly not within its effect on the result.
>
> ...The contrary state of mind, in which expectation is colored by hope and faith, is an effective force with which we have to reckon, strictly speaking, in all our attempts at treatment and cure. (p. 289)

Others emphasized the motivational function of hope as an integral component of the topographical structure of personality. Thus, French (1952) viewed hope as the activating force of the ego's integrative function. Frank (1968), discussing the role of hope in psychotherapy, defined it as a *"desire accompanied by expectation,"* and emphasized the differential effects of the presence versus the absence of hope on recovery from physical illness. Erikson (1964) defined hope as the *"enduring belief in the attainability of fervent wishes, in spite of the dark urges and rages which mark the beginning of existence"* (p. 118). Likewise, the concept of "basic trust" coined by Erikson (1963) in his developmental theory, can be viewed as congruous with the concept of hope.

Haynal (1985) defined hope as:

> Hope—the confident cathexis of an image of self and its future potentialities is the opposite of depression: it is the feeling that the hurt is not definitive, that reparation is possible, that there is no fait accompli. (p. 28)

Both Erikson and Haynal refer to the case presented by Freud, in which he described how his grandchild, who was unable to distinguish between temporary absence and permanent loss, learned, after repeated consolatory experiences, that his mother would reappear after her disappearance. Haynal saw in this case a description of the birth of hope. Menninger (1959) presented a more extensive analysis of hope, relating to it from a clinical perspective and attempting to integrate the concept within his general theoretical position. According to Menninger, hope reflects the working of the life instinct in its struggle against the destructive forces of the death instinct. Menninger distinguished hope from expectation and optimism: Optimism is not based on a realistic evaluation of the potential obstacles and, like pessimism, is self-centered. In contrast, hope is more strongly anchored in reality and is modest and self-less. Most importantly, hope implies a process and is oriented towards the future. *"It is an adventure, a going forward, a confident search"* (p. 484). Boris (1976) centered his discussion on hope on the distinction between hope and desire. Desire demands immediate gratification, a real object, and real fulfillment, whereas hope is within the realm of potential; it has no time or space boundaries and loses its meaning once its object, is attained. As stated by Bion (1961) *"only by remaining a hope, does hope persist"* (pp. 151–152). According to Boris, hope plays a central role in the process of separation from a loved object. In the face of loss, hope, unlike desire, does not resort to the easy solution of the problem by means of a substitute object, but rather internalizes the lost object.

Kanwal (1997) differentiates between hope and omnipotence: "If there is omnipotence, there is no need for hope. If there is frustration, omnipotence has failed, and then hope restores stability" (p. 138). He also claims that hope is linked to the capacity for reparation. Using Melanie Klein's theory as a metaphor he says "like reparation, hope functions as a bridge between the bad and the good breast" (p. 136) and he adds, "hope seems to repair the disruption of connectedness between mother and infant, patient and therapist, or a person and the outside world" (p. 138). Therefore he argues that hope is prelogical.

THE COGNITIVE-BEHAVIORAL APPROACH

The cognitive-behavioral theories treat hope primarily in terms of expectation. Stotland (1969), for instance, maintained that the concept of expectation encompasses hope because one cannot hope without having an expectation; "Hope can therefore be regarded as a shorthand term for an expectation about goal attainment" (p. 2). According to Stotland, individuals' expectations, desires, and preferences are determined by their history of successes and failures, so that each person continues to seek stimuli and behaviors that have led to success in the past and avoids those that were associated with failure. He emphasized the circularity of this process: expectation leads to a certain behavior; a success or a failure in obtaining the appropriate reinforcement or attaining the desired goal determines subsequent expectations. Stotland believes that "by translating the concept of hope into expectation about goal attainment," one can operationalize the concept of hope, which is otherwise entirely subjective.

Gottschalk (1974) defined hope as: "A measure of optimism that a 'favorable outcome' is likely to occur not only in one's personal activities, but also in cosmic phenomena and even in spiritual or imaginary events" (p. 779).

Lazarus and Folkman (1984) discuss the significance of morale, positive thinking, and hope in adjustment processes, with the assumption that positive emotions aid in coping with stress.

Scheier and Carver (1985) define optimism in terms of generalized positive expectancies for good outcomes and regard optimism as a mediator between stress and its outcomes (see Culver et al., 2002, chapter 2 this volume).

Seligman (1975), who studied the phenomenon of learned helplessness in animals and in humans during the 1970s, later developed his ideas on learned optimism (see Seligman, 1990), which he considers as a habit of thinking.

Snyder et al. (1991) define hope as a cognitive set that is composed of a "reciprocally derived sense of successful (a) agency (goal-directed determination) and (b) pathways (planning of ways to meet goals)" (p. 207).

Averill (1991) argues that hope is an "intellectual emotion." He bases his conclusion on an analysis of metaphors used to describe hope.

As can be seen from the above, the dynamic and cognitive-behavioral approaches treated the subject of hope from different perspectives based on different theoretical approaches. As a result, they had used diverse assessment techniques, making a comparison among them difficult. The major problem of this complex area of psychological variables, which are based on subjective experience, is the tendency of researchers to focus on a specific aspect of hope based on their theoretical assumptions and to regard it as representing the entire process (see also Chang, 2001, introduction).

BETWEEN STRESS AND HOPE: AN INTEGRATIVE APPROACH

Developmental theories have not explicitly addressed the subject of hope, but this concept is interwoven in all the theories that emphasize the importance of the primary child-mother bond and the importance of frustrating experiences for normal development.

In this section, I shall present my own conceptualization of the subject of hope, which derives, in addition to the approaches just surveyed, from some ideas and concepts introduced by developmental and existential theoreticians. The ideas evolved while I was conducting research on hope (Jacoby, 1987), based on material derived from two sources:

1. Interviews conducted with patients in surgical wards who coped with surgery, terminal illness, and so forth. From these interviews, I attempted to learn about the role of hope in coping with situations of severe stress and about the "devices" that enabled these patients to enact what will later be called the "work of hope."

2. Reports, stories, poems, and songs written by people who were exposed to severe danger and threats, yet struggled to overcome and survive them, such as songs written during the Holocaust, in the midst of war, and in prison.

Before continuing, it must be noted that among the many angles from which one can look at hope, I chose to focus on the psychological aspects dealing with the individual's personality and his or her primary relations, although I do not doubt that social-environmental, as well as cultural variables exert a significant influence that justifies a comprehensive investigation within the relevant disciplines.

Procreation

People bear children in order to continue the familial line, and this act is already oriented toward the future.[1] In animals, separation from parents occurs early in the life of the offspring. Young animals rapidly learn to become self-sufficient and to struggle for survival, exploiting the laws and resources of nature, such as the principle of territorial boundaries, which provide protection and signal impending danger (Lorenz, 1967). In contrast, human infants are helpless and require a long period of caring and protection. This need, by definition, leads to dependence on adult caretakers. Consequently, one of the most important tasks facing humans during development is to attain individuation, via the process of separation-individuation, at those stages when they can become independent. Only the process of individuation enables a view of orientation towards the future. If the symbiotic stage persists beyond its normal boundaries, one cannot attain a psychologically free future. Thus, when desertion, abandonment, or death of one object of the symbiotic bondage takes place, then the other "dies."

An infant's initial interaction with the world is via the senses: touch, vision, and hearing. Prior to the development of language, the infant's experiences do not undergo a process of symbolization and are imprinted in the body and in the zones of sensation (see also Fiener, 1998). If the experiences are good, nurturing, and supportive, they are like a "trust fund" from which it will be possible to draw in the future when need arises. A failure to form attachment to parents in the early years is related to impairment in psychological and physical development (Spitz, 1965; Bowlby, 1969).

Winnicott (1960, 1971) and Mahler (1968) emphasized the importance of mother's "holding behavior" for the child's healthy development, his or her capacity to form attachment, and as a primary component in the process of individuation.

A normal process of individuation can develop only if, after the experience of "good enough mothering," the parent allows the child to go through a process of separation without binding him or her through feelings of guilt and anger. This enables the internalization of the child's positive experiences, fostering his or her subsequent capacity to attain self-fulfillment.

In a talk delivered by Breznitz (1982) on "The psychology of hope," he presented some metaphors emphasizing the positive aspects of hope. The first metaphor was of "hope as a protected area." Breznitz referred to one of the dictionary definitions of the concept: *"Hope: a piece of enclosed land... in the midst of marshes,"* and developed the following theme:

> In the stormy sea of worries, anxieties and thoughts, the person searches for, and sometimes finds, a small island of peace, and he tries to reach this island and to cling to it—this is the protected area—and I am taking the liberty to suggest that the movement, the embrace—when a parent holds a child and protects him, shelters him, shields him—is the beginning of all hopes.

I would like to add that while the beginning of hope is indeed in the mother's protective embrace, its further development depends on the mother's ability to free the child to go his own way, carrying this protective embrace to guide him as he traverses the path of life.

Separation–Individuation

My first suggestion is that hope emanates from the experience of "good enough mothering" through the process of separation, as Lewis (1977) expressed in his poem:

How selfhood begins with walking away
 And love is proved in the letting go (p. 234)

The process of separation-individuation stressed in particular by Mahler (1968, et al. 1975), occurs gradually and requires several transitional stages, which were described by some theoreticians. Winnicott (1983) coined the terms "transitional object" and "transitional phenomena" to describe an intrapsychic zone ("intermediate area") lying between the internal subjective reality and the external objective reality. He stressed the critical role of this area throughout life "as a resting-place of the individual engaged in the perpetual human task of keeping inner and outer reality separate yet inter-related" (p. 230), and as a zone that contains the substance of illusion that enables imagination, creativity, religion, and cultural development. The first expression of the development of this area is the transitional object. This may be any object (e.g. a teddy bear, or a blanket) to which the infant becomes attached and that serves to calm him or her down, to soothe pain and to provide consolation. The principal use of this object is in the transition from alertness to sleep as a tranquilizing agent in the face of the anxieties aroused by this transition, particularly those of separation and desertion. Winnicott notes that the object represents for the child the transition from a state of symbiosis with the mother to a relation wherethe mother is an external and separate entity. According to Gaddini (1978), the transitional object represents the reunion with the mother and symbolizes her roles, in particular her calming function. Via this representation, the transitional object acts as a bridge between the mother and the infant: between elements from the past and, via the present, elements of the future; between hallucinations and reality; between illusion and disillusion; between the recognition of the mother and her retrieved memory; and between physical and psychological symbiosis and physical and psychological separateness. "Transitional objects are created in loneliness. They are based on feeling alone, yearning for past intimacy and the recreation of past togetherness, while weaving into it current wishes and hopes for the future" (p. 90).

The second metaphor used by Breznitz (1982) presented hope as a bridge between "darkness and light," and, I would add, a bridge from dependence to independence and from the past to the future. This is related to the first metaphor because an individual who was embraced in infancy will be able to be nurtured by this embrace in the future: "It is memory that gives us the power of foresight: we push into the future with images in which we fixed the past" (Bronowski, 1966). Indeed, from my clinical experience I have learned that under highly stressful conditions, such as imminent operations, individuals calm and encourage themselves using words and songs such as lullabies, which had been sung to them by their parents when they were young. Through the years the songs, which served to comfort the child, became a source of hope to cling to and a legacy to pass to future generations.

A Transitional Phenomenon

My second suggestion is that hope serves as a transitional phenomenon that represents the intermediate area between internal and external reality and aids in the process of individuation.

For centuries there was no consensus as to the nature of hope. In the "Pandora's box" legend, hope appeared together with evils and disasters to which humankind was condemned. The ancient Greeks considered hope as negative and harmful. According to the deterministic view, which was central to the global outlook of the Greek philosophers, destiny is unchangeable, and therefore hope is nothing more than an illusion, "the food of exiles." This fatalistic approach was espoused by the Greek-inspired poets and philosophers of the nineteenth century: "worse than despair, worse than the bitterness of death, is hope" (Shelly, 1819). "Hope is the worst of all evils, for it prolongs the torment of man" (Nietzsche, 1974).

Today, it is clear that hope is a positive and vital experience, but its definition, particularly the operational one, has remained a matter of debate. As we know, hope, like stress, depends on subjective experience and acquires different meanings in different contexts, schools, and cultures.

The psychoanalytic approach regarded the reality principle as a basis for mental health and treated fantasy negatively, similarly to denial. Therefore it is important to clarify the confusion that exists, even today, between different concepts, especially between hope and denial. Such confusion may have serious consequences when the mechanism of denial is unintentionally encouraged in the belief that it is hope. I have come across physicians who have spurred patients on to omit the mourning process after mastectomies, in the belief that they are encouraging hope. However, I believe that hope arises not from denial of pain but rather from confronting it. As Rollo May (1976) wrote on courage: "Courage is not the absence of despair; it is rather, the capacity to move ahead in spite of despair" (p. 3).

Thus, a number of writers (see Scheier et al., 1986; Taylor, 1989) argue that there is a conceptual distinction between optimism and denial, whereby they have different relations with the management of negative events and information. Aspinwall and Brunhart (1996) present results supporting this claim with regard to the way individuals attend to and recall threatening information.

According to Menninger, the role of the doctor is: "To inspire the right amount of hope, some, but not too much. Excess of hope is presumption and leads to disaster, deficiency of hope is despair and leads to decay" (p. 482).

Searls summarized his view on the role of hope in the therapist–client relationship as follows:

> ...Feeling of hopefulness proceeds in pace with the working through of progressively intense feelings of disappointment, discouragement, despair, grief and infantile omnipotence-based frustration—rage. This is a maturational process which is never completed.... (p. 502)

The question arises as to what is optimal hope. How is it to be defined beyond the subjective feeling? And how does one distinguish between hope and denial? In his article "Denial versus hope," Breznitz (1983) wrote: "By denying a threat, the person is also often denied the chances to consider some of its positive aspects." This statement may provide the basis for distinguishing hope from denial. Whereas in denial threat is ignored, or entirely negated (e.g. "this will not happen to me"), hope is a state in which reality is not ignored or escaped from. On the contrary, there is an awareness of the dangers and the difficulties, accompanied by an intention to cope and by active attempts to do so. As pointed out by Breznitz (1982) "a narrow bridge of hope is preferable than castles erected on the foundations of denial."

Threat and Pain

My third suggestion, then, is that hope, in contrast to denial, involves exposure to and confrontation with threat and pain, in an attempt to overcome them, as Tagore wrote: "Let me not pray to be sheltered from dangers, but to be fearless in facing them."

Numerous approaches, both physiological and psychological, emphasize the importance of the process in coping with stress. Selye (1956) described the process of physiological adjustment in dealing with prolonged stress, Janis (1958) developed the concept of "work of worrying," and Kubler-Ross (1969) referred to the "work of mourning." When we examine how hope actually "works," it is clear that in this case also we are dealing with an intrapsychic process that requires time and involves several stages. Thus, while one can talk about different tendencies of individuals, ranging from more hopeful to less hopeful, the critical issue is the process per se, which, by definition, implies change: "If it changes, it must be a process" (Lazarus and Folkman, 1985).

The Work of Hope

Thus, the fourth suggestion I would like to put forward is that hope should not be regarded as a discrete variable but rather as a process. Therefore, from a psychological point of view, we should speak of the "work of hope," rather than of "hope."

> The way Hope builds his House
> It is not with a Sill—
> Nor Rafter—has that Edifice
> But only Pinnacle—...
>
> Emily Dickinson

The "work of hope" requires several cognitive and emotional tools, namely, imagination, activity, curiosity, courage, and future time perspective.

According to Menninger: "There is no such thing as "idle hope." The thoughts and hopes and wishes that we entertain are already correlated to the plan of action which would bring this about" (p. 484).

Menninger (1959) describes the daily staff meetings held by imprisoned physicians in Buchenwald camp in which they discussed cases, presented articles, and made plans for improving the health conditions. They also managed to construct medical instruments from scrap metal, including an X-ray machine. Based on this, Menninger shows that activity, both at the intellectual-creative and the physical-concrete levels, is the foundation of hope. Stotland (1969) notes that activity includes thoughts and goal-oriented intentions. Scheier and Carver (1985) assume that optimism is a goal-based cognitive process and Snyder (1991) argues that hope focuses on moving toward desired goals. Henderson and Bostock (1977) reported that shipwreck survivors who spent 13 days on a rubber raft were preoccupied with thoughts, images, and plans about events that could happen, such as a ship coming to their rescue, meeting their family, and so on. Ghinsberg (1985), who found himself alone in the jungles of Brazil after having lost his friends, described how his hallucinations served him as "transitional phenomena."

An Active Process

In view of the above, my fifth suggestion is that hope is not a passive expectation for events to occur but is an active process oriented towards these events. Activity does not necessarily refer to actual behavior but also includes cognitive and mental activity emphasizing the role of imagination in problem-solving.

> The question was put to him (Aristotle) what hope is;
> His answer was: "the dream of a waking man."

In his illuminating paper on "The value of depression," Winnicott (1964) argues that depression, which is typically associated with a highly negative approach, is an important developmental stage, which aids in the process of maturation and must not be omitted. The "work of hope" also requires an active investment of the individual's resources after exposure to threat, pain, or life ordeals. Hope is not merely dependent on an external source of nourishment, but it grows out of struggle and emotional work that draws strength from within the person, while being oriented toward the future.

My final suggestion summarizes the points presented above: "work of hope" is an active mental process, which arises in response to a threat usually related to loss, and requires the process of separation-individuation, which involves emotional pain. This process fosters growth maturation and creativity in life's developmental and coping processes and therefore provides the means for coping with the ultimate threat, the threat of death.[2] Acceptance of reality frees one's energy, and enables the definition of new goals, more realistic and more attainable. The "Work of Hope" is a continuous process whereby the person repeatedly sets up new goals in which he or she is ready to invest effort and sometimes even take risks based on the belief and awareness of his or her capacities and strengths.

Before continuing I wish to summarize the assumptions that have been presented and that constitute the core belief of my therapeutic work.

1. Hope emanates from the experience of "good enough mothering," through the process of separation.

2. Hope serves as a transitional phenomenon, which represents the intermediate area between internal and external reality and aids in the process of individuation.

3. Hope, in contrast to denial, involves exposure to, and confrontation with threat and pain, in an attempt to overcome them.

4. Hope should not be regarded as a discrete variable, but rather as a process I term: "The Work of Hope."

5. Hope is not a passive expectation for events to occur, but an active process oriented towards these events.

6. The "Work of Hope" is an ongoing process that enables growth, maturation, and creativity in life's developmental and coping processes.

Based on these assumptions I wish to show how the "work of hope" can serve as a coping mechanism in stressful situations such as disease. I shall illustrate this process by using Michael Ende's book: (1983) *The Neverending Story,* which deals metaphorically with processes of development and growth and contains all of the elements that constitute the "work of hope." Indeed, I use this story in my therapeutic work with breast cancer patients, as a model of coping.

THE NEVERENDING STORY

The Neverending Story contains two parallel stories: the story of Bastian, the boy who experienced the death of his mother and has difficulties coping with this loss, and the story of Fantastica, the realm of fantasy, which faces the threat of destruction. Both describe the beginning of the process of individuation, which involves coping with the threat of death.

The Neverending Story begins with the description of the spread of the Nothingness, the Emptiness throughout the world. The Nothingness threatens to destroy everything, even Fantastica. As pointed out earlier, fantasy or imagination is one of the most important tools of the "Work of Hope," and therefore, its loss poses a grave danger.

At the heart of Fantastica, in the Ivory Tower, lived the Childlike Empress. She was the center of all life in the Empire. "Without her, nothing could have lived, any more than a human body can live if it has lost its heart" (p. 36).

Rumors were spreading that the Childlike Empress had become very ill and that there is a mysterious connection between her illness and the appearance of the Nothingness in Fantastica. This sentence contains metaphorically what is by now well known on the relationship between depression, helplessness, and the reduction of activity of the immune system, as a basis for the development of illness (see Weisse, 1992; Cohen and Herbert, 1996; Kiecolt-Glaser et al., 2002).

Four hundred and ninety-nine doctors had examined the Childlike Empress, and each had tried to help her with his skill. But none had succeeded, none knew the nature or cause of her illness, and none could think of a cure for it. "She doesn't cough, she hasn't got a cold. Medically speaking it's no disease at all," (pp. 37–38) said one of them.

Suddenly all fell silent. The great door had opened while Cairon, the far-famed master of the healer's art stepped in. "He was wearing a strange hat. A large golden amulet hung from a chain around his neck, and on this amulet one could make out two snakes, one light and one dark, which were biting each other's tails and so forming an oval. Everyone in Fantastica knew what the Medallion meant" (pp. 38–39). It was the AURYN, the symbol of the Empress, which is to be given to the hero who will not dread any dangers and will not surrender in the face of adversity and hardship.

The boy Atreyu is the hero who is destined to embark on the great quest to find a cure for the Childlike Empress and to save Fantastica. He must accomplish the "work of hope" and he is the only hope for Fantastica's inhabitants. Atreyu receives the AURYN, which will protect and guide him in his journey. Consequently, he must leave for the mission alone and unarmed. This is the road of the hero, full of dangers, adventure, and surprises, but one that promises emotional growth.

The journey is dangerous he is told, but if you fail, the Empress will die and our world will he destroyed.

Atreyu embarks on his journey riding his horse Artax. At the same time, out of darkness, the big black dragon begins his journey.

Atreyu rides during the days and dreams at nights without knowing where he is heading to and without finding anyone to advise him. He had been traveling aimlessly for almost a week when on the seventh day, the purple buffalo appears in his dream and advises him to find Morla the aged one, who lives on the Tortoise Shell mountain, which is located in the swamps of sadness, in the drowning marshland of sorrow.

Everyone knew that anyone who surrenders to sadness will drown in the swamps. Therefore, when Artax says to Atreyu: "with every step we take, the sadness grows in my heart. I've lost hope, master, and I feel so heavy, so heavy. It's the sadness that has made me so heavy. I can't go on" (pp. 60–61), Atreyu begs him: do not let the sadness of the swamps overcome you, do not surrender.

As noted earlier, the work of hope also often entails encounters with sadness and sorrow and painful visits to dark caves, and these cannot be prevented or detoured. Sometimes we learn that the wisdom resides somewhere in one's sorrow, in one's life experiences. However, while encountering sadness and sorrow, one must not surrender to them, but fight them, and emerge from the encounter as did Atreyu, and as is done by other warriors, including ill people with a fighting spirit, as has been mentioned by Greer et al. (1979).

Atreyu meets the old Morla. After the long years of loneliness, she is talking to herself. She is indifferent and allergic to youth. As far as she is concerned, everyone can die, and her response to Atreyu's plea that the Empress may die, is well, at last something will happen here.

After some time, Morla softens up in the face of Atreyu's entreaties and explains to him that the life of the Empress, who lives forever, is not measured in time but in names. The Empress needs a new name, and only the southern oracle that lives 10,000 miles away knows who can give the Empress a new name (this reminds us of the Jewish tradition to change one's name in order to confuse the angel of death).

Atreyu continues his journey. He encounters endless obstacles, including the land of the dead mountains from which few get out alive. But he knows all along that he must not give up because the life of the Empress and the existence of Fantastica depend on his success.

In the most difficult and helpless moment, Atreyu's savior appears. Falklor, the huge and white good-luck dragon arrives in a tremendous noise. Falkor rescues Atreyu from the impeding dangers and carries him on his back to the southern oracle.

We all know that good-luck dragons appear in legends. Our "Work of Hope" however, while being painfully aware of its constraints and limitations, embraces the patient and gives him or her faith and support, which enables him or her to continue the journey, even if only for the time that remains.

After days and nights of being unconscious, Atreyu wakes up, to find himself clean and his wounds healed. Close by he discovers a cave, in which there is a room that looks like an alchemist's laboratory, and which is inhabited by two small creatures: a man with big glasses on his nose, whom I will call the scientist and who represents knowledge, reason, and scientific investigation, and his wife who is busy preparing medicines from grass and small strange creatures, who symbolizes intuition, the senses, and sensitivity.

Atreyu learns about the interaction between them: "Woman," said the little man testily. "Get out of my light. You're interfering with my research!" (p. 88).

You and your research, said the woman, Who cares about that? The important thing is my health elixir.

The woman, who, as can be understood, specializes in traditional medicine, injects Atreyu with her medicines and explains to him the importance of pain: Without pain one does not heal. For the wound to heal, it must hurt.

The scientist, who has for years studied the mystery of the southern oracle, expresses his disappointment when he discovers that Atreyu is not familiar with his reputation: "Oh, well" he said, "apparently you don't move in scientific circles, or someone would undoubtedly have told you that you couldn't find a better adviser than yours truly, if you're looking for the Southern Oracle" (p. 90), and he recruits Atreyu to take part in his research.

On the top of the mountain, next to the cave, there is a small telescope through which one can see the gates one must pass in order to reach the oracle.

Two sphinxes sitting one facing the other make up the first gate to be passed. It becomes clear that the mission is not easy, and that many who tried did not come back.

Atreyu asks his friend, the scientist, whether he passed through these gates.

> "Don't be absurd!" He replies." I'm a scientist. I have collected and collated the statements of all the individuals who have been there. The ones who have come back, that is. Very important work. I can't afford to take personal risks. It could interfere with my work." (pp. 96–97)

This reminds us of some scientists who are secluded in their ivory towers and whose work is sometimes isolated from the human experience, whereas people who underwent the adverse experiences and overcame them can help and support others.

We learn from the story that as long as the Sphinx's eyes are closed, one can pass through the gate, but if the Sphinx's eyes are open, they fire on anyone passing through it. There are cases in which individuals succeed in passing the gate, but the crucial question that has not been answered until this very day is: why a certain person crosses the gate and another fails. As we often ask why one person succeeded to overcome a disease or a crisis, and another person did not, despite the fact that their clinical picture was similar.

We are told that the Sphinx's eyes remain closed until someone who is not aware of his value attempts to cross the gate. If a person has self-doubts, he or she is shot.

In the therapeutic process this is the stage when we focus on the positive resources, the strengths of the individual or the group, and the sources of support.

The second gate is more dangerous. This is the Magic Mirror Gate, in which you don't see your outward appearance. What you see is your real innermost nature. If you want to go through, you have to go into yourself.

Passing through this gate, good people discover that they are bad, brave people discover they are cowards, and most people who discover their true self escape in terror.

In the therapeutic process this is the stage when we work on the acceptance of limitations and on a sober and realistic view of reality, which includes looking at one's body and accepting its frailty.

Atreyu goes on in his journey and passes the gates. When he reaches the oracle he discovers that the Empress indeed needs a new name, but only a human child who can be found beyond the borders of Fantastica can give it to her.

Atreyu and Falklor fly to search for the borders of Fantastica but enter a storm and part. Atreyu meets the creature of the dark, Gmork, who presents himself as the messenger of the Nothingness. Atreyu asks him where can he find the borders of Fantastica. Gmork laughs at him:

> Fantastica has no borders, he says, it is the world of human fantasy. Each of its parts and axes are aspects of people's dreams and hopes therefore it has no borders.
> If so, asks Atreyu, why is it being destroyed?
> Because people lost their hopes and forgot their dreams, Gmork answers him.
> What then is the nothingness?
> This is the emptiness that remained, the despair that ruins the world.
> And Gmork adds:
> People who have no hope are easy to control, and those who control have power and strength.

Atreyu discovers his strength when he fights Gmork face to face and wins the fight.

This is the stage in therapy in which we deal with the hopes and the plans for the future, through awareness of capacities as well as of limitations.

Subsequently, Atreyu and Falkor unite again and discover that the land has disappeared. They set out to search for the Ivory Tower. They reach the tower exhausted and wounded and there meet the Empress, who asks Atreyu why he is so sad. Atreyu returns the AURYN to her and says: I have disappointed you. The Empress tells him he is wrong and explains to him that in his journey he established contact with a human child who has gone through the entire process together with him. This boy, Bastian, who had lost his mother, must give a new name to the Empress and call her by that name.

Bastian, the human child, hesitates. When the Empress asks Bastian: Why don't you do what you think? he answers: I can't; I must keep my feet on the ground, very much like those people who are incapable of using fantasy and imagination in their life.

At last Bastian calls the Empress by her new name. The new name represents the new parts that develop as the "Work of Hope" is being done. These are the parts that have learned to hope and have acquired the strength and conviction that liberation and victory of the spirit are possible and worth fighting for.

The Empress gives him a grain of sand and says: Only one grain of sand remained from Fantastica, but fantasy can be resurrected in your dreams and imagination. And she explains to Bastian that the more wishes he has, the quicker will Fantastica awaken to life. The grain of sand will turn into a seed, a shining seed that will begin to sprout.

Back to therapy, here we deal with the importance of initiative, courage, and creativity.

PERSONAL PERSPECTIVE

For the last 20 years, I have been working with cancer patients, and more recently, I have focused on psychotherapy with women who have breast cancer. After an encounter with my own fears, embarrassment, helplessness, and pain, I was looking for a way that would enable me to help my patients recruit internal strength and resources to cope with the immense threat these women face and their ability to go on. What had motivated me in my quest was my deep belief in the power of hope as a coping mechanism. Also, there has been accumulating evidence that a fighting spirit, hope, and social support have a profound influence on the patients' functioning as well as on survival and life expectancy (see Spiegel et al., 1989).

The question arises as to how hope develops and how one aids in its development. From a developmental point of view, it appears that hope develops in three stages (see Figure 14.1). In the first stage, hope is based on expectations of the individual that he or she will be saved by supernatural forces, such as gods, and he or she tries to reach them by using fantasy, magical words, or symbols. In the second stage, hope is based on the individual's expectation of getting help from a human figure on which he or she can depend, such as parent or physician. Finally, in the third stage, the individual finds hope within himself or herself, either by drawing on his or her internal strengths or by resorting to acquired strategies. In situations of severe stress, when the individual is not able to recruit inner resources or when they are not helpful, he or she regresses to previous

Figure 14.1
Hope: Three Developmental Stages

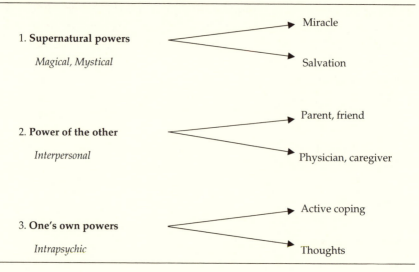

1. **Supernatural powers**

   Magical, Mystical

   → Miracle

   → Salvation

2. **Power of the other**

   Interpersonal

   → Parent, friend

   → Physician, caregiver

3. **One's own powers**

   Intrapsychic

   → Active coping

   → Thoughts

stages, of dependence on others, or relying on supernatural sources using magical thinking (see Keinan, 2003, chapter 6, this volume).

Back to *The Neverending Story*. In psychotherapy, we go through the different stages of Atreyu's journey, which serves as a model of coping, beginning with the encounter with the threat and the danger, through the encounter with pain and sadness, and subsequently facing the mirror, confronting the internal strengths and resources as well as limitations, and finally, the planning of activities towards the future, and by that, going out to the outside world stronger and better equipped to cope with stressful situations.

The unfolding of the process by means of a story while using metaphors, imagination, and creativity enables us to circumvent defenses and resistance and plant suggestions of coping, in both adults and children.

IN CLOSING

In this chapter I have put forward various points of view representing central psychological approaches to hope. My aim was to add another layer in the attempt to understand what is hope. However, as much as I have tried to grasp the concept, I realize just how intangible it is. It is still easier to describe hope in metaphorical terms or through prose or poetry.

In spite of that, hope should not be neglected in our empirical and thera-peutical endeavors, because:

Of all ills that men endure
Hope is the only cheap and universal cure.

NOTES

1. I would like to refer the reader to Gustav Klimt's paintings "Hope I" and "Hope II," in: Costanlino (1990).

2. For a stimulating analysis I would like to refer the reader to Becker, E. (1973). The Denial of Death. New York: The Free Press.

REFERENCES

Alsop, S. (1976). *Stay of execution.* Tel Aviv: Zmora, Bitan, Modan,

Amiel, S. (1979). *Ad klot: Unto the end of hope.* Tel Aviv: Ma'ariv.

Aspinwall, L. G., & Brunhart, S. M. (1996). Distinguishing optimism from denial: Optimistic beliefs predict attention to health threats. *Personality and Social Psychology Bulletin, 22(10),* 993–1003.

Averill, J.R. (1991). Intellectual emotions. In: C.D. Spielberger & I.G. Sarason (Eds.), *Stress and emotion* (pp. 3–16). New York: Hemisphere.

Bion, W. (1961). *Experience in groups.* New York: Basic Books.

Birenbaum, H. (1983). *Hope is the last to die.* Israel: Ghetto Fighters' House,

Boris, N. H. (1976). On hope: Its nature and psychotherapy. *International Review of Psychoanalysis, 3,* 139–150.

Bowlby, J. (1969). *Attachment and loss.* New York: Basic Books.

Breznitz, S. (1982). *The psychology of hope.* Paper presented at the Annual Con-ference of the Israeli Psychological Association, Haifa University, Israel.

Breznitz, S. (1983). Denial versus hope: Concluding remarks. In S. Breznitz (Ed.) *The Denial of Stress* (pp. 297–302). New York: International Universities Press.

Bronowski, J. (1966). *The identity of man* (p. 80). New York: American Museum of Science Books.

Chang, E. C. (2001). *Optimism & pessimism: Implications for theory, research, and practice.* Washington, DC: American Psychological Association.

Cohen, S., & Herbert, T. B. (1996). Health psychology: Psychological factors and physical disease from the perspective of human psychoneuroimmunology. *Annual Review in Psychology, 47,* 113–142.

Costanlino, M. (1990). *Klimt.* London: Bison Books (pp. 50 and 74).

Cousins, N. (1979). *Anatomy of an illness as perceived by the patient.* New York: Norton.

Dickinson, E. (1960). In T. H. Johnson (Ed.), *The complete poems of Emily Dickinson*. Boston: Little, Brown.

Ende, M. (1983). *The Neverending story.* New York: Doubleday.

Erikson, E. H. (1963). *Childhood and society.* New York: Norton.

Erikson, E. H. (1964). *Insight and responsibility.* London: Faber and Faber.

Feiner, A. H. (1998). Notes on touch and the genesis of hope. *Contemporary Psychoanalysis,* 34(3), 445–447.

Frank, J. (1968). Hope in psychotherapy. *International Journal of Psychiatry,* 5, 383–395.

Frankl, V. E. (1963). *Man's search for meaning.* New York: Washington Square Press.

French, T. (1952). *The integration of behavior.* Chicago: University of Chicago Press.

Freud, S. (1953). *Psychical (or Mental) Treatment. Standard Edition.* Vol. 7 (pp. 281–302). London: Hogarth Press.

Gaddini, R. (1978). Transitional objects origins and the psychosomatic symptoms. In S. A. Grolnick & L. Barkin (Eds.). *Between reality and fantasy: Winnicot's concepts of transitional objects and phenomena* (pp. 109–133). New York: Jason Aronson.

Ghinsberg, Y. (1985). *Back from Tuichi.* Tel Aviv: Bitan, Zmora.

Gottschalk, L. A. (1974). A hope scale applicable to verbal samples. *Archives of General Psychiatry,* 30, 779–785.

Greer, S., Morris, T., & Pettingale, K. W. (1979). Psychological response to breast cancer: Effect on outcome. *Lancet,* 2, 785–787.

Haynal, A. (1985). *Depression and creativity.* New York. International Universities Press.

Henderson, S., & Bostock, T. (1977). Coping behavior after shipwreck. *British Journal of Psychiatry,* 131, 15–20.

Jacoby, R. (1987). *On the "work of hope" in the recovery process after surgery.* Unpublished doctoral dissertation, Haifa University, Haifa.

Janis, I. (1958). *Psychological Stress.* New York: Wiley.

Kanwall, G. S. (1997). Hope, respect, and flexibility in the psychotherapy of schizophrenia. *Contemporary Psychoanalysis,* 33(1), 133–150.

Kiecolt-Glaser, J. K., McGuire, L., Robles, T. F., & Glaser, R. (2002). Emotions, morbidity, and mortality: New perspectives from psychoneuroimmunology. *Annual Review in Psychology,* 53(1), 83–107.

Kubler-Ross, E. (1969). *On Death and Dying.* New York: MacMillan.

Lazarus, R. S. and Folkman, S. Coping and adaptation. In W. D. Gentry (Ed.), *The handbook of behavioral medicine.* (pp. 282–325). New York: Guilford.

Lazarus, R. S., & Folkman, S. (1984). If it changes it must be a process: Study of emotion and coping during three stages of a college examination. *Journal of Personality and Social Psychology,* 48, 150–170,

Lewis. C. D. (1977). *Poems of C. D. Lewis,* 1925—1972. London: Jonathan Cape.

Lorenz, K. (1967). *On aggression.* London: Methuen.

Mahler, M. S. (1968). *On human symbiosis and the vicissitudes of individuation.* New York: International Universities Press.

Mahler, M. S., Pine, F., and Bergman, A. (1975). *The psychological birth of the human infant.* New York: Basic Books.

May, R. (1976). *The courage to create.* New York: Norton.

Menninger, K. (1959). Hope. *American Journal of Psychiatry,* 116, 481–491.

Mitchell, S. A. (1993). *Hope and dread in psychoanalysis.* New York: Basic Books.

Mowrer, O. H. (1960). *Learning theory and the symbolic processes.* New York: Wiley.

Nietzsche, F. (1974). *Human all too human.* New York: Gordon Press.

Pisar, S. (1981). *Of blood and hope.* Tel Aviv: Schocken.

Sacks, O. (1986). *A leg to stand on.* London: Picador.

Scheier, M. F., & Carver, C. S. (1985). Optimism, coping and health: Assessment and implications of generalized outcome expectancies. *Health Psychology,* 4, 219–247.

Scheier, M. F., Weintraub, J. K., & Carver, C. S. (1986). Coping with stress: Divergent strategies of optimists and pessimists. *Journal of Personality and Social Psychology,* 51, 1257–1264.

Searls, H. F. The development of mature hope in the patient-therapist relationship. In H. F. Searls (Ed.), *Counter transference and related subjects: Selected papers* (pp. 479–502). New York: International Universities Press.

Seligman, M. E. P. (1975). *Helplessness.* San Francisco: Freeman.

Seligman, M.E.P. (1991). *Learned optimism.* New York: Knopf.

Selye, H. (1956). *The stress of life.* New York : McGraw-Hill.

Shelley, P. B. (1819). The Cenci. In *The Poetical Works of P. B. Shelly.* (pp. 257–309). London: Frederick Warne.

Snyder, C. R., Irving, L., & Anderson, J. R. (1991). Hope and health: Measuring the will and the ways. In C. R. Snyder & D. R. Forsyth (Eds.), *Handbook of social and clinical psychology: The health perspective.* (pp. 285–305). Elmsford, N Y: Pergamon.

Spiegel, D., Bloom, J. R., Kraemer, H. C., & Gottheil, E. (1989). Effect of psychosocial treatment on survival of patients with metastatic breast cancer. *Lancet,* 2, 888–891.

Spitz R. (1965). *The First Year of Life.* New York: International Universities Press.

Stotland, E. (1969). *The psychology of hope.* San Francisco: Jossey-Bass,

Tagore. R. (1916). *Fruit Gathering.* New York: MacMillan.

Taylor, S. E. (1989). *Positive illusions: Creative self-deception and the healthy mind.* New York: Basic Books.

Weisse, C. S. (1992). Depression and immunocompetence: A review of the literature. *Psychological Bulletin,* 111(3), 475–489.

Winnicott, D. W. (1960). The theory of parent–child relationship. *International Journal of Psychoanalysis,* 41, 585–595.

Winnicott, D. W. (1964). The value of depression. *The British Journal of Psychiatric Social Work,* 7(3), 123–127.

Winnicot D. W. (1971). *Playing and reality.* New York: Penguin.

Winnicott, D. W. (1983). Transitional objects and transitional phenomena. *International Journal of Psychoanalysis,* 34, 89–97.

INDEX

ABOUT THE EDITORS
AND CONTRIBUTORS

VIRGIL H. ADAMS III is Assistant Professor of Psychology and Assistant Research Scientist of Gerontology at the University of Kansas. His scholarly interests center around well-being, hope, aging, and minority populations with particular interests in African Americans.

DANIEL BAR-TAL is Professor of Psychology at the School of Education, Tel-Aviv University. His research interest is in political and social psychology, studying psychological foundations of intractable conflicts and peacemaking. Specifically, he focuses on those societal beliefs and collective emotional orientations that feed conflicts and those that facilitate conflict resolution and reconciliation. He authored *Group Beliefs* (Springer-Verlag, 1990) and *Shared Beliefs in a Society* (Sage, 2000) and co-edited *Social Psychology of Intergroup Relations* (Springer-Verlag, 1988), *Stereotyping and Prejudice* (Springer-Verlag, 1989), *Patriotism in the Lives of Individuals and Nations* (Nelson Hall, 1997), *Concerned with Security* (JAI, 1998), *How Children Understand War and Peace* (Jossey-Bass, 1999), and *Patriotism in Israel* (in press). In addition he has published over 100 articles and chapters in major social and political psychological journals and books.

YAEL BENYAMINI earned her B.A. in Psychology and Biology and her M.A. in Social Psychology at the Hebrew University in Jerusalem, and her Ph.D. in Social and Health Psychology at Rutgers University, New Jersey.

She is currently a lecturer at the Bob Shapell School of Social Work at Tel-Aviv University. Her research focuses on subjective perceptions of health and their impact on ways of coping with various health threats, and on the role of resources, such as optimism and spouse support.

CARLA BERG is a Clinical Psychology doctoral student at the University of Kansas. Her research interests include health psychology, hope, and personality.

MELISSA BRIGGS-PHILLIPS is a doctoral candidate in Counseling Psychology at the University of Akron in Akron, Ohio. She is currently the Project Director of the National Institute of Mental Health, Office of AIDS Research grant concerned with HIV prevention in inner-city women. She has worked extensively with survivors of childhood sexual abuse and sexual trauma and plans to continue community-based research in a faculty position.

CHARLES S. CARVER is Professor of Psychology at the University of Miami. He received his Ph.D. in Personality Psychology from the University of Texas at Austin. Much of his current work examines the influence of personality on the manner in which people cope with life stresses, particularly medical stresses. He is also interested in the nature and functions of emotion. His work has been supported by the National Science Foundation and the National Cancer Institute.

JENIFER L. CULVER recently completed her Ph.D. in Clinical Psychology at the University of Miami. Her research has focused on stress, coping, and benefit-finding among breast cancer patients, as well as the ways in which clinical intervention changes these experiences. She is currently examining the role of emotional processing in adaptation to cancer. She has been supported in this work by the National Cancer Institute.

HAIM HAZAN is Professor of Sociology and Social Anthropology and the Director of the Herczeg Institute on Aging at Tel-Aviv University. His main areas of interest and research cover the life course, time, cultural and interactional aspects of old age, total institutions, community, nationalism, and collective memory. He published numerous articles and several books including "The Limbo People: A Study of the Constitution of the Time Universe among the Aged" (1980); "Paradoxical Community" (1990);

"Managing Change in Old Age" (1992); "Old Age: Construction and Deconstruction" (1994); "From First Principles: An Experiment in Aging" (1996); "Simulated Dreams: Israeli Youth and Virtual Zionism" (2001). His current work focuses on intergenerational relations and life stories.

LAURA HEINZE is a graduate student in the Clinical Health Psychology specialty program of the Clinical Psychology Program at the University of Kansas. She graduated from Drake University in 1998 with a B.S. in Psychology and a B.A. in English. She then earned her M.A. from the University of Kansas in 2000 in an exploration of the role of forgiveness in mediating the PTSD and hostility relationship among adult survivors of childhood abuse. Her current research interests involve the roles of coping and emotion in relationship to the cognitive functioning of patients with chronic diseases.

STEVAN E. HOBFOLL is Professor and Director of the Applied Psychology Center at Kent State University and Director of the Summa-Kent State Center for the Treatment and Study of Traumatic Stress. He has been involved with stress research for 25 years and is interested in both the course of stress and prevention of negative stress outcomes. He has also developed Conservation of Resources (COR) theory, which has been applied to the understanding of stressful circumstances ranging from burnout to severe trauma.

REBECCA JACOBY, is currently head of the Medical Psychology graduate program at the Tel-Aviv Yaffo Academic College and chair of the professional committee of Medical Psychology at the Israel Ministry of Health. Until 2002 she served as director of the postgraduate Medical Psychology program at the Department of Psychology, Tel-Aviv University and chairwoman of the Medical Psychology Division of the Israel Psychological Association. She is also Editor of the medical psychology section of the *Israel Journal of Psychotherapy: Dialogue*. Her main reserach and clinical interests are hope, coping with breast cancer, and doctor-patient communication.

MARIA JARYMOWICZ, Faculty of Psychology, University of Warsaw (Poland) has been full professor since 1989. She was a member of the Executive Committee of the European Association of Experimental Social Psychology (1996–2002) and co-editor of the *Polish Psychological Bul-*

letin (1970–1985). She was honored by the Polish Scientific Foundation with a grant "Affect and intellect in evaluative processes" for 1998–2001. Her research interests focus on the study of emotion, motivation, and personality. She has published numerous books, chapters, and journal articles on these topics in Polish. Among her publications in English are: *Perceiving One's Own Individuality* (1987), *To Know Self—To Understand Others* (Edited in 1993); chapters in Oliner et al. (edited in 1992), *Embracing the Other* and in Worchel et al. (edited in 1998), *Social Identity.*

RONNA F. JEVNE is Professor of Educational Psychology in the Faculty of Education at the University of Alberta, Canada, and Director of the Research and Programs for the Hope Foundation of Alberta. She was previously the head of the Department of Psychology at the Cross Cancer Institute, Edmonton, Alberta. Author/co-author of seven books, her most recent are *Finding Hope* and *Hoping Coping & Moping.* She has lectured extensively on hope.

KRISTIN KAHLE is a doctoral student in Clinical Psychology at the University of Kansas. She is currently a Trainee in Communication and Aging, supported by the National Institute on Aging. Her research and clinical interests center around the role of hope in the aging process.

GIORA KEINAN, Professor of Psychology, completed his studies in Clinical Psychology at the Hebrew University. Then he served in the Israeli Defense Forces as the Naval Chief Psychologist and the Head of the Diagnostic Branch. Since 1982 he has been a faculty member at Tel Aviv University and involved in stress research and instruction.

ELISA A. KING is a Clinical Psychology doctoral student at the University of Kansas. Her research interests include the psychology of hope, minority issues, and legal issues.

AMIA LIEBLICH was educated at the Hebrew University of Jerusalem where she is currently Professor of Psychology. Her academic work has been mostly dedicated to studies of the psychological aspects of Israeli society, focusing on the effects of the political situation, war and the military service, life in the kibbutz, and gender, using qualitative research methods. Together with Ruthellen Josselson and Dan McAdams she has edited the series "The Narrative Study of Lives" since 1993.

CHERYL L. NEKOLAICHUK Ph. D. is a counseling psychologist and research associate with the Alberta Cancer Board Palliative Care Research Initiative, Edmonton, Alberta, Canada. She is also an instructional associate with Athabasca University and an adjunct faculty member with St. Stephen's Theological College, Edmonton. Her master's and doctoral reserach focused on the nature of hope in health and illness. Her current clinical and research interests revolove around the biopsychosocial aspects of chronic and life-threatening illness, the experience of hope in the elderly and terminally ill, and the development of innovative assessment techniques.

ALBERT PESSO co-founded Pesso Boyden System Psychomotor with his wife, Diane Boyden-Pesso, in 1961. He is President of the Psychomotor Institute and has been Supervisor of Psychomotor Therapy at McLean Hospital in Belmont, MA, and Consultant in Psychiatric Research at the Boston Veteran's Administration Hospital. He is the author of several books and many articles, gives lectures at universities and hospitals, and directs training programs in PBSP in 11 countries.

KEVIN L. RAND is a doctoral student in Clinical Psychology at the University of Kansas. His research interests include positive psychology (e.g., hope) and depression.

ALICIA RODRIGUEZ-HANLEY is a doctoral student in Clinical Psychology at the University of Kansas. Her scholarly interests include hope, acculturation, and eating disorders.

MICHAEL F. SCHEIER received his Ph.D. from the University of Texas at Austin in Personality Psychology. He is currently Professor of Psychology at Carnegie Mellon University. His research interests fall at the intersection of personality, social, and health psychology. He continues to work on the health benefits of dispositional optimism and has developed additional interests in the adaptive nature of goal-disengagement.

DOV SHMOTKIN is a faculty member in the Department of Psychology and Research Coordinator in the Herczeg Institute on Aging at Tel-Aviv University. He is a senior Clinical Psychologist and served as head of the Clinical Psychology Graduate Program. His research interests relate to the psychology of adulthood and old age, focusing on subjective well-being and mental health, patterns of aging, long-term post-traumatic reactions of Holocaust survivors, and time perspective.

HAL S. SHOREY received his B.A. in Psychology from California State University, San Bernardino in 2001, and presently is a Self Graduate Fellow pursuing his doctoral training in the Clinical Psychology Program at the University of Kansas. He is researching the developmental antecedents of hope. The aim of this research is to facilitate the development of interventions to reach at-risk youth before they are forced to set goals and make choices that will guide the critical transitions into adult roles.

C. R. SNYDER is the Wright Distinguished Professor of Clinical Psychology in the Psychology Department at the University of Kansas, Lawrence. His scholarly interests center around positive psychology in general (e.g., his 2002 publication with co-editor Shane López is the *Handbook of Positive Psychology* by the Oxford University Press), and hope in particular (e.g., his 2000 edited volume *Handbook of Hope: Theory, Research, and Applications* by Academic Press).

LISA R. STINES is a graduate student in the Clinical Psychology doctoral Program at Kent State University. She is currently conducting research, under the advisement of Dr. Stevan Hobfoll, on the relationship between childhood abuse and PTSD in women. She also works as a psycho-educational group leader with inner-city women in an HIV prevention project, funded by NIMH, Office of AIDS Research.

LAURA YAMHURE THOMPSON is a Psychology Predoctoral Intern at McLean Hospital-Harvard Medical School. She was a 2001–2002 Ford Foundation Dissertation Fellow, and was Research Coordinator of the Heartland Forgiveness Project, funded by the Templeton Foundation, from 1998 to 2002. She received a B.A. in Psychology from the University of Virginia in 1996, an M.A. in Clinical Psychology at the University of Kansas in 1997, and presently is a Ph.D. candidate in the Clinical Psychology Program at Kansas University.